NATURE AND POLICY IN ICELAND
1400-1800

Nature and Policy
in Iceland 1400–1800

An Anthropological Analysis of History and Mentality

KIRSTEN HASTRUP

CLARENDON PRESS · OXFORD

1990

Oxford University Press, Walton Street, Oxford OX2 6DP
Oxford New York Toronto
Delhi Bombay Calcutta Madras Karachi
Petaling Jaya Singapore Hong Kong Tokyo
Nairobi Dar es Salaam Cape Town
Melbourne Auckland
and associated companies in
Berlin Ibadan

Oxford is a trade mark of Oxford University Press

Published in the United States
by Oxford University Press, New York

© Kirsten Hastrup 1990

British Library Cataloguing in Publication Data
Hastrup, Kirsten
Nature and policy in Iceland 1400–1800: an
anthropological analysis of history and mentality.
1. Iceland. Cultural processes, history
I. Title
306.094912
ISBN 0–19–827728–8

Library of Congress Cataloging-in-Publication Data
Hastrup, Kirsten.
Nature and policy in Iceland, 1400–1800: an anthropological
analysis of history and mentality / Kirsten Hastrup.
Includes bibliographical references.
1. Iceland—Civilization. 2. Iceland—Social conditions.
I. Title.
DL328.H35 1990   949.12—dc20   90–34623
ISBN 0–19–827728–8

Typeset by Joshua Associates Ltd., Oxford
Printed in Great Britain by
Biddles Ltd, Guildford & King's Lynn

ACKNOWLEDGEMENTS

THE idea of writing this book emerged in Reykjavík during the spring of 1982, when I held a scholarship at Stofnun Árna Magnússonar—the Manuscript Institute of the University of Iceland. I gratefully remember the scholarly milieu at the institute which was both cordial and broadminded enough to accommodate a social anthropologist. In particular I wish to thank philologist Stefán Karlsson who was so generous with his time, whenever I needed specialist advice. To the Icelandic Ministry of Education I express my gratitude for the grant supplied.

Later that year and for a shorter period in 1983 my field-work on an Icelandic farm and in a fishing village added an invaluable dimension of experience to the historical knowledge. The field results will be published in a separate work, but I wish to acknowledge my debt to my farming and fishing friends also in the present context. I should add that the field-work was supported financially by the Danish Research Council for the Humanities.

In the long and unsteady process of completing this work I have incurred other debts. One of them is paramount and owed to my teacher, colleague, and friend Edwin Ardener of Oxford University, who died so suddenly when this work was drawing to a close. My recurrent conversations with Edwin Ardener will remain an unlimited source of inspiration for years to come.

In 1985 I was appointed 'research professor' in anthropology by the Council for the Planning of Research in Denmark. With the appointment were invaluable privileges such as funds for travel and for employing a part time secretary. Both have been instrumental in the completion of the present work—among other works— and I gratefully acknowledge my debt to the source of these privileges.

Several people have provided valuable support and information at various stages of the process. I can mention only a few. Elise Pedersen fed the word processor from impossible drafts in handwriting or bad typing, and furnished my office with flowers at times of stress. Finn

Rindom Madsen helped check notes and bibliography, and bought ice-cream on hot summer days spent editing. Tom Nauerby prepared the index.

Colleagues from various fields have read the manuscript and supplied constructive criticisms, without which the book would have suffered in clarity. Peter Burke, Cambridge, Orvar Löfgren, Lund, and Kirsten Ramløv, Copenhagen, provided encouraging remarks on the first draft. Preben Meulengracht Sørensen, Århus, checked much of my Icelandic, and helped me translate some of the poems in the text. Loftur Guttormsson, Reykjavík, read the manuscript meticulously and gave me generous advice on all subjects. Malcolm Chapman, Oxford, did the final linguistic revision—in the course of which many themes became clearer. Finally, Niels Fock, Copenhagen, gave me some very useful hints towards improvement at the last stage. They all offered me expert advice, and whatever shortcomings remain in the book can only be blamed on me.

As always, my children Rasmus, Simon, Anders, and Frida must be credited for their presence. As experts in real life they have enabled me to pursue the odd intellectual problem through dusty archives and alien spaces without losing my sense of direction.

Last but not least I extend my affectionate thanks to Peter Elsass, who emerged on my private island and added life and warmth to it in the final phase of writing.

K.H.

Moesgård
June 1989

CONTENTS

FIGURES

TABLES

ABBREVIATIONS

AÍ	*Alþingisbækur Íslands*, i–xv. 1912–82. *Acta comitiorum generalium Islandiae.* Reykjavík: Sögufelagið
AK	*Biskop Arnes Kristenret.* In *Norges Gamle Love—indtil 1387*, i–v. 1846–95. Christiania: Det Norske Historiske Kildeskriftfond
Ann.	*Annálar 1400–1800. Annales Islandici. Posteriorum saeculorum*, i–iv. 1922–42. Reykjavík: Hið íslenzka bókmenntafélag
BS	*Byskupa sögur*, ed. Guðni Jónsson. Reykjavík: Íslendingasagnaútgáfan/Haukadalsútgáfan
DI	*Diplomatarium Islandicum. Íslenzkt fornbréfasafn*, i–xvi. 1857–1972. Copenhagen and Reykjavík: Hið íslenzka bókmenntafélag
Espolín	Jón Espolín, *Árbækur*, i–xii. 1943. Reykjavík: Lithoprint
ESS	*Encyclopedia of the Social Sciences*, ed. L. David. 1968. London and New York: Macmillan and Free Press
Grágás	*Grágás. Islændernes Lovbog i Fristatens Tidll*, i a, i b (1852), ii (1879), iii (1883), ed. V. Finsen. 1974. Odense: Odense University Press
IÆ	*Íslenzkar æviskrár* ed. Páll Eggert Ólason. 1948–51. Reykjavík: Hið íslenzka bókmenntafélag
IED	*An Icelandic–English Dictionary*, ed. Richard Cleasby, Gudbrand Vigfusson, and W. A. Craigie. 2nd edn. 1957. Oxford: Clarendon Press
ÍF	*Íslenzkt fornrit.* Reykjavík: Hið íslenzka fornritafélag
ÍL	*Íslenzkt ljóðasafn*, i–v, ed. Kristján Karlsson, *et al.* 1957–8. Reykjavík: Almenna bókafelagið
ÍM	*Íslenzkir málshættir*, ed. Bjarni Vilhjálmsson and Óskar Halldórsson. 1966. Reykjavík: Almenna bókafélagið
Íslb.	*Íslendingabók*, ed. Jakob Benediktsson. 1968. Íslenzk fornrit, 1. Reykjavík: Hið íslenzka fornritafélag
JÁ	Jón Árnason, *Íslenzkar þjóðsögur og ævintýri*, i–vi. 2nd edn., ed. Árni Böðvarsson and Bjarni Vilhjálmsson. Reykjavík: Bókaútgáfan þjóðsaga. 1954–61
Jónsbók	*Kong Magnus Hakonssons Lovbog for Island. Vedtaget på Altinget 1281*, ed. Ólafur Halldórsson. 1904. Copenhagen: S. L. Möllers bogtrykkeri
KL	*Kulturhistorisk Leksikon for Nordisk Middelalder*, i–xxii. 1956–78. Copenhagen: Rosenkilde og Bagger
Ldn.	*Landnámabók*, ed. Jakob Benediktsson. 1968. Íslenzk fornrit, 1. Reykjavík: Hið íslenzka fornritafélag

LI   *Lovsamling for Island*, ed. O. Stephensen and Jón Sigurðsson.
1853–89. Copenhagen: Höst og søn

LP   *Lexicon Poeticum antiguæ linguæ septentrionalis*. 1st edn., ed.
Sveinbjörn Egilsson, 1854–60. 2nd edn., ed. Finnur Jónson. Ord-
bog over det norsk-islandske skjaldesprog. Copenhagen: Det
Kongelige Nordiske Oldskriftselskab, 1931

NGL   *Norges Gamle Love—indtil 1387*, i–v. 1846–95. Christiania: Det
Norske Historiske Kildeskriftfond

OE   Old English

ON   Old Norse

SSÍ   *Safn til sögu Íslands og íslenzkra bókmennta að fornu og nýju*, i–vi.
1859–1939. Copenhagen and Reykjavík. Hið íslenzka bókmenntafélag

NOTE ON THE TEXT

ICELANDIC grammar is complex, and a brief note on orthographic peculiarities is required. Whenever single words in Icelandic are used in the text, they are given in standardized and nominative form. When connected to other words, they are inflected accordingly. Quotations are generally left unaltered, and they mirror the far from standardized language use in our period. This fact has caused me a few problems of presentation, and I am aware of a certain degree of linguistic inconsistency.

The letter þ ('thorn') is an unvoiced consonant pronounced as *th* in English *thorn*; ð ('eth') is its voiced counterpart, pronounced as *th* in English *weather*.

Icelandic second names are patronyms. Whenever an Icelander is mentioned in the text, both the first name and the patronym are given. The same applies to Icelandic scholars whose work I cite. In the bibliography they will be listed by their patronym, in accordance with international standard.

Often a particular Icelander is known by his first name and a nickname, like Jón *lærði* (Guðmundsson), and this usage has been adopted here. The nickname is translated when it occurs for the first time, Jón *lærði* ('the learned'), after which the Icelandic alone is given. When a person has been introduced by his full name, often only the first name will be used for the remainder of the paragraph; again this is in accordance with Icelandic practice.

In general, all translations from Icelandic have been made by myself unless otherwise stated.

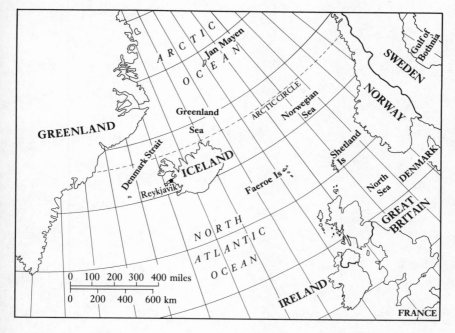

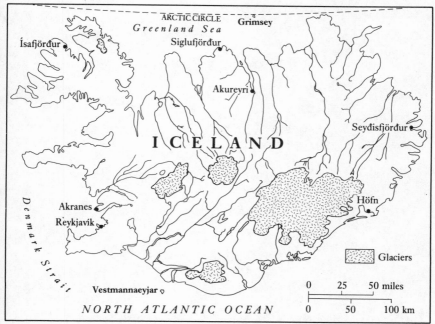

Fɪɢ. 1. *Map of Iceland*

Introduction

Island of Anthropology

THIS work is an anthropological analysis of four hundred years of social life in Iceland. In presenting a historical ethnography, my aim is to contribute to the development of anthropological theories of change and dynamism in human society. In the process I hope to shed new light upon the history of Iceland, which has provided me with privileged material for theoretical reflection. It is privileged both because it is rich, owing to the remarkable antiquarian interest of the Icelanders over the centuries, and because it is sufficiently limited to be known more or less in full owing to the comparatively small scale of the island community, with a population of only 50,000, or even fewer in parts of the period.

Another factor of importance to my project is the virtual isolation of Icelandic society. Although it was englobed by a larger order of social reproduction, as part of the Danish kingdom and of European Christendom throughout the period under concern here, the island was nevertheless sufficiently isolated to allow us to trace its *own* history. Icelandic history is unique—as are all histories. Comparative material would probably reveal many parallels to other rural populations of Europe, but here Iceland remains in focus. As we shall see, many external factors—natural catastrophes, foreign merchants, distant kings—also contributed to the particular course of Icelandic history during these centuries. It is a basic hypothesis of the present work, however, that we cannot even begin to understand the significance of these factors, until we know Icelandic culture from inside.

The purpose of writing a historical ethnography is to achieve this inside knowledge. As we know from the collective experience of anthropologists in the field, learning about a culture requires the laborious and detailed recording of facts whose relevance only gradually dawns upon the analyst. In the present case the mass of detail may sometimes seem to obscure rather than to clarify the issue. I have, however, found it necessary to provide the details, both in order to substantiate the more general points as fully as possible, and because there are no comprehensive works on this particular period of Icelandic history to which I could refer.

Icelandic history from 1400 to 1800 is mostly a silence, at least by comparison with the previous period of the Icelandic Freestate, dating from the settlements in the ninth century and until the surrender to the king of Norway in 1262–4. This is not to deny that Icelandic historians have dealt with the period, and among them we note Björn Þorsteinsson whose most recent work (in Danish) covers the entire period from the settlements until the present day (1985). Further, a new generation of Icelandic historians have begun publishing important analyses of selected aspects and lesser periods of this history. So far, however, no one has offered a comprehensive analysis of the silent centuries, and this is where my work may fill a gap in our knowledge of Icelandic culture during a very interesting period.

It is in the nature of anthropology to deal with wholes. Since the invention of field-work as the prime method of study, the whole has often been conceived as local cultures, forming 'islands of anthropology'.[1] Such 'islands' have been studied mainly from a synchronic perspective, since the original objects of study in anthropology were cultures without obvious written records. Even where records existed they were often ignored, and only recently have we realized that not only is anthropology historical, but history is also anthropological. Culture and history are adjective to one another (Hastrup 1985a: 246). Metaphor and reality merge and set society in motion (Sahlins 1981). The islands of anthropology have proved to be 'islands of history' as well (Sahlins 1985).

Iceland has predominantly attracted the interest of historians, philologists, and literary historians whose principal focus has been the Middle Ages.[2] This is mainly because the settlements and the period of the Freestate were so thoroughly described in the famous saga-literature of the twelfth and thirteenth centuries. Besides the sagas, a number of other documents from the same period supply important information on the highly sophisticated political organization, and the remarkable historical and linguistic awareness, of the Icelanders. The sagas have been described as the sole Nordic contribution to world literature (Hallberg 1974: 7). Assertions like this are of course debatable, but this one serves to identify a refraction of interest to Icelandic studies.

It is to redress this that I shall here approach Iceland, in the period from 1400 to 1800, as an 'island of anthropology'. Ultimately my aim is to reintegrate culture and history, or to 'explode the concept of history by the anthropological experience of culture'—to quote Sahlins on a similar issue (1985: 72). To reach there, I enter deeply into the ethnography of the island society, in the attempt to mediate the experience of Icelandic culture in a particular period. For reasons which will become clearer in the course of this work, this period has remained obscure. By comparison with the earlier period and its clear demarcation in time and space, the centuries from 1400 to 1800 seem to refuse bounding. They slip from our hands, leaving us with an apparently ill-defined time–space. This, however, is largely a *trompe l'œil*, owing to the refraction of interest and attention demanded by the previous period.

The contrast between our period and the previous one is not only an academic and arbitrary result of the one being relatively more studied than the other. Rather, the contrast reflects a real difference, or a real discontinuity in the development of Icelandic society. The present work will show how the non-distinct centuries actually make up an epoch with its own characteristics. On first judgement, the later epoch appears to be only a pale shadow of the original, honourable, and flourishing society of the first settlers. The Freestate was marked by political autonomy and by the high standards of social life achieved by its wealthier farmers. Its literature still captures the interest of modern readers. In the succeeding periods, Icelandic society was in a state of political submission, and social life in general was marked by impoverishment and decline. Moreover, this decline was recognized by people themselves; it was part of the ethnography in the period. The non-distinctness of Icelandic society was, so to speak, part of contemporary experience.

On the empirical level, there is evidence of decline or disintegration in almost all domains of history. There are, of course, notable differences within this period, and the centuries were not alike in all respects. Nor was development within the separate domains absolutely synchronized. Since my primary concern is with the general trends that can be elicited from the motley picture of detail during the entire period of four hundred years, I have probably under-communicated the internal differences between the lesser 'periods' within that time-span. As for the general trends we may note initially that old productive technologies were 'forgotten' or at least abandoned, and patterns of landownership entailed an increasing inequality among the Icelanders. Social reproduction was imperilled in several ways, landing Icelandic society in a more or less permanent demographic crisis. Nature impinged upon the island in ways which the Icelanders, given their perception of the crisis, could not avert.

Naturally, 'decline' can be measured only against some kind of normative standard. In this case the standard is set by the previous period of the Freestate. The important point is that this comparison is not only an external scale of measure; it was also part of the Icelanders' own implicit standard. In the repetition of the old literature, the people were continually confronted with a different and much more glorious state of affairs, which continued to shape their mentality. Without pre-empting the conclusions of this work, I will offer the preliminary suggestion that the Icelanders were actually imprisoned by their own mentality. As we know, 'mental frameworks can form prisons of the *longue durée*' (Braudel 1980: 31).

This idea of mentalities as prisons from which individuals cannot escape has been contested by Burke (1986: 444). It is untenable also from an anthropological point of view, because of the apparent paradox of the continuity between the social space and the individuals that constitute it—'they are defined by the space and are nevertheless the defining consciousness of that space' (Ardener 1987*a*: 39). In other words, 'social forms can never shape human beings completely, because social forms owe their own shape to the fact that human beings are social agents with ideas about social forms' (Hollis 1985: 232). This is the reason why I deliberately attempt to transcend the opposition between an approach that favours 'system' to the exclusion of individual action and creativity, and a kind of individualism that sacrifices the whole. A mentality is a prison to which the captives hold the keys.

However, in this particular historical case, and as I shall try to show, the Icelanders do seem to have been entrapped by a particular vision of the world, which made them prisoners of a mentality which was *in some ways* 'anachronistic' in the period under discussion. I must also stress that the mentality of the Icelanders should not be viewed as an autonomous set of ideas, which either has no relationship to society, or is only a distorted reflection of it (cf. Burke 1986: 448). My point of departure is a concern with the *relationship* between mentality on the one hand and the actual history of Icelandic society on the other. Neither has any meaning by itself.

It is the Icelandic mentality which accounts for the continuity between the earlier and later periods. It also provides an *ethnographic* reason for the recurrent references to the Freestate in the present work. By using the Freestate as an implicit reference for measuring later 'decline', I am only following contemporary Icelanders, whose culture I purport to study from inside. While concentrating the analysis on the period 1400 to 1800, and tracing actual changes in Icelandic society within this time span, I also want to elucidate cultural continuity across these centuries and beyond.

Studying a period of four hundred years allows us to deal with both continuity and change, and to assess the nature and origin of both. When Marc Bloch asserts that 'historical time is a concrete and living reality with an irreversible onward rush' (1954: 27), he is only partly right. Historical time also comprises the order of the *longue durée*, which orchestrates the conjunctures in the rush of irreversible time. Disparate events are connected through their integration into the reversible time-scale of a cultural logic, which seems to outlive all events. Social spaces are continually redefined by the individuals constituting them, often to construct an experience of continuity amidst the equally real experience of change. In Iceland the split between these two distinct experiences played a significant role in shaping the course of history. This is why we must attempt to trace history at both of these levels of dynamism.

This presupposes a notion of a *whole* which can be analysed at various levels. In anthropology the concept of 'worlds' has been used for the analytical wholes we are dealing with (Ardener 1975*b*; Hastrup 1987*d*). A world is not an arbitrary entity, which the analyst can isolate to his or her own taste, because it is also an experiential space in which real life unfolds and gains significance. Worlds are self-defining; they generate their own reality and identify their own events. For 'events' to be registered as such, they have to be significant from the point of view of the world (Ardener 1978). It is this internal significance which distinguishes them from mere happenings. 'An event becomes such as it is interpreted' (Sahlins 1985: p. xiv). This implies that some social spaces or some periods may seem to be either more event-rich or event-poor than other spaces or periods, which are equally rich in happenings. It is part of my argument in this work that the period 1400 to 1800 was a relatively event-poor period in Icelandic history, at least by comparison with the previous period, and that this is one reason why the later period has seemed so obscure to Icelanders and scholars alike.

Worlds also have distinct temporalities and generate their own causal systems. As Braudel has it: 'Each social reality secretes its own peculiar time, or time scale, like common snails' (Braudel 1980: 49). It is by recourse to the particular Icelandic temporality that we may eventually identify the system of causalities inherent in the Icelandic world. The identification of causalities is a construction upon past experience, and as experiences differ so do causal systems (Douglas 1975: 276). Thus we cannot properly deal with causation in history without a primary comprehension of the experiential spaces of people. Again, this is why an elaborate historical ethnography must precede the analysis of causation in any time perspective.

I approach Iceland 1400 to 1800 as a world in its own right. This implies that the history of this particular society is studied from its own centre, so to speak. Although Iceland was deeply involved in an external context whose centre was elsewhere, its history is still not the history of periphery. From the perspective chosen here, Iceland was at the centre of its own history—as well as of its own world. That is why we must enter so deeply into Icelandic culture during these centuries. The crux of the matter is that we need to 'understand the tradition and practices by which people's desires were once constructed if we are to recount precisely how they made (or failed to make) their own history' (Asad 1987: 604).

In anthropology, *culture* is an analytical implication, while *society* is an empirical category (cf. Knudsen 1989). My concern with culture is what distinguishes the present work from most social history, if I am allowed a simplification. While a social historian will seek to trace the developments at the level of the empirical, the anthropologist will also seek to trace the implications of this development at a non-empirical level. The social history of Iceland certainly furnishes us with the material for many of the chapters in this work, but the analytical scope lies beyond social history itself—in Icelandic culture. The concepts used will be further discussed below, but it is important to note the initial difference between an anthropological and a social history. At another level this is also a general difference between anthropology and historiography.[3]

This difference also extends to the use of sources and to the problem of veracity. Sources contain several levels of information, and different sources stress different aspects of social reality. Thus there are normative sources which may or may not reflect the actual social practice, and there are literary or poetical expressions, which may or may not reflect standard conceptions. In the present work, the normative sources and the general system of concepts have not been deemed inferior to the records of 'actual' life. Anthropological history grows in the area between these two levels of truth, and the assertions made on these levels must be considered to be of equal veracity, although they remain dissimilar.

In more than one way this work is a sequel to an earlier work of mine: *Culture and History in Medieval Iceland. An Anthropological Analysis of Structure and Change* (Hastrup 1985 *a*). In the first volume, I too dealt with the Freestate and showed how the extraordinarily coherent social and semantic system created by the settlers was gradually hollowed out with the passage of time. The present work is not only a chrono-logical successor to the previous one, however. It is also a consecutive theoretical work. In *Culture and History* I used the notions of synchrony and diachrony to organize the material in two distinct dimensions, and to illustrate the intersection between culture and history.

In *Nature and Policy* I add a more explicit 'panchronic' dimension. In the words of Saussure, who coined these concepts, the panchronic refers to a reality which outlives all events (Saussure 1974: 95). The synchronic and the diachronic are still important to the presentation; the synchronic relations bind together coexisting categories and realities in the collective representations of the people, while the diachronic relations bind together successive categories and realities, those that are substituted by one another in the course of time, and which do not form a system in the minds of people (cf. ibid.: 99–100). These classes of phenomena are both empirical, and comprise the tangible facts of history, and the principles for their development. By contrast, panchronic principles exist independently of concrete facts. One such principle is the fact of change itself; irrespective of time, place, and speed all societies do change. There is no way to stay the same, if nothing else then because new individuals are continually born and add their own consciousness to the space. Thus the fact of change outlives all events; it is a panchronic rule. In this work I am concerned with a qualification of this panchronic rule in my general discussion of causation in history. My aim is to contribute to the general understanding of how societies change—and how their specific histories are produced.

Actual changes have to be identified empirically by an investigation into the synchronic logic and the diachronic rules. 'Rules' are principles for change that seem to have a certain permanence, but they should not be reified. In history—unlike, for example, chess—no rules exist outside the game itself, but we may find a comparable set of principles or conditions for a movement, change, or breakdown of the system. These conditions are part of the collective representations of a people, and we should note that they are 'collective' only in the sense of being shared by the individuals, not in the sense of existing outside them, to paraphrase Burke on mentality (Burke 1986: 442). People are neither life prisoners of a mentality nor powerless victims of certain historical conditions. As we know, it is in the nature of culture to be able to recondition the conditions (Boon 1982: 114). In the Icelandic case this reconditioning did seem to pose a severe problem, however, and this work is an attempt to understand why—from a combined synchronic, diachronic, and panchronic viewpoint.

My approach has clear affinities both to the French Annales-school and to British social history. On the one hand, I share with the French an interest in 'total history'—I will mention here only Braudel's work on the Mediterranean world (1976), and Le Roy Ladurie's study of the peasants of Languedoc (1974a), which also traces the development of a region in a long time perspective. On the other hand, I am likewise concerned with the social conditions for human life and with the position of the individual in the larger social system. It is often difficult to make the connections between the various elements of the totality, and a critique against the French school has been propounded in these terms (Rabb 1982: 325). I have, however, the specific aim of providing a synthesis, and of making clear how individuals are not only defined by their space, but also its defining consciousness. A major point is

that to understand the behaviour of people in other cultures it is not sufficient to imagine oneself in their shoes, in their situation; it is also necessary to imagine their definition of the situation, to see it through their eyes. (Burke 1986: 442.)

In other words, we must enter their culture—which for them is a *synthesis* of stability and change, past and present, diachrony and synchrony (Sahlins 1985: 144).

Synthesis is also in part a feature of writing. We 'write cultures' (Clifford and Marcus 1986), and we certainly also 'write histories'.[4] It is the story that creates the sense of wholeness in both cases. The historical narrative establishes the context within which the various events and happenings gain meaning (Hastrup and Meulengracht Sørensen 1987). This context itself consists of textual representations; consequently all historiography is based on discursive constructs (Asad 1987: 596). Many metaphors have been used to describe the discursive mode which connects past and present; it has been seen as a dialogue of transference, for instance (LaCapra 1985). Transference is not accidental, and the present shaping of the past is informed by contemporary significances (Ardener 1989a). Historical presentations are structured by the past itself and are, therefore, non-arbitrary. But history as a whole only becomes visible through writing it; the disparate events of the past have to be connected in narrative.

The present narrative about Iceland 1400 to 1800 is an attempt to contextualize a wide range of texts or sources on the past, in order to make a comprehensive analysis of a whole—defined in both time and space. Through this analysis we may integrate a variety of events and happenings in a significant pattern of continuity and change. The title of the book indicates the main areas of concern. At the most general level *Nature and Policy* invokes both a set of specific conditions, and a set of strategies for coping with them. The title also reflects the fact that Iceland was rather badly trapped between an arid natural environment and an increasingly zealous foreign (Danish) policy. To study this from the perspective of history and mentality, as the subtitle of the book indicates, is to investigate the mutual influence between the 'objective' and discontinuous course of events and the 'subjective' visions of the world.

Throughout the work I am preoccupied with the interests of the people, and with the way in which dominant metaphors in their culture contribute to historical development. In this way I hope to avoid any implicit ethnocentricity in the study of 'mentalities' (cf. Burke 1986: 445). Even if Icelandic society 'disintegrated'—as the analysis will indicate—we are not allowed to treat this as a 'failure' on the part of the system. It was part of the system. And it was a failure only if one assumes that a normative development exists. Thus, whenever I use such value-laden concepts in the text, they indicate an implicit contrast with the general pattern of development in Europe on its way towards modernity. The 'failure' of the Icelanders to adjust their concepts to the early modern reality, which we may detect from an external point of view, is counterbalanced by the internal perspective and the logic of local culture. The Icelanders encompassed the existentially unique in the conceptually familiar as other peoples do (cf. Sahlins 1985: 146). Only in this particular case it seems that they embedded their present in the past to an extraordinary degree.

The book is organized in four parts, surrounded by an Introduction and a Conclusion. Part I comprises two chapters on the conceptual and the empirical contexts of the historical ethnography. We get closer to Iceland as we pass through these two chapters.

In Part II we are in Iceland, dealing with the social experience of the Icelanders. We start in the home, with a discussion of the significance of the household and analysis of development in the two dominant modes of livelihood (Ch. 3). In the succeeding chapter the pattern of landownership is presented, and we learn how the social order and the social categories were largely a function of this particular pattern (Ch. 4). At one further remove from the social centre provided by the household, the external relationships of the islanders are described, primarily with view to their local effects (Ch. 5).

In Part III the perspective shifts from the social experience to the human condition. Again we start very close to home with an investigation into matters of sexuality, procreation, and literacy— spheres that appear to be internally connected in a peculiar pattern of social reproduction (Ch. 6). Next, the collective representations of forces that might influence individual destinies are introduced in terms of magic, witchcraft, and healing—domains that form a particular field of knowledge (Ch. 7). Thereafter, concepts of the environment, hidden or visible, are discussed, and we end with a discussion of the Icelanders' concepts of nature (Ch. 8).

Part IV sums up the analytical results of the investigation. The separate histories told in the preceding six chapters of the ethnography are connected, and the logic of the course taken by the whole is elucidated (Ch. 9). In turn, this allows us to spell out some theoretical implications, and to deal with causation in history from a general perspective (Ch. 10). In the Conclusion I discuss the 'territory of knowledge' as a counterpart to the 'island of anthropology' presented in the Introduction. In this way the circle is closed.

Each of the chapters could have been expanded into a separate volume, but, as in *Culture and History*, I wanted to adopt a holistic perspective, in order to connect the disparate elements. I make no claim to have exhausted the sources, and my evidence is exemplary rather than representative.

Even though I have had to transform life to text, I hope that the real life of the Icelandic people may still be sensed in the following pages. They deserve our attention, as a category and as individuals, because they teach us what it means to be human—to be both defined by the social space, and the defining consciousness of that space. Ultimately, the study of Icelandic nature and policy during four hundred years shows how the objective and the subjective dimensions of history cannot be separated. Perhaps this is the principal lesson to be drawn from the explosion of the concept of history by the anthropological concept of culture.

I

PERSPECTIVES

Conceptual Framework

IF 'total history' is taken literally, it is of course impossible; the historian must always select (Burke 1980: 197). But we may use the notion as a shorthand for a history that is less limited by geographical or disciplinary boundaries than other kinds of history (ibid.). In the Icelandic case the word 'total' refers to the global perspective on Icelandic culture, by which no single topic or theme is given priority in the analysis of history. Concepts of magic are as important for the comprehension of Icelandic development, for example, as is the Danish rule. Like Le Roy Ladurie studying the peasants of Languedoc, I have come to realize that in order to understand the impediments to 'progress' during some long centuries of Icelandic history we must pursue the problem 'to the farthest reaches of the unconscious psyche' (Le Roy Ladurie 1974a: 301). This psyche is part of the collective 'unreal' of the people; it is their mentality.

The notion of mentality has been of current if not always consistent usage in French historiography in particular (Burguière 1982). This is not the place to review the literature on the concept, but I shall present it here as one of my principal analytical concepts in the study of the 'respiration of Icelandic social structure' (cf. Le Roy Ladurie 1974a: 4), and clarify it by relating it to other ideas.

In the second part of this chapter I shall deal with time and temporality in Icelandic history. The general point is that history contains several levels of dynamism, and that the relative speed by which history unfolds itself at these levels varies from one culture to another and from one period to the next. This may not be new, but once we are through the presentation of the material (which is also an interpretation, of course), I believe that we are able to reframe the problem in terms of a general theory of causation.

As I see it, writing a 'total history' implies that one operates with a unified concept of culture and history. In a previous work, I used the notion of 'state' for this unity, and showed how both culture and history gained meaning from the intersection between the synchronic and the diachronic—as defining parameters of the 'state' (Hastrup 1985*a*). In the slow respiration of a particular social structure, one state will succeed another almost without noticing at the empirical level. States, therefore, are units that emerge as a result of analysis, and we are intially faced with a problem of identification. The main problem is that, unlike a game of chess in which single moves can easily be depicted and states identified as the condition obtaining between two moves, social systems evolve in so many dimensions at the same time, that states must be defined by reference to a particular point of view (Hastrup 1985*a*: 244). In anthropology, worlds are identified by reference to the point of view of the people for whom the world is the experiential space. This means that the analytical bounding of units rests on real discontinuities. This must apply also to the definition of states in history, or of worlds in time.

In spite of conspicuous changes during the period of the Freestate, reflecting processes that did not end with the surrender of sovereignty to the king of Norway, it was a 'state' which could be identified by reference to the indigenous concept of *vár lög*, 'our law', as the defining parameter of Icelandic society. With the fall of the Freestate, 'our law' became irrelevant, as the proper definition of any society now rested on an idea of kingdoms (Hastrup 1984*a*). The period from 1400 to 1800 is not traditionally conceived of in terms of a well-bounded whole, but I argue that it can be studied as a state in a comparable manner. It is a phase of distinction, when compared to other phases in Icelandic history. This will have to be substantiated in the course of analysis, but the general concepts of continuity and discontinuity guiding this work will be presented in this chapter.

HISTORY AND MENTALITY

Drawing on Durkheim's notion of collective representations, the history of mentalities has had a long tradition in France. During the past two decades it has also become increasingly popular outside France, and the inconsistency of the term has become conspicuous (LeGoff 1974; 197; Burguière 1982; Burke 1986). Amidst various attempts at definition, it has been suggested that the history of mentalities is the history of 'the visions of the world' (Mandrou, quoted by Vovelle 1982: 5), or the story about the slowness of history (LeGoff 1974: 90). The former stresses the viewpoint of the people, the latter emphasizes its endurance. Both are important, of course. It is characteristic, however, that most discussions of this kind are discussions of the history *of* mentalities. Both the strength and weakness of the concept are located here.

For the strength, the history of mentalities opened up a new object for historical research, with at least three distinctive aspects—a stress on collective attitudes rather than individual ones, an emphasis on unspoken assumptions, and a concern with the structure of beliefs and categories (Burke 1986: 439). These features are implicit also in the present work, where Icelandic history is written to reveal the structure of the unspoken cultural assumptions of the Icelanders as a collectivity.

I do not conceive of this work as a history of a mentality, however, for the concept has also a serious weakness—the reification of 'mentality', and its isolation from social experience in general. It is this isolation which has led to the unsatisfactory notion of mentality as prison, discussed in the Introduction. From an anthropological perspective, history and mentality must be reunited. The Icelandic mentality was not an autonomous construct, it was an implicit part of the Icelandic world—which again was an entity of thought and action. Instead of studying mentalities as such, we should look at them as aspects of 'worlds in time'. From this perspective, the concept of mentality is one way of avoiding anachronism in Icelandic history (cf. Burguière 1982: 430). It is a means to interpret the social experience and the human condition of the Icelanders from the inside, on the assumption that their world is inherently 'foreign'. In this sense, perhaps this work is among those 'anthropological histories' which might claim to succeed and broaden the history of mentalities (ibid.: 427).

In the following chapters I am concerned both with material changes in Icelandic society and with collective representations. The latter are no less real than the former. In fact they are doubly real in the sense that they refer both to modes of conceiving and to the social facts conceived (Lukes 1975: 6–10). The relationship is not one of simple reflection; the mode of conceiving may be structured by metaphors which change at a different rate from the facts conceived. We shall see how in Iceland the collective representations could only with difficulty accommodate experience. While actual occurrences made old images crack, the ancient metaphors and settler values continued to structure thought. And, as we know, metaphors provide images in relation to which the social organization of action can take place (Fernandez 1986: 7).

Discussing history *and* mentality, therefore, is to discuss separate but equally real orders of reality that are distinguished by different temporalities (Braudel 1980: 49). The orders are not autonomous. In fact we may see the relationship between history and mentality as analogous to the relationship between society and culture. 'History' and 'society' are both empirical categories while 'mentality' and 'culture' are analytical implications. History and society are full of events and discontinuities; mentality and culture give them meaning by providing some kind of continuity and order beyond the empirical.

To clarify this proposition, we may organize the concepts according to the mathematical group structure (Barbut 1970).[1] In this way we get a more precise picture of the 'state' and the dimensions inherent in its definition (see Fig. 2).

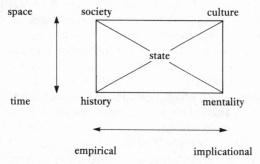

FIG. 2. *A State with Transformations*

As can be seen, the state comprises both a temporal and a spatial referent. It has an empirical manifestation in society and in history, and it has implied meaning in culture and mentality.

Apart from the definition of the whole, the model also serves the purpose of defining the interrelationships between the four polar concepts. At the empirical level, we note that history is society in time, and, conversely, that society is history in space. At the implicational level, I contend that mentality is culture in time, while culture is mentality in space. In the concrete analysis the emphasis may shift between these poles, but in anthropological history the four of them will always be implicitly present.

We should not mistake the distinction between the empirical and the implicational for a distinction between the material and the non-material. In principle, the material is inseparable from the non-material (cf. Le Roy Ladurie 1974*a*: 302). Implications are part of the materiality of categories (cf. Ardener 1982). The opposition dissolves in the anthropological analysis of worlds in space and time.

Cultures are inherently comparative and materialize only in contradistinction to other cultures (Boon 1982: ix). It follows that 'cultures interpenetrate symbolically, as they are constituted' (ibid.: x). This also applies to mentalities, defined as cultures in time. They can be identified only in contrast to implicational spaces of the same order.

As an implication, mentality is also a kind of mediation 'between the objective conditions of the life of men and the way they perceive them' (Vovelle 1982: 11). Phrased differently, the concept of mentality mediates between objective and subjective conditions. Like its spatial counterpart, culture, mentality also determines practical reason (Sahlins 1976). As a defining parameter of worlds in time, it also mediates between the irreversible order of events and the reversible order of structure. It is *duration*, but it is also an intersubjective category—always at risk in action (cf. Sahlins 1985: 145).

In Braudel's work the duration of structures is related to Durkheim's notion of society as a collective moral space, and of the exteriority of social facts (Bailey 1985: 15). This implies a latent risk of reducing individuals to passive carriers of culture, or to automatons in history. We have to realize, therefore, that the idea of exteriority cannot be upheld. People are defined by their world and their mentality, but they are also the definers. They are not only vehicles of collective representations, that are handed down from one generation to the next as entities, but are also actively engaged in a process of *re*presentation. This applies to the Icelandic case, even though—as we shall see—the Icelanders seem to have stuck to old metaphors far longer than they might. Their mentality was not a prison, however; rather, it was a bias in their view of the world, which they actively upheld. They accommodated—or tried to accommodate—the present in the past, or the existentially unique in the conceptually familiar. It was clearly an effort to do so.

'Culture is a gamble played with nature, in the course of which,

wittingly or unwittingly . . . the old names that are still on everyone's
lips acquire connotations that are far removed from their original
meaning' (Sahlins 1985: ix). If mentality is culture in time, we can
extend this point, and suggest that a mentality is a gamble played with
nature in a long term perspective. In Iceland between 1400 and 1800
the gamble was very real. It seems that the continuity in the Icelandic
mentality put history at stake. This will be substantiated in the course
of this work, although I must warn the reader that this is no mental
determinism, precisely because mentality is not a 'thing' that exists
and explains (cf. Spieser 1987: 83). It is an implication of history, and
both have to be explained simultaneously. If the old names remained
on the Icelanders' lips, their meaning must be elicited by reference
both to the order of history and the order of mentality.

TIME AND TEMPORALITY

I have already made points concerning time and temporality, and will
discuss them briefly here, with reference to Icelandic history in the
state of transition between the medieval and the modern eras.
Transition is one of the distinctive features of the epoch, understood
as a

particular stage in a society's evolution when it encounters increasing internal
and/or external difficulties in reproducing the economic and social relations
on which it is based and which give a specific logic to the manner in which it
operates and evolves. (Godelier 1987: 447.)

The Icelandic case is peculiar in that this 'stage' actually lasted for
some four centuries, making a conspicuous phase in history. Defining
it as a phase of transition calls for a study of the difficulties inherent in
social reproduction, and of the different time-scales involved.

The kind of history I am writing is an attempt to transcend the
single event, or rather, to absorb it and recycle it (Le Roy Ladurie
1979: 113). This does not imply a suppression of a time or of irreversibility. At the empirical level no events are exact replicas of previous
ones, and irreversibility is part of human experience. But the fact of
succession is not alone in shaping this experience, because it is constantly counterbalanced by the fact of repetition—belonging to the
implicational level. Thus there are immediately two time-scales
involved in this narrative of Icelandic history. Indeed, part of my aim

is to reintegrate the alleged opposition between the *faits de succession* and the *faits de répétition* (cf. Burguière 1982: 425).

The science of history has so far been perceived mainly as the science of the facts of succession, and of the unfolding of society in an irreversible time. This is a positivist view of history firmly linked with the idea that any event in history must be explained by its antecedents. In this model of history there are no rules for change, only actual changes. Before discussing the notion of 'rules' it is worth noting that in the natural sciences, the principal concern has been with the facts of repetition, while the historical, or irreversible, dimension has largely been excluded from the domain of rational thinking (Jaeglé and Roubaud 1987: 38). While searching for universal invariables and subjecting them to scientific thinking, world history continued to produce variations which could not and cannot be accommodated by the mechanical world view. In natural scientific thinking the goal has been to identify laws, and a law 'c'est la réalité moins l'histoire' (ibid.: 40). Today, natural scientists know that theories of movement in nature will of necessity have a historical component, because they always presuppose a certain set of conditions, without which the law does not hold. This is not the place to discuss the problems inherent in the natural sciences, but it is significant that, while historians discover the analytical limitations inherent in the exclusive focus on the irreversible dimension of time, natural scientists for their part become increasingly aware of the historical dimension of nature. Having grown in the interstices between the social and the historical sciences, social anthropology is familiar with both dimensions.

The point I am trying to make is that in order to comprehend the nature of continuity and change in Iceland from 1400 to 1800, we must have recourse to at least two time-scales. The first of these is the scale of 'states'—a scale of a particular and very slow dynamism, a reproduction of structure if never actually a repetition of events. We are beyond the empirical at this level, in the implicational space of Icelandic culture. One significant implication is that the Icelanders continued to define themselves as farmers, in spite of changing ecological, commercial, and organizational patterns which actually impeded the reproduction of farming life in the old settlers' sense of the word. The name of 'settlement' was still on the Icelanders' lips in our period, but it had become a signified without contemporary signifiers. While continuing to structure thought in the *longue durée* this aspect of Icelandic mentality was not realized in contemporary society.

The second time-scale implicit in this work is that of practice and events. At this level of dynamism we are concerned with the actual tracing of changes at the empirical level. Thus we are in the world of chronology and of successions. It is at this level that we find the evidence of a gradual process of internal disintegration, and of an increasing external influence. It is here also that we find a striking desuetude of old technologies, and a failure to keep up with the requirements of the environment. Apart from providing an ethnography of this development, I am also interested in tracing the diachronic 'rules' for change inherent in Icelandic culture.[2]

In general, we must reintegrate the facts of repetition with the facts of succession. 'Plus c'est la même chose, plus ça change' (Pouillon 1977), meaning that we can take neither the fact of continuity nor the fact of discontinuity at face value. They have meaning only in relation to one another; they are each other's implicit standard of measure. As exemplified by Sahlins, the real challenge to a historical anthropology is to comprehend how 'the reproduction of a structure becomes its transformation' (Sahlins 1981: 8). Repetition and succession are both of them part of reality, and the question put here is how the Icelanders' adherence to the old structure actually contributed to the changes of the experiential space, to the point where the Icelanders were almost checkmated by their own history.

In the following chapters we are going to see not only how in Iceland 'events are ordered by culture, but how, in that process, the culture is reordered' (ibid.). In order to understand this fully, we have to refer to both synchronic, diachronic, and panchronic dimensions of history. The synchronic dimension furnishes those structural patterns that seems to be true throughout the period; it refers to the 'ordering of events by culture'. In contrast, the diachronic dimension provides a framework for the tracing of changes that may eventually 'reorder culture'. The panchronic dimension contains the principles that seem to outlive all events, the features that remain constant irrespective of any cultural reorganization.

Speaking of diachronic rules for change is slightly more complicated in culture than in chess—which was the metaphor used by Saussure in 1916, when he coined the concepts (Saussure 1974; Ardener 1971b). In culture, rules are not laws, they are principles to which events seem to conform. Even 'conformity' has no precise referent in history, where no events are exact replicas of previous ones. Thus 'rules' must be taken as metaphors for recurring relationships between particular elements of the social. To the extent that we are at all able to identify such rules, all they tell us is that a particular kind of event or action 'as a rule' will be followed by a particular kind of reaction. It is no *law*, because people may redefine their culture precisely by overlooking the 'rule', that is by inventing new reactions to particular events.

It is part of the definition of states that a certain amount of continuity can be identified, or that certain rules seem to apply. In our period, one such rule is that priority was given to farming at the expense of fishing, in conditions of general labour shortage. This holds 'as a rule' throughout the period, while in the nineteenth century the fisheries suddenly gained momentum as a means for economic expansion in times of agricultural difficulty. A new state obtained.

Unlike a game of chess, the rules that we may identify in history do not exist outside the game itself. People enact them, but in the process they may actually redefine them. By the end of the eighteenth century Icelandic culture had been reordered to a point where we experience the end of an epoch, or the collapse of a state. Culture itself contained this transformation, just like the rule of checkmate is implicit in any specific game of chess. It is a rule which cannot be identified empirically until the last move of the game, but it is, nevertheless, the rule that defines its termination. We should not take the chess metaphor too literally, but it seems that in the Icelandic development there was a time when the Icelanders had to face a rule of mate. The old names on their lips had to be replaced by new ones.

States are defined by facts of repetition and moves by facts of succession. There is a particular kind of relationship which seems to connect them, which has been called an '*a priori* relation' (Vendler 1967). Imagine a chess board on which two pawns of the same colour stand in the same column. We can fairly reliably infer that at least one of them must have taken an opposing piece in a previous move. This must be so, *given the rules of the game* (ibid.: 17–21; Ardener 1971*b*: 216–17). Statements about hidden, or unobserved, moves of this kind are made via the framework of the game and its diachronic rules, and they hold a priori. In the study of history, the state and the recurrent relationships between succesive elements comprise the framework which allows us to identify a priori relations. Evidently the 'a priori' may be undermined, but to the extent that we are allowed to speak of duration and structural continuity at all, the a priori relations are keys to knowledge about actual changes even though they cannot be directly observed.

This brief discussion of rules and a priori relations serves as a necessary preamble to the implicit discussion of the panchronic dimension of any history. We shall return more explicitly to this discussion in Part IV, where the theoretical implications are dealt with. Already, however, in the presentation of the empirical material and the irreversible and reversible orders of history, there is a fundamental concern with causation in general. And that is where this particular work on Icelandic temporalities breaks away from traditional analytical history—and adds a dimension of general theory to the historical ethnography.

In the six chapters of Parts II and III on the ethnography I shall tell six separate histories, each with its own rhythm. The histories are interconnected in many subtle ways, but the point of separating them in the presentation is to avoid the facile idea of temporal causation. We have to experience the discontinuous development of the separate domains in order to perceive the multi-stranded causal relationships. Also, we must never forget that people are themselves agents in history, and we can see how this is true in many details of the lesser histories. We can see how choices were constantly made that affected the course of history. We can even see how it took an increasing effort to resist the radical reordering of Icelandic culture. The old names must have been pronounced with increasing difficulty, but the Icelanders persisted. Instead of producing a new history, they held on to old definitions and to a mythical reality.

The global perspective on Icelandic history is obtained through the juxtaposition of the separate histories, and the final analysis of the total development. But behind it all lies the Icelanders' own experience of continuity and discontinuity in their world.

Empirical Background

THIS work considers an epoch in Icelandic history. In speaking of an epoch, we give an impression of coherence and unity, and it is important to remember that this sense of 'wholeness' is to some degree analytically arbitrary. I intend to use the term 'epoch' in contradistinction to the 'period' of the historian—using epoch as an 'emic' periodization, a lived experience of coherence and unity, in contrast to the 'etic' periods of the historian.[1] In these terms, the comprehension of an epoch implies both that it can be seen as a systematic whole, and that this whole can be demonstrated to be of internal relevance.

With a period of four hundred years, and with no possibility of asking the Icelanders of the time about their views upon the unity of the centuries, I am obviously in the realm of conjecture when I speak of them as an 'epoch'. I do so mainly for heuristic purposes, and in order to contrast the perspective of the present work with the more traditional histories of Iceland. In these histories periodization is made with reference to particular events, which are then established as points of rupture in the dimensions of time. The events that are most often referred to in Icelandic history are the Reformation (1538–50), the Danish trade monopoly (1602–1787) and the advent of Absolutist rule (in Denmark, including Iceland) (1660). There is no doubt that these events were important markers in the chronology of Icelandic development, but elevating them to watersheds in the history of the Icelanders is to overlook the significance of continuities at another level.

By choosing to define an epoch which is at variance with those that are traditionally used to arrange the clusters of meaning by which chronologies are broken down to periods, we gain a fresh perspective upon causation in history. By evading the traditional watersheds (as watersheds, that is) we also dodge the facile identification between events and causes of development. As it happens, the major events cum causes by which Icelandic history is generally understood are all of them *external* causes. They represent measures taken by the 'colonial' power as against the Icelanders. The problem of internal versus external causes is a vital issue in the present work, and one that we are not allowed to pre-empt by any primary equation of political events and epistemological breaks. In the long run there is no doubt, for instance, that the Reformation contributed to a restructuring of Icelandic society, but there is no indication of Icelandic mentality changing overnight. In other words, there is no evidence of the Reformation being more than a new ideology phrased in the words of 'religion' which only gradually was to take root in the popular representations of right and wrong.

There is ample reason to choose an epoch like 1400–1800 as an object of analysis. It contains a series of major events, and because our view of the history implies that these events are *embedded* in a larger epoch, and not its boundaries, we are in a position to discuss causality from a more complex perspective than is usual. This, of course, will have to be demonstrated. Before I can adequately deal with the details of Icelandic history, I must present the empirical background of the larger history of the area. This amounts to positioning Iceland in physical space, and in European history. These two sections will be painted in rather broad strokes, meant only to prime the canvas for the motley and detailed picture to follow. The third section of this chapter, which serves to introduce specifically Icelandic history, is also rather sparse, and meant only to open up the epoch to the uninitiated.

THE NATURAL SETTING

Iceland is an island of about 103,000 square kilometres in the North Atlantic Ocean. It touches on the Arctic Circle towards the north, and generally the climate is sub-arctic. It was originally populated from the Scandinavian mainland, although more than 900 kilometres of dangerous seas separate it from the Norwegian coast to the east. Towards the south, Scotland is 800 kilometres distant; but towards the west, however, only 300 kilometres separate Iceland from Greenland, where Norse colonies were established about the first millenium, only to vanish some five centuries later.

This geographical position has important implications for the history of Iceland. It has fashioned patterns of trade and other kinds of communication, and also accounts for some natural limitations upon the social development. As we know, however, nature is no passive agent in history, because it is transformed by man and reacted upon according to particular conceptual schemes. For the moment, I shall concentrate on the purely natural parameters of Iceland—the objective features of nature. I am here following the lead of Braudel (*sans comparaison*) whose impressive work on the Mediterranean opens with a long narrative of the environment (1976). The environment is seen to provide that timeless reality in which both the history of structure and the history of conjunctures are embedded (ibid.: 1239). I appreciate his idea of distinct 'conceptions of time', or temporalities, governing the different histories, but perhaps the notion of timelessness for the natural environment is unwarranted. At least we have to distinguish between such eternal truths as the position of Iceland in the North Atlantic, and the fluctuations of climate that may actually affect history in the long run (Le Roy Ladurie 1979: 287–319). I am not here talking about changes occurring from one year to the next, but of those major fluctuations that can be detected over centuries and which may account for (without actually having *caused*) 'times of feast and times of famine' (Le Roy Ladurie 1972). Apart from yearly oscillations within the normal range of variations, such climatic fluctuations are characterized by a slowness which may make of their 'time' a more steady history than the history of structure. Climatic and structural changes may also coincide, however, as demonstrated for Danish prehistory (Jensen 1979); even for historical times with their much more detailed sources the possible association between the rhythm of climate and the rhythm of social structure should not be precluded.

The Icelandic climate is sub-arctic, cold and with a high precipitation. This holds true for the period 1400 to 1800, but it is of such generality that further discussion is needed. Climate has its own history (Le Roy Ladurie 1972: 7), and models have been made to describe climatological fluctuations in short- and long-term perspectives (Le Roy Ladurie 1970). Distinct periods of North Atlantic climate have been established as far back as 70,000 BC from measurements of the Greenlandic ice-cap, showing how cycles of different length (120, 940, and 13,000 years) have intersected (Dansgaard *et al.* 1969). On a smaller scale Lamb has investigated the alternation of climactic *optima* and *pessima* in Europe (1966). As far as our period is concerned, he has identified a *pessimum* from 1550 to 1700; this is the so-called 'little ice age'. On the basis of a tephrochronological method of dating, Þórarinsson shows how the glaciers of Iceland reached their maximum extension during this period (1949). Other evidence points unanimously to the same feature (Le Roy Ladurie 1972: 182–3, 222), including the internal evidence provided by the Icelandic annalists, who recorded recurrent bad winters and extreme amounts of drift-ice in the seventeenth century.

From the perspective of our 400-year period as a whole, the little ice age was a major climatic *pessimum*. However, as shown by Eyþórsson for the nineteenth and twentieth centuries, it is possible to trace significant changes also for shorter spans of time, such as 30–60 years (Eyþórsson 1949). Thus in the period 1925 to 1949 oats and barley ripened every summer in southern Iceland, while attempts to reintroduce grain in the eighteenth and nineteenth centuries had been unsuccessful (ibid.: 37). What is more, in a climate like that of Iceland, great fluctuations in temperature and precipitation can be expected from one year to another.

Climate fluctuates and the weather changes—in relation to history it appears to be an independent variable; there is no doubt, indeed, that climate influences the course of history. However, to link climate and history in a simple monocausal chain clearly would be an error. Any test of climatic influences on history must take into account other variables as well (de Vries 1981: 28). Climate may have its own natural history and meteorological measures, but it also has a social history, which is largely a history of adaptation to both short- and long-term fluctuations. In other words, the human context of climatic change, including the 'risk adverseness' of any social organization (ibid.: 46), is a crucial variable in considerations of climate. Thus it has been demonstrated how the decisive variable in the elimination of famine in Modern Europe was not the weather, but rather the ability to adapt to the weather (Appleby 1981: 83).

There are genuinely exogenous shocks which society can only respond to as crises, but generally the climatic fluctuations are absorbed by social adaptation. In Iceland from 1400 to 1800 there are numerous records of lean years and famines, and in the seventeenth and especially during the eighteenth century reports of mass deaths from starvation provide a sad picture. In 1783–6 a great volcanic eruption killed one-fifth of the population. This last example is an exogenous shock, and the crisis is explicable in these terms, but even here matters of administration and distribution of resources enter as an important variable in the scale of the crisis. As for the lean years and recurrent famines, climate cannot be treated as the sole cause either. A contributing factor was the extremely low security marginal—economic and social—which the Icelanders allowed themselves (Gísli Gunnarsson 1980*b*). As we shall see, the economic security marginal tended to decrease from the sixteenth to the eighteenth centuries, in positive and hence fatal covariation with climatic fluctuation.

From a climatological perspective the so-called *pessima* are not so much changes in the average temperature as they are indicators of lower extremes. With low security marginals in the Icelandic economy and society, the little ice age made catastrophe a recurrent phenomenon. But the cause for this and other declines was not solely climatic. Many good, even 'favourable' years interspersed the extremely cold winters, but social and economic structures were unfavourable to social reproduction, as we shall see.

Geologically, Iceland was formed during the Tertiary through volcanic activity. Today it is still among the most active volcanic areas, and from the earliest recorded history in Iceland, volcanic eruptions have been recorded as more or less damaging to society. Geysers and other thermal springs add to the picture of Iceland as an island of remarkable thermal activity. Place-names bear witness to an early exploitation of the natural hot-water supply.

The heat of the earth is in sharp contrast to the ice-caps covering vast areas of the land. These are old glaciers, and although they have displayed a certain pattern of contraction and expansion in historical time, they have been a very stable element in Icelandic geography. Some of the glaciers cover volcanoes, and occasional eruptions result in immense glacier torrents affecting large stretches of land. With one-tenth of the land covered in ice, and large stretches covered by volcanic sands and lava, only a very small proportion of the country is actually arable. There is evidence of a decrease of the tillable area during the two centuries following the first settlements, and while this decrease was owed in part to volcanic eruptions (like the one devastating the famous Þjórsárdalur), it also originated in human exploitation of the land (Hastrup 1985*a*: 158–65). Without going into the detail of this chain of gradual waste, we can note that during our period woods disappeared almost completely, and ensuing soil erosion laid many tracts waste.

The areas that are not covered in either ice or lava are generally mountainous with only smaller stretches of land habitable. Apart from one or two fiords in the north, it is only in the south-west that there are extensive areas of tillable lowlands; otherwise the general picture is one of narrow valleys separated by huge mountain ranges. The land is not very hospitable, and in spite of the size of the island its natural carrying capacity is low, and has probably decreased through human neglect.

Around the island the sea always provided another natural resource. Towards the south Iceland is hit by the Gulf Stream, while the north is touched by the cold East Greenland current. This accounts for internal variations in climate and also the seasonal variations in fishing. Apart from fish, the currents and winds at sea also brought driftwood to the shores of Iceland, without which the island would have been poorer. The huge distances across the North Atlantic and the unstable winds impeded communications for the better part of the year and defined the narrow limits of trade. Within these physical limits Icelandic enterprise flourished in certain periods, other factors permitting (Gelsinger 1981). Nature was demanding, but it was not all-important.

The two main sea currents touching Iceland account for the major difference between its two ecological zones (Gísli Gunnarsson 1980*b*: 21 ff.). The south and the west are affected by the Gulf Stream, and are characterized by mild winters and rainy and cold summers. The north and the east are touched by the Arctic East Greenlandic current, and suffer relatively greater fluctuations in temperature and precipitation. The two ecological zones are significantly different in their economies; in the south and west fishing was always an important assset to the economy, because cod came to spawn in the warm waters during the winter season when stores were getting scarce. In the north and east, fishing was limited and certainly no immediate security margin.

Both the fauna and flora of Iceland were always relatively poor in species. Of land mammals only small rodents and foxes were found; birds were abundant in numbers, but few in kind. Of plants, various grasses were the main species. Woods were few and far between, and consisted mainly of low birch. The sea contained whales, seals, and fish in plenty; streams and lakes supplied fresh-water fish as well.

There were, in general, important natural economic resources, in spite of the paucity of botanical and zoological species. The present work is largely concerned with the ways in which the Icelanders living in the period from 1400 to 1800 exploited nature. As will become evident, 'nature' is no objective category, and resources are not self-evident. They have to be conceived of as such before they can be exploited. Let us, therefore, terminate this brief discussion of the natural setting by remembering that nature may define ecological boundaries, but can never set absolute limits for human action.

THE EUROPEAN CONTEXT

Icelandic history from 1400 to 1800 was not only set in a particular natural environment, it was also englobed by a specific historical context. In spite of the geographical isolation and the socio-political marginality of the Icelanders, their lives were influenced by historical processes and dynamisms elsewhere in Europe.

In the ninth and tenth centuries Iceland was settled from Norway and from Norse colonies in the British Isles.[2] From then onwards its material and spiritual life was very much formed by Northern European realities, if not always concurrent with them. In the 1070s Adam of Bremen said of the Icelanders that they were somewhat anomalous compared with other peoples; they were primitive and lived in a state of nature, yet they were Christian.[3] Apparently, the Icelanders were less civilized than the other peoples of Northern Europe, but through their religion they were on the right track. Christianity took an increasingly strong hold in Iceland, and civilization took shape. Still, in 1247 the Cardinal William of Sabina expressed his misgivings, when he 'called it improper that Iceland did not serve under a king like all other countries in the world'.[4] An intensive campaign eventually made the Icelanders subjects of the king of Norway in 1262–4, and the entire socio-political context changed. A new and 'civilized' concept of society as a royal patrimony replaced the ancient Scandinavian concept of society as one with law and peace (Hastrup 1984*a*). This was a turning-point in Icelandic relations with Europe. In one stroke it had become part of a larger social order, redefined as an element in European civilization.

Formerly, the Vikings had swept all over Europe and enrolled distant southern neighbours in their world. This process, however, was now reversed, and Icelandic reality was englobed by Europe, Christianity, and the idea of kingdoms. Norway was united with Denmark in 1380 and Iceland was part of the deal. Denmark had made the transition to a kind of feudal society, a transition which the peculiar nature of Viking social structure had earlier impeded (Anderson 1974*a*: 173 ff.). Hierarchy had been introduced as the organizing principle *par excellence*, and land-rights were no longer allocated on the basis of the age-old allodial principle. By contrast to the feudal lords of central and southern Europe, those in Scandinavia had few privileges other than use-right of the land. Apart from a small category of princely estates, the feudal lands, *len* or *län* (from German *Lehn*, 'borrowing'), never entirely slipped out of the king's hands. Due to this and other 'anomalies' (when compared to central and southern European feudalism) Marc Bloch considers Scandinavia to be a blank space on the map of feudalism (1965: 445). This is not merely a matter of academic debate, but is of particular historical consequence. While European feudalism largely dissolved in the fourteenth century, owing to its own inherent process of sociopolitical fragmentation, the contradiction between the state and feudal principles never had the same consequences in the North.

Nordic feudalism was essentially a principle of administration, whereby the feudal lord collected taxes and such like for the king. This principle remained in force throughout the Middle Ages, but during the fifteenth century the structure changed. The greater *len* became fewer, while the number of smaller *len* increased. Christian II of Denmark and Norway (1513–23) changed the status of all fiefs from independent to 'accountable' fiefs, which were more profitable to the king.

Although Nordic society was not precisely feudal, the residual principle of European feudalism, whereby men exploit men and land-rights are strongly unequal, was a decisive element in Nordic policies during the entire period 1400 to 1800. Later, with the introduction, first of the Reformation, and then of absolutism, the legitimization of inequality changed its rhetoric. Hierarchy persisted and, in Iceland as elsewhere, an ancient social structure based on kinship and allodial right to land was consigned definitively to the past.[5] Once this passage had been made, the whole of Europe was set in motion towards absolutism, even though unevenly and discontinuously (Perry Anderson 1974*b*). In Denmark the absolutist state was declared in 1660. The king, Frederik III, managed to dismantle the system of aristocratic

power, and with the support of the growing bourgeoisie in Copenhagen, he replaced it with royal absolutism. The privileges of the
ancient nobility were demolished, and the land was redistributed to
bourgeois supporters. A stagnant agricultural system was thus
preserved and adscription was introduced in 1733. This was abolished
in 1788 partly as a consequence of changes in the European market
system (de Vries 1976: 59), and partly due to an internal and often overlooked peasant protest (Bjørn 1981).

Within the European economic system as a whole, the period from
1400 to 1800 contains the emergence and development of capitalism.
Whether actually determined by world-accumulation (Frank 1978) or
not, it is beyond dispute that European economic enterprises
gradually englobed the entire world in an unprecedented universal
history (Wolf 1982). Already by 1400 the Old World was internally
connected by trade routes, and after 1492 the New World gradually
became integrated into the same world-system (Braudel 1984: 28–9).
During the following centuries of European expansion, trade connections were gradually transformed into relationships of exploitation.
Hierarchy had become global. The movement of surplus was uni-
directional.

In the eighteenth century an emergent textile industry was to
become a major vehicle for capitalist growth (Wolf 1982: 267 ff.).
Gradually a new social category of labourers emerged, and urbanization changed meaning. In Iceland the industrial revolution did not
occur until the twentieth century; no urban centres were found at all
until early 1800, and even then they were on a very, very small scale.
But the new 'spirit of capitalism' (Weber 1970) engulfed Icelandic
reality in a range of subtle ways. Successive absolutist Danish kings
sought profit in this distant part of the kingdom, and new ways of pro-
cessing fish and woollens, and of exploiting minerals, were introduced
to the reluctant Icelanders. Despite obvious differences between
European countries, social developments had a tendency to be more
or less synchronized throughout Europe (Braudel 1982: 477). Western
civilization took shape in an all-embracing historical process, and
affected the structure of everyday life in even the most remote corners
of Europe (Braudel 1981). Where, in the early Middle Ages, Western
society had waged war against barbarism in the name of the Cross,
towards the end of the Middle Ages the same war was fought in the
name of civilization.

Apart from classical antecedents, the early modern concept of civilization as a unifying whole, was owed to Erasmus of Rotterdam who published a short treatise 'On Civility in Children' (*De civilitate morum puerilium*), in 1530. Although primarily an instruction for boys about proper behaviour, the concept of civilized as opposed to uncivilized was soon to cover much wider aspects of social life. As shown by Elias, the civilizing process occurred simultaneously both at the level of manners and at the level of thinking about social forms (Elias 1978, 1982). The individual and the social merge in that particular kind of transformation which we call civilization.

The period 1400 to 1800 embraces two stages in European history as identified by historians: medieval and early modern. The break between the two is obviously arbitrary and variable, and in Scandinavia it is normally defined by the Reformation, taking place in Denmark (and Iceland in part) in 1536. Shifting the focus to other parts of Europe, the early modern period may be defined as 1450–1720 (Clark 1966), or from *c.*1500 to 1800 (Burke 1978: 11). Whatever the chronological definition, there is unanimity that a unified European culture existed (with some regional variation, of course). There may be vertical differences, between élite and popular culture, but horizontally all European nations of the pre-industrial era were at some levels united in a shared system of thought and action.

The invention of printing was instrumental to this cultural unification. The printed book was not only a triumph of technical ingenuity; it 'was also one of the most potent agents at the disposal of western civilization in bringing together the scattered ideas of representative thinkers' (Febvre and Martin 1984: 10). The spread of printing was swift (ibid.: 184–5), and in the earliest days the most important task was to make the Bible accessible to everyone. Devotional literature was soon to be complemented by secular prose, and during the first part of the sixteenth century humanist interests led to a decrease in the proportion of religious works (ibid.: 248 ff.).

In Iceland, religious literature continued to dominate printed works (Loftur Guttormsson 1987*b*: 247–52). The bishops held a monopoly on printing until the mid-nineteenth century, and secular literature was continually copied by hand. This duality is a remarkable feature of the Icelandic pattern of literacy (Loftur Guttormsson 1981: 125–8).

By the end of the first millennium, most of Europe, including its northernmost fringes, had been incorporated into the Christian world. The pagans were converted, and so enrolled into Christian history. So also the Icelanders who had been converted in 1000. Apart from the conscious change of faith, 'conversion' may be read also as a metaphor of a particular historical transformation, which can only be identified retrospectively (Hastrup 1985c). By the beginning of our period, the transformation was complete, and Iceland was definitively part of European Christendom, which defined its own time-space (cf. Fabian 1983: 26–7).

When civilization replaced Christianity as the unifying concept of Europe, incorporation was no longer self-evident. Economically, politically, and historically, Iceland was indubitably integrated into the wider European context. However, in the eyes of many continental observers, the Icelanders lived on the fringes of civilization. It is a recurrent theme in sixteenth- to eighteenth-century travelogues that the Icelanders had very uncultivated habits. There were great intellectuals in Iceland during this period, but the general pattern of behaviour, according to contemporary reporters, was something wanting. In the course of this book I shall substantiate this image. I am not, of course, concerned to pass my own judgement on the Icelanders; rather, through detailed description of Icelandic material and spritual life, I shall let them be judged according to reigning contemporary ideas of civilization in Europe.

ICELANDIC CHRONOLOGY, 1400–1800

On the fringes of Europe peoples wrote their own histories in a more or less explicit dialogue with the history of the developing capitalism of the centres. Evidently, these were only centres in relation to industrialization and captalism, on the margins of which smaller cycles of social reproduction continued their autonomous existence, as in Iceland.[6] Although certainly tangential to European history, as depicted in the previous section, the development of Iceland is incomprehensible with reference to this history alone. To understand what happened and failed to happen in Iceland, we must look to its internal structures.

An internal view is also required in matters of chronology, since events judged significant from this point of view are not necessarily those visible from the outside. We are not able to ask contemporary Icelanders about their view of the relative importance of events in the fifteenth to eighteenth centuries, but there is an indigenous source which to some extent serves the purpose—the *Almanak fyrir Ísland*

(Almanac for Iceland), which has been published since the middle of the nineteenth century.[7] On the first page a list of *merkisár* ('marked years' or important dates in Icelandic history) sets the chronological frame for an internal view of history:

Fæðing Krists (Birth of Christ)	*á tímabilinu 7–4 f.kr.* (in the period 7–4 BC)
Upphaf Íslandsbyggðar (first settlements in Iceland)	*seint á 9. öld e.Kr.* (late 9th century AD)
Upphaf alþingis (Establishment of the Althing)	um 930 *c.*930
Kristnitaka á Íslandi (Acceptance of Christianity)	999
Upphaf konungsríkis á Íslandi (*Gamli sáttmáli*) (Establishment of the kingdom in Iceland) (The Old Treaty)	1262
Plágan mikla á Íslandi ('*Svartidauði*') (The Great Plague in Iceland) ('The Black Death')	1402–4
Siðaskipti á Íslandi (*Jón Arason hálshöggvinn*) (Reformation in Iceland) (Jón Arason decapitated)	1550
Einokunarverslun Dana á Íslandi (Danish trade monopoly in Iceland)	1602–1787
Móðuharðindin hefjast (The times of great hunger begin)	1783
Alþingi endurreist með tilskipun eftir hálfrar aldrar hlé. (The Althing re-established after a break of half a century)	1843
Ísland fær stjórnarskrá (Iceland gets a constitution)	1874
Ísland fær innlenda ráðherrastjórn (Iceland gets an internal ministry)	1904

Ísland verður fullvalda ríki   1918
(Iceland becomes an autonomous nation)

Ísland verður lýðveldi   1944
(Iceland becomes a republic)

On inspection this list of important dates in Icelandic history clusters around particular themes, each of which is prevalent in a particular period. After the birth of Christ, which for some reason is dated to 4–7 years BC!, the first cluster of dates concern the Freestate of Iceland—the period, that is, from the first settlements and the inception of the Althing, to the acceptance of Christianity, and onwards to the fall of the Freestate. The 'fall' was not necessarily as dramatic as it sounds, but it entailed an inclusion of Iceland into the kingdom of Norway and an agreement to pay tax to the king, as well as other mutual rights and obligations stipulated in the 'Old Treaty' (*gamli sáttmáli*). This is the period I have dealt with in my previous monograph (Hastrup 1985*a*).

At the 'modern' end of the list the dates recorded relate to the gradual achievement of sovereignty, from the re-establishment of the Althing in 1843 until the declaration of the Republic in 1944. The dates mark political events, and are symptoms of the victories won by the nationalist movement flourishing in Iceland as elsewhere in Europe in the nineteenth century.

In between these two relatively well-defined sub-series of dates we find four events of a different order, belonging to the period under scrutiny in the present work. The reason for claiming that the order is 'different' is that the recorded events are all externally imposed. Two of them are natural catastrophes, one is a foreign trade monopoly. The last one is the Reformation, which likewise was imposed by the Danish monarch, and although today the Icelanders would probably find no harm in this, the parenthesis indicates that at the time violence was needed to convince (part of) the people. Jón Arason was the last Catholic bishop, and although the Reformation had officially been announced in Iceland 1538 when the southern bishopric was converted, the northern bishop Jón Arason held on to Catholicism, until he was beheaded to convince him of the advantages of the new faith. Jón Arason is a national hero in many Icelandic histories, as he personifies resistance to the Danish hegemony. By referring to Jón Arason in the list of *merkisár* the Icelandic almanac makes the Reformation a transparently external imposition.

Thus, the four events recorded as *merkisár* in Iceland from 1400 to 1800 testify to an important point: that Icelandic history in this period is seen to have been caused by external factors of both natural and political kinds. My analysis will show that this is not the whole truth. Crumpling under the weight of these unhappy centuries, Icelandic society failed to react adequately, with Icelanders holding the view that they were powerless against external threats. These indigenous datings, therefore, give us a primary clue to the epoch from 1400 to 1800, although we must not forget that these *merkisár* were first construed in the nineteenth century, in a retrospective definition of meaningful 'history'.

A narrative history of Icelandic society during these years can be briefly set out. The period opens with a great natural catastrophe, the Black Death, ravaging the island from 1402 to 1404. The sources on the Black Death are few, the most important being Nýi Annáll; this relates the advent of the plague in 1402 and refers to 1403 as a 'great mortality year' (*Ann.* i. 9–10). As a curious detail the annalist describes how the nuns at Kirkjubæjarklaustur had to milk their cows themselves, owing to the loss of servants (ibid.). This gives a clue to the social effects of the plague; the normal order of things was quite upset. At the time the Church and monasteries owned about half the land, Icelandic yeomen and absentee landowners the other half. Among the latter the plague influenced patterns of inheritance and probably meant a redistribution of the land; in the first category normal patterns of tenancy were destroyed and much land fell into disuse; in the northern districts about 40 per cent of the farms were still laid waste in 1431 (Kristín Bjarnadóttir 1986: 61–2). The actual toll on the population has been estimated within the range of one-third (Þórkell Jóhannesson 1933: 57) and two-thirds (Arnór Sigurjónsson 1930: 174); the latest research suggests 40 to 50 per cent (Kristín Bjarnadóttir 1986: 61). Whichever is correct, the social effects in a population numbering less than a hundred thousand must have been remarkable. Björn Þorsteinsson may be correct, though, in suggesting that the plague had no fundamental impact on Icelandic society—if we refer to the social structure in general (cf. Björn Þorsteinsson 1980: 241). This cannot, however, explain away the very real drama of the Icelanders. Our epoch opens with a natural catastrophe of extraordinary dimensions, dislocating traditional patterns of landownership and cultivation. The ensuing century was to witness several catastrophes of a similar kind; smallpox epidemics, hard winters, and by the end of the century the 'later plague' hit Iceland (1494–5), with effects that were comparable to, if less severe than, the effects of the Great Plague of 1402–4 (cf. Kristín Bjarnadóttir 1986). The annalist who wrote of the later plague in *Fitja Annáll*, and its appearance in blue cloth and in the shape of a bird, compares it explicitly with the earlier plague, which was still living in the collective memory (*Ann.* i. 27).

The sources on matters of social organization in the fifteenth century are few, and inspired guesswork is necessary. In matters of trade and economy in general, however, we are more privileged. From a series of treaties and laws, we can identify a certain pattern. In the first half of the century, English merchants dominated trade, and the Icelandic economy improved. The period has been referred to as the 'English Age' (Björn Þorsteinsson 1970). Before this, trade had been governed by old Norwegian privileges, and by the Hanseatic league (Gelsinger 1981). In the second half of the fifteenth century, and after several 'cod-wars' (Björn Þorsteinsson 1976), merchants from Hamburg gained ground at the expense of the English. The Danish king played an important role, both in the distribution of privileges, and in maintaining the principle that no foreigners were allowed to winter in Iceland. While battles over cod went on at sea during the summer, the island had to be left alone during winter.

In the early sixteenth century, English and German merchants continued their fights over the Icelandic fish resources, and internal problems in Denmark prevented the monarch from intervening. In 1533 fishing was finally made free to everyone; only merchants of whatever nationality were told not to mark fish before they had paid for them, 'because all fights between merchants usually originate in this' (ibid.: 67). Earlier, the merchants had attempted to secure the landings for themselves by marking them the minute they were on shore. While foreign fishing continued to attract Icelandic labour the farmers strongly disapproved of it, and internal legislation gradually reduced the opportunities in fishing for Icelandic labourers.

The Reformation was a major event in sixteenth-century Iceland, and the history of the Icelandic 'conversion' has been told and retold by many historians. The Reformation was passed in Denmark in 1536–7, and formally this decision applied also to Iceland—at least since its announcement at the Althing 1538. Things were not that simple, however. Iceland was divided into two bishoprics—the See at Skálholt, established in 1056, and the See at Hólar, established in 1106; there were schools at both places which, with the monasteries, had controlled Icelandic education. In the decade before the Reformation, Ögmundur Pálsson had been elected bishop at Skálholt, and, after some controversy, Jón Arason was installed at Hólar. Ögmundur accepted the Reformation, but Jón Arason resisted it, and was eventually beheaded for his pains. This means that the Reformation in Iceland occurred in two parts, as it were. The south was converted in 1538, while the north remained catholic until 1550. Several episodes and small fights between the two groups took place between these dates. The problem most obviously affected the learned part of the population and the Church administration, but it evidently had repercussions among ordinary people.[8] At the level of 'belief' it is difficult to estimate the immediate effects of the Reformation, if for nothing else than because 'belief' as such is a highly problematic term (Needham 1972). Furthermore, 'conversion' may be regarded a metaphor which represents a gradual transition as an instantaneous switch (Hastrup 1985c).

One indisputable effect of the Reformation was to make the Danish king take a more active interest in Iceland. The church lands were annexed by the king, and a substantial proportion of Icelandic peasants thus became royal tenants, giving the monarchy more obvious interests in Icelandic farming than before. Further, the king engaged in a moral campaign to raise the standard of life in Iceland.

The seventeenth century began with the introduction, in 1602, of the Danish trade monopoly. This lasted until 1787, and although the monopoly was sometimes leased out to foreign merchants, for almost two hundred years the Danish king held ultimate rule over Icelandic trade.

It was in part due to this that the seventeenth century was marked by social and economic decline. Intellectually, however, the Icelanders remained active. Learning flourished in a small circle of intellectuals (especially under the influence of humanism), and among ordinary Icelanders literary entertainment was extensive. Copies of old manuscripts were made in large numbers, verses were composed, and old stories transformed into new genres. The seventeenth century also, and less happily, was a period of witch-prosecutions in Iceland, offshoots of the General European witch-craze (Hastrup 1988a).

By contrast to the seventeenth century, the eighteenth century seems historically indistinct. Farming and fishing coexisted on a poor technological level. In 1703 the first complete census of Iceland was made, and the population numbered 50,300 Icelanders. Almost immediately after this the population was reduced to about 35,000 by a smallpox epidemic, and it was more than a hundred years before 50,000 was reached again. This demographic condition is part of the reason why the eighteenth-century Icelanders appear to be such passive agents in history. As the following analysis will show, this 'passivity' was correlate with a peculiar attempt to stick with old concepts. Already in 1786, a German observer noted this peculiarity of the Icelandic 'character', as he called it. 'Kurz—der Character der Isländer ist eins der *allermerkwürdigsten Phänomen in der heutigen Geschichte der Menschheit*' ('In short—the Icelandic character is one of the most remarkable phenomena in the modern history of humanity') (Eggers 1786: 44, original emphasis).

By the mid-eighteenth century, a campaign had begun for improving the standard of living in Iceland, and new technologies were gradually introduced. Intellectually, the effects of the European Enlightenment begin to be noticeable towards the end of the century. For the peasants, however, the effects of this are more or less un-measurable until well into the nineteenth century. A major obstacle to progress was the great famine of the 1780s, following a volcanic erup-tion in the Skaftá area in south-east Iceland. The effects of the spread of lava and ash upon an already fragile economy, led to the death of half the livestock and one-fifth of the population, from hunger and epidemic diseases. This catastrophe led some people to suggest that the surviving Icelanders should be transferred either to Denmark or to Finmark (Björn Þorsteinsson 1985: 191). This did not happen, how-ever, and an important step towards improvement of the Icelandic economy was taken in 1787 when free trade was introduced. A series of other measures followed, designed to restore Icelandic society, and (later) to regenerate an Icelandic 'nation'. Skúli Magnússon was particularly important in this.

Restoration was accompanied by the abolition of age-old institu-tions. The See and the school at Skálholt were abolished in 1785, and a new school started in Reykjavík, by then the only urban centre in Iceland (although its population was still only 500). The See and the school at Hólar were abolished in 1801, and henceforth Iceland became one bishopric. In 1804 the Latin school was moved to Bessastaðir, outside Reykjavík. The Althing, or people's assembly, which had ruled in Iceland since 930, under changing conditions and with varying functions, was moved from the ancient site of Þingvellir to Reykjavík in 1798. In 1800 it was finally abolished, and a new assembly was set under Danish ruling. So it is that 1800 marks the end of an epoch, and the beginning of a new era.

We can leave Iceland at this intersection between two periods. By doing so, however, on the eve of restoration, we are left with an inkling of a new kind of mentality to replace the old—the old medieval mentality which had gradually become dislocated from the world.

II

THE SOCIAL EXPERIENCE

3

Modes of Livelihood

IN *Laxdœla saga* the reason given for the emigration of Ketill *flatnefr* and his family from Norway is the expansionist policy of King Harald Fairhair.[1] The author of *Laxdœla saga* thereby reaffirms the tradition that the tyranny of Harald was the main reason for leaving Norway in the ninth century.[2] However, would-be emigrants not only had to decide to leave; they also had to decide upon a proper destination, and *Laxdœla saga* gives us some reasons for choosing Iceland. There is no unanimity among the main characters; Ketill's sons Bjǫrn and Helgi opt for Iceland because they had heard the place so highly praised, and because 'land was so abundant and one did not have to pay for it; there was much stranding of whales and salmon-fishing, and places to fish all the year round' (*Laxdœla saga*, *ÍF*: v. 5). Ketill was not convinced, however, as he felt that at his age he would have little pleasure from fishing-places (*veiðistǫð*). Thus while the younger generation settled for Iceland, Ketill went to the British Isles 'where life was good'—where, that is, there were good conditions for farming (ibid.). According to the tradition established by the thirteenth-century author of *Laxdœla*, then, there were two reasons for making Iceland a new home besides the tyranny of Harald Fairhair: abundance of land and abundance of fish.

Farming and fishing were to remain basic pillars of the Icelandic economy until modern times. As one eighteenth-century reformer observed,

the Icelandic economy is founded on only two gifts of nature: cattle-breeding and fishing, holding out their hands towards one another, since the latter gets life and power from the former, which again is supported by the latter. (Skúli Magnússon 1944*b*: 37.)

The gifts of nature were not always plentiful or reliable, and nature herself was subject to change over the centuries, but the dualistic economic pattern persisted, such that ethnographic reports from the fourteenth century to the eighteenth century all refer to it as a distinctive feature of Icelandic society. Thus in 1350 the abbot Arngrímur Brandsson introduced his *Guðmundar saga Arasonar* with a brief general description of Iceland, in which he says that *fiskr sjádreginn ok búnyt er þar almennings matr* ('fish from the sea and milk from cattle are everyman's food' (*BS*: iii. 161)). This statement about food-habits is echoed by the Revd Bishop Oddur Einarsson in 1589, who says that 'after milk-produce and meat from the cattle, the greater part of the food of the Icelanders consists of fish' (1971: 124); and Eggert Ólafsson, in his extensive report on Icelandic society in the mid-eighteenth century, says much the same (1772: 24 ff.). There is no doubt that these reports reflect an actual complementarity between farming and fishing at the level of subsistence. In the words of Skúli Magnússon quoted above, the two 'support each other'.

The annals provide additional evidence that both economic activities were absolutely vital to the country. If failure occurred within one of the domains, hunger was likely, even if the other domain was of ordinary yield. If both failed, the consequences were likely to be fatal to the population, as abundantly testified to by Hannes Finnsson when in 1796 he set out to extract from the annals as well as other sources the evidence of 'population decrease in lean years' (Finnsson 1970).

Although recognized as complementary at the level of consumption, farming and fishing as two distinct systems of production apparently did not occupy equal positions in the minds of the Icelanders. They were never simply alternative ways of making a living, because they held asymmetrical positions in the (social) system of classifications. This was implied also by Ketill's answer to his sons: whereas farming was conceived of as a *sine qua non* of the 'good life', fishing was subsidiary, a source of income which might or might not be exploited. In another thirteenth-century source there is even a hint that too much fishing might be detrimental to the people; in *Landnámabók* (*Ldn.*)[3] it is said of the settler Flóki Vilgerðarson and his men that they failed to harvest hay in time 'because the fjord was so full of catch'. All Flóki's cattle consequently died during the winter, and Flóki abandoned the island, leaving behind only the name, Iceland, which is attributed to him (*ÍF*: i. 38). Although evidence like this comes from a literary tradition whose historicity is arguable, nevertheless this tradition was to have very literal historical repercussions in the centuries under study here.

The aim of the present chapter is to investigate the nature of the dual economy, and to explore the apparent discrepancy between the actual economic complementarity of farming and fishing, and their conceptual asymmetry.

The basic unit of production and consumption for our period was the household. The composition and the size of the household varied, but its paramount significance persisted; it outlived all events, so to speak. In this chapter, therefore, I deal first with the household, which provided the social frame for farming and fishing, both of which shall be dealt with in turn. The chapter ends with an analysis of the relationships between the elements of the economic order. As promised in the Introduction, I attempt to trace developments and changes in the diachronic dimension, while simultaneously working within a pan-chronic frame of reference, where the constants of the period are elicited.

THE HOUSEHOLD

In Icelandic the household is referred to by the concept of *bú*, whence the notion of *búandi*, and later *bóndi*, meaning 'farmer' or 'yeoman'. To the Icelanders of the early Middle Ages, the *bú* was a cherished token of personal autonomy, as testified to by the ancient Norse god Oðinn's speech:

> *Bú er betra*
> *þótt lítit sé,*
> *halr er heima hverr,*
> *þótt tvær geitr eigi*
> *ok taugreptan sal,*
> *þat er þó betra en bænn.*
>
> (*Hávamál*, v. 36
> (Bugge 1867: 47))

(A *bú* is better, even if a little one, a man is somebody at home, even if he owns only two goats, and his house is thatched with fibre, it is still better than begging.)

From the time of the settlements, to establish an independent household was to claim autonomy for oneself and one's family. To be a *bóndi* was also to have access to political power, although the privileges of the *bóndi* varied in the changing social structure of the high Middle

Ages (cf. Hastrup 1985*a*). In many ways the household was a micro-cosm, reflecting the larger order of cosmology and society at the only relevant 'local' level (Hastrup 1981*a*).

Although there were some changes in world view between the Middle Ages and the end of our epoch, certain major structural patterns remained constant; one of these was the conception of *bú* and farmstead, *bær*, as the pivot of social organization, in relation to which more peripheral orders were 'measured'. This remained true right up to the end of the nineteenth century, for no urbanization took place until then. This is one of the main differences between Iceland and the other Nordic countries, for in the latter the social division of labour was reflected in geographical separation. In Iceland all specialist tasks had to be carried out within the household during the entire period. The focus on the household, and the atomistic social structure result-ing from it, have had important implications for the conception of history in Iceland. As observed by Ker:

There is no sense of those impersonal forces, those nameless multitudes, that make history a different thing from biography in other lands. All history in Iceland shaped itself as biography or as drama, and there was no large crowd at the back of the stage. (Ker 1923: 315.)

The establishment of a household, however, was not an option open to everyone. The two goats mentioned by Oðinn would not, in reality, have been a sufficient basis for setting up an independent household. Thus, in *Jónsbók* (of 1281), there is a clause about 'what men must possess if they want to found a *bú*' (1904: 234). This passage in the law is interesting not only for its statements about the legal, economic requirements for becoming a *bóndi*, but also for its implication that it is everyone's desire to become so. It was difficult for the farmers (*bændr*) to get labourers *því at allir nær vilja þá búa fara* ('because almost everybody wants to have their own households'); and to redress this situation the requirement of five 'hundreds' (the value of five milking cows), was imposed upon would-be farmers (ibid.).[4] This was not within reach of most of the population, which had become gradually impoverished during the last years of the Freestate.[5] To the Ice-landers, therefore, the clause was unacceptable, because it prevented them from realizing what was dearest to them—their individual in-dependence. The Norwegian king Eiríkr made a series of amend-ments to the law of *Jónsbók* in 1294, after consultations with local Icelandic legal experts. Among the amendments (*réttarbœtr*) was an annulment of the clause referred to above (ibid.: 283; *LIL* i. 19). Despite this amendment, it was still well-nigh impossible to found a *bú* with only two goats, and strong impediments against the penniless setting up their own households persisted, however differently expressed. The impossibility of the two-goat household is related to the fact that a *bú* had to be absolutely self-sufficient. Even with some fishing to help, Eggers noted in 1786 that it required two cows or twelve sheep for three adults to subsist (Eggers 1786: 60).

The social and conceptual significance of the *bú* as a microcosm was related to its relatively isolated position in the landscape. Towns were entirely absent, and so were villages. This meant that each farm was the centre of its own world, and such 'worlds' were conceptually mapped as if they were serially placed, either along the coastline or in the narrow valleys (see Hastrup 1985*a*: 55–6). In some tracts the farms were closer than others, but they never clustered in real villages. Churches were connected to particular farms, and known by the proper names of these, frequently names with the suffix *staðir* (meaning 'place', a direct translation of the Latin *locus*, and referring to the site, that is, the farmstead to which a church was attached).[6] At an abstract level the church may have served the purpose of creating a kind of centre for the *sveit* ('district') or the *hreppur* ('commune') (these terms referring respectively to a social and an administrative reality). This can be inferred from the co-operation of clerical and secular officials in the administration of poor relief (Lýður Björnsson 1972: 65–6). This emergent possibility of a social community beyond the farm is acknowledged in the Danish royal legislation for Iceland; in the so-called *Píningsdómur um tíundir* (on tithes) from 1489, the Church and the support of the paupers are explicitly linked (*LI*: i. 39).

Although the *hreppur* had a host of functions, and a relatively well-defined statute set down in *Jónsbók* (1904: 109–10), the scattered farmsteads of the *sveit* were not actually integrated by it. Rather, they 'added up' to it, so to speak, just as they pooled their tithes, parts of which were meant for the poor (ibid.). The farm remained the centre of gravity in the social organization; it was a localized, domestic unit of production and consumption.[7] Its importance is testified also by numerous clauses in the laws forcing people to take up *lögheimili* ('legal home') at a farm. 'Vagrants' were generally a much despised category of non-social beings, encompassing all those who did not live permanently at a farmstead; in various periods the category covered different kinds of people, such as beggars, loose labour, lawless

people, and others classified as semi-humans.[8] Law, society, and the
entire cosmology, had their centre in the *bú*.

The physical frame of the *bú* was the farmstead, or *bær*. *Bær* could
refer to either the assembly of houses on their own, or to the houses
and the fenced infield close to them (Valtýr Guðmundsson 1889: 2).
This second definition associates the *bær* directly with the notion of
innangarðs ('inside the fence') which is opposed to *útangarðs* ('outside
the fence'); this opposition is conceptually equated to an opposition
between 'the social' and 'the wild', confirming the importance of the
bær in the cosmology of the Icelanders.[9]

The *bær* itself consisted of several 'houses', forming two separate
categories, *innihús* ('inner houses') and *útihús* ('outer houses'). The
inner houses were for dwellings, while the outer houses contained
stables, barns, and workshops of various kinds. Between the settlements and the close of our epoch, there were remarkable changes in
the construction of the farmstead. The settlers had constructed large
houses, with wooden pillars supporting a high mounted roof (Bruun
1928; Stenberger 1943). From a relatively simple Nordic long-house,
an Icelandic farmstead consisting of several semi-detached houses
developed (Hörður Ágústsson 1968). Shared walls were to remain a
constant feature of Icelandic farms throughout the period (Valtýr
Guðmundsson 1889: 69 ff.).

Timber became increasingly scarce, and the size of the farmhouses
decreased. While *eldhús* ('kitchen'), *skáli* ('sleeping-room'), and
baðstofa ('bathroom' meaning 'living-room') had been separated in the
High Middle Ages, they tended to fall back into one room (*baðstofa*)
during most of our period. There were internal variations, but for the
main part of the population housing was very simple; the walls were
constructed from stone and turf, and the roofs were generally made of
driftwood covered with turf.

In 1589 Oddur Einarsson remarked that in spite of the fact that the
farmsteads were neither large nor beautiful, they were not as poor as
people tended to believe (1971: 93). He describes the construction of
stone walls and roofs, and notes variations in roofing. Roofs were
made from either boards, if people had enough wood, thin stones, or
slashes; all of it was then covered with turf (ibid.). Most importantly
Oddur notes the great variety of farms: some small and poor, others
big and rich. Whatever the size, they shared one unpleasant feature;
they had no smoke-hole, and the *baðstofa* was always full of smoke
(ibid.: 94).

Oddur Einarsson strongly rejects the notion that the Icelanders lived in earth-holes and the like, a view that was currently entertained among foreigners. In 1640, for example, a German traveller, Daniel Vetter, noted that the Icelanders 'have their houses under the soil' (Vetter 1931: 172). Certainly, by comparison with urban European house-styles, the turf and stone constructions of Iceland may have appeared rather earth-bound to outsiders. Vetter, however, goes on to describe the Icelandic house-type as a fine adaptation both to the climate and to the natural lack of timber (ibid.). The Icelanders were not a healthy people, and one reason given for this by another traveller in about 1730 is the poor and cold housing (Jochumssen 1977: 23). This view is further substantiated by Eggers, who gives a rather detailed description of the typical farmstead in 1786. According to him, the houses were primitive and unhealthy, however well adapted to the environment. According to Anderson (1746: 122), the houses were humid and foul and people sleep together in one 'bed', itself nothing but a raised platform made of earth. The *baðstofa* was the central room, and in some places this was adjoined by *eldhús*, *búr* ('store room'), and *skáli* (Eggers 1786: 50–3). Even the poorest among peasants had a separate house for the animals (ibid.: 55). While the number and specialization of the *innihús* might have decreased, the fundamental distinction between *innihús* and *útihus* was never blurred.

Changes also occurred in the composition of the outer houses. I shall postpone the discussion of this until the treatment of farming, but we can note here that the outer houses, like the inner houses, decreased in size and number during our period. In the nineteenth century this process was reversed for both categories (Jónas Jónasson 1961: 438ff.). This was partly due to a growing consciousness of the importance of housing to health and hygiene in general (Jón Péturs-son 1791), and partly to a general improvement of farming techno-logies.

Irrespective of size, the *bær* englobed the domestic economy, and represented a microcosm. The farmstead was society writ small and concretized. During the entire period there was no social division of labour except *within* the household, apart from small and unsuccess-ful attempts to establish fishing-villages in the fifteenth century. This means that whatever class-structure there was, it was more or less internal to the *bú*, which was thus populated by a variety of social categories.[10] The *bóndi* was the head of the household, and his position was as much legal as economic. The *bóndi* was the *de facto* and *de jure* leader of the small community which made up the household.

While legally set apart from other members of the *bú*, the *bóndi* was socially and economically very much part of it. To translate this dual relationship into anthropological terms, the *bóndi* was related to the *bú* in both a metaphorical and in a metonymical way: in the first sense he represented the entire household, he *was* it; in the second he was just a part of its labour force. It is in the first sense, which had made the *bændr* their own rulers, and the administrators of national law, since the founding of the Freestate, that we can find the rationale for the prohibitions against petty peasants establishing their own independent households. If you were not worth five cows, you were not entitled to the civil status of *bóndi*, so highly esteemed.

The most inclusive term for other members of the household was *hjón*. The semantics of this term makes it complementary to that of *bú*. *Hjón* (pl.) may refer to a married couple, the family, the members of the household, and the servants or farm-hands (cf. Fritzner 1954: i. 832; *IED*: 267–8; Blöndal 192–4: 330). Etymologically, *hjón* (*hjún*, or *hjú*) was related to the first part of the word *híbýli*, meaning 'house', 'homestead', or 'home', and even in some contexts 'the members of a particular household' (*IED*: 265). When, from a legal point of view, home had to be precisely defined the notion of *lögheimili* ('legal home') was used; this abstract notion covered the same reality as the (spatial) *híbýli*, and the (social) *bú*, framing the lives of the household members (*hjón*) in various dimensions.

The linguistic coalescence of married persons, members of the household, and farm labour, is significant. It indicates that marriage (*hjúskapr*) was the starting-point of a new household, and also suggests that marriage was in some way subsumed by the economic order. In *Grágás*, there are clear rules as to who may marry at all. A certain amount of wealth (6 *alnir*) was required unless the woman was infertile (*Grágás*: i *b*. 38, ii. 167). The important thing was clearly that any married couple could cater for their offspring. This was in the interest of the commune (*hreppur*) upon which catering for the paupers (*ómagi*) would otherwise fall.

In *Jónsbók* of 1281, and in the *rettarbœtr* of 1294, 1305, and 1319 there are no parallels to this rule of marriage limitation. There is here, as we have seen, a minimum property rule for the establishment of households. In *Jónsbók*, marriage among the dispossessed is actually an implied possibility, as we can see from a passage dealing with the division of property after the death of one or the other *hjón* (spouse): *nú ef øreigar ii koma saman at landslǫgum réttum* ('now, if two "without property" have been [married] together according to the proper law of the country') (*Jónsbók*: 75). Historically, this may be seen as a consequence of Bishop Árni Þorláksson's Christian law of 1275, which allowed no limitations on marriage.

The law could no longer prevent people from marrying on account of poverty, because marriage was essentially a holy union. The semantic unity of marriage and household, however, still prevented the marriage of the poor by implication. This is confirmed by the census of 1703, which furnishes us with the proportion of married and unmarried persons among the household heads and others. Thus among the married men less than 2 per cent are *not* household heads in the age group 25–54; among married men over 60, 5 per cent are not household heads, indicating that old married persons had handed over their status to the next generation (Loftur Guttormsson 1983: 106).

Within the *bú*, a social differentiation emerged. The early medieval pattern of a dual 'class-structure' (free farmers and slaves) had long since been replaced by a more complex picture (Hastrup 1985*a*: 107–18). Degrees of dependence had replaced kinds of people. By 1400 the social structure presented a motley picture of farmers, tenants, cottagers, and labourers, all of whom were, in principle at least, englobed by the social microcosm of the *bú*.

To quote from *Hávamál* again:

> *Bú er betra,*
> *þótt lítit sé*
> *halr er heima hverr*
> *blóðugt er hjárta,*
> *þeim er biðjá skal*
> *sér í mál hvert matar*

Hávamál, v. 37

(A *bú* is better, even if a little one, a man is somebody at home, bleeding are the hearts, of those, who shall pray for the food at each meal'.)

Independence is praised, while dependence on others for food is demeaning. If dependence includes having to work for others to win food, then most Icelanders living in the period 1400 to 1800 must have had bleeding hearts, at least according to the Eddaic standard.

54 *Modes of Livelihood*

Social relations within the *bú* were regulated by the *búalög* ('household law'), which was an important supplement to the national law of *Jónsbók*. The oldest known *búalög* is found in a manuscript from the mid-fifteenth century; from then onwards several revised manuscripts and later printed versions testify to (changing) social and economic conditions, right up to the end of the eighteenth century.[11] The persistent regulatory influence of the *búalög* is noted by von Troil in 1780 (115 ff.). The 'household law' laid down the rights and duties of *bóndi* and *vinnuhjú* ('farm servants'), specifying the length of the working day, the amount of work to be done in a day (in weaving, hay-harvesting, peat-digging, and so on), and the correct payment for this. The *vinnuhjú* were to be given daily meals of fish, butter, milk-produce, and (occasionally) meat, and were to be provided with clothing. Men were to have twice as much food as women; the men's ration was one dried fish of two pounds, half a pound of butter, and a little whey—according to Jochumssen (1977: 51). Judging by traditional proverbs, feeding the farm-hands was something of a burden: *góð væru hjúin, ef ekki væri maturinn, sagði kerlingin* ('It would be fine with the servants if it was not for the food, said the old woman' (*ÍM*: 145)).

As if this were not enough, the farm-hands were also to be paid. According to the norm established by the Althing in 1722, men were to have 60–120 ellens a year, women between nothing and half this amount—more often nothing it seems (Jochumssen 1977: 50). A cow's worth was 120 ellens, and it appears that during the fifteenth and sixteenth centuries, farm-hands were encouraged to work by the prospect of eventually being able to set up their own households (Eggert Ólafsson 1772: 38). This was an important ambition throughout our epoch, although it is probable that it became increasingly unrealistic some time in the sixteenth century, as a result of general impoverishment (ibid.). Related to this, we find that as time went by the legal day's work as defined in *búalög* became hopelessly over-estimated. In the latter part of the period no one could keep up with the requirements, allegedly because of deteriorating farming conditions (ibid.: 35; Skúli Magnússon 1944a: 76).

The *búalög* organized the domestic economy, including the relationship between *bóndi* and *hjú*. In the proverbial wisdom of the Icelanders the importance of this relationship is much stressed: *hjúanna trú styrkir bóndans bú* ('faithful servants strengthen the farmer's *bú*' (*ÍM*: 45, 145)). The social well-being was defined by household ethics.

The household framed the lives of the Icelanders, socially and economically. It also encompassed them in a strict legal sense. In a law of 1404, this was made explicit for the first time. All labourers (*vinnumenn*) were obliged to take up residence at a farm by *krossmessa* (one of the first weeks in the summer half-year, that is, in the beginning of May). Labourers who would not work for the farmers were in effect outlawed (*LI*: i. 34–5). The law amounts to a law about compulsory farm service, even for the seasonal fishing population (ibid.); it is also an affirmation of the social significance of the *bú*. Every Icelander was required to live within the *bú*, even though seasonal fishing elsewhere was allowed.

In 1490 this theme is repeated. The Althing agreed that *engir búðsetumenn skulu vera í landinu, þeir sem eigi hafa búfé til at fæða sik við, so þó, at þeir eigi ekki minna fé en iii hundruð, svo karlar sem konur, og skyldir til vinnu hjá bændum allir þeir, sem minna fé eigu en nú er sagt, konur og karlar* ('No *buðsetumen* should be in the country, who have not livestock (*búfé*) to provide for themselves, that is who have at least three 'hundreds', men as well as women, and those who have less than now said must work for the farmers, men and women alike' (*LI*: i. 42).[12]

Búðsetumenn ('cottagers') is a social category which came into existence some time during the Middle Ages (Hastrup 1985*a*: 110ff.). Cottagers were contractually related to farmers, who could demand labour from them. During the twelfth century the category was further subdivided, according to kinds of contract. Some time during the 'English Age', that is the period of flourishing fishing enterprises in the fifteenth century, the notion of *búðsetumaður* changed meaning, and came to refer to people with no direct access to land. In contrast to the *bú* of the *bóndi*, the *búð* of the *búðsetumaður* ('man sitting on a *búð*') was conceived of as a temporary abode (cf. Hastrup 1985*d*), and as such they could not provide a focus of social-spatial organization. During our period, they came to be known as *þurrabúdir* ('dry abodes'), defined by their lack of land and consequently their lack of hay for livestock (whence 'dry').[13] This lack of agricultural autonomy was a serious negation of the legal and economic order, which is why *búðsetumenn* were not wanted. They were conceptually 'dangerous' outsiders *vis-à-vis* the cosmological structure (cf. Douglas 1966).

Despite their small number the *búðsetumenn* continued to be a conceptual nuisance. In 1612 this was noted again and provisos made (*AÍ*: iv. 191–2). Even worse, for conceptual security, were the *lausamenn* ('loose people', day labourers), who, although they were actually migrant workers, were categorized with vagrants and beggars. In 1685 they were judged blasphemers, and sharply distinguished from the farm-labourers (*vinnufólk*) who were clearly attached to particular farmers (*LI*: i. 428–37). In the census of 1703 only seventy-three *lausamenn* are recorded out of a population of 50,000, most of them in Grindavík and in the Westman Islands, the two most important fishing centres. The distinction between proper *vinnufólk* (or *vinnuhjú*) and *lausamenn* (or *lausgangarar*) was still relevant in 1720, when Icelandic law was updated by local sheriffs (*Aĺ*: x. 557–77). In this update, it was stated that only someone in possession of ten cows (three times the amount required to set up a *bú*) could choose to be a free, unattached labourer (ibid.: x. 558).

Compared to the mere 73 *lausamenn* of 1703, there were many *vinnuhjú*. In 1703 the category embraced 17.8 per cent of the total population; in the age group 25–9 the figure was as high as 45.1 per cent (Loftur Guttormsson 1983a: 105, 122). During the eighteenth century and for the better part of the nineteenth century, some 25 per cent of the population were listed as *vinnuhjú* (Guðmundur Jónsson 1981). Despite the numbers of farm-labourers, however, there seems to have been a perceived lack of farm labour throughout our period—from 1404 when the nuns at Kirkjubæjarklaustur had to milk their own cows, right up to 1784, when Skúli Magnússon takes it for granted that most farmers are short of servants, and that some may take in day labourers during the hay-harvest (1944a: 77). There would, of course, have been fluctuations in the alleged labour shortage (cf. Loftur Guttormsson 1983a: 127–8).

The *bú* remained the pivot of social organization, and it continued to be associated with marriage. Only a *bóndi* was supposed to enter the holy union. This link is again explicitly noted in 1720, when sheriffs wrote to the bishop suggesting that marriage be denied the dispossessed, since they were unable to feed their children, and contributed to the impoverishment of the country. The clerical response was ambivalent. The Church could not officially refuse marriage to non-relatives, but the bishop agreed that the blessing should only be given to people who could give their children a reasonably decent Christian upbringing. This ability had to be confirmed by the local governor, and the ball was thus played back to the civil authorities (*Aĺ*: x. 570–3). The clause from *Jónsbók* had been removed, but marriage and household independence remained privileges enjoyed by a strikingly low proportion of the adult population.

According to the eighteenth-century observer Skúli Magnússon, it was the recurrent famines which had made the authorities take measures against marriage in 1720 (1944*b*: 32). The same authorities, however, were also lamenting the decline of the population and the general economic weakness. Poverty may have been the reason for preventing too many marriages at the level of 'intentional meaning', but with respect to the 'implicational meaning', I believe that the close association between *bú* and marriage must share the blame.[14] Given the all-pervasive significance of the independent household in the social, economic, and conceptual order of the Icelanders, the *bú* could not be taken lightly.

To terminate this discussion of the household as a permanent feature of Icelandic history from 1400 to 1800 I shall quote one more proverb. It goes: *hjú sem herra, bú sem bóndí* ('servants as the master, household as the farmer' (*ÍM*: 145)), and signals the structural dominance of the *bóndi* in the domestic mode of production. It also confirms the ideology of the self-contained household, representing the sole relevant unit in an atomistic social organization, where organic solidarity (Durkheim 1893) was to be found only within the *bú*.

FARMING

The domestic unit was first and foremost engaged in farming or *land-búnaður*. There was a fine balance to maintain between arable and stock farming. Grain was grown, and also hay, the latter being vital for the livestock. Natural grazing was adequate only from June to September; for the rest of the year the animals had to be kept at the farmstead on stored hay. The balance between animal numbers and labour-input in the fields was, therefore, delicate.

Grain-cropping, although of minor importance compared to animal husbandry, provides an interesting chapter in Icelandic history; the fate of grain-growing in Iceland can also serve as an indicator of much wider features of Icelandic society. We are discussing mentality as well as barley in what follows.

In the period of the settlements grain-cropping was known all over Iceland, as place-names and literary evidence show (Sigurður Þórarinsson 1956: 15–16). It was abandoned in the northern and eastern parts of the island relatively quickly—probably before the end of the twelfth century (ibid.). By 1350 the situation is described thus: *korn vex í fám stöðum sunnan lands en eigi nema bygg* ('grain grows at a few places in the south, but then only barley' (*Gudmunðar saga*, *BS*: iii. 161)).[15] It is also towards the south (-west) that the place-names referring to grain-fields (*akur-*) are most common. This pattern is slightly enigmatic because climatic conditions for grain-cultivation were actually more favourable in the north-east where the average summer temperature was higher.

There are very few direct references to grain-cropping in the sources from our period. There is, however, an important statement from 1589, which echoes Arngrímur Brandsson's statement in his *Guðmundar saga*. In his thorough description of Iceland, Bishop Oddur Einarsson writes that although grain-cropping was quite common in earlier days, as can be inferred from old books, traces of fields, and place-names, it has now fallen into disuse (1971: 126). He then adds that the people of some southern places cultivate grain even today, and make much use of it (ibid.).[16] Generally, however, the Icelanders had to import grain in order to make bread, if they wanted any (ibid.).

Oddur's brief statement is the last (known) evidence of grain-growing in Iceland. In 1640 the absence of grain-fields in Iceland is noted by a German traveller (Vetter 1931: 170), while the Icelandic observer Jón Eggertsson notes about the same time that the furrows are still visible.[17] When in the eighteenth century observers were sent to Iceland by the Danish king to report on the economic conditions in Iceland, grain-growing belonged to the distant past. Olavius describes how in some places one can still see traces of ancient ploughed fields (1780: 14, for instance), and suggests that a reintroduction of the old agricultural techniques might be attempted (ibid., *et passim*). Others make similar statements (Eggert Ólafsson 1772: 235–6; Skúli Magnússon (1944*a*: 31).

In Jónsbók references are made both to *akr* and *engi* ('field' and 'meadow'), indicating that grain-fields were still of legal significance in 1281 (e.g. *Jónsbók* 113ff.). It is possible that when *akr* is used in contradistinction to *engi*, it refers to the home-field in general, including the tilled and manured hay-field (*tún* or *taða*), while *engi* refers to the out-field. There are, however, passages in the law where *akr* is explicitly opposed to *tað*, and it seems probable that, within the context of *Jónsbók*, *akr* means grain-field (e.g. *Jónsbók*: 121).

It is difficult to assess the quantitative importance of home-grown grain even during the early centuries. In the thirteenth-century *Þorgils saga ok Hafliða*, a feast at *Reykhólar* in 1112 is described; the author notes how the fields (*akrar*) at Reykhólar were always fertile, but that nevertheless fresh flour was a delicacy for special occasions only.[18] From the treaty of 1262 between the Icelandic farmers and the king of Norway, we can infer that Iceland was already short of grain in the thirteenth century. The treaty contains a clause that the king must ship six shiploads of grain to Iceland during the (first) summers (*DI*: i. 620; Hastrup 1985a: 233–4). On the whole it seems that the earlier self-sufficiency, noted by Oddur Einarsson in 1589 was already over in the thirteenth century, and that by the end of the sixteenth century Icelandic grain was of negligible economic significance. In the popular view of Icelandic history (as represented, for example, by Espólín, writing in the early nineteenth century), grain cultivation had disappeared in the fifteenth century, together with almost everything else of traditional national value (Espólín 1943: ii: *Formáli*, unpag.).

Also disappearing was the plough, which had been in use in the Middle Ages (Björn Þorsteinsson 1966: 116). Modern archaeologists and contemporary travellers have noted furrows in many parts of the island, proving that ploughs were used in the early Middle Ages. For some reason they fell into disuse, and are not in evidence during our period. In the mid-seventeenth century Jón Eggertsson complained that if only the Icelanders could get hold of ploughs, they would be better off (MS Thott 1738: fo. 6). When the Enlightenment reformers started their redressment of Iceland in the late eighteenth century, ploughing was one of the things they wished to introduce. However, when the German legal historian Konrad Maurer travelled around Iceland in 1858, he could only find one plough (Maurer 1858: 281).[19] Ploughing and grain-fields were linked, and both had disappeared. The former left its furrows in the soil, and the latter remained as a wild variety of grain, known as *melur*. *Melur* descended from the cultivated stock, and when cultivation ceased, *melur* continued to be a source of flour in some parts of the country (von Troil 1780: 105–6; Eggert Ólafsson 1772: 236, 773; Olavius 1780: 204; Horrebow 1752: 87–9; Eggers 1786: 25). In other places it was used only for animal fodder (Olavius 1780: 449; Eggert Ólafsson 1772: 673–4). Generally, it was badly exploited and, as Jón Eggertsson remarked, the Icelanders did not fully understand how to use this valuable resource (MS Thott 1738: fo. 6).

While semi-wild horses with no economic significance grew fat on *melur*, the Icelandic people suffered a permanent lack of grain.

Climatic changes played their role, but cannot of themselves explain why grain-growing and the use of *melur* were abandoned. Equally unsatisfactory is a simple cost-benefit analysis, as provided by Gísli Gunnarsson (1980*b*: 23–4), distantly echoing Stefán Þórarinsson who said in 1793 that grain-growing would not pay.

To end this brief discussion of agriculture in the narrow sense of grain-growing, I will quote a native point of view. In the mid-seventeenth century Stefán Ólafsson, a poet notable for his concern about the decline of Iceland (Stefán Einarsson 1957: 199) wrote a poem entitled *Um þá fyrri og þessa öld* ('About the Former and the Present Century'):

> *Mjög var farsæl fyrri öld í heimi*
> *undi sér við akurplóg,*
> *af honum þóttisk hafa nóg,*
> *fráskilin þeim illa óhófs keimi.*
>
> (Stefán Ólafsson 1885–6:
> i. 297)

(In former times people were very prosperous in the world, they were happy by the field-plough, they found themselves satisfied by it, and were free from the distaste of excess.)

The important thing to note here is that the happiness and prosperity of former times were linked to the plough.

Happiness is one thing, food another. The sources leave us in no doubt about the utmost importance of animal husbandry and hay-cropping in the domestic economy of the Icelanders. The livestock were cattle and sheep, of which the latter were quantitatively dominant. Cows, however, were perhaps conceptually dominant, since they had been used as a standard of value ever since the early Middle Ages, as expressed in the notion of *kúgildi* ('cow's worth'—see *KL*: vii. 85). In addition to cows and sheep, horses were kept for riding and transport. After the introduction of Christianity, horse-meat was no longer eaten. Fowl and pigs were found in the early Freestate, but in our period they survived mainly in some place-names. Oddur Einarsson mentions pigs as a feature of farming at a few places, and he connects their scarcity to a shortage of their natural food—wild nuts and grains (1972: 101–2). In *Jónsbók* there is a clause concerning restitution to be paid for damage caused by straying pigs (287). Although very limited in number already in the sixteenth century, and in no evidence later, pigs once played some part in Icelandic farming (Anderson 1746: 39; Eggert Ólafsson 1772: 202). Probably they were in too direct competition with humans over scarce vegetable resources. The same may have applied to fowl, which also disappeared (Anderson 1746: 39).

Cows and sheep were dependent on grazing in the summer, and fodder in the winter, and the farming cycle was determined by the needs of the animals. Natural grazing was available for only four or five months a year and during the same short summer hay had to be grown and harvested to provide for the winter. For the animals summer was a period of expansion, a movement into 'the wild', with a return to the domesticated social space of the farmstead during winter.

The sheep went farthest afield, to mountain pastures, soon after the spring lambing season. Beyond the boundaries of the single farmsteads were common pastures, or *almenningar*. For a few months each summer, sheep were left untended in these commons. Use of commons was regulated by the law; in *Jónsbók* commons are defined, and rules about their usage are laid down. *Almenningar* belonged to all people living in one quarter, who had the right to let their animals graze, to hunt, and to collect birds' eggs freely (*Jónsbók*: 185–6, 193–4).[20] The grazing part of this use-right was regulated by the community; no one was allowed to send animals out into the commons before eight weeks of summer (that is, the 'summer-half' of the year) had passed, and animals had to be collected when four weeks of summer remained (ibid.: 176, 181). The importance of these regulations was emphasized in a statute of 1682 (*LI*: i. 394). The rounding up of sheep was a communal task from which no sheep-owner could withdraw (*Jónsbók*: 181). Sheep had to be marked by the owner, so that they could be identified in the autumn. Unmarked stray sheep could be claimed by anyone (ibid. 177–81).

There is some semantic confusion between the two notions *almenningar* and *afréttir*. Generally *afréttir* is used to denote the common pastures of the *almenningar*, comprising also the common rights to driftwood, fish, and other catch (*IED*: 8; *KL*: i. 103). In *Grágás*, *afréttir* are defined as shared property: *þat er afréttr, er ii menn eigo saman eða fleire* ('that is afréttir, which is owned by two or more men together' ii. 479), and this is echoed in *Jónsbók* (177, 184, 187). The word *eigu* ('own') is slightly confusing, and seems to be at odds with the notion of 'commons'. In some passages of *Jónsbók* the concepts *almenningar* and *afréttir* are used indiscriminately, but they seem to connote different kinds of relationship. *Afréttir* refers to shared ownership, denoting a particular social relationship between two or more peasants, while *almenningar* refers to common rights, defining a particular relationship between people and their resources. The legal historian Maurer seems to share this opinion, when he says of *afréttir* that they were private, if shared, property, while *almenningar* were pastures that could be used by people who had no grazing of their own (Maurer 1858: 308; see also Gunnar F. Guðmundsson 1981).

More important, perhaps, than distinction between these terms, is the fact that both were conceptually contrasted with the *heimaland* ('homeland') or *tún*. In our period, the former were left unfenced, that is unbounded against nature, while the latter were fenced and defined as within 'the social' (see Hastrup 1985a: ch. 5; 1982). However, Olavius reports in 1780 that *afréttir* could not have been held cheap in earlier times since in that case the ancestors would not have taken the trouble to put up those stone fences between rock walls, which are still in evidence somewhere (Olavius 1780: 25). In his time *almenningar* were part of the conceptual 'outside'.

Closer to 'home' were the saeters or summer shielings (Hastrup 1989b). Saeters were individually owned, and facilitated a transhumant pattern for milk cattle. In Iceland, the saeter was known as *sel* (cf. Hitzler 1979). The basic meaning of this term was 'a small hut', used as a temporary dwelling, and (perhaps later) the pasture around this hut (*KL*: xv. 104–5). The *sel* in Iceland was close to the main farmstead, often within walking distance (Ólafur Lárusson 1944: 99–101). In *búalög* it is presupposed that at least some of the dairymaids working at the *sel* had to return to the farm by noon to do *heimavinna* ('homework') (*Búalög* 1915–33: 22, 34, 61).

If close to home, the *sel* was also part of the privately owned land, on the fringes of 'the social' though it might be. In *Grágás* it was explicitly prohibited to establish a *sel* within the common pastures (*afréttir*) (i *b*. 113; ii. 478). This is repeated in *Jónsbók*, where the Norwegian word *sætr* has replaced the notion of *sel* (176). (Apart from the legal text, *sel* remained the term in use.) Before our period, it was not uncommon for the entire household to move to the *sel* during summer; in some places the saeter was explicitly contrasted to the winter-dwellings (see, for instance, *Laxdœla saga* (ch. 35), and Eggert Ólafsson 1772: 179). Later, only part of the household moved. In the fifteenth- or sixteenth-century versions of *búalög* it is stipulated that 3 women had to be at a *sel* in addition to the housekeeper (*matselja*) in order to milk

80 sheep and 12 cows (1915–33: 22, 34, 61). In the seventeenth century the work-rate seems to have gone up; then 3 maids were supposed to manage 90 sheep and 15 cows, besides *heimavinna* and *heyvinna* ('hay-work') (*Búalög* 1915–33: 191). This number of livestock suggests that the *sel* was a feature of large-scale farming, for few ordinary peasants would own such a herd.

The use of saeters was consistently defined as an internal household matter, in contrast to the use of the *afréttir*. The farmers were not completely at liberty to exploit the saeter-lands, however. The law stated that livestock had to be brought to the saeter when two months of summer had passed, and to be returned to the home-fields before the month of *tvímánuður* (*Jónsbók*: 172–3). This makes a total of about two months (mid-June to mid-August), although doubts have been raised about the length of this period (*KL*: xvii. 718). The ancient month-name *selmánuður*, comprising the time of activity at the saeter, suggest that the period was actually less than two months.

Extensive reference to saeters is found in place names with the suffix -*sel*, suggesting that the transhumant pattern was fairly common in the Middle Ages, especially in the north and north-east (Finnur Jónsson 1907–15: 475–8; Ólafur Lárusson 1944: 43, 47). Gradually, however, it seems to have lost its momentum (Hitzler 1979: 236ff.; Hastrup 1989*b*). Some *sel* were turned into permanent dwellings for an emerging cotter class already in the early Middle Ages (*KL*: xvii. 178).

There is other evidence for the decline of saeters during our period, leading to near abandonment by the eighteenth century (Eggert Ólafsson 1772: 178; Olavius 1780: 247–8; Eggers 1786: 120). In 1754 the Danish king issued a decree reinforcing the traditional rules about saeters, thus reminding ordinary peasants of the valuable practice of transhumance (*LI*: iii. 191). In spite of the relatively consistent reference to *sel* in household law, however, all that was left by the eighteenth century was the word. Even words had become fewer it seems. Von Troil, listing month-names that refer to economic activities, has no mention of *selmánuður* (1780: 117–18). It was for the Enlightenment reformers to recommend a reintroduction of saeter use (Eggert Ólafsson 1772: 178–9), as part of a much more comprehensive attempt to improve the exploitation of the land.

The infields (*tún*) were not for grazing, but for growing hay. As such, they had to be fenced to keep out the cattle (*Jónsbók*: 282). Hay was of two kinds, *taða* and *úthey*. The first kind was grown in the *tún*, which could also be referred to as *taða*; the second kind grew in the outfields or meadows outside the fencing. The notion of *taða* indicates that the home field was manured with animal dung (*tað*). The field was manured in early summer, when stable dung was spread out and levelled by means of a simple harrow made of woodsticks and stones (Jónas Jónasson 1961: 57–8). Cow-dung was the main ingredient, since sheep-dung was needed for fuel in this woodless island. Horse-dung was allowed to waste in the outfields, where the horses spent most of the year. When grass appeared on the *tún*, still visible field manure was raked back into small heaps, and this *afrak* ('raked off') also was used for firewood (ibid.: 58–9).

After lambing, the sheep were sent up into the *afréttir*, apart from a small herd of milking sheep. Wool was collected during *stekktið* ('lambfold-time') when ewes and lambs were still in the fold. The wool was never cut but more or less left to fall off on its own (ibid.; Oddur Einarsson 1971: 97; Eggert Ólafsson 1772: 199; Skúli Magnússon 1944a: 37; Vetter 1931: 171). The wool was processed during winter, and made into clothing of different kinds (Vetter 1931: 171).

One of the peaks of the agricultural cycle was the hay-harvest. The period in which this took place was referred to as *heyannir*, and governed by a number of specific laws. Thus if a farm-hand fell sick he would normally be excused for a month; during *heyannir*, however, he was only allowed three days. After three days *skynsamir menn* ('reasonable men') had to decide whether the case was breach of contract (*Jónsbók*: 283). Hay was the vital resource of the country, and the amount of hay determined the amount of cattle that could be kept for the winter. In turn, this influenced the amount of manure for the following summer. There was a circular logic to the economy, and a fine balance was needed.

Hay not only had to be harvested, it also had to be properly stored to preserve it during the winter months. Simple though this seems, the Icelanders failed to meet the requirements. This was a marginal agricultural area, where minor climatic changes had more severe effects than elsewhere in other Atlantic economies (Davis 1973: 122–4); neglect in storing techniques was likely to prove fatal. The annals bear extensive witness to shortage of hay, resulting in starvation and death. Vetter in 1640 (1931: 171) describes the use of dried fish as fodder for the animals in replacement of hay, but this was not always possible.

In the early Middle Ages, barns were used for storing hay. This is seen from archaeological material (for example, Stenberger 1943) as well as from literary sources (Valtýr Guðmundsson 1889: 253–4). *Sturlunga saga* has several references to a *hlaða* ('barn') (1946: *passim*). Gradually, however, it seems that barns became fewer. The fate of one single farm is illustrative of the trend (although evidently no general proof of the decreasing number of barns). In 1431 a probate court is set for a farm on Tjörnes, comprising two barns (*DI*: iv. 436–7); in 1685 the same farm once again appears in a diploma, but now it has only one barn (*AM*: 255, fos. 71^r–72^r).[21]

In the mid-seventeenth century the observer Jón Eggertsson remarked that the hay never dried up properly because of the rain; when it was collected and put into barns, it was still moist, and subject to internal combustion (MS Thott 1738: fo. 2). Possibly, then, barns became of less currency as a result of bad experience. Again, this experience may be related to a previous handling of hay which left much wanting. It had, after all, rained in the Middle Ages, when barns were in common use.

In the nineteenth century the folklorist Jónas Jónasson notes that hay was stored as it had always been, in turf-covered stacks in the *heygarður* ('hay-yard'), while barns were very few and known mainly in eastern Iceland (1961: 85–6). During our period, then, it seems that the technology of hay-storing declined; even *heygarðar* were found only in the southern parts of the island in the nineteenth century (ibid.). In 1858 Maurer also noted some regional differences: in the southern tracts of the western quarter people were experimenting with a new kind of stack (*heystakkir*), while further north barns (*hlaðir*) were used. The new stacks were assembled in *heygarðar*, leaning against house walls and more or less enclosed by walls themselves (Maurer 1858: 379–80). The interesting thing to note is that Jónas Jónasson mentions this handling as an age-old custom, while Maurer's local informant calls it a new experiment.

The fences around the *tún* were also falling apart. Fences around the infield were compulsory, and certainly also in the interest of the peasants, but they nevertheless gradually disintegrated. In 1776 an ordinance was issued by the Danish king demanding of the Icelanders that they reconstruct their fences, offering the threat of fines and also promise of rewards (*LI*: iv. 278ff.). Judging from later decrees, it was not an easy task to convince the Icelanders of the necessity of this restoration and the sheriffs were urged to keep track of length of fence rebuilt at individual farms (*LI*: v. 72). It was also suggested that exemplary fences be built in all regions for the Icelanders to study

(*LI*: iv. 426); the old technology was apparently forgotten. Eggert Ólafsson considered the absence of fences to be a decisive element in the
poverty of eighteenth-century Icelanders (1772: 178), while Eggers
argued that rebuilding the fences would not in itself improve the conditions of Iceland; the fields would also have to be ploughed and
manured (1786: 113). On the whole, eighteenth-century observers give
life to the dry evidence of the law, in their general lamentation of the
pitiable conditions of farming in Iceland.

During our period the fences disintegrated; there is enough
evidence for this general statement, even though a few farmers may
have kept up with repairs. When and why this happened is more difficult to assess. The consequences were clear, however. If the infields
were not protected against animals, the hay was likely to become
scarce. And animals were not the only creatures to encroach on the
tún. In some places, people themselves contributed to the reduction of
the infield by cutting up parts of it into turf for roofing for houses or
haystacks (Olavius 1780: 472).

Reduction of the fields was one thing; another was the preparation
of the soil which left more and more wanting (cf. Eggers's statement
above). Ploughs disappeared completely, and even spades were completely lacking; in 1776 the king promised to provide the Icelanders
with necessary tools (*LI*: iv. 287). Hoes were used, but with decreasing efficiency it appears. One recurrent complaint among late
seventeenth-century commentators concerns the number of tufts
growing in the fields (see, for instance, Olavius 1780, and Eggert
Ólafsson 1772). Hummocks hampered hay-harvesting considerably,
and yield diminished; the king, recognizing this, urged the people to
remove the tufts using proper spades (*LI*: iv. 284 ff.). The historical
development had an interesting semantic counterpart in the notion of
banapúfa ('tuft of death'); originally referring to the mound upon
which a dying person was laid; this gradually came to mean a tuft *causing* death (Strömbäck 1929). Tufts grew out of nature in more than one
way.

The history of the infield area during these four centuries can be
summed up in the word 'deterioration'. Olavius says that, in many
parts of Iceland, the people had forgotten the old farming skills (1772:
592). Collective forgetfulness is a fascinating phenomenon for the
analyst, and one which I shall pursue. For the Icelander, however, it
was less stimulating. Disintegrating fences left the *tún* unguarded
against animals, hummocks seriously reduced the yield, and the

storage of hay became poorer. These are very general statements, but the long-term trends are well documented. The combined effects of changes in farming practices *innangarðs* (inside the fence) and *útangarðs* (outside the fence) were multiple, and reached far beyond the strictly economic order. Before we can pursue this, we must turn to fishing—the second pillar of the Icelandic economy.

FISHING

Settlers went to Iceland for land and for the abundance of fish. Fishing was, however, subsidiary to farming upon which the entire social organization was based. The *bú* was the centre of the Icelandic social world, and remained so until the twentieth century.

In the period of the Freestate and well into the fourteenth century, the external historical context favoured this dominance of farming over fishing. Foreign trade was dominated by farm produce, notably woollen cloth (*vaðmál*). From the eleventh century trade was in the hands of a Norwegian merchant class, who shipped grain and timber to Iceland in return for *vaðmál* (Gelsinger 1981). It was this major export that gave Iceland its early standard of value according to which prices were set and values measured, in *alnir*, or 'ellens' (of cloth).

In the fourteenth century the Hanseatic League replaced Norway as Iceland's main trading partner, and a new market opened. This was an important precondition for the transition from 'the age of farming' to 'the age of fishing' (Þorkell Jóhannesson 1933). This transition is discussed at length elsewhere (Ch. 5, below), and it is sufficient to note here that by 1400 fishing had assumed a new importance. Dried fish, or *skreið*, had always played a considerable part in the subsistence economy of the peasants, as can be inferred, for instance, from an amendment to the law (*réttarbœtr*) made by (Norwegian) King Eiríkr in 1294 and which was restated in 1319: *Eigi uilium ver at mikil skreið flytiz heðan meðan hallæri er i landinu* ('we do not want much *skreið* to be sent from here, while there is a lean year in the country' (*DI*: ii. 287; cf. *Jónsbók*: 287). Fish had to be used mainly as a local food supply. By 1400, however, it was acknowledged as an important export commodity, and a separate development of fishing began. Trading ports gradually turned into tiny villages, and a category of professional fishermen emerged. While earlier there had been no specialist groups, the fourteenth century witnessed an incipient division of labour between farmers and fishermen. In 1404 *fiskimenn* appear for the first time in the documents. Characteristically, the document does not seek to define the fishermen as a feature of proper Icelandic society, but attempts rather to subsume them under the original farming structure. In the wake of the Black Death that ravaged Iceland from 1402 to 1404, farm-labourers had become scarce. This was the reason behind a law of compulsory farm service passed in 1404, obliging *vinnufólk* ('workers') and *fiskimenn* ('fishermen') to settle with and work for the *bændur* ('farmers'); if they refused, the landowners had to exile them from their land (*LI*: i. 34–5).

Fishing continued, but fishermen disappeared from the records. They were subsumed under the general category of *vinnuhjú* ('servants') or *vinnufólk* ('workers'), and lived within a *bú*, at least in principle. Fishing was never defined exclusively by the habitat and the fish; it was defined, rather, by special kinds of relationship to the prey (cf. Hewes 1948: 239). The relationships changed, as did technology and catch, but some elements were constant and formed an unchanging frame of reference. These were the category of 'fishing' itself, the fishing rights, and the seasonal movements of fish and men.

Fishing was designated by the general term *veiði* (sg.) or *veiðar* (pl.), which was in conceptual opposition to *landbúnaður* ('farming'). *Veiðar* comprised all kinds of 'hunting' and 'gathering', and could be specified as *fiskiveiðar* (fish), *fuglaveiðar* (birds), *hvalveiðar* (whales), *eggveiðar* (eggs). In the folk taxonomy of economic activities *veiðar* formed a comprehensive category of all direct exploitations of nature, and fishing was one among other kinds of 'hunting' (see, for instance, *Jónsbók*: 188ff.).

In *Jónsbók* the stipulations concering *veiðar* were related to rights in land. Landowners had an exclusive right to *veiðar* on their own land, and in the streams and lakes within its confines (ibid.: 188). If a stream separated two estates the owners had equal rights (ibid.). In common lands, by contrast, *veiðar* was open to everyone: *Fiskivǫtn ǫll í almenningi eru ǫllum jafnheimil; þar megu menn fiskja ok fygla* ('all people have equal rights in all fishing waters in the commons; men may catch fish and birds there' (ibid.: 193)).

As for the sea and the beach, the landowners also had privileged access to resources. *Landsdróttin* and his *bú* had exclusive rights in fish caught within the *netlǫg*, 'the net area'. This was defined as follows:

þat eru netlǫg utast er selnet stendr grunn xx mǫskva djúpt at fjǫru ok koma þá flár upp ór sjá ('it is *netlǫg* where a seal-net of twenty meshes takes the bottom of the sea, while the floats are still on the surface' (ibid.: 196)). The *netlǫg*, is also mentioned in *Grágás* (for example, i*b*. 125; ii. 514; iii. 384).

Operatively, the fishing limits or *fiskhelgi* were defined by that distance from the coast where a flattened cod could no longer be seen from the shore (*Jónsbók*: 203). Perhaps flattened cods were more ready to hand than seal-nets, and would provide no excuse for trespassing on another man's rights. Beyond the *fiskhelgi* the sea was defined as *almenningar* ('commons'), to which everyone had access. The model for conceiving of fishing rights and rights in *veiðar* in general was set by rights in land. Farming was socially and conceptually dominant, while *veiðar* was a subsidiary means of income and food-accumulation. With increasing concentration of land the possibility of subsisting as a free-enterprise fisherman declined.

Until the Reformation, the Church was one of the biggest land-owners, and there were continual disputes between the clergy and the *bændur* over fishing- and stranding-rights (for example, *DI*: v. 562–4; vi. 107–8). Catches and strandings were important contributions to the household economy at all levels of society throughout our period. The 'legal time' used for the proper administration of this is an apt indicator of its consequence.

Another permanent feature of Icelandic fishing was its seasonal character. The ecology of the sea waters has its own cycle, with stocks of fish being closely linked to the production of plankton (Cushing 1975: 84). In the temperate or sub-arctic zone around Iceland there is a definite peak in May (ibid.: 20). There is a remarkable regularity over the centuries in the seasonal cycle of Atlantic fisheries (ibid.: 85), although climatic changes may modulate the fish population through the link of plankton production. In the pre-industrial fisheries of Iceland there was no risk of over-exploitation by man, today a major problem in North Atlantic fishing (Andersen 1979: 17). This meant that the natural regularity of the seasonal cycle was undisturbed by the fishing population of Iceland throughout our period.

The Icelandic cod, which was the principal catch, were thought to circulate clockwise around the island, and a cod was considered to be at its best when it had made the tour six times (Skúli Magnússon 1944*a*: 42). In the south and west the main season was from January to April, while in the north the best catches were during summer. The migration of the fish had important social parallels in the labour migrations that were a continuous feature of Icelandic society. Oddur Einarsson writes in 1589 how, during the *vertið* ('fishing season'), any farm-hand that could be spared was sent off to the southern and western coasts (1971: 108–9; Eggert Ólafsson 1772: 181). To reach the southern *veiðistöðvar* ('catching places') some northerners in the fifteenth and sixteenth centuries even crossed the great glaciers in central Iceland (Þórarinsson 1956: 36).[22] Oddur Einarsson records how in 1588 many emigrant fishermen lost their hands and feet on their way as a result of the cold (1971: 109). They had no choice, however (ibid.). Seasonal fishing was a necessary supplement to farming, and an integral feature of the social order. In the winter of 1633/4, known as Hvítivetur ('the white winter'), heavy snow made the mountains impassable and 'no northerners came to the sea at south' (Hannes Finnsson 1970: 53); this was clearly an anomaly. It was also a serious threat to the population, and when the hay harvest also failed in 1634, starvation followed (for example, *Ann.* i. 240).

In the north where fish were plenty only in summer large-scale fishing conflicted with the demands of *heyannir*. Fishing was still important, however, if we can judge from the annals, where notifications of fishing conditions in the north are often made (for example, ibid. i. 191, 192, 232). On the whole, the northern and eastern parts of the country were more dependent on farming, with the added possibility of sending off migrant fishermen to the *verstöð*. In the south and west, the dual economy could more easily be pursued from home. The northerners thus made less profit from fishing than the southerners, because their costs were higher (Skúli Magnússon 1944*a*: 67–8). Seasonal fishing, however, was of established importance for all Icelanders, even though the *verstöðvar* were closer to home for some than for others.

The fishing cycle was invariable but variations in stock and catch nevertheless occurred from one year to the next. The annalists bear witness to this, with recurring references to *fiskiár litið* ('bad fishing year'), or *fiskileysi* ('fish-lessness'), or *fiskiár mikil* ('good fishing year') (*Ann.: passim*). A letter of supplication from the Icelandic peasants to the Danish king Frederik II in 1579 also emphasized the importance of fish. The peasants asked for indulgence in matters of taxation, due to lean-years, decimated herds, and 'because the fish is disappearing from the country' (*Al:* i. 393–6; Espolín: iv. 29). Hannes Finsson explicitly mentions poor fish catches as one of the main reasons for starvation in Iceland (1796: *passim*). Nature was not always generous with gifts from the sea in spite of the prayers made by fishermen for a safe journey and a fine catch (Lúðvík Kristjánsson 1983: 209–21). Prayers were not the sole technology of fishing, of course, even if rituals and magic were important features (Lúðvík Kristjánsson 1986: 317ff.). From the eighteenth century we have extensive records of fishing technologies made by active reformers such as Horrebow (1752), Eggert Ólafsson (1772), Olavius (1780), and Skúli Magnússon (1944*a*; 1944*b*). Before that the state of fishing technologies has to be inferred from other sources.

A brief note of the inland fishing must be made before the extensive discussion of the sea-fishing. Salmon, trout, and the like were caught in lakes and rivers, according to well-established rights. Nets were stretched out across the river (Oddur Einarsson 1971: 108). It was illegal to block off the rivers in the spawning season when the salmon went upstream (*Jónsbók*: 188–90). When rivers froze and nets could not be used, freshwater fish were caught by hook and line (Oddur Einarsson 1971: 108). Traps were also used; rivers were partially blocked with stones and traps placed in the free passages (Horrebow 1752: 237–8; 1966: 171–2). Already Ketill and his sons knew that salmon abounded in Iceland, and it seems to have continued to do so. In the mid-seventeenth century, however, Jón Eggertsson remarked that salmon was poorly exploited (cf. n. 17 above). Other evidence points in the same direction, namely, to a decreasing importance of inland fisheries.

Sea-fishing was mostly from boats. During our period and up to the late nineteenth century, boats were never used for long-term fishing, only for day trips. They were open plank-boats, most often designed for eight or six oars (Lúðvík Kristjánsson 1982: 91).[23] In an earlier period larger ships are often mentioned in the records, but in the fifteenth and sixteenth centuries the commonest size was six to eight oars. In the eighteenth century, these had even been replaced by two-oar boats in the south-west (Skúli Magnússon 1785; 1944*a*: 59ff.). Elsewhere bigger boats were still in use (Eggert Ólafsson 1772: 339–40). The size of the boats determined the distance that could be travelled—journeys of between 3 and 6 miles were common (Skúli Magnússon 1944*a*: 53). The first nation-wide registration of boats in 1770 gave the results as seen in Table 1. None of these was designed for deep sea-fishing, and the lack of timber (and the price of it) made construction of a truly sea-going fleet impossible. In addition to this, local landing facilities were poor, and outside the few larger merchant-controlled harbours, boats

TABLE 1. *Boat Sizes in 1770*

Size	No.
12 oars	2
10 ,,	20
8 ,,	386
6 ,,	310
5 men	223
4 ,,	278
3 ,,	41
2 ,,	604
1 man	5
TOTAL	1,869

Source: Lúdvík Kristjánsson 1982: 101.

had to be lifted ashore. Lightness of construction was essential (Eggert Ólafsson 1772: 343).

Fish were caught at sea by hook and line. Nets were not used until the late eighteenth century, when they were introduced by Skúli Magnússon (1785; 1944a: 54–5; Olavius 1780: pp. xcviii–xcix). We know that in the Middle Ages seals were caught in nets (whence comes the notion of *netlǫg*), and in 1589 such nets were still common (Oddur Einarsson 1971: 111). By the eighteenth century, however, seal-nets had been abandoned in most places (Olavius 1780: 172–3; Skúli Magnússon 1944a: 49–50, 56). They were only in use in one northern district; elsewhere harpoons and clubs were used (Horrebow 1752: 234–5; 1966: 169–70). Once again we get a glimpse of a collective amnesia.

Nets were not used for catching cod or other sea-fish until the late eighteenth century; in some places they were not introduced until the twentieth century (Lúðvík Kristjánsson 1983: 434–6). This means that during our period hand-lines and hooks were virtually the only fishing implements. They were handmade, either at the farm, or sometimes at the *verstöð* (ibid.: 401–15).

The lines were relatively short; seventeenth-century reports suggest lengths between 40 and 60 fathoms (*Aí*: v. 12), while in the eighteenth century line lengths of between 40 and 60 metres are reported (Skúli

Magnússon 1944*a*: 54). In the fifteenth century there is evidence of longer and more 'efficient' lines; thus in 1482 a line of 180 fathoms with a hundred angles is reported (*DI*: viii. 71). Probably this scale of fishing, which was rare, had been learnt from the visiting English fishermen. When, later, the English were banned, this was largely because their fishing techniques were so effective; in a judgement of 1500, English boats using sinker lines with several hooks (such lines were known as *lóðir*) which had no other commercial purpose for visiting Iceland apart from fishing, were deemed *ófriðhelgir* ('outlawed') and everyman's prey (*DT*: vii. 497). The Icelanders themselves were generally small-scale fishermen. While the Icelanders deliberately prevented their own fishing industry from developing, and were stuck with small and inefficient boats, they always had the foreign fishermen's large-scale fishing within sight. As early as the eighteenth century, Jochumssen commented on this historical irony (1977: 30).

On the whole, efficiency in fishing deteriorated, and during the sixteenth century there was distinct resistance to technological innovations. Court verdicts prohibited the use of lines with more than one hook; the *bændur* feared that fishing, if returns increased, would be too attractive to the farm-hands (*AÍ*: i. 432–4; v. 122). In 1699 the rules were modified, and the use of *lóðir* permitted, but only during the *vertíð*; outside this period it is prohibited because of its allegedly damaging effects on farming (*LI*: i. 546–7). To judge from eighteenth-century evidence, the use of these more sophisticated lines was only sporadic. Thus, Skúli Magnússon makes a strong case for the reintroduction of sinker-lines with up to thirty hooks, and gives a detailed description of how to make them (1944*a*: 55–6). In his time lines with only one hook were the most common instrument, and he complains about the deterioration of fishing in general (1944*b*).

The main catch consisted of cod, haddock, and halibut. The first two species were dried, and used for both home consumption and export. From the *búalög* we know that fish was a regular part of the diet, while meat was a rare food. Some species of fish, that might have contributed to subsistence, were considered inedible, like herring (Jochumssen 1977: 43) and eel (Skúli Magnússon 1944*a*: 48).

Dried fish (*skreið*) was the main export article in our period. There were two ways of producing it; either it could be hanged to dry in the air, or it was left on the ground (Anderson 1746: 81 ff.). Both methods had their drawbacks, for rain and snow could cause the uncovered fish to rot (Jochumssen 1977: 19). The two drying methods were not equally to the taste of the authorities. In 1691 the king complained that some inhabitants in 'our land Iceland' had reintroduced an old method of cutting fish up the back and hanging them to dry. He demanded that this method should be abandoned, since fish dried in heaps on the rocks was more marketable (*LI*: i. 497).[24] Salt was scarce and salted fish was unknown. This lack of salt was lamented by many travellers (Vetter 1931: 154; Jochumssen 1977: 15, 18).

The hunting of seals was a common feature of medieval Iceland. In *Grágás* (ii. 32) and *Jónsbók* (181) there are references to *selveiðar*, and we know that normally nets, and sometimes traps, were used for catching them (*Jónsbók*: 206). In 1481 the economic importance of seals is indirectly evidenced by a papal letter allowing the Icelanders to eat seal, both during fasts and otherwise (*DI*: ix. 39–40). Christian law forbade this, but the bishop at Skálholt had made a supplication to the pope. A century later Oddur Einarsson emphasized the value of seals in lean-years, which suggests that by this time they were no longer considered part of the normal diet in ordinary circumstances (1971: 111). Prices on seal-meat seem to have gone up in the same period—to judge from the evidence of *búalög*. In the oldest manuscript (mid-fifteenth century) the price is 3¾ ellens per firkin of salted seal meat; later it is 6 ellens (*Búalög* 1915–33: 2, 4, 40, 46, 50, 67, 86, 105). By 1700, however, seal hunting had declined considerably, and was completely abandoned in many places (Lúðvík Kristjánsson 1980: 314–16).

Stranded whales also played an important part in the Icelandic economy. *Jónsbók* has rules about rights in them, which leave us in no doubt about the significance of strandings (*reki*) (194 ff.). Disputes over strandings (*reki*) were common in court. Certain shores were known as *rekastrandir*, and clearly to have access to such a place was an invaluable economic asset, often claimed by the Church (Lúðvík Kristjánsson 1980: 199–235). Little was left as *almenningar*.

In addition to various kinds of 'hunting' (*veiðar*), a fair amount of gathering was practised. Shellfish and seaweeds were used (ibid.: 35–182), birds' eggs collected; berries, mosses, and wild grass were used in the diet. Drift-wood, too, was much in demand. Farming was paramount, however, and it is curious that we sense a more or less conscious effort by the farming population to keep fishing to a minimum, and to prevent technological innovations. The eighteenth-century observers consistently report a decline in Icelandic fishing and their views are substantiated in the records. Fish remained as a significant part of the household economy and in the normal diet. Yet on the whole, from the fifteenth to the late eighteenth century, the *veiðistöd* gave less and less joy to Iceland—just as Ketill *flatnefr* had prophesied.

From 1400 to 1800 fishing and farming coexisted in a dual economic system. The system was framed by the household, in a kind of 'domestic mode of production' (Sahlins 1974). The system persisted, but there were remarkable changes in the economic order. Having dealt in some detail with continuities and discontinuities in the domestic organization of farming and fishing, I shall here attempt an analysis of developments within the economic system as a whole, in order that we may, eventually, approach the larger issues of cause and effect in history.

The basic pillars of the household subsistence pattern were farming and fishing. Farming consisted of several elements, between which certain historical choices were made. We may visualize the system as in Figure 3. These were the ingredients, but the Icelanders did not evaluate them equally. At all taxonomic levels, there was a 'choice' which favoured the right pole in the scheme.

At the most inclusive level, we have seen how farming was favoured at the expense of fishing, right from the law of 1404 forbidding full-time fishing as a way of living. In spite of occasional upswings and of new markets for fish, legislation recurrently points to the primacy of farming, especially when labour was short. Fishing was seen as a diversion from proper interests, in spite of its domestic and export value. Fishing technologies declined, boats became smaller, multi-hook lines were partially prohibited, and fishing places were abandoned (Olavius 1780: 395). The fishing population had a reputation for uncleanliness (Eggers 1786: 32). Perfectly edible sea animals were not exploited (such as herring and eels) or fell out of view (like seals), in spite of recurrent famines. The general trend is one of gradual decline (noted as early as the sixteenth century; see Friis 1881), which is partly explained by the countermeasures taken by landowners.

Farming, however, was also in decline. Leaving aside matters of causation, we can remember that grain growing was abandoned, with the subsequent disappearance of the plough. Pastoralism remained

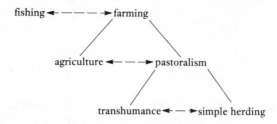

FIG. 3. *Taxonomy of Economic Activities*

the pivot of farming, but even here a choice between two strategies had to be made. The use of saeters and the transhumant pattern in general was abandoned, leaving the milking cattle to graze on the home fields. This reduced the return of *úthey* (hay grown in the non-manured meadow). Fences disintegrated, tufts sprouted, and the yield of *taða* or hay from the *tún* diminished. Hay-storage techniques worsened. Farms fell into waste in great numbers, although some of the recorded *eyðibýli* ('waste farms') may actually have been abandoned saeters (see Björn Teitsson and Magnús Stefánsson 1972). Horses had not been eaten since the eleventh century, and a great number of 'surplus' horses were allowed to eat the wild grain.

There is a logic to the general displacement of balance between the separate poles of the economic order. I have generalized the trend, but there is no doubt that development systematicaly favoured the *less-intensive* parts of the complex economy, in spite of deliberate attempts to concentrate labour in farming. In a simple economic model, agricultural growth and increasing population density go together, permitting a more intensive exploitation of the soil (Boserup 1965). 'Intensity' in this sense is characterized by high productivity from the soil and high input of labour. By contrast, 'extensive' farming is defined by a poor yield and a low input of labour. There seems to be a direct correlation between population and technology in European history, with a clear pattern of oscillation between intensive and extensive modes of exploitation concordant with population densities (Boserup 1982: 93 ff.).

Correlation is one thing, causation another. In Norway, which found itself in an economic condition comparable to Iceland, population increased tenfold from around 150,000 to 1.5 million in the period

1500 to 1850 (Dyrvik 1979: 9). Population growth clearly does not then, of itself, *cause* intensification of farming, and the economic model seems too simple to account for both the Icelandic and the Norwegian development.

Certainly, there *was* a general labour shortage in Iceland, but only relative to an ideal model. In Iceland, the difference between the intensive and the extensive modes of farming was small; certainly far smaller than Boserup's model presupposes. This was because of the duality inherent in farming itself—in the coexistence, that is, of grain-growing and of a pastoralism which presupposed a regular cropping of hay. Grain and hay were in competition for the *tún* (the prepared infield), the size of which was limited both by the arid nature of the land and the amount of labour available. If grain was favoured, the production of hay would decrease, and the stock of animals diminish. This, in turn, would have a negative influence on manuring and on the return from the soil in general.

Grain-growing, the most intensive mode of farming, was never of much consequence in Iceland. Within pastoralism itself—at a lower taxonomic level—the difference between the intensive and extensive pole was similarly small. A consistent use of saeters would allow all the home fields, including the unprepared meadow (*engi*), to be used for hay to be stored for winter fodder, and would thus permit larger flocks at each farm. Simpler herding, however, meant that the home meadows were used for summer grazing, while only the *tún* was cropped for hay. The transhumant pattern was more productive, but also more labour-consuming, and the *per capita* return does not differ much in the two modes.

Turning Boserup's model upside down, then, we may ask why the Icelanders did not intensify their modes of living, making the way for an increasing population. This would have been possible through a concentration of labour in bigger and fewer farms. Labour *was* a critical factor from an economic-historical point of view, but the organization of labour has more aspects than the strictly economic.

The stress on the independent *bú* is important here. *Bú er betra* accounts for the mental priority of farm-life to fishing, and for the continuous domestic nature of the economy. The *bú* and the *bóndi* epitomized everything properly Icelandic, like independence, power, and honour. They were also associated with marriage and, ultimately, with social (as well as biological) reproduction.

The domestic mode of production, according to Sahlins, is characterized by a general underproduction (1974: 41 ff.). In the household regulated economy, labour is often in excess when measured against the actual production (ibid.: 68–9). This domestic economic 'failure', however, cannot be understood without reference to social and cultural values. In Iceland, the *bú* was extremely valued, and wealth was measured in farm produce. It is tempting even to speak of an honour-and-butter complex, which was recurrently expressed in tradition. In *Skíðaríma*, a very popular and much-reproduced *ríma* ('popular verse') from the fifteenth century, this finds a neat expression; Óðinn, whom the tramp Skíði is visiting, sends for butter lest his household should be regarded without honour. Although Skíði has clearly overstepped the limits of hospitality by asking for butter, Óðinn in his turn makes a potlatch of the event when he showers butter on Skíði.[25] According to *Landnámabók*, one of the first Norwegians to visit Iceland in the late ninth century reported that 'butter dropped from every straw in the country'—and thereby attracted settlers in multitudes (*Ldn.*, *ÍF*: i. 38).

The decline in the economic conditions of Iceland during our period is not only measurable by external standards. Contemporary Icelanders also felt it strongly; apparently they failed to perceive the nature of their crisis, however, and continued life after a preconceived *bóndi*-model. To end this chapter, I shall cite three generations of poets on the developments in Icelandic modes of livelihood.

Einar Sigurðsson (1538–1626), who largely wrote within a pre-Reformation tradition of religious poetry (Stefán Einarsson 1957: 194–5), made a plea for consolation in his *Hugbót* ('mind comforter') in which he begs the Lord to take care of his flock (*ÍL*: i. 340). Others blame the country for the decline, he says, but retorts that the land is good. His son, Ólafur Einarsson (1573–1651) (the younger brother of Bishop Oddur Einarsson whose work I have quoted previously), is more direct in his long poem *Ættlera-aldarháttur* ('degenerating conditions'), in which he compares the present misery to former plenty, and asks God for advice to reverse the trend (*ÍL*: i. 349–54). The father's brighter view on the national conditions has been replaced by a more sinister one; 'like most, he looked back wistfully to the good old days and had harsh words to say about the trade monopoly and the sloth of his country men' (Stefán Einarsson 1957: 195). Thereby he also anticipated his son Stefán's satire of lazy farm-hands and useless crofters (ibid.). In his *Ómenskukvæði* ('Song of Inhumanity') Stefán

Ólafsson (1619–88) explicitly condemns the Icelanders for their vices, and for their inability to keep up with their own traditions (1885–6: i. 261–78).[26] From grandfather to grandson, the tone has sharpened.

The theme of decline is repeated by the religious poet Hallgrímur Pétursson (1614–74), in, for example, his poem *Aldarháttar* (1887–90: ii. 355). It is perhaps most forcefully expressed by the eighteenth-century Eggert Ólafsson, whose poem *Búnaðarbálkur* ('on farming') is an emotional attack against the Icelanders, who are accused of wasting their land and their lives (1832a).

'Underproduction' was clad in many different (and more vivid) words in contemporary Iceland, but there is little doubt that it was part of the social experience. Whether one can blame the people, as Eggert Ólafsson does, it is clear that development within the economic order was not solely an effect of material causes such as demography and ecology. Nature, erosion, and climate were important contributing factors, but there were social and cultural conditions as well; perhaps even a certain 'mentality', which we will pursue further.

Meanwhile, we may conclude that 'economy is rather a function of the society than a structure' (Sahlins 1974: 76). The Icelandic economic order was a function of an atomistic society, with no division of labour, and no organic solidarity outside the household, which for centuries was the only relevant social unit. The household was society writ small and concretized in the landscape; society was the household writ large. The economic order was largely a function of this particular cosmology; it was an order, nevertheless, which worked to the detriment of the very social space which it purported to reflect and uphold.

4

Landownership

GIVEN the central position of farming in Iceland, access to land was of primary social concern, and land the vital resource of both the economic and the cosmological order. In this chapter I shall deal with landownership, and the social categories which were a corollary to the distribution of land.

From the earliest settlements rights in land were central to social thinking. It was when the land was *albyggt* ('fully settled') that Icelandic law was drawn up according to the twelfth-century *Íslendingabók* ((*Íslb.*) ch. 3). Among other things the law regulated rights in land. The laws were written down in 1117–18, a few decades before *Landnámabók*, 'the book of settlements'. This latter work, which was compiled in several versions, has been interpreted by some as a means of establishing individual rights over land on the basis of genealogical relationships to original settlers (Sveinbjörn Rafnsson 1974). Probably, however, this is taking too pragmatic a view. The genealogical information is too sporadic to support such an interpretation, and there is no explicit interest in ownership (cf. Jacob Benediktsson 1974).

As the title indicates, it is the *landnám* ('land-taking') which is of direct concern. The point is that around 400 named people settled on Iceland, founded Icelandic society, and became ancestors of Icelandic kin groups. In other words, *Landnámabók* is concerned with origins and beginnings (Bruhn 1985: 37). In this way the origins of 'Icelandicness' were tied to the land, and this was to remain an important feature of Icelandic self-understanding. We have seen how farming was conceptually dominant over fishing in the dual economy. It seems appropriate, therefore, to begin discussion of landownership between 1400 and 1800 with the twelfth-century myth of origin.

In the twelfth century the social structure was changing in Iceland. Large landowners and thrall labour were being replaced by much more variegated groups of farmers, smallholders, tenants, and servants (Hastrup 1979; 1985*a*). In this situation *Landnámabók* may have served the purpose of bounding the 'real' landowners from other categories of peasants (Bruhn 1985: 40). By reference to origins, and to the antiquity of particular kin groups, the truly landowning class could distinguish itself from the up-and-coming class of people (including freed slaves) who could now buy or rent land. The bounding of social categories was to remain a problem throughout our period.

The first *landnámsmaðr* ('settler') was Ingólfr, who—according to *Landnámabók*—*tók ser bústað þar sem ǫndvegissúlur hans hǫfdu á land komit* ('settled down where his high-seat pillars had driven ashore') (*ÍF*: i. 45). The procedure of throwing the high-seat pillars overboard and let them determine the immigrants' home, was a way of linking men to particular places through fate. By 1400, when my analysis begins, access to land was still to some extent a matter of fate. It was no longer augured by high-seat pillars but rather by birth into a particular natural and social environment. In this environment the landowners were in a minority. Other categories dominated numerically, but as every Icelander had to belong to a farm, the landowners retained their structural dominance.

In the first section of this chapter I shall deal mainly with the constants of landownership. These are expressed in laws which legally framed the entire period under study here. There were changes at the concrete level of course, and I will touch upon some of them. In the second section, I introduce the landowners as the (conceptually) most important dramatis personae in Icelandic history. The sources allow us to perceive the distinct categories of owners, and the differentiation of farm sizes. Thirdly, I deal with 'the others'—the large and complex non-landowning population of Iceland.

The chapter terminates with a general outline of the social order in terms of social categories and mental structures.

THE LAW

In 1281 *Jónsbók* was introduced as the new Icelandic law, and until the nineteenth century it codified social action and legal rights. Numerous amendments and additions were made during the period 1400 to 1800, largely as the result of interest taken by the Danish monarch. *Jónsbók* remained, however, and circulated among the Icelanders in innumerable manuscripts, from which many young people were taught to read.[1] By contrast, the additional clauses and royal decrees never formed part of this popular reading. From an internal perspective, the law persisted, even though the way it was administered by external rulers changed. To illuminate the permanence of landownership, we must look again at the *landnám*.

In Norway, from where most of the settlers came, rights over land were expressed in the principle of *óðal* or allodial land. This principle implied a particular relationship between a kin group and a plot of land, which could not be removed from the kin group without its consent. Within the cognatic kin group, agnatic kinsmen had precedence over uterine kinsmen as heirs to land (*Gulaþingslǫg*, ch. 275; *NGL*: i. 92).

In spite of this rule of precedence, the kin group was a cognatic kindred, which logically could not possess land in common. The *óðal* right was not actually a form of ownership, like the Roman *possessio*, but rather a right of pre-emption. The 'heirs' were the ones to be given first option should a *bóndi* die or want to sell his land (ibid.: ch. 276; *NLG*: i. 92). Land could be bought and sold, but the law protected the interests of the *ætt* or kin group.

On arrival in virgin Iceland, the Norse settlers had no traditional claims in land. History did not favour any kin groups or persons at the expense of others, whence the principle of *óðal* became irrelevant. It remained a dormant principle for the social organization of access to land, however, as I have shown elsewhere (Hastrup 1985a: ch. 7). In *Grágás* it survived in the notion of *aðalból* ('main farm'), for instance, which was inalienable in the same way as the ancient *óðal*-land (*Grágás*: ii. 226). A consequence of this was that specific farms could remain the property of particular kin groups for centuries.[2] When generational depth had been established, the principle of *óðal* re-emerged locally in Iceland.

Meanwhile the Church gained more and more influence, and along with this notions of property changed (Gurevich 1977). From being essentially a social relationship, the idea of ownership was transformed into a relationship between persons and objects. This paved the way for the gradual concentration of land in the hands of the Church. However, in *Jónsbók*, the notion of *óðal*, which was absent from *Grágás*, reappears. The use of the term is somewhat inconsistent, though. In some places it refers simply to privately owned land in general (*Jónsbók*: 3, 20), while elsewhere it is used in contradistinction to movables (ibid.: 41). In other passages it has retained the traditional meaning of privilege by kinship (ibid.: 78, 82). No problems of interpretation arise out of the first two kinds of usage, which reflect the Roman notion of *possessio* and imply little more than landownership.

Concerning the third kind of usage, the matter is less clear, at least when viewed within a historical context. First of all, not all manuscripts transmitted refer to *óðal*. Some have the notion of *hǫfuðból* ('main farm') instead, where inheritance is concerned. Thus, it is stated *en effaðir á jarðir eptir, þá skulu synir snúaz til hǫfuðbóla, en dœtr til útjarða eða lausafjár ef eigi eru jarðir til* ('if a father leaves land behind him, then his sons should inherit the *hǫfuðból*, while daughters should have the *útjarðar* ('outlying land' 'farms') or movables if no such farms are found') (*Jónsbók*: 78). The precedence of male heirs is conspicuous. To the passage quoted above, a further note about primogeniture was added which is otherwise absent in the law. This testifies to the special position of the *hǫfuðból*, which was further underlined in a royal decree of 1481, entitling heirs to redeem a *hǫfuðból* which for some reason or another had gone into Church possession (see Magnús Már Lárusson 1970: 44).

Óðal (*Gúlaþingslǫg*), *aðalból* (*Grágás*), and *hǫfuðból* (*Jónsbók*) are concepts from one and the same semantic field, relating kinship and land. Reflecting certain historical changes, these concepts also point to a continuity in the Icelandic representations of their world, and in attitudes towards landed property (cf. Gurevich 1985: ch. 6 *et passim*).

This semantic continuity was not upheld without practical debate. A much-disputed passage in *Jónsbók* illustrates this. The law contained a so-called *óðalscapitulum* (*óðal*-chapter) in which the principle of *óðal* was defined.[3] When the law was introduced, some Icelanders, among whom was Bishop Árni who was responsible for Icelandic Christian law, voted against the reintroduction of the *óðal*-principle, understood as a right of pre-emption, and interpreted as an invalidation of free purchases of land if these lands had not first been offered to kinsmen. The bishop protested *um þat, ef sá byðr eigi frændum land, er selja vill, at fyrir þat megi eigi þat kaup rjúfa* ('that even if a person does not offer his kinsmen the land he wants to sell, it should still not invalidate the selling') (*Árna saga biskups*, ch. 28; *BS* i. 364; cf. *DI*: ii. 207). It is not clear whether the clause was actually enforced or not; the *bændur*, at least, are recorded as having been in favour of it (*Árna saga biskups*, ch. 28; *BS*: i. 364–5; *DI*: ii. 208).

Old disputes over the contents of this particular chapter of *Jónsbók* are matched by modern disputes over its authenticity (see *KL*: xii. 501; Ólafur Halldórsson 1904: xi–xv). The chapter is found only in some of the *Jónsbók* manuscripts, and it may be read as a survival from Norwegian law, which was used as a template for *Jónsbók*. For the present purpose, however, we can note these ideas fitted well into the semantics of kinship and landownership in Iceland. *Ætt* (kin group) and *óðal* were explicitly linked in a series of diplomas dealing with matters of inheritance in the fifteenth and sixteenth centuries (*DI*: iii. 761 (1415); *DI*: vii. 319, 401 (1496); *DI*: vii. 647 (1503); *DI*: xiii. 32 (1555)). In 1620 a court case about the selling of *óðal* land led to the re-establishment of the principle, after reference to several sixteenth-century manuscripts of *Jónsbók* (*AÍ*: v. 27–35). Whatever the legal status of the *óðalscapitulum* in 1281, it certainly penetrated the administration of landownership for the centuries to follow.

The Danish monarch, Christian IV, who had 'learnt about the unsuitabilities in our land Iceland' ratified the *óðal*-chapter in an ordinance of 1622 (*LI*: i. 209–11). He objected, indeed, to the Icelandic practice of excluding half a chapter of the *óðalsbálkur*—the *óðalscapitulum*. In due course such negligence, he said, would entail a pernicious disorder in the population in general, a contempt for the authorities and the law, and above all oppression and destruction of the ordinary man (ibid.: i. 209). To avert these sinister developments Christian IV emphasized the legal status of the *óðal* principle, and demanded that land always be offered first to the nearest kin. At the same time he forbade the *sýslumenn* and other authorities to buy land before matters of inheritance and kinship rights had been fully determined (ibid.: 210). In 1646 the issue reappeared in a decree of clarification. Due to misunderstandings and uncertainties as to the relevant range of kinship, the king specified that first option on land should be given publicly at the annual assembly to kinsmen in the first and second degrees only (*LI*: i. 233–4).

Óðal in Iceland, then, does seem to have been an enduring, if sometimes latent, concept of privileged access to land through kinship. It coexisted with notions of private and freely disposable property, to which the Church in particular adhered. After the Reformation in the mid-sixteenth century the Danish monarch took a renewed interest in Iceland, and the *óðal* principle was reinstated. Seen from feudal Denmark where the Crown gave privileges to the *aðal* (nobility), the relationship between kinship and patrimony, like a large-scale *óðal*, did not seem strange.

In practice the ambiguous definition of rights in land was an inevitable source of conflict. The fifteenth century in particular witnessed innumerable court cases concerning inheritance, and the legitimacy of wills and testaments. Such cases could run for years and years. The possible reasons for the concentration of conflict in the fifteenth century are many. The Black Death (1402–4) seriously disrupted social organization; the Church, as well, seems to have become increasingly perverted in its thirst for power at this time, suffering from its own moral decline.[4]

A famous case of disputed inheritance followed the death of Björn *ríki* ('the rich') Þorleifsson, killed by English pirates on Snæfellsnes in 1467. His wife was Ólöf Loftsdóttir, daughter of the renowned Loftur Guttormsson (d. 1432) who was also designated 'rich'. Ólöf died in 1479.[5] Of Björn it was said that he was the wealthiest man ever in the country, leaving 'hundreds of hundreds' of *kúgildi* ('cow's worth') behind him.

At his death, the estate had to be passed on to his heirs (*DI*: v. 497–503). So far there were no problems, because he had four legitimate children who had to share the inheritance according to the principles of the law; this excluded at least three illegitimate children, and possibly a daughter who had had a child while still unmarried and living in her father's house (Arnór Sigurjónsson 1975: 143). The original property of his wife Ólöf, who had brought lands with her into the marriage was to remain in her hands, however. Among her lands was Skarð at Skarðsströnd, '*elzta óðal á Íslandi*' ('the oldest *óðal* on Iceland'; Ólafur Lárusson 1925), which she had inherited from her father. The rules of inheritance entitled the daughters to half the amount of the sons (*Jónsbók*: 78) and Björn's estate was divided between his three sons and one daughter on this principle.

When the mother Ólöf died in 1479, however, the problems started. By then one son had died in military service for the Danish king. The daughter, Solveig, had had an affair with a man below her own rank; because of their unequal standing marriage was denied them. Normally a father was the marriage guardian, but in his absence the mother and the brothers took over (*Jónsbók*: 70). In Solveig's case her brothers refused her permission to marry this man by whom she had children. At the death of Ólöf these illegitimate births were held against Solveig. The two surviving brothers referred to the passage in the *Jónsbók* where it is stated that if a daughter is *legin* ('lain with') in her father's house, she is entitled to no inheritance whatsoever

(_Jónsbók_: 79); this is also the case if she marries without the consent of her father, mother, brothers, or any other marriage guardian (ibid.: 71). Thus her brother claimed Skarð for himself to the exclusion of Solveig, even though she was entitled to this farm, as well as other lands, through the bequest of her father.

Solveig had, in fact, finally married a man, Páll, of equal standing, and the mother Ólöf had given her consent to this marriage just before her death (_DI_: vi. 182). This meant a reconsideration of the inheritance claims, after which Solveig received Skarð (Ólafur Lárusson 1925: 238). The problems did not stop there, though, because it became known that Solveig and Páll were _fjórmenningar_, kinsmen related in the fourth degree. This meant that the bishop had to give a dispensation for the marriage to be valid. The case was delayed, and two children were born to Solveig, before her marriage was confirmed and she could finally claim Skarð. However, born out of wedlock, her children were not considered her legitimate heirs and when Solveig died in the 'later plague' in 1495, the old case was renewed.[6] Her testament was disputed, and the descendants of her brothers made claims on her lands (see _DI_: vii. 238–47, 256–7, 347–54, 357–66, 367–8 for details).

The point at issue is not only the conflict of interest between kinsmen, but the contradictions inherent in the laws about access to land, and to the _höfuðból_ in particular. Last wills and testaments may have been legal documents, but the law sometimes went against them. Amidst everything else, we also note the clerical power to permit, detain, or prohibit particular unions.

Ownership, as _óðal_ or _possessio_, was not the only means of establishing rights in land. It could also be rented, and ever since the Freestate there were numerous specifications in the law about the rights and duties of tenants (_Grágás_, _landsleigubálkr_). In principle no land was allowed to lie waste, and if an owner could not exploit his lands properly he was legally compelled to lease them to someone else (_Jónsbók_: 171–2). Thus, from an early stage in the history of Iceland we find an important distinction between _aðalból_ and _leiguból_. The _leiguból_ ('rented farm') was an independent farmstead where the tenant was himself a _bóndi_, with all that implied in terms of rights and duties.

The relationship between owner and tenant was one of free contract. The tenant took possession of the farm on the 'parting-day' at the end of May, and held the lease for one year (_Jónsbók_: 130). The contract was oral, and made in the presence of two witnesses. In 1705 the Crown decreed that a written contract was necessary for the lease to be legal. It was stated also that no other payments could be imposed on the tenant apart from those written down, nor could the owner evict a tenant who paid his rent in due time (*LI*: i. 623–4). Importantly, King Frederik IV also stated that no landowner could claim more rent than had been customary 'since time immemorial' (*Arildstid*). Age was the hallmark of legitimacy.

In the Freestate the land rent was 10 per cent of the real value of the land (*Grágás*: i*b*. 140, 148, 248; ii. 213, 224). In the era of *Jónsbók* it was variable. There is no general clause of the *Grágás* kind; only the hire of dairy cattle is mentioned. Such cattle were leased with the farm, and for every *kugildi*'s worth of *leigufé* ('rented cattle'), two farthings' worth of butter, or the value of winter fodder for four lambs, had to be paid (*Jónsbók*: 224). As Björn Lárusson has shown, the rate of interest on the hire of cattle amounted to some 16 per cent, while otherwise interest rates during the fifteenth century were between 5 and 10 per cent (1967: 45). For lands possessed by the Church, the Crown, or the monasteries, the rent was generally 5 per cent (*KL*: x. 282). In spite of variations from place to place, the rent for particular plots was fairly constant because it had to be *eins og að fornu verið hefur*, 'like it has been in the old times' (ibid.). Again, age defined the rights.

Provided the tenant paid his rent and exploited the land properly, there were no limitations on his usufruct rights. These included rights to fish, fowl, birds' eggs, seals, and turf (*Jónsbók*: 134–5). There were some restrictions on driftwood and stranded whales, but they were not very clearly formulated. To clarify the issue the Althing stated in 1604 that a tenant was now fully entitled to driftwood (*LI*: i. 145). It is worth adding that a tenant had no right to sublease any part of his farm, but that this prohibition was widely disregarded, the comprehensive land register of Árni Magnússon and Páll Vídalín from the early eighteenth century shows. Tenants commonly leased smaller plots of land to cottagers, from whom they then collected rent (Björn Lárusson 1967: 42).

Aðalból and *leiguból* were treated as separate farmsteads for inheritance purposes, and were also individually valued for tithes. In that sense they were both *lögbýli* ('law-farms'). Contrasted to the *lögbýli* were the *hjáleigur* (Ólafur Lárusson 1929: 36–7). A *hjáleiga* was a kind of *leiguland* ('rented land'), but unlike the *leiguból* it was not independent of the main farm, of which it was considered a part. *Hjáleigumenn* ('cottagers') had their own *tún* ('infield') but no separate pastures.

Their animals grazed on the pastures of the main farm, and in the commons. Whether attached to an *aðalból* or a *leiguból*, the *hjáleiga* was defined as 'of' or 'with' (*hjá*) the farm for which the cottagers had to work. In the preceding chapter we saw how some saeters (*sel*) were transformed into *hjáleigur* during our period, and on the whole these seem to have become an ever-more significant element in the social landscape of Iceland. In some parts of the country the *hjáleiga* comprised almost half the land in 1703–12, when the land register was made (Ólafur Lárusson 1929: 37). This was in the south-west, where farms were relatively big, and where the dual economy was more easily practised. On average, the *hjáleigumenn* amounted to one-fifth of the farming population (excluding servants) (Björn Þorsteinsson 1978: 243–5).

In the chronology of Icelandic history, *hjáleigur* are first documented after 1200.[7] They were to gain importance in our epoch, for they furnished the landowner with farm labour, while not alienating the land from the main farm. Also, they helped people of limited means to set up some kind of independent household at reduced cost. From an economic perspective, the introduction of *hjáleigur* meant an intensification of farming, an increase in yield per area, and ultimately an increase in land-rent (*KL*: vii. 677).

Given the importance of land in Iceland it is small wonder that access to it was regulated by detailed rules of inheritance, lease, purchase, and gift-giving. Even in cases of inheritance or gift, the receiver had to vindicate the land publicly and in the presence of witnesses (*Jónsbók*: 117–18). Landmarks were to be carefully made, leaving no one in doubt as to the extension of the farm (ibid.: 120, 124). Within its boundaries, the farm had to be well maintained, and no infields were to lay unattended; in contracts of tenancy it was further stipulated that the tenant had to employ sufficient labour to exploit properly the hay of the outfields (ibid.: 133–4). If hay was allowed to waste for three successive years, the tenants lost all rights in the land.

The contract of tenancy was traditionally for one year, from *fardagur* to *fardagur* ('moving day'). While there was certainly no shortage of land, however, landowners often refused to renew contracts, thus illegally letting land waste and leaving people without means of subsistence (Olavius 1780: 393). In 1591 the king, hearing of this practice, on his own farms as well as others, instructed that tenants had a right to remain on their farms, provided the land rent was duly paid (*LI*: i. 126–7). No '*Bonde eller Boemand*' (peasant or cotter) should be sacked without good reason. In 1607 this decree was followed up with a more precise statute giving royal tenants life contracts—for the sake of both the peasants and the land (*LI*: i. 149–50). Under these contracts, tenants were required to maintain their own housing (ibid.); normally, it had been the duty of the landowner to restore the buildings on the *leiguland*, or at least to provide the tenant with wood for the construction (*Jónsbók*: 131–2; Oddur Einarsson 1971: 87). Apparently it took some time before this new state of affairs was internalized by the sheriffs, to judge from a repetition of the royal decree in 1619, wherein it was further stated that also tenants' widows should have a right to continued tenure (*LI*: i. 182). It was clearly felt necessary to maintain farming activities at the highest possible level at this time, and a further decree of 1705 (cf. above, pp. 86–7) again reinforced the rights of the tenant (*LI*: i. 623–4).

An indigenous voice from half-way through our four centuries gives a vivid portrayal of the lot of the tenant. Oddur Einarsson tells of the destitute *leiguliðar*, who are little better than beggars (1971: 86). Probably, he uses the term *leiguliði* as opposed to land*owner*, and thus includes in it the *hjáleigumenn*. He notes how these people have to rent land and cattle and pay interest in butter 'as stated in our lawbook' (ibid.: 87). Often, he says, they are so impoverished that they prefer to send their children away rather than have them grow up in destitution, with its potential of misery and evil (ibid.). We can return to these people later; here, I wish to pursue the discussion of the law.

The farmers not only had rights; they also had duties. Landowners and tenants alike had to pay tithes. These were first introduced in Iceland in 1096 (*Grágás*: i*b*. 205 ff.; ii. 46 ff.; iii. 43 ff.), and included in Bishop Árni's Christian law of 1275 with only minor changes (*AK*: ch. 21; *NGL*: v. 32 ff.). Anyone in possession of more than ten *aurar* and free from debts had to pay one-tenth of his income (that is one-tenth of the potential rental value of his property) to the Church.

Church property was, of course, exempted from tithes, and this was one reason why wealthy farmers 'donated' part of their property to the Church, through building churches in the twelfth and thirteenth centuries.[8] In *Grágás* the exemption was explicit, although Bishop Árni's Christian law makes no mention of it. It remained common practice, however, until 1479, when the bishop at Skálholt, Magnús Eyólfsson, decreed that all land that had come into the possession of the church within the last twenty years was liable to tithing (*DI*: vi. 458–68). This was eventually passed by the Althing and the priests' council (*prestastefna*) in 1489 (*DI*: vi. 663–76; xii. 62–4). From this time church lands became tithable, with the proceeds ostensibly directed towards social welfare.

The Church divided tithes into four—a quarter for the bishop, a quarter for the local church, a quarter for the local priest, and a quarter for the poor (*AK*, *NGL*: v. 35). The quadripartition of tithes was reflected in the different kinds of acceptable payment. The parts for bishop and priest were to be paid in *vaðmál* ('homespun'), sheepskin, gold, or silver; the part for the church could be paid in timber, wax, incense, or cloth. Tithes for the poor, administered by the *hreppur* ('commune'), could be paid in cloth, sheepskin, wool, food, and livestock (except horses) (ibid.).

In the fifteenth century, when church lands had become very extensive, but were still exempted from tithes, the community had very little surplus for its paupers. This put a heavy load on the ordinary farmers who had to board and lodge the poor. In *Jónsbók*, a passage from 1305 required a farmer to house poor people for one night for every ten hundreds of capital in his possession (291 ff.). The maximum was eighteen nights per year irrespective of wealth—unless the community leader suggested something else (ibid.). In addition to this, the peasants also had to pay a relatively higher land-rent and tax, while the Church amassed one estate after another. This could not continue, and eventually rents began to fall, both in relative and absolute measures.

Table 2 illustrates this trend:

TABLE 2. *Cattle Hire and Land-rent for 58 Farms Owned by the Cathedral Church of Hólar*

Year	Cattle hire	Land rent	Total rent
1388	—	171	—
1449	67	142	209
1550	58	120	178
1569	54	117	171
1665	51	104	155
1686	54	105	159
1695	50	100	150
1710–13	37	75	112

Source: Björn Lárusson 1967: 49.

In practice both tenant and landowner paid tithes, although according to the law only the landowner was obliged to do so. After all, the tenant paid the farmer the rent, of which 10 per cent was to be paid in tithes. In 1619 the king affirmed the one-sided obligation by referring to 'old custom' (*LI*: i. 181–2; *Aĺ*: iv. 490). He was cautious enough, however, to submit that the decree would be valid only if it did not conflict with traditional law. It did, at least, contradict local practice, and at the Althing of the same year (only two months after the royal letter had been issued) the *bændur* reasserted their own traditional custom. Thereafter, tithes were to be levied on those 'who live on the land' (*LI*: 183–4; *Aĺ*: iv. 500).

In summary, the law of land rights had two main aspects—ownership and lease. Ownership in our period balanced between *óðal* and *possessio*, in a fashion which illustrates the persistence of the early medieval world view, in which ideas of time, space, and property were closely connected with the concept of kinship and 'belonging' (Hastrup 1985*a*; Gurevich 1985). Leases were generally annual, and only became life-long at a later stage, and then only for the royal estates. Contracts were of two kinds: ordinary *landleiga* ('tenancy'), where the *leiglendingur* (or *leiguliði*, 'tenant') was conceived of as an independent *bóndi*; and *hjáleiga* ('sub-lease') where the *hjáleigumaður* ('cottager') stood in a relationship of dependence to the landowner and had to supply labour as well as land-rent.

Land-rent varied between 5 and 8 per cent of land-value, while cattle-rent was considerably higher. The concept of *leigubúfé* referred both to rented livestock and to rent paid in livestock, suggesting that livestock were both capital and interest. Livestock certainly had a key-position in the economy (Ólafur Lárusson 1944: 40), and the old notion of *kúgildi* ('cow's worth') was commonly used as a standard of value, emphasizing the continuity between landed property and movables.

THE OWNERS

In spite of various adjustments the legal framework of landownership remained fairly constant throughout the period. Ownership was caught between a 'modern' clerically inspired notion of private property on the one hand, and a traditional and local idea of kinship-based relations to the land on the other. This contradictory situation made of 'the owners' a composite category. It comprised individual farmers, the Church (including the monasteries), and the Crown.

The actual number of farms in Iceland remained surprisingly constant. In 1311 when the tax-paying farmers were counted, they numbered 3,812 (Björn M. Ólsen 1910: 295–307). By the end of the seventeenth century, when the first land registers are found, there were 4,020 farms (Björn Lárusson 1967: 33). The numbers are comparable, even if the measurements were different, because both enumerate independent households. Even today the number of farms in Iceland is roughly 4,000, and whether or not this number reflects the ecological capacity of the island (and the widely varying farm-sizes would obscure such a conclusion), it certainly seems to be the Icelandic 'measure'.

Farm-size varied considerably, although we know very little about this on a national scale before the land-register of 1686. This was made on the king's demand, and his interest was in the tax-value of the farms. Tax-values were measured in 'hundreds' according to the ancient duodecimal system. One (long-) hundred was equal to 120 ellens of homespun (*álnir vaðmál*), or one cow's worth (*kúgildi*). There is little evidence about the principles of valuation. They may have been based on the number of livestock that a farm could feed, as some sources suggest (for example, in 1565, *DI*: xiv. 431–2). The tax-value was also the price for buying and selling, and the impression we get is one of strikingly stable values through the centuries. In 1446, 123 farms had a reported value of 2,085 hundreds; in 1695 the same farms had a combined value of 2,077 hundreds (Björn Lárusson 1967: 32). We might recall that the king, in his decree of 1705 concerning land-rent, forbade landowners to claim more rent than had been usual since 'time immemorial' (*LI*: i. 623). The stability of valuation was the result of a more or less explicit ideology of 'age' and 'tradition', taken to be hallmarks of value also in a broader sense.

The tax-values of farms in the late seventeenth-century land register are shown in Table 3. Three-quarters of all farms had a value of less than 24 hundreds, a significant concentration on small-scale farming, whether on the basis of tenancy or of private ownership.

This numerical frame set, we can approach the composition of the category of owners. Table 4 gives a perfunctory idea of property ownership based on the tax-value distribution of the 4,000 or so farms. It is interesting that the value of private property remained more or

TABLE 3. *Tax-values of Farms in the Late Seventeenth Century* (expressed in hundreds)

Tax-value	Number of farms in each value category (% in parens.)	Total tax-value (% in parens.)	Tax-value/ mean value
1–12	1,374 (34.2)	13,094 (14.8)	9.5
13–24	1,597 (39.7)	30,816 (34.8)	19.3
25–36	485 (12.1)	14,560 (16.5)	30.0
37–48	274 (6.8)	11,114 (12.6)	40.6
49–60	223 (5.5)	12,697 (14.3)	56.9
61–	67 (1.7)	6,235 (7.0)	93.1
	4,020 (100.0)	88,516 (100.0)	

Source: Björn Lárusson 1967: 33.

TABLE 4. *Distribution of Land* (%)

Year	Private	Ecclesiastical	Crown
1540/50	53	45	2
1560	50	31	19
1695	52	32	16

Source: Based on Björn Lárusson 1967: 60.

less constant. Redistribution between Crown and Church can be attributed to the Reformation.

Once again we must look back to the history of the Freestate, where many historical movements recorded from 1400 to 1800 began, and where many later distortions had their origin. It will be clear that I do not subscribe to the idea that Iceland up to the eighteenth century 'was at a standstill, almost petrified, in the forms it had inherited from the peak of the Middle Ages' (Björn Lárusson 1967: 28); the continuity, nevertheless, is remarkable. In order to 'measure' the historical movements in our period, this continuity has to be identified.

At the time of the *landnám*, anyone could become a landowner, because no claims existed prior to the colonization. After these first claims, land then began to be bought, sold, inherited, or rented, and apart from the resulting variation in farm-sizes, the development also entailed a new type of landlord—the Church.

We may date the Church's entry into the landowner's category in a relatively precise way. The first bishop had been appointed to Iceland in 1056, and the farm of Skálholt was given to the diocese. It was the law of tithes from 1096 (*Grágás*: i*b*. 205; ii. 46) which paved the way for large-scale ecclesiastical landownership. Because church land was exempted from tithes, this made the farmers donate their land to the Church by building a church at their farmstead.[9] For the *bóndi* the 'donation' was a temporary gift, leaving him free of tithes, and en-titling him to collect tithes paid by others for his church and his priest. From the point of view of the Church, the donor was but a warden of the property that now belonged to the Church. A contradiction between the different concepts of property (*óðal* and *possessio*) is evident.

In the thirteenth century the contradiction ended in open conflict between the Church and the farmers. The Church fought not only for a general *libertas ecclesiae* (freedom), but also for *libertates* (rights and privileges). The conflict, *staðamál*, was finally settled in 1297 with the *sáttargerð* ('settlement') at Ögvaldsnes.[10] It was agreed that churches owning more than half the land of particular farms were to gain possession of these farms. If the *bóndi* himself still owned half or more of the land, the farm remained his private property (*LI*: i. 22–3). This settlement confirmed the Church's ownership of large amounts of land, while alienating quite a few *bændur* from their ancient *óðal* land. They were not necessarily entirely dispossessed, since farmers at this level of the social hierarchy often had both an *aðalból* (which had usually been redefined as church land) and one or more outlying farms.

The displacement of landownership produced by the settlement of 1297, was further cemented during the fourteenth century. Sees and monasteries were arid purchasers of land for which they exchanged *lausafé* ('movables'). In addition to the *lausafé*, the seller often retained some of the original usufruct rights—such as a lifelong right to collect stranded whales and driftwood, for instance (see *DI*: vi. 16–17 for an example from 1364).

Farms were also bequeathed to the Church; this had become possible since the Christian law of 1275, which introduced new rules concerning wills (*AK*: chs. 16–17; *NGL*: v. 27–8). In the legislation of the Freestate, giving away land was virtually illegal because any diminution of an estate was an offence to the heirs. Only in connection with the payment of tithes and with soul's gifts (frankalmoins) was an owner entitled to dispose freely of his land; otherwise he had to procure the permission of his heirs (*Grágás*: i a. 246; ii. 84). Again, the *óðal*-principle is evident.

Jónsbók of 1281 also extended the possibilities of gift-giving. The *erfðabálkr* ('law of inheritance') permitted people to give away one-fourth of their possessions, and one-tenth of their inheritance, without the consent of the heirs (*Jónsbók*: 100). Another clause made it possible to leave one's entire estate to a convent or a See, if the closest heirs consented to this, and if dependent children were catered for (ibid.: 109). The Church was thus increasingly favoured by legislation, restated and further specified in the *réttarbœtr* ('law amendments') of 1280 and 1309 (*DI*: ii. 196 ff.). Private persons could also profit from the new rules of gift-giving, but the Church was the landowner to gain the most.

Another source of ecclesiastical wealth were payments in land made by landowners for the clerical education of sons or other male relatives. From the fourteenth century there are quite a few contracts of this kind, giving farmsteads to monasteries in payment for the boarding and teaching of a candidate for the priesthood (for example, *DI*: vi. 10–11, 13–14). This practice belongs to a kind of intermediate space between gift-giving (in the legal sense) and inheritance.

Meanwhile, lesser income continually flowed in from fines. In the Christian law, it was left to the clergy to administer the rules of marriage and related rules, and to collect penalties for breach of these rules. The combined result of the law concerning tithes (1096), new rules about testaments (1275) and gift-giving (1281), the settlement at Ögvaldsnes (1297), and the continual accumulation of fines, was that by 1400 the Church had become a major landowner.

In the fifteenth century, the process of accumulation continued. The shadow of the Black Death induced people to donate more and more land *til sáluhjálpar* ('to help the soul'). In 1484 the abbot at the monastery of Munkaþverá wrote of the growth of the monastic property during his time as an abbot: *tuo hundrud hundrada ok sextigi hundrud at auk ok þar til mikill skogur j hnoskadal j uaglajordu. er hier ecke til reiknud jorden jlhugastader er hann hafde til feingit* ('two hundreds and sixty hundreds in addition and to this many woods in Hnjoskadalur in Vaglajörð. The farm Illugastaðir which he had also got is not counted here in' (*DI*: vi. 526)). Munkaþverá was not unique. Surviving sources show that the monasteries of Viðey and Helgafell doubled their property from *c*.1400 to 1540, as did the See at Hólar (Björn Lárusson 1967: 65–6).

In the early sixteenth century the accumulation of ecclesiastical property began to look like straightforward exploitation and oppression. In 1513 the landowners of the West and North made an extensive complaint to the king about the clerical encroachment on their rights (*DI*: viii. 429–52). When Espolín (shortly after 1800) says of his fellow countrymen from three centuries previously, that their own ignorance was the reason why their land was claimed by the bishops, he is perhaps too hasty (Espolín: iii, *Formáli* (unpag.)). From the massive complaint in 1513 we can see that the people not only knew that they were being exploited, but also knew how to react.

Ecclesiastical property was of different kinds: private church farms, *beneficia* (that is, those farms that were surrendered to the Church by the settlement at Ögvaldsnes), monasteries, and Sees. Immediately prior to the Reformation, when the ecclesiastical property amounted to about 45 per cent, there were around 570 Church farms, while the monasteries owned 580, and the Sees some 670 farms (Björn Lárusson 1967: 64–9).

At the Reformation all monastic property was confiscated by the Crown (cf. Table 4). Church farms and Sees, however, retained their property. For the remainder of our period the Church owned and administered about one-third of Icelandic farms, although a small decline in property is noted for both Sees in the century following the Reformation (Björn Lárusson 1967: 68–70). This was as a result of farms being returned to private ownership or being reclaimed by the Crown.

Crown property was negligible prior to the Reformation. According to Björn Lárusson it amounted to a mere 1.7 per cent of the total tax value (Björn Lárusson 1967: 70). Royal claim to Icelandic land, however, had begun very early. During the campaign for Norwegian supremacy in the mid-thirteenth century, the king's representative had confiscated the land owned by Snorri Sturluson, who vigorously opposed the idea of submission. Snorri's property included Bessastaðir, which was to remain the residence of the king's representative in Iceland. It was the treaty of 1262–4, known as *gamli sáttmáli*, which finally paved the way for Crown property on a larger scale. The king of Norway now had claims in taxes and fines, and in the case of *níðingsverk* ('libel'), for instance, the king was entitled to half the property of the convict, in real estate and movables (*Jónsbók*: 40–2).

With the *rettarbœtr* of 1294, the king was explicitly acknowledged as a landowner, and rules were laid down about living and farming on Crown land (ibid.: 287, 288–9). In matters of tenancy, and contractual relations in general, there was no difference between private and royal estates. In matters of tithing, Crown land seems to have been exempted from payment until 1487, when this privilege was abolished for Church and Crown alike (*DI*: vi. 661–75).

Although the king was potentially a landowner since the fall of the Icelandic Freestate in 1262–4, he in fact showed no particular interest in the accumulation of land before the Reformation. Farms confiscated by the Crown were sometimes sold to private persons, and on the whole Crown property was scattered; an exception was the district of the Westman Islands, owned by the Crown in its entirety (Björn Lárusson 1967: 70). This district alone amounted to one-fifth of the royal property.

After the Reformation the picture changed. The Crown confiscated monastic property and retained it.[11] In 1560 Crown property amounted to one-fifth of the total tax value in Iceland (ibid.). It was managed by representatives at various levels. The *landsfógeti* ('governor') managed all the land of the monastery of Viðey around the western fiord, Faxaflói. Sheriffs managed quite a few farms that were earlier privately owned, while the remaining Crown land (about one-half) was leased to private persons on life-contracts (*LI*: i. 149). During the seventeenth century, Crown property declined somewhat, as we saw above (Table 4). This was largely because about seventy farms were sold in the 1680s on account of the Danish Lord Admiral Henrik Bjelke. He had disbursed some 1711 *rigsdaler* in order to maintain some poor priests, and in a decree of 1674 the king reimbursed him in land (*LI*: i. 351). He was entitled to sell it for the ordinary price in Iceland, that is, a hundred of land for eight *rigsdaler*, and each *leigubúfé* for three *rigsdaler* (*LI*: i. 356). In this scale of value, the land is more highly priced than the movables, although in principle one *kúgildi* would be the shared standard for both one hundred and one cow.

For all this, however, Crown property was of minor importance in the total context of landownership in Iceland. The royal estates amounted to less than 2 per cent of landholdings before the Reformation, and never exceeded 20 per cent thereafter. Crown property was

sold, leased, and farmed like other land. Half of it was farmed by
tenants according to custom, with the difference, as we have seen, that
by the late sixteenth century Crown tenants gained the protection of
life-contracts instead of annual ones.

During our period about half the land was privately owned (cf.
Table 4). The small decline in the years of Reformation was owed to
some farms being confiscated by the Crown because of the stir
aroused by the Reformation.

We know very little about the actual distribution of land among
private owners until the first land registers in the late seventeenth
century. The original landownership was established at the *landnám*,
when the idea of equality among the yeomen also had some practical
implications. During the Middle Ages, however, inequalities grew
markedly. This process was probably furthered by the disruption of
hereditary succession after the Black Death, which must have had
demographic consequences of very unequal impact (*KL*: vii. 673). The
diplomas from the fifteenth and sixteenth centuries confirm a pattern
of great inequality of wealth. Oddur Einarsson notes (in 1589) that
some hardly owned 'up the cat's nose, as the saying goes', while others
possessed about twenty farms in addition to the *höfuðból*, where they
lived themselves (1971: 88–9).

Table 5 shows the pattern as depicted in the 1695 land-register
(which was not complete). The inequality of distribution is clear: 68 per
cent of the owners had less than 20 per cent of the property value; two-
thirds of the landowners controlled less than one-fifth of the land,
while one-third controlled four-fifths.

There are two other striking features of private landowning. One
concerns the distribution between men and women owners. Again,
Björn Lárusson provides the figures (see Table 6). Women owners
constituted about one-third of the total group, and generally their
property is of equal standing to the men's. Considering the precedence of sons in the laws of inheritance, women appear to be well
represented.

Another feature of the land-register is that on average only about
30 per cent of the landowners lived on their own farms. Within the
group of owner-occupied farms, the smaller holdings were in clear
majority. Of a total sample of 1,212 farms, 349 were occupied by their
owners, among whom the smallholders dominated the picture as
Table 7 shows. Evidently this pattern left many farms to tenancy even
among the privately owned lands.

TABLE 5. *The Value of Privately Owned Property According to the 1695 Land Register* (expressed in hundreds)

Tax value	Number of owners (% in parens.)		Total tax value	Mean tax value
1–12	483	(47.2)	3,463	7.1
13–24	213	(20.8)	3,693	17.3
25–36	85	(8.3)	2,472	29.1
37–48	56	(5.5)	2,298	41.0
49–60	45	(4.4)	2,479	55.1
61–72	19	(1.8)	1,269	66.8
73–84	17	(1.7)	1,331	78.3
85–96	13	(1.3)	1,163	89.5
97–108	9	(0.9)	913	101.4
109–20	9	(0.9)	1,017	113.0
121–240	48	(4.5)	7,545	164.0
241–360	19	(1.9)	5,577	279.1
361–480	5	(0.5)	1,961	392.2
481–600	2	(0.2)	1,138	569.0
601–720	1	(0.1)	617	—
	1,024	(100.0)	36,936	

Source: Björn Lárusson 1967: 73.

Before we leave the landowners we should make some further observations, however. The distinction between *höfuðból* and *útjarðir*, introduced above (p. 83), was relevant only to a minority of land-owners. The majority had plots that could hardly support a family. Even landowners often owned only part of a particular named farm and had to rent other shares to support a proper household (Björn Lárusson 1967: 72). In areas where sea-fishing was readily available as a supplementary income, households could be supported on less land, of course. As we saw in the previous chapter, this applied to the south-west in particular.

Generally, it was a common feature that farms, which were legally defined as one unit, could be in the joint possession of several farmers, who were equally classified as *bændur*. Thus one *lögbýli* could contain

TABLE 6. *The Value of Private Property Held by Women and Men in 1695* (expressed in hundreds)

	Tax-value		
	1–120	121–720	Total
Number of women owners (% in parens)	323 (31.5)	21 (2.1)	344 (33.6)
Tax-value of women owners (% in parens)	6,627 (17.9)	4,608 (12.5)	11,235 (30.4)
Number of men owners (% in parens)	626 (61.1)	54 (5.3)	680 (66.4)
Tax-value of men owners (% in parens)	13,471 (36.5)	12,230 (33.1)	25,701 (69.6)
Total of men and women owners (% in parens)	949 (92.6)	75 (7.4)	1,024 (100.0)
Total tax-value (% in parens)	20,098 (54.4)	16,838 (45.6)	36,936 (100.0)

Source: Based on Björn Lárusson 1967: 73.

TABLE 7. *Numbers of Owners Living on their own Property* (expressed in hundreds)

Tax value	Number of owners (% in parens.)
1–12	162 (46.4)
13–24	115 (33.0)
25–36	36 (10.3)
37–48	17 (4.9)
49–60	13 (3.7)
61–	6 (1.7)
	349 (100.0)

Source: Björn Lárusson 1967: 75.

two or more *bændabýli* (Björn Teitsson and Magnús Stefánsson 1972: 135–6). In 1696 there were about 4,000 *lögbýli*, as we have seen. The number of *bændabýli* in the census of 1703 was 5,915, making an average of $1\frac{1}{2}$ *bóndi* per *lögbýli* (*Manntalið* 1960: 21).

The category of landowners was composite, and although we have detected a dormant principle of *óðal* in the law, social practice made land-owning the privilege of a small group of people, akin to the *aðal* ('nobility') elsewhere in the Nordic countries. There were differences, however. Icelandic society was never feudal in the same sense as Denmark, for example. In 1640 the German traveller, Daniel Vetter, made the significant observation that the Icelanders, unlike his own people, were not bowed down in submissiveness or villeinage (1931: 174). Every *bóndi* was his own master, ruling a household that was both socially and geographically autonomous.

Landownership as inherently ennobling ideally appertained to every *bóndi*. In practice, however, the big *bændur* were more ennobled than the rest, and they were in charge of the affairs at the Althing. We have seen how the *bændur* impeded fishing activities—as one among other manifestations of the structural dominance of the big landowners in need of surplus labour.

In a very interesting report from 1647 on Iceland and its institutions, the royal official Gísli Magnússon actually suggested that the old and mighty *ættir* ('kin groups') be given privileges like the nobility elsewhere. Allegedly, this would be to the benefit of the country (Gísli Magnússon 1647: 53). He related how Icelandic 'knights' still set the standard in all domains of Icelandic life and referred to Arngrímur Jónsson's *Crymogæa* of 1609 for genealogical confirmation of their ascendancy among the first settlers.[12] Ever since the beginnings of Icelandic history, he argued, the distinguished *ættir* had been greatly important to the country; now, however, the king's men and the merchants seemed to disregard their ancient status. This status was tied to hereditary property, 'which we call *óðalsgarðar* (*'óðal*-farms'), while the Norwegians call them *óðalsjarðir* (*'óðal*-lands)*' (ibid.: 60).

What Gísli Magnússon suggested, in fact, was that the leading landowning kin groups in Iceland be further ennobled, on the basis of their ancestry, wealth, and proficiency. At this point the *óðal* could have become transformed into a true *aðal*, or nobility in the Danish fashion. This did not happen, however. In the social structure, the *bændur* remained the dominant category, with no other social category above it, except the Danish king himself. In spite of the internal differentiation, the private landowners remained one category.

THE OTHERS

As we have seen, landowners in our period were only a minority of the population. Others were in majority, even if they did not have a separate occupational structure; there were no fishermen, no artisans, and no merchants, as elsewhere in Europe. In a society economically and conceptually centred on farming, all social categories were defined by their relationship to the land, whether positively or negatively. When the household was discussed, some of these categories were introduced. Here we shall pursue the matter more fully, presenting the social categories according to their relative position *vis-à-vis* the land.

Tenants had a relatively close connection with the land, and from the Middle Ages onwards tenants had been classified as *bændur*. In the *Grágás* there is no notion of landowner as such apart from the *bóndi*, a designation which could apply also to a tenant. The tenants emerged as a category after a few generations, when leasing land had become a necessary way of acquiring land, after the whole country had been claimed and divided by the first immigrants. Tenants were named *leiglendingar* ('lease-landers'). As I have shown elsewhere, once the category of *leiglendingar* had emerged it became more and more densely populated, as it were, and increasingly differentiated internally (Hastrup 1979; 1985a: 175). This was accompanied by changing notions of property.

This development may explain a change in terminology from *Grágás* to *Jónsbók*. In the latter, a new character has emerged, namely *landsdróttin* ('the landlord'). He is contrasted to the *leiguliði*, or tenant. In a few passages the term *leiglendingur* is retained, but the general notion, here as elsewhere in the relevant documents, is *leiguliði*. This is significant because it seems to reflect a semantic displacement. A *lið* refers to the train of attendants, the *liði* being one among them (Fritzner 1954: ii. 499, 505). The *leiglendingur* was primarily defined as a leaser of land; the *leiguliði*, however, was defined by his relationship to the landlord. Problems of naming aside, we note that between 1400 and 1800 tenants were by far the largest category of people. For the Westfiords, for example, it has been suggested that the tenants amounted to 90 per cent of the population from the fifteenth century onwards (Arnór Sigurjónsson 1973: 112).

Tenants had contractual rights and duties, default in which entailed loss of land. We noted before how land- and cattle-rent had to be paid according to a fixed scale. The rent was paid in kind, either in farm produce or fish. The balance between exploitation of the land for hay and the size of the herd was, as we have seen, precarious, and natural catastrophe could destroy any surplus overnight. We know very little of precautions taken against such catastrophe in the early part of our period, but we have some knowledge for the seventeenth century, when natural conditions seemed to worsen. In 1662 the Althing acknowledged the *force majeure* of nature, and legislated that the *leiguliði* could not be held accountable for any *leigubúfé* ('rented cattle'—being both capital and interest) destroyed by *skriður, jökul-hlaup eða eldgang* ('avalanches, glacier bursts, or volcanic eruptions' (*AÍ*: vi. 695)). There are other examples of a similar kind, and in general we find an increasing formal acknowledgement that natural forces were an uncontrollable element in Icelandic farming.

Before leaving the contractual situation of the tenant, it is worth noting what Skúli Magnússon, the Enlightenment reformer of the late eighteenth century, had to say about the rent. According to *Jónsbók*, he wrote, rent was originally quite arbitrary, and a matter for negotiation between landlord and tenant (1944a: 81). Gradually, however, from the early sixteenth century individual arbitration was replaced by fixed values (ibid.). This varied background to rent figures explains why sizes of farms and land-rents are not directly proportional.

Another category of people were cottagers, or *hjáleigumenn*. In the sources they gradually 'replaced' the *búðsetumenn*, who had been deplored by the lawmakers ever since the Freestate (cf. above, p. 55). The two categories speak of different realities, and there is a semantic displacement from *búðsetumaður* to *hjálegumaður*. The first—and oldest—category emphasizes the non-permanence of the dwelling (*búð*), and by implication the impermanence of the relationship to the land. We have seen that *búðsetumenn* had to have the permission of a local community to settle, however impermanently. The later category of *hjáleigumenn*, however, invokes a slightly different associative field; *hjá* is a preposition meaning 'at', 'by', or 'with', and the semantic focus of the term is on the rental of land, from a landowner or at a particular farm. In the land-registers *hjáleigur* were registered as appendages to the farms, and they were always sold with the farm. In the sources a farm is valued with outhouses and *hjáleigur* (for example, *DI*: vii. 300 from 1493). This association is reflected also in the occasional use of the term *heimamenn* ('home-men') for both *hjáleigumenn* and *húsmenn* ('house-men') (cf. *DI*: iv. 454, for instance, for a case from 1431). Both are members of the *lögheimili*, although not necessarily part of the same *bú* (household). From *búðsetumaður* to *hjáleigumaður*, therefore, there is a shift of emphasis from a particular relationship to the physical environment to a social relationship, which is a parallel to the shift from *leiglendingr* to *leigulíði*.

Whatever term was used, a cottager was required to meet certain minimum property requirements. This was stated, first, in the so-called *Píningsdómur* of 1490, wherein the requirement is 'three hundreds' (*LI*: i. 42). This was restated by the Althing in 1531 (*DI*: ix. 580, xi. 807, 829). It is hard to assess the actual significance of such rules, but we know that in 1528 all *hjáleigumenn* who possessed less than the minimum were forced to leave the Crown property of Vestmannaeyjar (*KL*: vii. 149). This, however, was not simply an automatic enforcement of an old rule, but very much tied to immediate circumstances. During the late fifteenth and early sixteenth centuries English merchants and fishing vessels operating in Iceland had attracted many Icelanders to the Vestmannaeyjar, where they earned their living in diverse fishing jobs. When the Crown took measures against the English enterprise, the suddenly redundant cottagers became a burden to the local community. It was only then that the rule of minimum property was enforced.

The *hjáleigur* of Vestmannaeyjar and other fishing places were of a particular kind—*þurrabúðir* (cf. above, p. 55). Originally the *hjáleigur* had had their own home fields; they apparently had to pay *hey-tollur* ('hay-toll') to the Church like the *bændur* (as evidenced in a verdict of 1510; *DI*: viii. 307ff.), and land rent to the landowner according to contract. Gradually, however, *hjáleigur* without grazing or fields appeared. These were the 'dry abodes', or *þurrabúðir*, and they were a feature of the fishing places in particular. In the sources, *þurrabúðarmenn* are closely associated with fishing and the drying of fish along the coast (Lúðvík Kristjánsson 1980–5: *passim*). Again, it is significant that the non-permanence of the dwelling was underlined by the term. Although such dwellings were often permanently inhabited, the semantics of fishing (and the law) prevented this fact from being acknowledged.

In the population census of 1703, a distinction between *hjáleigur* and *tómthús* is made; the former refers to outlying small-holds with 'grass', the latter to dwellings without any fields, and thus identical with the *þurrabúðir*.

TABLE 8. *Status of Household Head in 1703*

	Bændabýli (assessed farms)	Hjáleigur (outlying farms)	Tómthús (cottages)	Hús- mennska (lodgers)	Total
Male	5,345	1,045	286	382	7,058
Female	570	136	57	370	1,133
TOTAL (% in parens.)	5,915 (72.2)	1.181 (14.4)	343 (4.2)	752 (9.2)	8,191

Source: Based on Manntalið 1960: 21.

TABLE 9. *Average Size of Households in 1703*

	Number	Average size (people)
Bændabýli (assessed farms)	5,895	6.0
Hjáleigur (outlying farms)	1,175	4.3
Tómthús (cottages)	308	3.3
Húsmennska (lodgers)	244	2.5
TOTAL	7,622	5.6

Source: Manntalið 1960: 2.

Table 8 shows the distribution of the categories in 1703. 'Lodgers' were associated with a farm and working for it without being actually englobed by it like the *vinnufólk* (servants); they represented a kind of truncated household.

The average size of the various households is telling (Table 9)—the lower the status of the category, the smaller the household. The difference is due mainly to the absence of farm-hands and servants in the lower categories. In the category of *húsmennska*, it is interesting to note that a relatively larger proportion of these 'households' had a female head. Most of such households consisted of one woman and one child (ibid.; cf. also Loftur Guttormsson 1983a: 122–4).

Still closer to the *bú* in the order of englobement were the *vinnufólk*, or *vinnuhjú*. They were the farm-hands and servants, and as such they

TABLE 10. *Paupers in 1703 by District*

	Number of paupers (% of total population in parens.)			
	a *Niðursetningar*, apportioned among the households	b *Lagt af sveit*, in receipt of parish relief	c *Flakkarar*, vagrant beggars	d Total
Gullbringusýsla	430 (16.5)	10	50	490 (18.8)
Kjósarsýsla	203 (15.8)	25	2	230 (17.9)
Borgarfjarðarsýsla	297 (14.3)	37	6	340 (16.4)
Myrasýsla	216 (12.1)	40	3	259 (14.5)
Hnappadalssýsla	50 (7.8)	—	8	58 (9.1)
Snæfellsnessýsla	388 (9.9)	130	38	556 (14.2)
Dalasýsla	184 (9.5)	8	13	205 (10.6)
Barðastrandarsýsla	175 (6.5)	13	30	218 (8.1)
Vestur-Ísafjarðarsýsla	68 (2.9)	13	27	108 (4.5)
Norður-Ísafjarðarsýsla	112 (8.0)	16	4	132 (9.4)

Strandasýsla	109 (10.6)	1	—	110 (10.7)
Húnavatnssýsla	289 (10.9)	11	35	335 (12.6)
Skagafjarðarsýsla	323 (10.4)	1	51	375 (12.0)
Eyjafjarðarsýsla	370 (12.1)	—	34	404 (13.2)
Þingeyjarsýsla	341 (11.6)	—	31	372 (12.6)
Norður-Múlasýsla	178 (15.0)	9	4	191 (16.1)
Mið-Múlasýsla	313 (23.5)	—	5	318 (23.9)
Suður-Múlasýsla	289 (18.5)	25	2	316 (20.2)
Austur-Skaftafellssýsla	228 (20.8)	142	5	375 (34.2)
Vestur-Skaftafellssýsla	440 (23.4)	—	9	449 (23.9)
Vestmannaeyjasýsla	45 (13.8)	7	8	60 (18.5)
Rangárvallasýsla	772 (18.2)	—	4	776 (18.3)
Árnessýsla	969 (18.6)	129	25	1,123 (21.5)
TOTAL	6,789 (13.5)	617	394	7,800 (15.5)
Of this:				
Gullbringusýsla				
Borgarfjarðarsýsla og N-Múlasýsla-Árnessýsla	4,164 (18.3)	384	120	4,668 (20.5)
Mýrasýsla-Þingeyjarsýsla	2,625 (9.5)	233	274	3,132 (11.4)

Source: Manntalið 1960: 23.

were subsumed by the household (cf. above, pp. 54). There was still another category of people in Icelandic society, however. The *ómagar*, or paupers, were embraced by households, but often on a far from permanent basis. They were shuffled around the community, and farms took their turn in providing shelter and food.

The census of 1703 (see Table 10) shows that paupers were not equally numerous in all districts. In the eastern parts of the country there were up to 34 per cent *ómagar* (Austur-Skaftafellssýsla), and about 20 per cent was quite a common proportion. In a long-term perspective this proportion may be a short-term 'anomaly', owing to the combined effect of various critical factors (Loftur Guttormsson 1983a: 11–16). Yet the geographical differentiation is also telling. In some western parts the proportion went down as low as 4.5 per cent. The low average percentage of paupers in the western districts reflects the fact that in the west fishing was a much more stable asset to the economy, and even landless people could make a living there.

The conceptual association between *ómagar*, *lausamenn* ('loose men'), and *flakkarar* ('vagrants') is significant. These were the 'unstable people', and while the *lausamenn* often provided vital labour on the farms in summer, during the winter they could easily become a burden. During the Middle Ages and right through our period, strong measures were taken against vagrancy of any kind, and in 1589 Oddur Einarsson blamed vagrants for the evils of the country. They are the hordes of beggars who infest the countryside and impoverish the peasants (1971: 85). Often they were also invalids, sick, and brought infections to the healthy and settled people (ibid.: 86).

Lausamenn, or (later) sometimes *kaupamenn* ('hired men') Eggert Ólafsson 1772: 183), constituted an incipient working class in Iceland, but it was not until the late nineteenth century that this class became conspicuous as such (Finnur Magnússon 1986). Before that day labourers and the like were subject to continual restrictions, and had to register with a *bú* and thus let themselves redefine as *vinnufólk*.

Lausamenn were always to some degree dependent upon the *bændur og búfastir menn*, whom they worked for. If they had horses, they were also in need of hay; this is the implication of a verdict from 1504 concerning tenants who cannot pay their rent:

Those *lausamenn* who have been housing with the tenant and bought hay from him and given it to their own horses . . . have to swear that they have not let the horses eat of the outstanding rent on the land. (*DI*: vii. 727.)

Apart from the problems of the tenant, we can see from a passage like this that the *lausamenn* were perceived to be in competition with the landowner about the resources of the smallholders.

In 1555 a *sýslumaður* ('sheriff') took steps to reduce this competition. He noted the untimely and illegal habit of men and women settling independently as cotters (*setia sig niður til sialfræðis og búðsetu* (*DI*: xiii. 20)), and stated that all *lausamenn* had to work on the land according to the rates for ordinary farm-hands. Likewise, *búðsetumenn* who had not enough cattle to live from were not allowed to make themselves a boat, nor to employ people on the sea, except family members (ibid.: 21). The linkage of *lausamenn* and *búðsetumenn* is not accidental. Both categories belonged to the mobile marginal population, and they had to be tied down to earth in a very literal sense. Otherwise they represented a threat to resources in both hay and labour.

As we have seen, the category of non-landowners was composite, if still englobed by the household. Table 11 shows the composition of the population in the 1703 census in relation to their varying positions in the household.

Entirely outside the household structure, and even more mistrusted and feared than the migrant labourers was the category of *útilegumenn*, 'outlying men', consisting of people who had been exiled from society for one reason or another (cf. Hastrup 1985*a*: ch. 5). *Útilegumenn* played a prominent part in the oral tradition (Einar Ó. Sveinsson 1931*a*; Briem 1959). Although the category was in part 'mythological', it did include real people, mostly robbers (of whom there were remarkably few in Iceland). The annals mention a horde of robbers in 1454, qualifying them as *útilegumenn*, and in 1638 Gísli Oddsson tells how such people make their lives in remote caves in the mountains (1942: 122).

Generally, the *útilegumenn* were conceptually associated with other inhabitants of the wilderness, to whom we shall return at a later stage. At this stage, however, we can note an important feature that *útilegumenn* had in common with the supernatural *huldufólk* ('hidden people')—both were a threat to women. Some folk-tales relate how the *útilegumenn* captured beautiful young girls, forcing them to do women's work in their hidden dwellings in remote valleys, and to marry them (for example, JÁ: II. 189ff.). In comparison with the *huldumenn*, the *útilegumenn* seemed to be less of a threat to the *sel*-women ('saeter-women') in the popular opinion (Jónas Jónasson 1961: 63). The endangered girl was characteristically the lone and sometimes

TABLE 11. *Population by Position in the Household in 1703*

	Males	Females	Total
A. *Fjölskyldan* (the family)			
Húsráðendur (heads of household)	7,046	1,131	8,177
Húsmæður (housewives)	—	5,670	5,670
Börn heima (children at home)			
Innan 15 ára (under 15 years)	4,895	4,995	9,890
15 ára og eldri (15 years and over)	2,850	2,886	5,736
Fósturbörn (foster-children)	437	474	911
Ættingjar og einkaómagar (relatives and dependants)	895	2,227	3,122
TOTAL	16,123	17,383	33,506
B. *Vinnufólk* (servants)			
Ráðsmenn og ráðskonur (bailiffs and house keepers)	32	293	325
Vinnufólk í vist (work-people in service)	372	19	391
TOTAL	4,251	5,418	9,669
C. *Sveitarómagar* (paupers)			
Niðursetningar (apportioned to households)	2,273	4,516	6,789
Flakkarar (vagrant beggars)	220	174	394
TOTAL	2,493	4,690	7,183
A–C. *Öll þjóðin* (Population Total)	22,867	27,491	50,358

Source: Manntalið 1960: 19.

lost wanderer far away from her farm. Men, also, were sometimes endangered by the *útilegumenn* (ibid.: 189 ff.). In the mid-eighteenth century a reporter notes how people in the southern parts of the country never went to the mountain pastures except in large groups, for fear of *útilegumenn* (Eggert Ólafsson 1772: 159).

A final social category deserving of mention are the *útlendingar* ('foreigners'), in Iceland. Apart from a small number of administrators, the *útlendingar* were mainly merchants of varying origins. They are interesting not for their numbers but for their position in relation to Icelandic society. The concept of *útlendingur* explicitly connotes a person from 'outside the country'. 'Outlanders' were welcomed in Iceland during summer, but wintering was banned. This was stated clearly in 1490 in the so-called *Píningsdómur*:

> No foreigner should be allowed to winter here unless out of extreme necessity, and in that case he must trade nothing more expensively during winter than summer, and take no Icelander in his service, and take neither ship nor men to sea. Anyone housing or maintaining a man who does not follow these rules, will be pursued as if he housed an outlaw. (*LI*: i. 42.)

Several themes arise here. In the first place, trade had to be regulated, and Icelandic labour was reserved for Icelandic farmers. There is a deeper concern, however. Outlanders were forbidden from taking up residence in Iceland, and this theme is repeated again and again in decrees and provisions made at the Althing. In 1573 a man was allowed to winter provided he mastered 'the Icelandic tongue'(!), after a decision made by the Danish governor-general (*AÍ*: i. 170). However, in the very same year the *lögmaður* ('lawman') made a speech at the Althing in which he reminded the Icelanders that it was against the law to house foreigners over winter (*AÍ*: i. 211). A few years later, dispensation was given to a cooper on condition that he learnt the Icelandic language (ibid.: 333). In 1545 *bartskerar* ('barber-surgeons') were exempted from the prohibition, on account of their usefulness (*DI*: xii. 427).

The treatment of foreigners in Iceland speaks of a general difficulty in accommodating 'outlanders'. In the experience of local people there was nothing of much good to be expected from foreigners. Either they were merchants exploiting the impoverished peasants (and we shall return to this in the next chapters), or they were pirates and slave-raiders. The latter were generally referred to as 'Turks', and in the sixteenth century Turks were a real threat to the coastal population of Iceland. In a magnificent document from the seventeenth century the priest Ólafur Egilsson tells the story of a raid made by Turks in 1627 on the Vestmannaeyjar. Together with around 300 other unfortunates, Ólafur was taken to Algiers, where he experienced the strange ways of a barbarian people. Unlike most of the others he returned to Iceland and produced an account of the event (Ólafur Egilsson 1969).

A certain Guttormur Hallsson, who was likewise captured in 1627 and sold as a slave in Algiers, in that part of Arabia 'which is called

Barbaria', wrote a letter to his friends in Iceland in 1631 (Sverrir Kristjánsson 1969). He tells of the passage to Algeria, and of the slave-market. He adds, 'they call us *bestian*, that is wild beasts. But we know more than they do . . .' (ibid.: 147). For Guttormur knowledge was a derivative of Christianity. From the perspective of the 'Turks', however, the Icelanders were the wild ones.

This note of reversal finally leads us to the concluding section of this chapter.

THE SOCIAL ORDER

We have now reached a point where we can make a preliminary sketch of the social order in Iceland from 1400 to 1800. When analysing the economic order in the preceding chapter, I concluded that it was a function of a particular social system centring around the independent household, the *bú*. From earliest times the *bú* was the pivot of Icelandic social structure. In theory every Icelander was englobed by this structure, and every farmstead was a complete social universe in miniature.

In actual fact, however, the social order became increasingly complex. Access to land was an unquestioned right of any settler at the time of the *landnám*, and later it was the birthright of their descendants. By 1400, however, only a minority of the population belonged to the category of landowners, and could claim the full rights of ownership, household leadership, and *bóndi* status. Tenants had emerged, and had become an increasingly variegated group. Cottagers had appeared as well, especially along the southern and western coasts, and in spite of restrictions they had come to stay. *Lausamenn* had cut themselves loose from the settled world, and made their living on a migrant basis. Consequently they tended to merge with the category of vagrants, who—like outlaws and foreigners—were on the outskirts of society.

While Church and Crown owned half the land in shifting proportions, the other half remained private property. As we have seen, property sizes varied greatly, and by far the largest proportion of Icelandic landowners were smallholders, and possessed only a small fraction of the land. The society was not strictly feudal, but by 1400 it had certainly become hierarchical. The status and property hierarchy was implicitly matched by an ideological model which positioned the social categories on a scale of relative purity or danger (cf. Douglas 1966).

In the traditional cosmological model of the Icelanders, the central part of the world was inhabited by humans, while the periphery was inhabited by non-humans of various sorts (Hastrup 1981*a*; 1985*a*: ch. 5). Every single farmstead was its own local centre, which had to be fenced off against the external wild. This model, however, actually alienated a large proportion of the Icelanders from the centre of the world (Hastrup 1987*a*). The centre, and with it the *bú*, was associated not only with farming, permanence, and the social order, but also with Icelandicness, as it were. In the mental image of the Icelander, the fishermen, cottagers, *lausamenn*, and so forth had no immediate position. The recurrent attempts made by administrators to tie these marginal categories back into the structure of farming households are clearly attempts to re-centre these people.

There is a definite pattern here. The pure categories were the landowners or well-to-do tenants. They were the stable elements in society; they *were* society—as it saw itself in institutionalized form. Just as labour was concentrated in the farm at the expense of fishing, so the social *order* was a function of attachment to the land. The looser the attachment, the greater the moral problem, the more measures were necessary to ensure order. The more mobile people were, the more 'dangerous' they seemed, according to this mental model. Mobility was actually a structural feature of the farming society, but it was associated with migrant fishermen, *lausamenn* and vagrants, who by their movements in space were perceived, by those *bændur* who administered the law, as a threat to social order. Even more threatening were the *útilegumenn*, who were explicitly beyond the social order, inhabiting the external wild.

The attitude towards *útlendingar* confirms this pattern on a national scale. While history made their temporary presence an absolute necessity, for merchandise in particular, Icelandic cosmology could not accommodate them on any more permanent basis. If an individual was not *of* Iceland, there was no mental space for him in the country. If he had to stay for some reason or other, he had to learn Icelandic. This was a minimum prerequisite for being accepted.

We can conclude that in the relative positioning of social categories there were two measures—both of them mental corollaries of landowning. One measure was relative distance from the centre, as represented by the *bú*. The other measure was degree of mobility. By their mutual enforcement, these measures progressively alienated more and more people from the concept of Icelandic society, and reduced most of the population virtually to non-human status. While the increasing impoverishment of the Icelanders set more and more people on the move, they were also and simultaneously defined out of Icelandic social order. They became part of disorder.

Foreign Relations

ALTHOUGH virtually isolated in the North Atlantic, Icelandic society was always part of a larger cycle of social reproduction. In the early Middle Ages Icelanders were engaged in extensive commerce, linking Scandinavia, the British Isles, and the North Atlantic communities through trade (cf. Foote and Wilson 1970; Gelsinger 1981). The import of grain and timber was vital to Icelandic society, and the concurrent cross-cultural dialogue was equally vital to the maintenance of a distinct Icelandic identity (Hastrup 1985a: 227ff.).

After the surrender to Norway in 1262-4, the integration of Iceland into a larger order became more explicit. The Icelanders acknowledged a foreign king and agreed to pay tax to him in exchange for provisions of grain—and peace. As we shall see, the interpretation of the treaty between the Icelanders and the Norwegian king was far from unanimous. In spite of this, the treaty of 1262-4 definitively marked an Icelandic integration into a European context on foreign terms. Our epoch, then, is marked by the external world from the very beginning.

In Chapter 2 the European context was presented as the ground against which the figures of Icelandic history stood out. The European context was more than a backdrop, of course; it was also an active factor in the shaping of Icelandic history. Changing markets in Europe had a significant impact on Icelandic trade, and ultimately on the entire economy. Icelanders, learned and otherwise, travelled abroad, and were engaged in correspondence with foreign scholars, exchanging knowledge and literary images (see, for example, Seaton 1935: 179ff.). New ideas from abroad were transplanted to the arid Icelandic soil. The Reformation, Humanism, and the Enlightenment, to mention only a few larger tendencies, all had consequences in Iceland. Moreover, the political subordination of

Iceland to Denmark entailed a continual attachment to an unstable political order.

In this chapter I shall discuss the nature of Icelandic integration into the larger order. My focus is on the internal implications of external relations; and my emphasis is on structural propensities, rather than the historical development of the various relationships.

I shall deal successively with the constitution, the Church, and trade, all of which were areas of alien power and influence. Developments within each of these areas, and their implications for the Icelandic populace could all of them be the theme for extensive separate histories. Aspects of such histories have already been provided, and I shall rely on the scholarship of others for part of my presentation. My own aim is more analytical than narrative. I shall break down the discourses of Crown, Church, and commerce—each commenting upon the relationship between Iceland and the rest of the world—to discover their most salient features *within* Icelandic society.

CONSTITUTION

Iceland had been part of the Norwegian kingdom since 1262(–64), and when Norway came under Danish rule in 1380, Iceland went with it. During this early period of the centralization of power in the Nordic countries, political conditions were far from stable, and the constitutional realities of regal power were ill-defined. This was certainly true in Iceland's relationship with Norway (Líndal 1973). In the transition between the old system of petty chieftaincies, and the new system of hereditary kingship, there was incessant conflict amongst the many aspirants to power throughout the Nordic countries. By the end of the fourteenth century, however, power was concentrated in only a few hands.

In 1359 the Danish king Valdemar had betrothed his daughter Margrethe to Hákon, son of the Norwegian king Magnús. This was one of the more spectacular elements in an alliance between Valdemar and Magnús, designed to exclude another of Magnús's sons, Erik, who had taken the throne of Sweden.[1] The details of the alliance are complicated, but the consequences for Iceland were relatively clear. Valdemar died in 1375, leaving the throne to 5-year old Oluf, son of Margrethe and Hákon. Since Oluf was a minor, the actual ruling was left to his mother. When Oluf's father Hákon died in 1380, the

Norwegian throne was added to Margrethe's rule, in the name of her son. At this point Norway and Denmark became one, with little thought of Iceland. Oluf died in 1387, after which Margrethe declared herself ruler. Later, she included Sweden in her patrimony, and in spite of occasional allegations of scepticism, the famous Nordic Union (the Union of Kalmar) was declared in 1397. It lasted for a couple of centuries, although Sweden was always slightly rebellious, and finally declared itself out of the Union. Later, in 1814, Sweden took over Norway, but Iceland remained 'Danish'.

The point to note is that Danish rule over Iceland was established more by accident than through a conscious colonial strategy. The basis for the Danish rule remained the old treaty with Norway, which the Icelanders had signed in 1262–4. This treaty is named *Gizurarsáttmáli* ('the treaty of Gizzur'), and it marked the end of the autonomy of the Icelandic Freestate (cf. Hastrup 1985*a*: 232ff.). The treaty was signed at the Althing, not so much by Iceland as a state or nation, but rather the decision of individual chiefs (Berlin 1909: 45–58). In the nineteenth-century nationalist movement, the proper status and interpretation of this *gamli sáttmáli* ('old treaty') became a major issue. Jón Sigurðsson was a major force behind movements towards Icelandic sovereignty (Einar Arnórsson 1949; Líndal 1973). He was anxious to stress that the union of Iceland and Norway had been a deliberate union between two equal partners. Iceland was *not* a province of Norway; rather, it was an autonomous country, that for its own reasons had favoured a larger union (Jón Sigurðsson 1951: 120–1).

This point of view is constitutionally arguable, but it is sustained by a certain measure of reciprocity in the treaty. The full text runs like this:

Gizurarsáttmáli

This is what the yeomen [*bændr*] of the North- and South-lands agree upon:

1. They, under sworn oath, grant to the Lord King Hákon and King Magnus permanent tax and rights in land and subjects [*þegnar*], 20 *alnir* from each man due to pay *þingfararkaup*. This payment [*fé*] is to be collected by the commune leaders [*hreppstiórar*] and taken by them to the [King's] ships and handed over to the King's representative [*umbodzmaðr*], after which their responsibility for this ceases.

2. In return, the King shall grant us peace and Icelandic law [*friði og islendskum lögum*].

3. Six ships are to sail from Norway to Iceland in the first two summers; after that as many [ships] as the King and the best among the yeomen of this country consider most beneficial for the country.

4. Icelanders shall receive their inheritance in Norway, if true heirs or their legal representatives [*umbodzmenn*] come forward, no matter how much time shall have elapsed.

5. *Landaurar* are to be discontinued.

6. The rights of Icelanders in Norway shall in no way be inferior to those they had previously. You yourself [i.e. the King] have, in your letter, offered to maintain peace over us, as God provides you with strength.

7. We want the Earl [Gizurr] to rule over us as long as he keeps faith with you and peace with us.

8. We and our heirs will remain faithful to you as long as you and your heirs keep this treaty [*sattargjörd*]. We shall be released from it [*lausir*] if the best men consider it to have been broken [on your part].

(Icelandic words inserted in the text are all from the text printed *DI*: i. 620.)

In my book on the Icelandic Freestate I analysed the content of this treaty in some detail (Hastrup 1985*a*: 232–7). Here I shall merely stress that while the Icelanders swore allegiance to the Norwegian king as his subjects (*þegnar*), and agreed to pay tax, he also had some obligations towards them. The obligations were political ('he shall give us a law and maintain peace'), economic ('he shall guarantee our provisions of grain'), and judicial ('the rights of Icelanders in Norway are to be respected').

The last clause introduces the question of time, through the mention of the 'heirs' of both parties. Berlin has argued that the Icelanders thereby acknowledged the right of succession held by Norwegian kings also as far as Iceland goes (1909: 89). Icelanders of the nineteenth century, however, preferred to interpret the passage as an escape clause. It may be so, but it is neither specific for Iceland nor does it dislocate the central power of the kingship as an institution (Líndal 1973: 601). Maurer has pointed out that such a clause was quite ordinary in medieval coronation charters (1874: 476), and concerned the behaviour of the individual king rather than the abstract power of the Crown.

The importance of the crown in Iceland is evidenced by a passage in *Jónsbók*, which emphasizes the grave nature of any kind of treachery against the king; that is the gravest offence: *þat er níðingsverk hit mesta, ef maðr ræðr lǫnd ok þegna undan konungi sínum* (*Jónsbók*: 36). The power of the king was expressed also by the clause that he should 'give the Icelanders a law'. The law was to be 'Icelandic' but it should be designed by the king. As we know, *Jónsbók* (of 1281) was the result, and one of far-reaching importance. It was the basic law of Iceland until the nineteenth century.

Jónsbók owes its name to the Icelandic 'lawman' Jón Einarsson, who took part in the framing of the law in Norway, and who brought it back for confirmation at the Althing. A relatively detailed account of this event has been handed down (*DI*: ii. 206–10). It appears that there was considerable resistance towards many passages of the law, and although these were eventually passed almost unaltered, the event revealed a major contradiction between the internal and the external view of legislation. This was to remain an important theme in the orchestration of Icelandic law.

While the Icelandic farmers present at the Althing thought it their right to adopt or reject any law as they saw fit, the king's representative Loðinn *leppr* denied them this right. He was of the opinion that only the king had a legitimate right to legislate and the law was passed with little deference to the peasants' objections (*DI*: ii. 209–10). Although his speech may have been more of a tactical manœuvre than a correct interpretation of the royal privileges, there is no doubt that the majority of the Icelanders had a different view from the king's men. Already, in 1281, the proper interpretation of the second clause of *Gizurarsáttmáli* posed a problem; what did it mean that the king should provide the Icelanders with peace and Icelandic law? In spite of this problem the contract was explicitly renewed in 1302 (*LI*: i. 23–4) and 1319 (ibid.: 32–3). In these renewals of the contract of subjugation, the Icelanders were careful to state, however, that they did not want any more burdens imposed, and that they wanted the old taxation rules upheld due to the poverty of the country. They might have become 'subjects', but they were still not submissive.

Nor did they ever quite become so, it seems. They could be destitute, and starved nearly to the point of extinction, but they apparently maintained a degree of self-esteem amidst it all. Thus the Norwegian Peder Claussøn Friis, reporting from Iceland in 1580, stated that 'since the first times . . . the Icelanders have been an insolent and headstrong people, who have held the Norwegians in little esteem' (Storm 1881: 194–5). 'Norway' had troubles in accommodating the Icelanders in their own straightforward world view, and the 'marginal' Icelandic population remained untamed.

The letter of the law might have been open to various interpretation, but even in 1589 Oddur Einarsson was in no doubt about its
spirit. He stated definitively that in secular ruling, Iceland was
governed by the principles in force when she first entered into the
union with Norway (1971: 140). 'Because the Icelanders agreed to the
king of Norway on the condition that they could continue to live with
the old customs, laws and habits' (ibid.). He then described the
various offices of government. At the top of the hierarchy the king's
representative, or governor-general, had the prime function of levying
taxes. Next, the *lögmenn* ('lawmen'), had the duty of keeping law and
justice in the country; there were two such *lögmenn*, one for the eastern
and southern quarters, another for the western and northern quarters.[2]
In addition to the *lögmenn*, Oddur enumerated twelve *sýslumenn*, or
local sheriffs, who were locally responsible for the execution of
verdicts, rules, and judgements. It is important to note that the *lögmenn* acted on behalf of the Icelanders to keep up *their* law. They were
not the king's representatives, any more than were the *sýslumenn*.

A similar emphasis on Icelandic autonomy in legislative matters is
found in Arngrímur Jónsson's *Crymogæa* of 1609.[3] He comments upon
the old treaty, and propounds that King Magnús as well as his father
Hákon had portentously promised to maintain Icelandic laws
unaltered; any changes had to be approved by the Icelanders themselves (Jakob Benediktsson 1985: 228–9; cf. also Maurer 1968a: 14–16).
This remained true in practice through the sixteenth and well into the
seventeenth centuries, even if Arngrímur's final listing of certain
problems in his own time indicates some discrepancies in the interpretation of the law. However, he is probably correct when he closes
his book on the history of Iceland with an assertion of King
Christian IV's love of justice (Jakob Benediktsson 1985: 282). Royal
justice around 1600 involved leaving the Icelanders alone, while
collecting from them tax which they themselves had agreed to pay.

Élitist though Arngrímur's view may be, the Icelanders had
managed to rule according to their own conception of autonomy until
then. They assumed that the king would pass no laws without their
consent (*AÍ*: i. lxxxvi). It was part of the original constitution of 930
that the *lögrétta*, that is the legislative body of the Althing, had the
supreme right to legislate in Iceland. The *lögrétta* and the *lögmenn*,
were still important features in the constitution of *Jónsbók*, although
their position by then had become slightly ambiguous.

Thus in the section on the Thing-order it reads:

what is not stated in the lawbook should in each case be decided upon by the *lögréttumenn* in unison. If they are not in agreement then the *lögmaðr* and his supporters will decide, unless the king together with wiser men find something else more lawful. (*Jónsbók*: 10.)

We notice that the *lögrétta* is subordinate to *Jónsbók*, and that the king has the right to overrule any decision.

Yet the *lögrétta* was there, and in force. As a result, it was not until 1630 that the Althing adopted any law against its own will (*AI*: i. lxxxvi). Obviously, the Althing did not 'represent' all the Icelanders equally and in unchanged fashion during the entire period. We have seen how farmers gradually outruled fishermen, and how the landowners alienated the others. Further, in the seventeenth and eighteenth centuries, when the 'central' Danish power became increasingly manifest on this most peripheral island of the kingdom, the class of public servants actively feathered its own nest, a nest it shared with the big landowners (Gustafsson 1985). The ambiguity inherent in the legislation also had local dimensions.

Be this as it may, *Jónsbók* set the frame of secular administration in Iceland. Until 1800 the focus remained the annual Althing: *vér skulum lǫgþingi várt eiga at Øxará á þingstað réttum á tólf mánuðum hverjúm* ('we shall have our law-thing at the proper thing-place at Øxerá once every twelve months (*Jónsbók*: 5)). A certain number of representatives from each of the (former) lesser things were to be present. Their travel expenses were to be paid by their local sheriffs, *sýslumenn*, themselves a new element in the law.

The payment of Thing-expenses, *þingfararkaup*, was to be collected among the taxpaying farmers—farmers, that is, in possession of ten hundreds or more (ibid.: 7). In 1311 a census of taxpaying farmers was made on behalf of the king, and they then numbered 3,812 (*DI*: i. 373–5; *DI*: iv. 9–10). These were the foundation of the constitutional structure, both in terms of external taxation and internal legislation. The legislative functions of the Althing gradually diminished, however, and by the time of Absolutism (1660), the Althing was reduced to being a mere symbol of independence (cf. Maurer 1968a: 18). The law of taxation remained in force from the introduction of *Jónsbók* until 1877 (Björn M. Ólsen 1910: 310). By inference from proportions of taxpaying and other peasants in the nineteenth century, it has been suggested that the Icelandic population was about 72,000 in 1311 (ibid.: 341; cf. also Lárusson 1936: 126–7; Hastrup 1985a: 171). The

Black Death probably caused at least one-third to die in 1402–4. Whatever the actual population size, however, the number of representatives at the Althing remained constant; according to *Jónsbók* the number was 84. When the representatives were first actually enumerated in 1678 there were 81, and in 1679 84 (*Aĺ*: i. lxxxii). In the eighteenth century this changed; in 1764 there were only 20; in 1770 their number was reduced to 5, and in 1796 to 4. By then their function was reduced to a mere witnessing of the official procedures. In 1800 even the legal court functions of the Althing were closed down, and symbolic autonomy ended by the same stroke. When in 1850 the Althing was re-established in Reykjavík, it was very much as a consequence of the nationalist movement.

A close reading of the laws and ordinances issued by the Danish monarch reveals an increasing interest in Iceland, from the introduction of absolutist rule in 1660 and onwards. Irrespective of the degree of interest there was a continued, if sometimes latent, contradiction between external and internal rulings. The balance between the opposing elements in this contradiction was far from stable. During the first centuries of our epoch, the Icelanders had effective home rule, while in the seventeenth century this became more and more of an illusion, to be completely overthrown by 1800 (Maurer 1968a: 1–32). However, the principle of autonomy remained latent in Icelandic self-understanding, and formed the principal basis of the nationalist movement in the nineteenth century (Hastrup 1981c), pushing the balance back again. Whatever current interpretation of the ruling principles was in vogue, an Icelandic perspective of keeping privileges and individual autonomy remained constant (Líndal 1973: 608–11).

In 1640 Daniel Vetter remarked, in an implicit contrast to his own European knowledge, that the Icelanders had little use of the king:

> The Icelanders acknowledge the king of Denmark as their sovereign; they have for a long time been his subjects and he remains their hereditary master. They have only little use and pleasure from the king, however, because he does not care much about this faraway island. (Vetter 1931: 159–60.)

The king exploited Icelandic natural resources, but did not care about the Icelandic people. Arngrímur Jónsson saw this as justice; Daniel Vetter denounces it as a dereliction of duty.

In 1555, when the Swede Olaus Magnus wrote his history of the Nordic peoples, he argued that Iceland was badly administered, and its citizens thus caused distress (Olaus Magnus 1976: ii. 90–1). From the Scandinavian point of view, Iceland was not only on the geographical periphery, but also on the social margin. In their own way, both Arngrímur Jónsson and Daniel Vetter confirmed this a century later.

By the mid-seventeenth century, however, the king of Denmark had begun to take an increasingly active interest in Iceland. It was the growing power both of the king and of the merchants which prompted Gísli Magnússon, in 1647, to suggest that more privileges be given to the Icelandic 'nobility' (Jakob Benediktsson 1939: 2–3).

One reason for the renewed interest in Iceland, was the increasing number of travel reports and other foreign comments upon the Icelandic condition. Iceland began appearing on European maps in the late sixteenth century, literally, on the maps by Ortelius (1590), Mercator (1595), and Hondius (1611) (Nørlund 1944; Haraldur Sigurðsson 1971–8). The maps were accompanied by descriptions of the island. The geographical positioning of Iceland entailed a simultaneous mental mapping of Iceland as a 'wild' area of Europe. Writings by Gories Peerse (1561), Dithmar Blefken (1607), and David Fabricius (1616) left no room for doubt about the savage nature of the Icelanders (cf. Þorvaldur Thoroddsen 1892–1904).

It was in reaction to this that, in 1647, the two Icelandic bishops were asked by the king to produce evidence of the Icelandic condition. They immediately provided information both on the present population and the history of Iceland (Jakob Benediktsson 1943). Their information is pretty neutral, while Arngrímur Jónsson's work had been explicitly directed towards a refutation of the false foreign impressions of the country (cf. Jakob Benediktsson 1957). Both reflect the growing external interest in matters Icelandic in the seventeenth century.

Locally, the administration of royal privileges, and, indeed, of law in general, was left to the *sýslumenn*. Some were more zealous than others, and certainly there were great discrepancies in their executive functions. While most remained almost 'invisible' and left everything to the Althing, others entered the drama in full force.

Formally there was a hierarchical administrative structure. Central power resided in Copenhagen, and was represented in Iceland by a governor-general. Until 1684 Iceland was a 'land' under the Danish Crown; in 1684 'our land Iceland' became a *stiftamt*, or a district. This meant that a *stiftamtmand* now represented the public authorities, while the *landsfoged* was in charge of the taxations. The latter was also supposed to control the *sýslumenn* (Gustafsson 1985: 42 ff.), the next level in the hierarchy; originally twelve they were later to number about twenty. According to *Jónsbók*, they had to attend the Althing, and on their way back home they had to hold a local *leiðarþing* to announce the new decisions (*Jónsbók*: 12–13). This practice was abandoned in the eighteenth century, when the office of *sýslumaður* changed considerably.

In 1721 the *sýslumenn* were instructed to obey the (*stift-*) *amtmand*, and in subsequent letters and ordinances their status as executives of the royal interests was further enforced. It was they, for example, who were required to ensure that the farming reforms of the last half of the eighteenth century were implemented (Gustafsson 1985).

While centralization was a dominant theme in the formal administration of Iceland in the seventeenth and eighteenth centuries, the local communities retained a fair amount of self-government in some respects.[4] From the first, the smallest administrative unit in Iceland was the *hreppur*, headed by a body of five local governors, or *hreppstjórar* (*Jónsbók* 1904: 109). In the census of 1703 the number of *hreppstjórar* was 670 (*Manntalið* 1960: 54–5). These men were in charge of poor relief, and of communal tasks connected to sheep-rearing, for instance. A very detailed instruction concerning the office of *hreppstjóri* is available from 1573 (*Aĺ*: i. 197–201). He was supposed to help the *valldsmaður* ('power man', that is, the official) in the levying of tax, punishment of criminals, and other such matters; the priest might expect help from him in connection with payment of tithes, the observance of holidays, and so forth. Apart from this he had independent functions in the administration of the *búalög* ('household law'), and in everything connected to the proper communal spirit of various kinds of work. In addition to the administration of poor relief (being one-fourth of the tithes), the *hreppstjóri* also inspected the circulation of paupers and other poor people among the farmers.

Thus at this level of social reproduction in Iceland, age-old principles of autonomy prevailed. They were not untouched by external changes, of course, and in the eighteenth century the *hreppstjórar* were explicitly required to assist the *sýslumenn* (for example, in 1746, *LI*: ii. 619). Later still, in 1809, they became royal officials.

The point is, however, that while centralization occurred at the upper levels of the administrative hierarchy, giving more and more influence to the class of civil servants (recruited from the upper strata of society) (Gustafsson 1985), local 'centres' survived.[5] These provided a sense of continuity in belonging.[6] Even when external power impinged most forcefully on Icelandic society, the internal control of allocation of resources still provided an experience of local community.

In 1800 the Althing was abolished, and the symbol of autonomy at the national level disappeared. Between Copenhagen and the Icelandic peasant communities there was only a void. Thus at the close of our period, the defining element of the Icelandic order from its first construction in 930 was destroyed. Iceland was definitively included in a larger order—only to react against it a few decades later, when a nationalist movement started to voice a demand for independence.

CHURCH

The Icelanders converted to Christianity through an agreement at the Althing in the year 1000. The story of the conversion has been told many times, first by Ari *inn fróði* in his *Íslendingabók* from *c.*1120.[7] The conversion was not only a local event, but signalled Iceland's entry into the larger scene of European Christendom. In the Icelandic world as first founded and conceived of by the Norsemen, the Church was an alien element. It represented a 'centre' outside Iceland, and the conflict of values between Rome and the Althing was a contributing factor in the fall of the Freestate (cf. Hastrup 1985*a*: 178 ff.).

The conversion symbolized a far-reaching social change in Iceland; the very concept of society changed, from being synonymous with the law, to an equation with the (divine) kingdom (Hastrup 1984*a*). This paved the way for the entry of the Norwegian king, and for a new concept of hierarchy in social relations. The discrepancy between the 'old' and 'new' ideas was to remain a source of drama, not only in property relations but also in ideational matters. When the witch-craze hit Iceland in the seventeenth century, it was very much a consequence of old ideas of magic being translated into the current language of European demonology (cf. Chapter 7).

The point at issue here is that ever since the conversion of the Icelanders there was a latent contradiction between two scales of value, one internal, one, the Church, external—even if the latter took strong root in Icelandic soil, establishing itself as a landowner and lawmaker.

A Christian law was first made in the early twelfth century, to supplement the local laws of *Grágás*. The two laws were different in many respects, and when they were written down the discrepancies could no longer be hidden. Two and a half centuries after the Althing had adopted Christianity as the national religion, native Icelandic law finally conceded to Christian (canonic) law. In 1253 it was agreed at the Althing that 'in case of discrepancy between God's law and the law of the nation, the law of God shall obtain' (*DI*: ii. 1).

This defeat was soon followed by the treaty with Norway, conceding sovereignty while, perhaps, still entertaining ideas of autonomy. Church and Crown were both external powers, and they went hand in hand into the Icelandic world. When, after the surrender, new laws were made, the secular laws of *Járnsíða* (1271) and *Jónsbók* (1281) were backed up by the Christian law of Bishop Árni (1275). Bishop Árni's Christian law was to remain the foundation of the clerical law at least until the Reformation, but in some cases also beyond it.[8] Bishop Árni, in the opening passage of this law, says: 'It is the foundation of our, the Icelanders', law . . . that we shall have and uphold the Christian faith' (*AK*, *NGL*: v. 16). Like all other Christian nations, the Icelanders had to obey the commandments of the Church. Fortunately, God had given the people two servants to help them in this, the king and the bishop (ibid.: 17).

The intimate connection between the divinely installed king and the bishop is conspicuous. Yet secular and clerical laws were not always in accord. In principle, the Church had to legislate and judge in all matrimonial matters, and administer sacred rituals of baptism, confirmation, marriage, and funeral—quite apart from its own internal affairs. The people had to be served according to prescribed rules, and to pay their dues respectfully. If they did not, it could be owed to failure on the part of the bishops, who took things too lightly. This, at least, is the impression given by a royal ordinance of 1354, urging the bishop of Hólar to enforce Christian law in the northern bishopric. Practice there had apparently become too lenient, and the king was obliged to remind the bishop of his duty to collect tithes and make visitations according to the law (*LÍ*: i. 33–4).

I do not intend here a history of clerical administration, but wish only to stress the external position of this administration *vis-à-vis* the Icelanders. The people were Christian, yet they were also Icelandic, and often their own sense of justice and autonomy clashed with the rulings of the Church. In 1431 this was made quite explicit. At the Althing, the *hirdstjóri* (governor), the *lögmenn* (lawmen), the *lögrétt-umenn* (lawmakers), and the *almuga* (peasantry) agreed to send a letter to the king, Erik of Pommern. For some decades Iceland had suffered severe commercial problems, and the bishops had played no small role in these, usurping huge profits. This was the background to the following letter:

First we promise to be true and loyal to our venerable lord Erik, by the grace of God king over Norway, Denmark, Sweden, and the Goths and Duke of Pommern, and to keep that law which Saint Olaf has given, and which his rightful descendants have since then passed in agreement between the kingdom and those who inhabit the land, both the lawbook and the Christian law and the king's law amendments. But all new burdens which the bishops and other men of power want to impose upon us we want to prohibit with a ban. (*DI*: iv. 461.)

There are several important themes in this document. While swearing allegiance to the (new) king, the Icelanders also manage to emphasize—verbally, at least—their age-old autonomy in legal matters: those who live in Iceland have as much say in Icelandic matters as the king. They swear to obey the laws stated in the *lögbók* (*Jónsbók*), and in the *kristinréttur* (Bishop Árni's Christian law), and the *réttarbætr* (law amendments, passed by subsequent kings in 1294, 1305, and 1314, as additions to or clarifications of *Jónsbók*). The bishops, however, had apparently gone too far beyond the law. We saw in the preceding chapter how the Sees and monasteries had amassed disproportionate amounts of land by the early fifteenth century, and the secular administration represented by the Althing now wanted the king to stop this. From the local centre, the two external powers were played off against each other. At the time the Icelanders favoured the distant, absent, and careless king, and mistrusted the all too obvious presence of zealous bishops.

There were, as well, real conflicts of interest between Crown and Church, at least until the Reformation when they merged into one. In 1480 the king reminded the Icelandic clergy that they were not supposed to collect debts to the Church from the rent due to the king (*LI*: i. 38). Payments continued to be a problem for the peasantry, while in 1490 the king relieved Crown and Church lands from tithes in the so-called *Píningsdómr um tíundir*, named after *hirðstjóri* (Governor) Didrik Píning (ibid.: 39). As we saw in the preceding chapter, this contributed to an aggravation of the distorted pattern of landownership.

Before the Reformation, the Church in Iceland suffered from the same debasement as elsewhere in Europe. Large landowners and profit-makers among the clergy give an impression of secular interests, as does the disregard for celibacy and other Roman commandments. For the better part of the fifteenth century at least, the Church was in a poor spiritual state, according to some standards. The bishops were foreigners, an Icelandic historian notes, and were but little concerned with the Icelanders (Arnór Sigurjónsson 1930: 191–2). The priests were violent and had mistresses (ibid.). The *libertates ecclesiae* had developed into a more or less autonomous Icelandic Church. On the other hand, learning and devotion among other clerics also reveal a continual concern with the sacred.

The Latin alphabet and writing had been introduced in the early twelfth century. Since then schools had been associated with the two Sees, and scholarly pursuits remained among the prime diocesan functions. Astronomy and 'magic' knowledge mixed with legend and homily. Some of the monasteries also pursued scholarship, and no doubt many of the works transmitted from the late Middle Ages originated in clerical centres of learning.

From the beginning of our epoch and until the Reformation, there is little religious literature. The high point of sacred poetry from the fourteenth century, *Lilja*, 'The Lily', written by a monk, was not matched until after the Reformation. The sacred poems of the fifteenth century are few, most of them being, like the *Lilja*, in praise of the Virgin Mary (Einarsson 1957: 76–7). In the sixteenth century Jón Arason, the last Catholic bishop of Hólar (1522–50), wrote some memorable poems, both sacred and secular. Most probably Jón Arason also introduced printing to Iceland (ibid.: 82–3).

A poem by Skáld-Sveinn from about 1500 brings us back to history outside the sacred concerns. In a long satire (*Heimsósómi*) he describes the lawlessness of the chieftains, and the vicious conditions of the second half of the fifteenth century.[9] The clerical exploitation of the peasants was an element in this. More important, perhaps, is the indirect testimony to a collective experience of changing social conditions.

Once again a 'conversion' expressed the change, although there is little evidence that the break was, in the first place, anything other than an official declaration. The élite and the ideologists may have taken the declaration seriously, but the people experienced no immediate change in their personal salvation. The Reformation was imposed from Denmark, and, again the northern bishopric went its own way.

In Copenhagen the new religious order was made law by an ordinance of 1537 (*LI*: i. 43 ff.). This ordinance obtained for Iceland as well, but as we saw in a previous chapter, it was not until 1550 that it overtook both bishoprics. Until then, Bishop Jón at Hólar resisted the change. When the game was up, the annalist could note '*Hoggvin byskup Jon og ij synir hans af Cristian umbodsmanne kongsens j Skalahollti eptir festum omnium sanctorum*' ('Bishop Jón and two of his sons were decapitated by King Christian's representative at Skálholt after all Saints' Day') (Storm 1888: 375). A new era began.

The interesting thing about Bishop Jón was not so much his resistance, but rather his immense popularity. He was to become a national hero, and in the popular recollection he personifies resistance against foreign domination. Histories are never constructed from scratch; the collective memory is not solely a matter of retrospective structuring (Ardener 1989a). It is a simultaneous registration of contemporary significances. Jón's fame in later nationalist periods probably reflects a contemporary perception of significance. Although materialized in a religious discourse, his significance is 'social' in a much broader sense. From this perspective, we may infer, from the enthusiasm for the memory of Jón, a general resentment towards external rule. Arngrímur Jónsson indirectly testifies to this in his treatise of 1609. He had been educated at Copenhagen University, a stronghold of the Reformation, and was heavily influenced by the ideas circulating there (Jakob Benediktsson 1957). Even so, his account of Jón Arason's end conveys a clear disapproval of the fact that Jón and his sons had not been properly convicted, and that the authorities had resorted to a *coup de main* (Jakob Benediktsson 1985: 241). Arngrímur's text is very controlled, but his account of Jón reveals his ambiguity in the matter, if nothing else than because of its brevity and slight distortion of the facts (cf. Jakob Benediktsson 1957: 57–8).

The sequel of the Reformation was an intensified impression of foreign rule. In the sphere of landownership the consequence was immediate. The monastic estates were annexed by the king, whose property soon outweighed ecclesiastical wealth. Through legislative change, the major sources of the Church's income were diverted into the royal treasury. The many decrees and ordinances following the Reformation are firm evidence of an intensified concern not only with the Icelanders, but also with royal power in Iceland. Among them were new rules of marriage, breach of which entailed fines to be paid to the civil authorities.

Although the new laws were still expressed in terms of religion or of its negation, heresy, they had far-reaching secular implications. Some of the religious doctrines conflicted with the Icelanders' view of their own world. An interesting example was the Lutheran doctrine of marriage, with its notion of a worldly union under the sovereignty of God. In Iceland, worldliness was to become paramount in the concept of marriage; God was repressed to the point where marriage was conceptually cut completely loose from the Church (Björn Björnsson 1971: 78–9).

In 1587 an ordinance was issued reinstating the Church as the principle arbitrator in marriage matters (*LI*: i. 113–24). A priest had to ascertain the propriety of marriage. In spite of this, Icelanders continued to regard marriage as their own affair, with their long tradition of secular engagement and private marriage negotiation (Björn Björnsson 1971). Again, this points to an immanent independence in Icelandic thinking about religion.

As an external power the Church was unrivalled before the Reformation. After it, the Danish king emerged as the main authority. His inroads into traditional spheres of ecclesiastical concern, and into local definitions is well illustrated by the *stóridómur* of 1564 (*LI*: i. 84–90). This was a law against heresy of all kinds, notably against sexual misconduct, and it imposed heavy penalties on deviant behaviour. The royal impact on civil life culminated in the introduction of the trade monopoly in 1602 (see below). The combined effect of all this was a steady flow of value out of the country, in the form of profits made by Danish merchants, and taxes collected by the king. Before the Reformation much wealth had been consumed and reinvested by the Church and the big landowners; so there was not necessarily greater social 'justice' then, but at least a larger proportion of the national wealth had remained in Iceland.

If we inspect more closely the position of the Church and of religion in general there is a strange inherent paradox. On the one hand, the Church is acknowledged by the Icelanders as a significant institution; on the other hand, it is often completely neglected or even contradicted by them. Adam of Bremen noted a similar paradox in the late eleventh century: 'the Icelanders treat their bishop as a king and take his words for their law. Yet they were exceedingly primitive and lived in a state of nature' (Henrichsen 1968: 289).

In the sixteenth century this was echoed in a less philosophical tone by Gories Peerse, a German observer, whose description of the

Icelanders leaves us in no doubt of their savage nature. Thus: 'Ten of them or more sleep together in one bed, and both women and men lie together. They turn heads and feet towards each other, and snore and fart like pigs under the homespun' (Sigurður Grímsson 1946: 27). About the priests he says: 'Many priests and clerics in the country often make only two sermons a year' (ibid.: 25).

The veracity of such statements is not open to assessment, but there is a striking continuity from Peerse's observation on the priests and up to Anderson's observation in 1746 that 'the Icelanders entertain the Evangelical-Lutheran religion—but hardly seriously. Very often the priest arrives at the church so drunk that the service must be given up' (1746: 135–6). Like other peasant societies Iceland was incorporated into European Christendom, but the Icelanders retained a freedom to do what they thought fit. They continued to marry, to make love, to give birth, and to drink as they pleased, although the *stóridómur* certainly had some effects. Even in the Catholic times priests disregarded their instructions about celibacy.

There is much direct and indirect evidence of the mixed religious feelings of the Icelanders. Although it is difficult to discuss belief as an objective category (Needham 1972), there is little doubt that the Icelandic world view accommodated religious beliefs of variegated origin, as did other European world views at the time. Oddur Einarsson noted in 1589 that superstition prevailed alongside proper faith (1971: 144). This echoes the critical voices of foreign commentators of the late sixteenth and early seventeenth century, like that of Dithmar Blefken, who said of the Icelanders that 'they are all prone to superstition and have demons and spirits in their service. Some of the men with luck in fishing are woken up at night by the Devil to go fishing' (Sigurður Grímsson 1946: 37).

Arngrímur Jónsson strongly resented the foreign impression that the Icelanders were impious, which was a common view in Northern Europe in the late sixteenth century (Jakob Benediktsson 1957: 32 ff.). In *Crymogæa* (of 1609) he also described the initiatives taken by the Danish kings after the Reformation to improve the standards of the Icelanders (1985: 242 ff.).

An observation from 1640 confirms the Icelandic ambivalence towards religion. Daniel Vetter noted that the Icelanders had been Christian for a long time; the king of Denmark had helped them to become Lutheran, and they held their bishops in high esteem (1931: 158–9). The priests, on the other hand, were very lax about their sermons; they repeated the old ones incessantly, or read directly from the Book, as people wished them to do. They had strange customs in Holy Communion, prostrating themelves on the earth floor of the Church; they even received the blessing in that position (ibid.).

In a similar spirit Eggers related in 1786 how the people had retained more ancient Nordic customs than elsewhere, because of a low level of external communication; he took this to be a very positive feature, and noted that the Icelanders were the happiest people in the world due to their freedom (1786: 40–3). In spite of living under a strong foreign power, the Icelanders, he claimed, had remained un-authoritarian (ibid.: 42).

Of course, the Icelanders complied with many rulings of the Church, and were baptized and buried according to current standards. They were not rigorous, however, in thought and practice, to say the least. As we shall see later, some bishops were directly involved in the art of magic, and in popular imagery there was no sharp distinction between religion, magic, and witchcraft (cf. below, Ch. 7). This endured far beyond the Reformation. Certain religious concepts like the 'soul', which was invoked by the Church in order to get donations, had some currency but it is impossible to establish the popular meaning of this concept. In a popular verse about elves, we learn that they are like men except that they have no soul, 'but that is the lesser part' (JÁ: i. 4, cf. below, Ch. 8). In the *þjóðsögur* (ibid.: i–iv) both churches and priests recur as centres of gravity in tales of the supernatural.

Until the Reformation almost all education had been in the hands of the Church, and European humanism was little known. Theologians in general were only concerned with theology. After the Reformation a major change in the intellectual climate occurred, but it only gradually revealed itself. The education of the Icelanders was still taken care of by the two episcopal seats, where regular cathedral schools had been established according to royal instructions (1537, *LI*: i. 48–9; 1552, *LI*: 66–9). The bishops were warned not to favour their relatives, but to choose the best educated clerics for teachers (*LI*: i. 67). Education had a new kind of significance beyond the local level; a selection of pupils from the cathedral schools was to receive further education in Copenhagen.

Until then higher education abroad had been infrequent, and no single university had preference. The centralization and intensification of learning in Copenhagen had a strong impact in Iceland. As early as 1579, subsidies were given to penniless students (*LI*: i. 109), and later the Icelandic bishops were urged to send at least one student a year to Copenhagen (*LI*: i. 179). Although few in numbers, perhaps, the Icelandic students in Copenhagen became familiar with European ideas to an unprecedented degree. The humanist concern with history was one such idea, and it was to take firm root among the Icelandic élite.

A prominent person in the Icelandic intellectualist movement after the Reformation was Guðbrandur Þorláksson (1542–1627), who was among the first Icelanders to study in Copenhagen after the Reformation.[10] He soon became rector of the school at Skálholt, and was eventually appointed bishop at Hólar (1571). In addition to numerous translations of learned foreign works, Guðbrandur also published the first complete Icelandic translation of the Bible in 1584, and a hymn-book in the vernacular in 1589. He was the originator of the privileges obtained for Icelandic students in 1579, and of the rule that the teachers and rectors of the cathedral schools in Iceland were to be native Icelanders. We can see that Guðbrandur, prime mover as he was in bringing external sophistication to Iceland, was nevertheless still keenly concerned with Icelandic autonomy.

The second generation of Icelanders educated in the humanist spirit included Arngrímur Jónsson among others. His writings were mainly in Latin and directed towards an international audience and did much to make Icelandic history known abroad (Jakob Benediktsson 1957). In his Icelandic history of 1609, *Crymogæa*, we detect the afore-mentioned paradox; the monarchy remained a divine institution for Arngrímur as for the other humanists, but Arngrímur also emphasized the element of free will in the old treaty with Norway. The contract, according to him, was mutual, and confirmed Iceland's ancient constitutional rights of self-government. If the king did not fulfil his part of the obligations, the Icelanders had the right to repudiate the treaty (*Crymogæa* (Jakob Benediktsson 1985: 226)). Arngrímur was no separatist, but he *was* an Icelander.

Through his work a romantic preoccupation with the past was disseminated among the Icelandic readership, which was thereby given a national history to rank with the best. Arngrímur's work was much admired in Denmark, and he was largely responsible for the growing antiquarian interest in old Icelandic literature, and for bringing Icelandic studies into the international scholarly arena.

Neither the inclusion of Iceland within the European intellectual

world, nor Iceland's distinct history, were of much concern to the
Icelandic people in general. At the level of common social experience,
people undoubtedly experienced the tension between intensified
external ruling and a traditional world view, but in other ways: they
chanted new hymns, but in their own old language; they still went to
church, but missed Mary who had been their principal saint; they
became more and more literate in their own vernacular, but had to
read a foreign edifying literature.

The century immediately after the Reformation witnessed a
veritable fight between two standards of value, fought with the
weapons of law and conviction. Numerous court cases testify to this
trend, which culminated in the witch-craze of the seventeenth century
(cf. below, Ch. 7). In the eighteenth century, the gap between the two
standards seems to have diminished, and the king could then direct
his efforts towards development from a truly reformed basis.

In an ordinance on household discipline dating from 1746, the king
stressed that people were under obligation to verse themselves in the
Catechism, and to read aloud from the Bible every evening (*LI*: ii.
605–20); the obligation to read the Catechism was actually first
imposed in 1635 (*LI*: i. 218–19). If no one at a particular farm could
read, and the neighbouring farmstead was too far away, then the
people should memorize psalms and biblical stories. The *bóndi* was
responsible for his children's and servants education, and the priest
should examine them regularly. Rules were given about proper
behaviour towards parents, servants, and masters; swearing was
forbidden, and priests were to warn people against making up untrue
narratives for the purpose of entertainment (cf. Loftur Guttormsson
1983a).

Religion, education, etiquette, and propriety in general merge in
this ordinance. The 'heretics' of the previous century have been
replaced by a populace whose main fault was to be rather ill-informed.
While the 'heretics' had to be killed or converted, the people now
simply had to be taught and improved. The digital 'either-or', through
which the clerical authorities saw everything in black or white, had
been transformed into an analogue 'more or less', where the Icelanders were perceived in all shades of grey. By the end of the
eighteenth century, Bishop Finnur Jónsson could sit down and peacefully write the *Historia Ecclesiastica* of Iceland (1772–8)—even as if this
history was single and continuous, distinguished only by separate
periods. Unity prevailed once again.

COMMERCE

In Europe the wheels of commerce propelled a particular development of capitalism during the period 1400 to 1800 (Braudel 1982). The mercantile system pushed European society towards modernity, albeit by different routes and in different stages (ibid.: 542). The system integrated Europe, and in some respects it also englobed the world outside Europe, Old and New (Wolf 1982).

Iceland was part of this commercial world, but its route towards modernity was long and difficult. It was also distinct from the routes taken by other European societies, if nothing else then by virtue of its peripheral position. European peasantry had many features in common during this period, most particularly the precariousness of their living, which induced them to engage in many other supplementary trades. The peasants supplemented their income from the soil through crafts, mining, forestry, iron-work, fishing, and so on. There were great regional variations, but structurally, European peasantry shared the condition of a complex economic order. This theme of unity and variety was played out also within the domain of popular culture (Burke 1978: 23–64). Whether we focus on form or content, however, Iceland was very much apart, and moved only very slowly towards modernity.

Iceland was absolutely dependent on long-distance sea trade, which was subject to serious limitations of a purely physical kind, quite apart from anything else. During the early Middle Ages the winds prevailing on the North Atlantic seem to have changed, for instance, impeding smaller boats in their passage between Iceland and Norway, and complicating the passage even for larger boats (cf. Hastrup 1985a: 162, 227). The sea was often violent and unpredictable and certainly only navigable during the summer. External communication was to remain unstable until the age of steam. The Icelandic annals from 1400 to 1800 contain many references to years when no ships at all called at Iceland. Trade was difficult under such circumstances.

Another peculiar feature of Iceland which, as it were, delayed modernity, was the absence of local commercial centres. There is evidence of a rather permanent commercial port at Hafnarfjörður from the thirteenth to the fourteenth centuries—and at least until the sixteenth century (Gísli Sigurðsson 1960–3). This was singular, however, and was finally abandoned. No villages or towns emerged until the nineteenth century, and there could be no interplay between rural and urban areas as elsewhere in Europe. This prevented a proper market economy from developing, and also contributed to a stagnation within the peasant economy. Although certainly tied up with European development in general and the Scandinavian order in particular, Iceland remained marginal to the capitalist development, for better and for worse. Here I shall investigate the local implications of this position. The centre of the analysis is still situated in the periphery itself.

Since the period of the settlements travel had been part and parcel of the Icelander's life. The passage to the new land emphasized this. Historically, the primordial journey to Iceland was among the last large-scale manifestations of the Vikings. *Víkingr* in Old Norse referred to the traveller, trader, and pirate. The unruly Viking gave a name to an epoch in Scandinavian history, when the majority of people were still sedentary farmers. The Vikings disappeared, and Nordic society entered the Middle Ages. At the point of intersection between these epochs Iceland was discovered and settled.

The descendant of the *víkingr* was the *farmaðr*, being both 'traveller' and 'trader', and a key-person in early medieval Icelandic society (Hastrup 1985*a*: 224–5). Trade was vital to social reproduction; grain, timber, iron, and other items had to be imported, while woollens were exported (Gelsinger 1981). With the changing conditions in the North Atlantic, the Icelandic *farmaðr* lost ground. He could no longer direct his own trade for want of proper ships and capital. His enterprise was taken over by a specialized category of merchants, mainly from Norway. This is directly reflected in a terminological shift from *farmaðr* to *austmaðr*, literally, 'man from the east', denoting Norwegian and other Scandinavians whose appearance in Iceland was owed to commerce (cf. *Grágás*: iii. 587).

When *Jónsbók* replaced *Grágás* the *austmaðr* was replaced by the *kaupmaðr* ('merchant'). Trade had become a specialized profession, and it was never again to become simply a subsidiary to travel in general. It was not until the nineteenth century, moreover, that trade was back in Icelandic hands. In this sense among others, trade was part of Iceland's foreign relations.

It will be recalled how foreigners, including merchants were generally met with scepticism in Iceland. Even though the Icelanders had recognized their need for regular imports ever since *gamlí sattmáli*, they did not permit any prolonged presence of foreigners. Outlanders should not delay their return to where they came from. Thus in the pattern of trade we detect an immanent ambiguity on the part of the Icelanders, which corroborates the paradox in their relationship to the Church. The following exposition will be organized around this theme.

Icelandic trade from 1400 to 1800 falls into more or less distinct periods. 'The English Age', *c.*1400–1500, was dominated by English merchants, who took over the market from the Norwegians. A German interregnum, *c.*1500–50 was followed by a Danish intervention in the second half of the sixteenth century. This was reinforced by the trade monopoly introduced by the Danes in 1602, which lasted until 1787. The monopoly was leased out to various agencies in this period, but ultimately it was under royal control. Whatever the nationality of the foreigners, they were always impatiently attended in the summer, and not really welcome when they came.

In *Jónsbók* it is stipulated that ships had to leave by *Maríumessa* (8 September) at the latest (240). The ships referred to were bound for Norway almost by implication, and one would have thought that the captains themselves could be left to arrange their own safe passage to Norway. The Icelanders, however, were continually preoccupied with the leaving of foreigners. In their letter of allegiance to King Erik of Pommern in 1431, authorized at the Althing, they repeated the rule that no *útlendzker menn* ('foreigners') should be in the country after *Maríumessa* (*DI*: iv. 461). The *Piningsdómur* of 1490 confirmed the prohibition on foreign wintering (see above, p. 111), and for centuries to come this was often referred to as the supreme authority on the matter.[11]

This state of affairs lasted through the seventeenth century. From charters of 1602, 1619, and 1662 we gather that wintering could be allowed only exceptionally, for merchants' servants who had urgent business (*LI*: i. 141, 197, 281). In 1682 this was overruled by a decree stating that a trade company may leave neither merchants nor their servants behind, whatever the circumstances (*LI*: i. 392).

In 1701 the Crown attempted to abolish this rule. Wintering by merchants was now deemed useful for the country (*LI*: i. 561). By 1702 the Icelanders were asking the king to reintroduce the ban (cf. Aðils 1971: 319–20) and he yielded to their petitions in 1706 (*LI*: i. 633). It was not until the mid-eighteenth century that native Icelanders themselves began to express doubt about this rule. Thus in 1757 Skúli

Magnússon, who was responsible for the collection of royal taxes, voiced the idea that Iceland would be better off if merchants stayed and if trade was allowed all year round; regular commercial centres could then develop (Aðils 1971: 321–2). Skúli seems to have had a vision of ports developing into towns, as a basis for a badly needed boost for the Icelandic economy.

In 1770 a commission was appointed to reorganize Icelandic trade (Gísli Gunnarsson 1983: 132–6). Skúli argued for a liberation of trade, but the Icelandic ruling class opposed this, and was seconded by an official royal objection, ostensibly based on the fear that commerce would completely fail in years of bad need. It was also argued that if merchants were allowed to settle in Iceland they would upset law and order. It was not until after the great catastrophe of 1783–5 (*Móðuharðindin*), when a volcanic eruption and its consequences caused a quarter of the population to die, that free trade was finally permitted (1786/7) and a new era could begin (*LI*: v. 305–16).

The above sketch is not meant as an exhaustive account of centuries of Icelandic trade.[12] It serves as a necessary preliminary, however, to the discussion of the inherent ambiguity in the trade relations of the Icelanders. They could not survive without being engaged in some sort of commerce, yet they resented the presence of the merchants.

The merchants were foreigners, and the animosity towards them can be partly explained through a typically Icelandic fear of losing autonomy. Another underlying problem was competition for the labour force. If merchants were allowed to stay over winter, they could engage in fishing, and thus be in competition with the locals for scarce labour. It was a recurrent theme in the decrees on wintering that merchants should never take Icelanders into their service.

Most fishing took place during winter as a supplement to farming, and if Icelanders were allowed to work on foreign vessels and for foreign merchants on the shore, the 'umbilical cord' between farming and fishing would be cut (Gísli Gunnarsson 1983: 23). The conceptual dominance of farming, and the social importance of the *bú*, helps us to understand Icelandic ambiguity towards foreign merchants. In this way the 'social infertility' of the Icelandic people and the resulting more or less permanent demographic crisis combined with a cultural emphasis on farming life and impeded economic growth. Ultimately it delayed modernity.

Trade patterns were important contributing factors, and the pricing system contained an anomaly which confirmed the ambiguity towards foreign trade. We have noted before that Iceland's primary export after the fourteenth century was dried fish, or *skreið*. In consequence *vættir*, or 'pounds', of fish became the standard of value, but only in external commercial relations. Internally, the standard was a derivative of farming.

Since the settlements the basic unit of value was the cow. We saw in the preceding chapter that the value of farms was measured in *kúgildi*, or the value of one fertile cow 3–10 years of age. Other prices were fixed relative to this standard. Another standard used since the oldest times was that of *alnir*, or 'ellens'. Originally the *alnir* referred to ellens of homespun (*vaðmál*), the coarse cloth which dominated export in the earlier period. Eventually, the ellens became a more abstract standard of value. Thus in the *búalög*, the price of 40 ellens of long *vaðmál* is 120 ellens. The ellens remained the basic value in domestic trade.

The two scales, the internal scale of farm produce and the external scale of fish, were measured against each other. In general the Icelandic economy was organized in a very complicated system of relative pricing. The main complication was that while real prices changed, due to external market conditions, relative prices had to remain constant (Gísli Gunnarsson 1980*c*; 1983). The changes were, therefore, expressed in other ways than price. One example is the relative price of grain. During the fifteenth century the supply of grain increased considerably, and the price fell accordingly. That is, the import price became much lower than the legally fixed relative price of grain in the internal market. 'Consequently, the barrel in the law-stipulated price list was doubled in size but the new grain barrel had the same price in relation to other products as the small barrel had previously' (Gísli Gunnarsson 1983: 18).

Pricing was not only an abstract game. It had some very real consequences for people. One result of the dual pricing of grain was that tenants could buy grain from the merchants and pay their land-rent with half of its 'value'. The effects of this 'overvaluation' were eventually met by royal restrictions on imports (Gísli Gunnarson 1980*c*).

The *vættir* fish were also measured against other commodities. One cow was equal to one 'hundred', and the number of *vættir* amounting to a hundred varied according to external market factors. Until 1200, 10 *vættir* made one hundred; in the period 1350–1400 it was 6. From 1420 to 1550 the price of fish increased further, so that $3\frac{1}{2}$ *vættir* valued one hundred. The price of fish effectively increased by 286 per cent from 1200 to 1550 (Gelsinger 1981: 189; Þorkell Jóhannesson 1933: 63). Thereafter, the prices went steadily down and again, and some time during the monopoly period in the seventeenth and eighteenth centuries, 6 *vættir* became equal to one hundred.

To add life to these general remarks on pricing, Table 12 gives a scale of relative prices from 1619 (when one hundred equalled 3 *vættir*), introduced by Christian IV (*LI*: i. 184–94). The following scale was enjoined on the merchants, operating at this period under royal privilege:

TABLE 12. *Relative Prices in 1619*

Commodity	Price (in fish)
Barrel of grain	50
Barrel of good ale	50
Barrel of salt	40
Barrel of Danish biscuits	60
Unit of iron	10
Set of horseshoes	5
1 mark or half a pot of spirits	2
12 marks of tar	10
1 ellen of linen	6
Handaxe	15
Keel timber, 12 ellens	60
Keel timber, 8 ellens	40
Oar, 10 ellens	12
Oar, 6 ellens	6
Good knife	8

Source: *LI*: i. 187–90.

The list gives a vivid impression of the import needs of the Icelanders, which are specified in detail. It also demonstrates the position of fish as a standard of value.

The standard varied somewhat within Iceland. According to the decree on prices in 1619, there was a major distinction to be made between the southern and western parts on the one hand, the northern and eastern on the other. The reason was that the population of the former were able to pay directly in fish, while northerners and easterners apparently paid in cattle, butter, cloth, and socks (the knitting of which had been introduced in the sixteenth century). This is a clear reflection of the two ecological zones of Iceland (cf. above, Ch. 2), and one of the consequences is that the people paying in farm produce had to pay relatively more. Thus, a southerner paid 80 fish for one barrel of grain, while the northerner paid 90; similarly, a barrel of good ale cost 70 fish in the south and 80 in the north (ibid.: 191).

Changes in 'real' prices on the external market, whether owed to free fluctuation or to the monopoly, were more or less covered up by the fixed system of relative pricing in the internal market. Here, the principle of one cow equals 6 ewes equals 120 ellens equals 240 fish seems to have remained the implicit duodecimal standard of relative value. Among other things this meant that Iceland experienced very little 'inflation' during our period (with the exception of the temporary change in the size of the grain barrel and other measurements that were essentially external to the 'price').

The distinction between external and internal pricing reflects another feature of Icelandic society. No money was used. Internal exchange was carried out in the form of barter. In 1640 Daniel Vetter wrote that the Icelanders 'need no money to buy and sell but received one thing for another' (1931: 172). If they get any money from the merchants for their goods these could only be used for tax; otherwise they were of little use (ibid.: 171–2). Anderson confirms that all payments are made in goods (1746: 130), and a generation later von Troil observed that due to the mountainous nature of the country 'there is no agriculture, and no commerce, except that carried on by bartering of the various commodities on the arrival of Danish ships' (1780: 56).

There is no need to pile on the evidence on this. In spite of the fact that Iceland was in many ways a highly 'mercantile' society, in the sense that it was heavily dependent on foreign trade (Gísli Gunnarsson 1983: 27), its internal economic structure remained archaic. It was founded on a medieval subsistence economy to which external trade had to adapt, rather than the other way round.

There is little doubt that external trade in general and the Danish monopoly in particular had a flavour of exploitation. The exception was perhaps found in the English Age, where the profits of the merchants were balanced by an internal growth in wealth as well. After this period, the profits made by others were correlated with increasing poverty among the Icelanders. Many modern scholars have seen the external trade, and notably the monopoly, as the single major *cause* of the impoverishment and disintegration of Icelandic society.[13] No doubt it contributed, and the Danish Crown in many ways legitimized the commercial exploitation. We need, however, to be a little more careful in our search for causes.

Mathias Jochumssen, writing in 1731, gives a clue:

> Because the Icelanders have lived with the trade monopoly for so many years, they have become so unused to all trade, dealing, correspondence, and conversation with other people, that they have had no opportunity to see or learn anything to the improvement of their country, or to exploit those useful products which the country provides in addition to fish, meat, woollens, and other goods specified by the Company. (1977: 72.)

They had not discovered the values of their country, he added. And they knew nothing of trade; the very few people that went abroad studied theology and not commerce (ibid.).

While Jochumssen acknowledged the detrimental impact of the trade monopoly, he supplemented the 'cause' with a qualification of the Icelanders' own stage of knowledge. In many ways this point of view was corroborated by other eighteenth-century observers such as Eggert Ólafsson (1772), Olavius (1780), Eggers (1786), and Skúli Magnússon (1786). The critical voice of Johann Anderson stated that the Icelanders were idle—they were not stupid by nature but had neither desire nor will to learn except what they could learn from parents and grandparents (1746: 125).

Anderson's statement is important for one reason: it imputes that the Icelanders had become non-inventive, and continued to regard social reproduction as essentially a household matter.

At one level Icelandic trade 1400–1800 was governed by foreigners; at another it was ruled by a local ambiguity. Since the *farmaðr* ('travelling man') had given in to the *austmaðr* ('eastman') and, later, the *kaupmaðr* ('tradesman'), commercial enterprise had been in the hands of foreigners. It was externalized from Icelandic society, originally settled by Vikings, and navigated by Icelandic *farmenn* until the late twelfth century. While travel until then had been part and parcel of Icelandic life, history was no longer in favour of this definitional parameter. The merchants who took over had intruded on the Icelandic world in much more than an economic sense. Consequently, the foreigners became suspect to the Icelanders, and were defined out of the Icelandic world. Commerce itself was alienated from the social.

So, although Iceland was decisively part of a larger cycle of social reproduction, its inhabitants were very reluctant to admit this. By separating internal pricing and barter from foreign trade, they symbolically emphasized the boundaries of the social. When, later, external commercial power tightened its grip around the country during the period of monopoly, the Icelanders reacted by closing even further the boundary around their small cosmological units: the households. The externalization of trade was mirrored by an ideology of the self-sufficiency and independence of every *bú*. The concentration on the reproduction of the *bú*, including the maintenance of the integrated farming and fishing economy, was both caused by, and subsequently effected, external developments. From the centre of the *bú*, all commercial enterprise beyond its confines was potentially threatening to the social order—as defined by the Icelanders themselves.

THE RULING ORDER

Our inquiry into the foreign relations of the Icelanders in matters of constitution, Church, and commerce has unveiled a dual structure of inclusion and autonomy. There is a feel of contradiction in this, even perhaps of impossibility; yet there is also a logic and a cultural necessity, as I will try to show.

In each of the three spheres there was a discrepancy between the internal and the external ruling. Politically, the Icelanders were increasingly implicated in Danish rule, and in the king's sphere of interest. This sphere was one of power, of course, but also one of civilization. Losing ever more of their sovereignty during our period, the Icelanders nevertheless maintained a kind of autonomy. The farming community never ceded completely to the external power, and the Icelanders remained masters within their own households. Indeed, most of their negotiations with successive rulers were directed towards the simple goal of maintaining individual autonomy (Líndal 1973: 608–10). The scope of this autonomy shrank but in domestic, religious, and other matters, Icelanders continually struggled to retain power over their own reality. Two standards prevailed. Only very slowly did the Icelanders come to comply with external Christian teachings; only at the close of our period did internal and external moral standards become unified.

A similar pattern of a double standard was found in commercial matters. Internally, the exchange relationship between people was one of barter; externally, a larger market defined the terms of trade. The double standard of exchange was related to an ideology of self-sufficiency on the one hand, and badly needed imports on the other.

If we consider the historical process in all of these matters there is a definite trend towards centralization in an external power centre. Law, religion, and commerce all became increasingly governed from Copenhagen. In this sense, Iceland became more and more integrated into an outside world. Inside Iceland the process was also one of concentration—at an ever lower level of social organization. The law-court, the Althing, continued to function until 1800, but in reality the relevant local centre was the individual *bú*. This was a corollary to the fact that the representatives of the Althing no longer represented anything but the external ruling order.

We may comprehend this dual reality of inclusion and autonomy by reference to the Icelandic world-view. Ever since the Freestate, Icelandic self-definition had been locked into a taxonomic space of several levels of inclusion (cf. Hastrup 1984*a*: 238ff.). In this taxonomic space the Icelanders were both part of a larger Scandinavian order (in which they originated) and contrasted to other peoples of that order. By the treaty of 1262–4, the Norwegian king had won a taxonomic victory, so to speak. Politically, the Icelanders were subsumed by the Norwegian kingdom. At that very moment, however, the Icelanders intensified their literary efforts to maintain cultural autonomy.

In cosmology, this was mirrored in the coexistence of a vertical and a horizontal model (Hastrup 1981*a*), a simultaneous realization of hierarchy and equality. In the horizontal model of the world, Iceland (and by implication every single household within it) was the centre of an autonomous world. Vertically, the Icelanders were defined by hierarchical relationships. The nature of the hierarchy differed from one period to the next, but the principle persisted. The Icelanders were subsumed and defined by a larger order, while also always stressing their distinctness from it.

The continuity at this level of conceptual modelling is striking. The local centres were permanently emphasized. Confronted with the external centralizing tendencies belonging to a higher level in the taxonomic hierarchy, the Icelanders reacted by redefining the external order as marginal. From each of the centres, the 'other' was defined as periphery. The civilized and the wild were continually counter-specifying one another.

The double standards, the multi-levelled taxonomic space of identity categories, and the stress upon the autonomy of the local centre within a larger context of ruling, ultimately generated two separate histories. From outside, the Icelanders became part of a history which was shared with Europe and directed towards progress and modernity. From the perspective of this history, the Icelanders were barbarians. Internally quite a different historical order prevailed. It was not based on an idea of progress but of conservation. The Icelanders certainly *had* a history of their own, but Icelandic society as such did not *produce* history.

Indeed, it is as if the Icelanders bathed in history, just as their island floated on the ocean, but that they refused to let it in. In that sense, their world was as 'cold' as their climate, and only slowly was it heated up to the point of entering into the steaming 'hot' history of capitalism and civilization in Modern Europe.[14] This was not to happen until the end of our epoch.

III

THE HUMAN CONDITION

6

Patterns of Reproduction

THIS chapter is concerned with the reproduction of human life in Iceland within the context of the social experience of the Icelanders. 'Social reproduction' does not necessarily imply repetition. The reproduction of culture may contain its own transformation (Sahlins 1982; 1985), and 'events' are never exact replicas of previous ones, even though they may be realizations of the same structure (Ardener 1972).

Reproduction occurs at several levels, and there is a sense in which all studies of culture in time are studies of reproduction for the simple reason that things go on. We can begin our investigation of reproduction at the level of biology and study the patterns of sexuality and procreation. This will give important clues to the human condition, including an understanding of how humans perceive themselves as agents in and of life. Subsequently I shall deal with reproduction at another level, and explore how the morals of sexuality and procreation were matched by a particular pattern of literacy. Dealing with literacy in this way is not so much a study of percentages of readers as it is a way of hearing the voice of the Icelanders; for what is literature other than voices turned into letters?[1] In the literature, we can hear the Icelanders voicing their own indigenous views upon humanity. Literature, moreover, is also a field of reproduction in its own right. In literature images of past and present conditions are expressed. If, as happened in Iceland, literature is truly popular, this kind of cultural reproduction is vital in the self-definition of a people, quite apart from its entertainment value.

Through investigation into these matters we are able to approach the question of how the Icelanders conceived of humanity—how they named themselves and set themselves apart from non-humans on the one hand and non-Icelanders on the other. Both of these boundaries are vital in the reproduction of a distinct social system.

SEXUALITY

The field of sexual relations is a field of emotions, desire, and pleasure, but it is also a field of interest, deprivation, and legislation. It is a field of encounter between the individual and society, between the body and the moral order. In short, it is a total social fact where gifts are permanently exchanged, linking together people in a moral community (cf. Mauss 1950). From this perspective, we are far removed from the minimal condition of sexual reproduction, that is, from that merely sufficient contract between the two sexes which allows them to exchange genetic material (Fox 1985: 1).

We are not so much interested in the flow of genes as in the code for this particular exchange. Codes are expressed in actions of various kinds. Because we are removed from the people under study by some centuries, we cannot witness sexual behaviour, nor can we spy on courtship and secret meetings. What is left for us to study are the dead stretches of laws and verdicts, and a certain amount of love-poetry. The two kinds of sources differ in important ways. Love-verses relate positively to the field of sexual relations, while laws and verdicts relate negatively to this field. Love-verses deal with emotional content, while laws and verdicts deal with legal boundaries. Poetry may express a longing for the unobtainable, while legal verdicts tell us about the inadmissible.

In the legislation of the Freestate it was a criminal act to address love-songs to a lady; it was considered an aggression towards her male guardian, and towards the honour of the kin group (*Grágás*: i*b*. 184). There is no parallel clause in *Jónsbók*, although other passages show that a similar concept of honour still existed. Legally, at least, after *Jónsbók* the way was open for the making of love-poetry.

Love itself has often been depicted as the invention of the West, and more specifically of the medieval court poets: 'the passion and sorrow of love were an emotional discovery of the French troubadours and their successors' (Curtius 1953: 588). It is possible that the French troubadours were among the first ones to translate this emotional discovery into the language of courtly poetry, but the idea of their representing a wholly new conception of love is surely wrong (Dronke 1968: 2). Icelandic scaldic poetry, at least, displays a similar concept of love which by some centuries antedated the advent of Occitan courtly poetry, and which cannot be explained by an impact of the Mediterranean mind (ibid.: 39ff.).² There are also, of course, many Classical precedents.

The parallels between French courtly poetry and traditional scaldic poetry have often been noted. In his introduction to the thirteenth-century *Kormáks saga*, Einar Ó. Sveinsson describes Kormákr as 'the forerunner of the southern troubadours . . . in his sensibility and in the relation to his art there is a parallel between him and them' (*ÍF*: vol. viii. p. lxxxix). Kormákr's passion for his lady Steingerðr makes him equate her with the whole world in a verse which leaves nothing of the courtly poetry wanting (ibid.: 8). Kormákr experiences love as all-embracing. He clearly realized that his passion would 'bring harm both to me and her' (ibid.: 3), but even denounced the fear of death in face of it (ibid.: 54). Love being everything, he would be nothing without it. Kormákr is certainly heralding a 'romantic' concept of love, but whether he was a forerunner to the troubadours, or inspired by them, is an open question (cf. *KL*: ix. 142–4).

Love-poetry from our period is not abundant, but what has been transmitted shows considerable continuity with the scaldic imagery. A famous poem in the genre is *Háttalykill* ('metrical keys'), attributed to Loftur *ríki* Guttormsson, who died in 1432. Allegedly he wrote his poem, which is both a praise of the beloved one and an exploration of the metrical forms, to his *fylgjakona* ('concubine') Kristín Oddsdóttir. *Háttalykill* has been transmitted in one sixteenth-century and a number of seventeenth-century manuscripts, and the question whether Loftur actually composed it is still unresolved.³ Whoever the original author, the poem exists in several slightly different and some-what inconsistent versions, all of which are an exploration of metrical forms as well as a love-song (cf. Finnur Jónsson 1932*a*: 287–8).

In his discussion of *Háttalykill*, Finnur Jónsson demonstrates the likelihood that an original early fifteenth-century poem (by Loftur?) was added to by later writers (ibid.: 311–12, esp.). This testifies to the 'popularity' of the poem from the fifteenth through to the eighteenth centuries. The number of manuscripts also suggests that the poem was much read. On this basis, we can classify *Háttalykill* as popular poetry, that is, poetry which 'is composed not by a people but for it' (Dronke 1968: 1). As such *Háttalykill* need not be a direct expression of the Icelandic *Volksgeist* and a wholly anonymous creation, but whoever the author (or authors), the people had made it their own. Even if it was not for everyone to indulge in the pleasures of extra-marital love, nor in every Icelander's power to write love-lyrics, the idea of love and passion was probably part of the popular imagery of the time. Through this imagery, the legitimacy of extra-marital love was mediated. It seems that in the popular view there was nothing 'immoral' about having a mistress, or in begetting children by her; an early nineteenth-century narrator of Icelandic history gives us some idea of this (Espolín 1943: ii. 22).

One poem is not much evidence for a set of collective representations of love, but although *Háttalykill* is exceptional in form it is not unique in content. *Víglundar saga*, for instance, has been bluntly characterized as 'a love story of the 15th century' (Jón Helgason 1953: 165). Even though the creation of secular prose literature virtually came to a halt in the fourteenth century, the reproduction of the medieval sagas for centuries afterwards continously brought forward similar notions of passion (and of social conflicts resulting from it). It has been argued that the leitmotiv in the saga literature is the conjunction of 'chaos and love' (Bredsdorff 1971).

No less important was the creation of a more or less independent subgenre of the popular *rímur* ('verses'), the so-called *mansöngvar* ('love-songs'). Generally speaking, *rímur* were rather epical in their form, while the *mansöngvar* were more lyrical in tone (Stefán Einarsson 1957: 89; Jón Helgason 1953: 170). By one of the authorities of early Icelandic *rímur*, the *mansöngur* has been described as 'man's love song to or about a woman' (Björn K. Þórolfsson 1934: 256). These love-songs had a quite distinct position in relation to the *rímur* more generally. They opened a *ríma*, which was thereby 'dedicated' to a particular woman (ibid.: 276–8). In this form they had wide circulation, and—at least until the Reformation when their purpose was obscured—the *mansöngvar* were as indispensable to the *rímur* as the refrain to the ballad (Stefán Einarsson 1957: 89). The art of making love-songs was widespread; some of the poets themselves refer to 'many men doing so' (Björn K. Þórólfsson 1934: 277). The tradition of love-poetry was firmly rooted in an Icelandic tradition of scaldic poetry, and the context of its transmission was specifically Icelandic. It gave voice to a particularly Icelandic 'battle for chastity' (cf. Foucault 1985) which in spite of a differing social context had strong parallels in other societies, notably England (Macfarlane 1986: 174–208). Wherever romantic love was originally invented, it was known and talked about in late medieval and early modern Iceland.

If lovers were the heroes of a certain genre of literature, they were often the villains of community life. Passion was not only an object of lyrical praise, it was also an object of shame and derision. The old Norse institution of *nið* was particularly defamatory in its implied sexual perversion (Meulengracht Sørensen 1980). Sexual slander of this kind was of public concern (*Jónsbók*: 66). The semantics of *nið* changed during the Middle Ages; from the allegation of femininity, to homosexuality in general (under the impact of Christianity), the main problem from the fifteenth century onwards was the accusation of adultery. Public charges of adultery or fornication were highly insulting and required restoration through court or by means of *tylftareiður* ('acquittal by a jury of twelve lay persons'). In 1440 a man swore *fullan bokaræidh ath hann hefdi aldre a sina lifs dagha lægit likamliga med fyrgræindræ helgo þorlæifsdottor huorckcæ fyr næ sidar* ('on the Bible that he had never in his life lain bodily with the aforementioned Helga Þorleifsdóttir') (*DI*: v. 13). Eleven other men swore with him, and he was acquitted.[4]

Court actions were only allowed if the slander had no truth in it: *Engi á søk á sønnu rógi* ('no one can bring an action for true slander') (*Jónsbók*: 66). This had a general validity, apparently, as implied by later court verdicts (for example, 1504, *DI*: vii. 709 ff., and 1533, *DI*: ix. 659 ff.). If untrue allegations were made, and this had to be publicly established, the slanderer had to pay full compensation to the injured person. In 1579 a man lost half his estate for having accused another man of incest with his sister, to mention but one example (*AÍ*: i. 381–3).

With this I shall move from the discussion of personal sexual honour towards the sexual relationship between man and woman. Within marriage, sexuality is invisible in our sources. Sex was so much part of marriage, that lack of it (due to impotence, for instance) was, and remained, a legitimate reason for divorce.[5] To discuss the sexual code, therefore, we cannot investigate the sexual life of married couples. This is indeed the silent background, but it gives us few clues about sexuality; the study of illicit relationships, by contrast, provides us with rich material concerning the moral order.

The cases brought to court were mainly of two kinds, concerning adultery and incest. Since the introduction of Christianity, and certainly after Bishop Árni's Christian law (1275), the holy institution of marriage was the only legal framework of sexual intercourse. In practice this was not so, and sexual offences were of public concern. Private and immediate vengeance was not allowed according to *Jónsbók*, as it had been in *Grágás* (*Jónsbók*: 67, 68–9).

In the Christian law of 1275 adultery was graded; *tvefalldr hórdómr* ('double adultery') involved two persons who were both of them married to somebody else, while *einfalldr hórdómr* ('single adultery') involved a married and an unmarried person (*AK*, *NGL*: v. 39). The presupposed symmetry between the sexes is remedied by a male advantage elsewhere in the laws. A man had to pay no atonement to his wife after he had had an illicit love-affair, while a married woman found guilty of infidelity would lose her dowry (*heimanfylgja*) to her husband (*Jónsbók*: 75–7). Somewhat paradoxically, she lost her only token of economic independence if she chose sexual autonomy. Also, the inheritance of an unmarried daughter who had been 'lain with' in her father's house was at stake in case of premarital love (ibid.: 79). This was the case of Solveig Björnsdóttir, as we have seen above, Ch. 4), but she was not unique in this respect (see, for instance, *DI*: v. 555–6).

If a man, whether married or not, committed adultery with a married woman, and if the injured husband took action against him, a court of twelve men was set to judge his case. If the injured party had had sexual intercourse with his wife after the case had been put forward, however, the case could not be pursued (*Jónsbók*: 67). By using the wife sexually, the husband apparently nullified the adulterer's offence. By mounting what was a polluted body, he implicitly denied that his honour had been derided; otherwise he would have waited until the boundary around his sexual privileges had been restored through judgement. Similar rules obtained if the parties were betrothed or 'promised' to each other (ibid.: 77).

Until the Reformation, cases of adultery or other sexual offences were in the hands of the Church. Ever since the appearance of a separate Christian law (probably 1123), the clergy had had the ultimate say in matters of marriage and related topics. In 1253 it was legally agreed by the Althing that in case of discrepancy between civil and canon law, the latter should prevail (*DI*: ii. 1). In 1275 a new Christian law was made by Bishop Árni Þorláksson, and in 1277 a treaty between the king of Norway (who since 1262–4 had also been the sovereign of Iceland) and the archbishop gave statutory rights to the Church to judge in matters concerning marital and sexual conduct (*DI*: ii. 139–55). Some problems of interpretation still caused conflict, however. In 1458 the king issued an ordinance which confirmed the privilege of the Church to judge in cases of *hórdómur* ('adultery'), *frændsemisspell* ('incest'), *meinsæri* ('perjury'), *frillulífi* ('concubinage'), and *fadderscap* (or *faðerni*, 'paternity') (*DL*: v. 158–9). The privileges of 1277 were repeated on the occasion. Thus, it was for the Church to judge in cases of adultery, and to inflict the appropriate punishment. This was a fine of three *merkr* on the first occasion, and six on the second (*AK*, *NGL*: v. 39). It is explicitly stated that a woman had to pay out of her *heiman-fylgja* (dowry) and not out of her husband's property (ibid.). Adultery could legitimize divorce if the injured party wished it, and if the bishop permitted (ibid.).

The clergy could more than banish and fine, however; it could also absolve the guilty parties, once the fines had been paid. In a case where both husband and wife had committed fornication, the bishop had to excommunicate them until they had once again resumed marital relations (ibid.). After this they were expected to live happily ever after, with the sexual boundary around their marriage restored. If an adulterer was absolved by the Church, the offended party could still claim satisfaction through the civil court. It will be recalled that each case had to be judged by a jury of twelve men, who were supposed to adjust the compensation to be paid to the injured person with due regard to his social standing and the relative loss of dignity (*ráðspell*). That this was not mere lip-service to a principle of relativity in justice is documented by the verdicts following different cases of *legorð*, where compensation is weighed out according to status, wealth, and so forth (cf., for example, 1478, *DI*: vi. 138–40; and 1505, *DI*: vii. 797–9).

After the Reformation (1538/1550) things changed completely. First of all, the Church lost the power to judge in marital matters, and to give absolution for sins committed. Adultery now became a matter of civil jurisdiction. Generally, the Reformation made the king (now of Denmark *and* Norway) take a more active interest in his 'colony' in the North Atlantic, and a series of laws from the late sixteenth century testify to his intent to stop sexual promiscuity. In 1558 a law concerning adultery was passed in Denmark: the first offence was to be punished by fines, the second by fines and expatriation, and the third by execution (*LI*: i. 76–7). This law was made statuate in Iceland in 1563, with reference to cases that were not explicitly dealt with in Icelandic law already (ibid.: 79–80). Allegedly, this was because the king had heard of many Icelandic vices which were not properly punished (ibid.). This so-called *koldingske reces* ('the recess made in Kolding') was followed by the *stóridómur* ('big verdict') of the Althing in 1564 (*LI*: i. 84–9). The purpose of the *stóridómur* was to establish unequivocal rules about sentences in cases of incest, adultery, and debauchery. There was, allegedly, a great need for such clarity (ibid.: 85).

The crimes were finely graded. Unmarried persons had to pay 6 *merkr* for their first illicit love-making. Married persons committing adultery for the first time had to pay a fine of 12 *merkr* (pl.). If payment had not been made by the *fardagr* ('moving day', that is, early summer) following the verdict, the culprits would receive one blow with a stick for each *mörk* (sg.) unpaid. For repeated sins, fines would be augmented by 50 per cent and accompanied with flogging. If the culprits were generally incapable of paying they would be flogged right away and be otherwise bodily inflicted as a twelve-man jury would decide. If caught in adultery for the third time, execution would follow. Men were to be beheaded, women drowned.[6] The property of the executed would pass to the legal heirs 'for the sake of the poor country' (*LI*: i. 87–8).

In 1565 this *stóridómur* was ratified by royal decree (*LI*: i. 89–90) and henceforward it framed judicial practice for the remainder of our period, although it was in some respects 'un-Icelandic' when compared to the traditional leniency over matters of sexuality (Þorgeir Kjartansson 1982: 5). This 'leniency' was not easily removed. In 1585 the king had to remind the Icelanders that adultery and incest were to be dealt with according to the law (*LI*: i. 111–12). Even this, apparently, was not enough to keep a seemingly flourishing promiscuity in check, and in 1587 a new ordinance about matrimonial cases was issued (ibid.: 113–24). In 1674 an agreement at the Althing shows us that the *stóridómur* was still in full force (ibid.: 357), and certainly the great number of court cases from the seventeenth century show promiscuity as being one of the main targets of administration. In a statistical inquiry into court cases taking place in Iceland 1641–50, Þorgeir Kjartansson found that of all crimes committed and brought before the court, no less than 92.5 per cent were sexual offences (1982: 10–11). Of the sexual offences, 79.9 per cent concerned extra-marital sex (*frillulífi*), 13.1 per cent concerned adultery (*hórdómur*), and 6.4 per cent concerned incest (*frændsemisspell*) (ibid.). These figures speak for themselves. Eighty years after the *stóridómur*, the Icelanders were apparently still not ready to accept its ruling, however rigorously applied.

After the turn of the seventeenth century court practice relaxed a little, as shown by a case of 1710 when a verdict was passed showing (for the first time?) a certain relief of punishment—flogging was to be omitted (*LI*: i. 671). The spirit of mercy also broke through in 1753, in the case of a married man having twice committed adultery; according to the *stóridómur* he was to be flogged, to pay 12 *merkr*, and to leave the district; with a view to his poverty and to his physical fitness, however, he was sentenced instead to penal servitude in road-work (*LI*: iii. 160–1). In general, the eighteenth century saw a change in the administration of the law, and sexual offences tended to be punished with ordinary imprisonment. The validity of the *stóridómur* was not questioned; the verdicts were still somehow measured by the scale of 1564, but new ideas of clemency, and/or changing notions of corporal punishment, are clearly evidenced.

The nature of the sources is one reason why the juridical practice in cases of sexual offence stands out more clearly after the Reformation than before. It was not until the late sixteenth century that a systematic recording of the Althing procedures commenced. There is no doubt, though, that sexual offences were generally overlooked until the Reformation—something which can be inferred from the (indirect) evidence of post-Reformation legislation if nothing else. There is, however, a further reason why sexual offences became so conspicuous in the late sixteenth and seventeenth centuries. With the Reformation of 1550, and especially after *stóridómur* in 1564, the scale for 'measuring' such offences became unified.

Until the Reformation, matrimonial cases in particular were subject to the double standard of Christian and civil law. As late as 1514 King Christian II, in a decree addressed to the Norwegians, gives statuary power to the Church in these matters; referring to the Christian law (of 1275) and to the treaty between king and bishop (of 1277), the king holds the local sheriffs responsible for dealing with sexual charges according to these ancient laws (*DI*: viii. 503–5).

In 1517 a specific case illustrates how the decree was interpreted. A man who had fornicated with a woman, whose mother he had been involved with earlier, had the following judgement passed: either he had to swear himself free of the accusation by *tylftareiður* before ten weeks had passed, or he would lose his property to the king and the Church according to the rules (*DL*: viii. 629–31). This was normal procedure. No doubt persons of influence in civil life could more readily produce twelve witnesses to their innocence than could peasants at the bottom of the social scale.

When the 'moral order' of society was more permissive than the holy principles of the Church, a *tylftareiður*, issued by lay-persons, could acquit 'adulterers' who by the standards of the Church were guilty of grave violations of the sexual code. A clash between two incongruent standards was, therefore, always likely. The clergy, who officially had the last say, seem to have adapted themselves to the less rigorous standard of interpretation, however. Their own ways of life were rather closer to the permissive civil code than to the strict clerical order. Priests, who were not supposed to 'know' women (carnally) at all (*AK*, *NGL*: v. 38), often had mistresses who bore them children; this applied also to some of the more distinguished post-Reformation bishops such as Guðbrandur Þorláksson and Oddur Einarsson—who (by then) *were* permitted to 'know' women—in marriage. In general, clergymen were not infrequent actors in court cases of *legorð* (for example, 1505, *DI*: vii. 797–8). Thus in 1440 the abbot of Þingeyra-klaustur was said to have lain with someone else's wife, and was acquitted on the basis of his swearing full *bókareiður* ('book-oath') his innocence (*DI*: 13–14). Public opinion clearly would not put it past an abbot to indulge in illicit affairs. In 1545, when the rights of inheritance for priest's wives and legitimate children were established, the king referred rather reproachfully to the debauchery in which Icelandic priests had previously indulged (*LI*: i. 59). Even if it is just a standard formula, demonstrating the necessity of the law, it seems that the reasons for the king's disappointment continued—in the seventeenth century, the priests were still recorded as having worldly desires (see, for instance, Thoroddsen 1892–1904: ii. 18). This was no doubt one reason why the Church was prepared to be merciful as regards sexual offences, even if mercy was somewhat casually distributed.

Concerning mercy, one more case shall be referred to here. In 1530, close to the waning of the power of the Church, its ministers pardoned a couple having an incestuous relationship which had resulted in children, not only once but twice (*DI*: ix. 508–9; 616). Quite clearly, the double standard was not always a trap between a sacred and a profane code of sexual conduct; sometimes, rather, it could be a liberation. The servants of Christ were often rather sacrilegious themselves, and the double standard could thus become one—of permissiveness (Hastrup 1985*c*).

The unification of the moral standard, and the restrictions on individual sexuality, met little explicit opposition among the Icelanders. It was not until the mid-seventeenth century that voices were raised against the *stóridómur*. Before considering this, we can look at the problem of incest, which was another target of the administrators.

Incest is one of the major offences against the moral order in any society. All societies have prohibitions on sex and marriage between relatives of various kinds. In some cases the prohibition makes a distinction between sexual intercourse and marriage, which we must also separate analytically. In Iceland this distinction was propagated in Bishop Árni's Christian law from the thirteenth century, where reference is made to man taking a woman either for *eiginkóna* ('own(-ed) woman', 'wife') or for *líkamslosti* ('bodily pleasure', 'sex') (*AK*: ch. 27; *NGL*: v. 40). Characteristically, the point of view adopted is wholly male; in the Christian world view female desire is left unspoken, while male needs are acknowledged to the point where the main purpose of marriage is to prevent fornication (Flandrin 1985).

From the male perspective of Bishop Árni Þorláksson the inadmissible women were classified according to degree. The first class contained the mother, sister, daughter, stepmother, son's wife, brother's wife, son's daughter, stepdaughter, brother's daughter, sister's daughter, daughter's daughter, father's mother, mother's mother, mother's sister, father's sister, wife's mother, wife's sister. In Christian law sexual relations within this category were absolutely inadmissible and transgression of the taboo entailed excommunication (people were deemed *friðlaus*), a confession had to be made with the bishop, and they lost all property, half of which would pass to the Church, the other half to the king (*AK*: ch. 27; *NGL*: v. 40). However, the accused could be acquitted through a *tylftareiður* in his favour (ibid.).[7]

This first category of 'forbidden' women contains both consanguine and affinal relatives. In the legislation of the Freestate, these were distinguished by separate terms. *Frændsemisspell* ('kinship spoiling') referred to an incestuous relationship between consanguines, and *sifjaspell* ('affinity spoiling') was incest between affines. In *Jónsbók* no separate clause on incest is found, since this was now a matter for the Christian law, but the traditional social distinction between the consanguine and the affinal relationships was generally maintained in these matters (*Jónsbók*: 22, 83).

The second category of forbidden relations contained women at one further remove, and comprised first cousins among others. The taboo could be broken by *líkamslosti* ('sex'), only, since marriage in the sense of an officially recognized union was unfeasible. If a man had intercourse with a first cousin he would be fined $4\frac{1}{2}$ *merkr* (to be paid to the bishop) and compelled to confess to the bishop (*AK*: ch. 27; *NGL*: v. 40). The third (and last) grade of incest involved *prímenningar* ('relatives in the third degree'), and the offence was punishable by a fine of 3 *merkr* and a confession (ibid.). The confession is not further qualified in this case, and we can assume that it was to be taken by the local priest.

Sexual relations with the forbidden degrees were thus internally distinguished, and the offences could be more or less easily redressed. Outside the boundary set by the *prímenningar*, more distant relatives were available for sex or marriage. This was established as common canon law after 1217, until when Icelandic law had forbidden sexual relations between kinsmen related up to the fifth degree. Even within the more narrow boundary of third-degree relations, however, the Church often administered the law rather liberally.

The *stóridómur* of 1564 was an attempt to stop this sexual 'liberalism'. The *stóridómur* explicitly refers, in matters of incest, to 'ancient Church-law', and makes almost the same distinctions between categories of the offence. The first category is defined as before, but the sentences were new; sex between relatives of the first category was now punishable by death: men were beheaded, and women drowned (*LI*: i. 85–6). Further, half the culprit's estate was confiscated by the king, who, by his grace and mercy, let the legal heirs have the other half.

The second and third categories of relatives with whom sexual and marital relations were forbidden were defined as before, if slightly more specified. The sentences were graded according to the number of offences committed. Punishment itself was modernized, now including blows with a stick and flogging in addition to fines. In a sense, the advent of the *stóridómur* is less of a change in the legal codification of proper sexuality than it is a change in context and in the discourse on sexuality. The reference made to the ancient Christian law in the *stóridómur*, and its demarcation of similar prohibitions clearly demonstrate this. With the Reformation, however, the context and the rhetoric of power had changed. The Church was replaced by the king, excommunication by decapitation, confession by flogging.

The legal definition of the moral order was, of course, not always quite matched by social practice. The Church was always rather liberal, and absolved sinners; even with the *stóridómur* the king had the power to allow people who were related in the third (and fourth) degrees to marry (*LI*: i. 87). The people themselves showed even less respect for the law, and incestuous relations as defined by this law were frequent. In the period 1641–50, for which a quantitative analysis has been made, a total of 113 cases of incest were brought before the court (Þorgeir Kjartansson 1982: 10). Such was the general picture of the seventeenth century. Even incestous relations of the first degree, between father and daughter (and stepdaughter) or brother and sister, were not rare. In the oral tradition, brother–sister relations were a popular motif; while they were pitied (because they had to flee to the uninhabited regions to avoid the law) they were not morally condemned, to judge from the tone of the stories.[8]

Among the cases of father–daughter incest, one from the late fifteenth century is particularly famous. In 1480 some people bore testimony to the fact that Bjarni Ólason of Hvassafell in Eyjafjörður had had intercourse with his daughter when she was only 13 years old, and this testimony was repeated to the bishop by some priests (*DI*: vi. 297). Later it was followed up by yet another testimony to the two having lain naked in bed under the same cover (ibid.: 289). A month later, four priests stood forward and reported having heard Bjarni saying—in the presence of the bishop—that he had lain with his daughter Randidi so many times that he could not tell (ibid.: 301). A court of twelve priests was set. The verdict, to which lay and clerical power both agreed, sent Bjarni to prison—and the case was to be pursued according to traditional clerical laws (ibid.: 302–4). Caught and put into custody at the See of Hólar, Bjarni admitted having slept with his daughter, now 15 years old, and he asked for mercy, promising to observe the rules of the Church ever after (ibid.: 308). Testimonies continued to pile up against him, and his property was sequestrated by the king's representatives (ibid.: 341–56). The clerical court ratified this (ibid.: 355–6), although a new verdict was passed on the king's part, admitting the rights of the heirs (ibid.: 365–6). The wife of Bjarni had legal claims, and later evidence shows that she did not lose anything (in terms of real estate) in the deal.[9]

In the judicial institutions the case continued. Bjarni's offence was difficult to ignore, even though technical details of his intercourse with Randidi were provided, so as to mitigate the gravity of his offence. First, when Randidi was only 13, Bjarni had just 'tried her' with his little finger, and she was 14 before he had actually penetrated her, and then only half-way. Also, Bjarni claimed, he had never let the semen out in her, but in his hand. When asked why, he explained it as a contraceptive device (ibid.: 372). If this showed some degree of consideration on his part, it was not enough for Bjarni to escape the charge of incest.

The main remaining problem was whether Randidi should be tried as well. She had been excommunicated by the bishop, but taken into custody by Hrafn *lögmaður* Brandsson. It is not clear whether he took her as a mistress as well as a ward; according to Espolín: *Rafn héldt Randydi á heimili sinu, sem fyrr, oc samneytti henni sem ósekum manni* ('Rafn kept Randidi in his home as before, and "used" her like a non-convict' (Espolín: ii. 98). The term *samneyta* refers to the sharing of a meal, but also has some implicit sexual associations. Hrafn used the case as a way of formulating his opposition to Ólafr *biskup* Rögnvaldsson. At the Althing in the year 1481, the so-called Hvassafellsmál was a major issue, since it came to symbolic conflict between clerical and secular power. Originally excommunicated, Randidi was allowed to swear herself free by *tylftareiður* (the jury consisting of twelve women). She stated her innocence, arguing that she had simply been the powerless object of her father's desire (*DI*: vi. 377–8); she was acquitted.

When Hrafn suggested that Bjarni should be allowed the same privilege of *tylftareiður*, this was felt to be going a bit far, although Bjarni actually won the oath (ibid.: 378). Both defendants, the *lögmaður* and the *biskup*, made up their separate statements of the case, and no final solution was reached (ibid.: 379–84). The bishop then collected new evidence, and sent the case to the Archbishop of Nidaros, who reacted by banning Hrafn for having violated Church regulations (ibid.: 404–7). Bjarni was urged to leave the country, but there is no evidence that he did. On the contrary he continues to appear in various documents, as if he had never been sentenced at all (see, for example, *DI*: vi. 524). The case continued to lurk under the surface, and in 1491, for instance, ten years after the major court verdicts at the *Althing*, a certain priest was suddenly excommunicated, and his property confiscated, because he had sworn false oath in Bjarni's case (ibid.: 735). More remarkable is the fact that as late as 1574, in a court case of inheritance involving Randidi's grandchildren, somebody suggested that their claims should be forfeit because of her crime. The grandchildren won the case, on the basis of Randidi's acquittal (*AÍ*: i. 242 ff.). The popular recollection is extraordinary, and bears witness to the small scale of the society.

It is of some note that the *lögmaður* was prepared to tolerate incest in the first degree, in order to manifest his opposition to the clerical

authority structure. In Hvassafellsmál the double standard of jurisdiction was perhaps more conspicuous than in any other court case
concerning a sexual offence. The case also illustrates the arbitrary
nature of the legal process. The institution of *tylftareiður* was obviously
open to manipulation, as Bjarni's acquittal demonstrates; he was
acquitted by *tylftareiður* in spite of his own admission of guilt. Bjarni's
social status was important here, for he was a prosperous *bóndi*. The
structurally 'muted' groups of small-scale peasants and landless
tenants were less likely to provide a focus of conflict between clerical
and secular courts. Bjarni, indeed, was already marked as an opponent
of the clerical authorities, having been involved in a court case against
the monastery of Munkaþverá over rights to strandings; that was in
1477, and the agreement reached favoured the monastery (*DI*: vi.
107–8).

In studying social and administrative responses to incest, then,
Hvassafellsmál is thus particularly instructive. As an example of the
violation of sexual taboos, however, the case was not unique. The
recorded cases of *frændsemisspell* in varying degrees are more numerous after the *stóridómur*, and the nature of the sources accounts in part
for this. Another reason was that traditionally the concept of *legorð*
comprised all kinds of illicit sexual behaviour, which in the Middle
Ages made of incest a rather shadowy phenomenon. Generally,
authority in matters of the social organization of sexuality was in the
hands of the clerics until the Reformation; the clerics, partly due to
their own fallibility, seem to have become increasingly permissive.
The notion of sex as distinct from marriage was part of the cultural and
clerical heritage, as we have seen from Bishop Árni's Christian Law.
After the *stóridómur*, incest was more conspicuous, and a regularized
feature of the sexual order. Incest, even in the first degree, appeared
again and again in the courts.

It has been argued by Claude Lévi-Strauss that the incest taboo is
what distinguishes humanity from the rest of the animal world. The
incest taboo is universal in human society, and its establishment
marked the step from nature to culture (Lévi-Strauss 1949). Rodney
Needham questioned this on the grounds that even the universal
phenomenon of social rules for sexual behaviour is subject to
cultural (conceptual) transformation according to particular
standards (1971). According to Needham, 'incest' hardly exists; what
is found is a variety of taboos on sexual behaviour. As far as I
am able to judge, the two points of view rather complement than

contradict each other, and when reading the Icelandic case both should be kept in mind.

The Icelanders had rules regulating sexual conduct, among which were quite clear demonstrations of 'forbidden' relations. They also had a judicial structure, which laid down rules that were, in principle, unambiguous. In actual practice things were different; the Icelanders regularly transgressed the legal rules, and the authorities would turn a blind eye. Perhaps due to the double standard of jurisdiction, 'incest' fell through the net originally spun by the social organization of sexuality. The gap between the two authority structures allowed for an increasing 'permissiveness' in the field of sexual relations. The Reformation closed this gap, and the *stóridómur* was an attempt to revert to a single standard—a standard of strict ruling rather than permissiveness. It was followed by one royal decree after another. These, along with the court cases, bear witness to an extreme disorder in the social organization of sexuality.

The disorganization was correlated with an increasing unwillingness on the part of mothers to tell who the fathers of their illegitimate children were. This may point to an increasing indifference to matters of kinship. *Ættleiðing* ('introduction into the paternal *ætt*') had traditionally been very important. The social status of any individual would depend on it, as would inheritance; by the sixteenth and seventeenth centuries, however, this seems to have been of less importance. In 1612 the king tried to oblige women to confess the name of the genitors of their illegitimate children, by issuing a law allowing for mild torture; the suspicion was voiced that the reason for their silence was that the children were the results of incestuous relations (*AÍ*: iv. 185–7). This suspicion may not have been totally unwarranted. While the community would 'cover up' the cases, the king wanted them dealt with according to the law, so that immoral persons could be duly prosecuted.

Incestuous women were drowned as a consequence of their offence. They had at least one escape, however. There is not much evidence of this in actual court cases, but there is at least one example in the annals of an extraordinary acquittal of the accused woman. *Ein kvinna ól barn og kendi huldumanni, sú kom til alþingis, stóð á sama* ('A woman got a child by a *huldumaður* [a man of the 'hidden people'], came to the Althing and maintained that vehemently' (Skarðsárannáll 1624; *Ann.*: i. 218)). Possibly due to her success in maintaining this, in 1625 the king once again felt compelled to stress the necessity for inclemency regarding women who refused to reveal the fathers of their children; if they continued to refuse they had to be sent to Copenhagen for proper punishment (*LI*: i. 211–12).

Incest, now also referred to by the Danish term *blodskam* or by the comprehensive notion of *ketterie* ('heresy'), did not disappear, however. The taboo was often broken and cases brought before the court were likely to be severely dealt with. In 1671 a man, having begotten a child by his stepdaughter chose to take his own life rather than be publicly executed (*Ann.*: ii. 227, 451, 500). This allowed the daughter to maintain that she had been taken against her will, and she escaped prosecution (ibid.). Year after year cases of incest are recorded; in some years they virtually abound. For instance, in 1705 no fewer than six people lost their lives on this account: three men were beheaded and three women drowned at the Althing because of incestuous relations; to add to this, a fourth woman was drowned for having had a child by a married man, who himself succeeded in escaping (Vallaannáll 1705; *Ann.*: i. 471–2).

Gradually, during the Enlightenment, social practice contributed to changes in the law, and in 1770 a royal decree admitted of new definitions in matters of sexual relations in Iceland. Referring to the old laws, according to which marriage had been forbidden in second- and third-degree relations (even if possible in the third degree after application for dispensation), the king issued a general permission of marriage in these degrees 'to save the expenses and time required for such an application' (*LI*: iii. 692–3). From then onwards marriage between first and second cousins was allowed, and by the same stroke a widower was permitted to marry his deceased wife's sister, or her sister's daughter. Otherwise, the rules of forbidden relations remained the same (ibid.). At long last, it seems, legislation partly caught up with social practice. So far, Needham's argument of the rules and regulations of incest being a culture-specific concept and not a universal seems perfectly valid (Needham 1971: 24ff.). Notions or concepts are always embedded in a particular historical context, and are likely to change with history. In that sense, the 'abundance' of incestuous relations in Iceland in the sixteenth and seventeenth centuries is so only in relation to what were already outdated rules, and it may be doubted whether we can speak of 'incest' at all from the perspective of the collective representations of the ordinary Icelanders. It is certainly also a question whether the Icelandic case was unique by comparative European standards.

However, we are still left with a number of cases of sexual relations between primary consanguine relatives. Thus, the allegedly universal incest taboo, or the prime marker of humanity in Lévi-Strauss's terms, seems to have been disregarded in Iceland in the period under consideration, as it may have been elsewhere. By their sexual behaviour, at least some Icelanders questioned one of the basic features of human society, the exchange of spouses.[10] There were other reasons than sexual for the apparent irrelevance of alliance, as we saw in the discussion of landownership (above, Ch. 4).

While it is difficult to assess the actual number and frequency of cases, we have enough evidence to suggest that during the entire period the incest taboo was under some attack from social practice. By keeping sexuality 'within the family', so to speak, the most important means of social integration was ignored. We do not know why that was, but a seventeenth-century Icelander gives us a clue. Guðmundur Andrésson formulated a general protest, *Discursus Oppositivus*, against the *stóridómur* and indirectly against the royal rulings (Jakob Benediktsson 1948). He invoked the law of 1253 which gave God's law primacy over man's law in case of discrepancy between them (ibid.: 15; cf. *DI*: ii. 1). *Stóridómur* conflicted with God's law, he argued, and he listed a number of discrepancies. First, the limits of incest were too wide; nieces were not prohibited in God's law, for instance (Jakob Benediktsson 1954 8: 24). Marrying a deceased wife's sister ought likewise to be allowed (ibid.: 25), and on the whole the natural love between kinsmen should be held in esteem (ibid.: 28). Even for incest in the first degree, the punishment was far too severe. Life sentences should be completely avoided; no man had the right to take another man's life. Life was given by God, and only he could reclaim it (ibid.: 24).

Guðmundur Andrésson also argued that the definition of fornication given in the *stóridómur* conflicted with both God's law and ancient Icelandic practice. *Frillulífi*, he argued could be just as moral as marriage, and a man and woman could choose to cohabit in mutual affection; institutionalized marriage was no precondition for a legitimate relationship (ibid.: 34ff.). Details from biblical texts were used as evidence of the unnatural foundations of the *stóridómur*, and the general question raised

who knows better than God himself about the most righteous way to live? I know so much that it is neither the bishop in Rome, the pope, nor some

Icelandic prelates, and least of all is it 24 un-learned lay-persons down south at Öxará. (ibid.: 19.)

Öxará is a name for the Althing, which the author clearly despises.

Discursus Oppositivus argued a strong case for reform in the regulation of sexuality; it was also an Icelandic voice (albeit formulated in a curious mixture of Icelandic, Danish, and Latin) raised against a foreign legislation. Morality should be defined by internal Icelandic standards, and by God's. Both of these have scope for mercy in sexual offences.

So, if sexual relations were founded in love and mutual respect, they were not necessarily immoral, even if they were between relatives; such was Guðmundur Andrésson's view at a time when the *ætt*, the kin group, had lost meaning among the common Icelandic people. It was still a significant institution among the highest class of landowners, but in other social spheres it had dwindled in importance. If there were no *ætt*, no kin group, then there were no kin-group boundaries to be transgressed, which entailed the revision of the boundaries of incestuous relations as we have observed. The absence of the *ætt* also ruled out, except among the highest social classes, an ancient aspect of Icelandic social structure—exchange and mutual alliance between kin groups.

PROCREATION

A necessary minimum condition for social reproduction is the recruitment of new members to society. Procreation is a means to this end; the continuation of the species may appear a 'natural' propensity of mankind, but ways of achieving this continuity are as heavily culturalized as anything else. In this sense, patterns of procreation are not only preconditions for the reproduction of particular social systems, they are also consequences.

The Icelandic population only barely regenerated itself. In 1402–4 the Black Death took a heavy toll and the population hardly recovered until the late nineteenth century. It has been widely discussed whether the European plague disrupted the normal order of history at all, and whether it was a welcome check on too-prolific populations (see, for example, Carpenter 1962). Questions on this scale cannot be answered in brief, and suffice it to note that in Iceland it seems that ever since

1402 the population was stagnant and even in a more or less permanent state of reduction. This is the long-term perspective of our period; in the short term, there were striking fluctuations due to epidemics and other catastrophes. The first census of 1703 shows a population in decline (Gísli Gunnarsson 1980*a*: 5–6; Hajnal 1965: 137). Contemporary observers were worried about this decline of Icelandic society (Jochumssen 1977: *passim*). We know that a smallpox epidemic in 1703 reduced the population from *c.*50,000 to *c.*35,000; and it is probable that the population size varied within these limits during most of our period.[11] Tomasson speaks of a 'millenium of misery' (1977), and states that 'the population of Iceland saw no sustained growth from after the Black Death (1404) until the end of the 1820s' (1980: 68).

Demographic features are both causes and consequences of particular social structures (Godelier 1975: 5; Harrison and Boyce 1972: 1). They are also to some extent consequences of features outside the social structure, and few will deny that the Icelanders have had their turn with the elements. Starvation and death followed natural catastrophe, and, as elsewhere in Europe, there was a link between climatic change and population fluctuation which was not concordant with the simple Malthusian view that population is the active factor and the environment the passive one (Utterström 1955: 3). However, we also know that people more or less subconsciously could redress changes in population by changes in morality—already in pre-modern times (Utterström 1954: 159); they could even avert demographic crisis by administrative measures (Sogner 1976). Mortality crises, and these were a fundamental characteristic of the demographic structure of pre-industrial society (ibid.: 114), could be outweighed by changing rates of nuptiality and fertility, although there was rarely any 'direct link between reproductive behaviour and contemporary events' (Macfarlane 1978: 100). In looking at these matters in the Icelandic context, therefore, we must first let the data speak for themselves.

To be a full member of Icelandic society one had to be born in wedlock. Illegitimate offspring appear in the *erfðatal* ('law of inheritance') in *Jónsbók*, but their rights are inferior to a whole range of other consanguine relatives (78–86). Clearly, this is a consequence of the ancient ideology of the *ætt* ('kin group') and its alienable relationship to the land (Hastrup 1985*a*: 202–4). Rules of *ættleiðing* ('leading into *ætt*') existed; in the legislation of the Freestate these referred primarily to the establishment of paternity (ibid.: 73), while in *Jónsbók* they were explicitly concerned with establishing a new order of inheritance. To *ættleiða* someone, the assent of the otherwise closest heirs was required (*Jónsbók* 87–8). Illegitimate children were not the only ones who could profit from this; distant relatives of other kinds could also make steps up the ladder of inheritance in this way. The comparison between the old and the new concepts of 'coming into *ætt*' suggests that the semantics of kinship had changed from an emphasis on group affiliation to an emphasis of economy.

Marriage was still the only legitimate framework for procreation, although the laws of inheritance had little meaning for the majority of poor people. This may have been one reason for Guðmundur Andrésson's suggestion that legitimacy and the institution of marriage should be redefined. Within the landed class, however, marriage was important because 'kinship' was still an important means of transmitting status and property. The case of Loftur Guttormsson will illustrate this.

We met Loftur in the previous section as the alleged author of *Háttalykill*, the love-poem composed for his mistress. Here we meet him again as a married man, and compare the consequences of his two relationships. Three illegitimate sons and one love-poem were the outcome of his first union, while three sons and one daughter resulted from the second. The two broods had different positions in the laws of inheritance. Illegitimate children could be given legal 'gifts' as a kind of compensation for the lack of inheritance. In this case Loftur made a *gjafabréf* ('gift-letter') in 1430 to meet this. He gave his three illegitimate sons three 'hundreds' each and added: *svo skipa ég mínum löglegum erfingjum, að ómagi skal fæðast ævinlega á öllum þeim höfuðbólum, er þeir erfa eftir mig* ('I demand of my legal heirs that a dependant is to be permanently catered for at all the main farms that they inherit from me' (*DI*: iv. 404–6; Magnús Már Lárusson 1970: 47)).

This *gjafabréf* is the first one to use the notion of *höfuðból* ('main farm'), which is known also from *Jónsbók*. As we saw in a previous chapter the notion of *höfuðból* implied an inalienable relationship to the land. Only among the upper strata did social reproduction imply a continuity of this relationship. For tenants, the location of their *bú* was of less moment; there is evidence that they were geographically very mobile (Björn Teitsson and Magnús Stefánsson 1972: 177). For Loftur, however, it was important not to alienate his illegitimate sons completely from his estate (*höfuðból*), which by law was to go to the sons (*Jónsbók*: 78). He had sired six sons, but only three had a definite position in the cycle of social reproduction. Before the Reformation, 'marriage' itself was open to some interpretation. There were originally three steps in the process of establishing a marriage; negotiation between the man and the legal guardian of the woman, betrothal, and the wedding itself (Björn Björnsson 1971: 41–6). The two first steps were outside the control of the Church, although the Church was prepared to recognize betrothal as a legal union. Children born after the contract of betrothal were considered legitimate (*AK*: ch. 23; *NGL*: v. 37). Guðmundur Andrésson clearly felt, from this perspective, that the restrictions imposed after the Reformation would be a thorn in the flesh of Icelanders.

The Reformation transferred the ultimate power of interpretation in matters of marriage to the 'State'. The Lutheran doctrine of marriage somewhat paradoxically meant that once again marriage became (also) a worldly affair (Björn Björnsson 1971: 21–5). The ordinance of 1537, which inaugurated the new era in Denmark, was accepted by the Icelandic Althing in 1541 for the southern diocese, and in 1551 for the northern (*LI*: i. 43–54). New rules for marriage and related matters were established. A piece of writing from the last Catholic bishop in the southern diocese suggests that reform was timely; in a letter to his colleague in the north, he wrote—that the holy union in sixteenth-century Iceland was under the most severe attack since it was first instituted by God in Paradise (*DI*: x. 600).

In 1552 an *alþingissamþykkt* ('agreement of the Althing') on marriage was passed: first, the prohibited degrees should be strictly observed; secondly, the clergy should ban cohabitation between persons for whom public announcement (*lýsing*) of their union had not been made three times, and who had not been betrothed and married immediately after with the consent of the parents (*DI*: xii. 439). Betrothal and marriage were conflated (temporally), and the earlier status of betrothal was completely changed. Sexual intercourse was now forbidden until the full process of marriage had been completed.

Although marriage was now formally a secular affair, a way for an ecclesiastical rule was paved by this agreement (Björn Björnsson 1971: 51). This was further substantiated by a decree of 1559, which adduced the old Christian law of 1275 'which in many places is still useful in matters of marriage' (*DI*: viii. 432). Meanwhile the Icelanders continued to take sex and marriage lightly, and in 1560 the king asked the Icelandic bishops for advice (*DI*: xiii. 480). The bishops produced an answer akin to the decree of 1559, and asked to be relieved from giving any final opinion on the matter (ibid.: 497). The final outcome of this dialogue was the *stóridómur* (1564), including all its foreign elements. In 1587 a law about marriage and divorce was finally passed (*LI*: i. 113–24).

Marriage was still the only legal framework for sexual relations and procreation. It could be dissolved, however. Grounds for divorce were fornication, desertion, and impotence (this last if it had preceded marriage and been kept secret from the wife). If impotence occurred at a later stage, the married couple had to bear the cross (ibid.: 121–2). These rules were in force until 1824, but they were not strictly followed either by the priests or the people. In 1746 another decree was given concerning the observance of the marriage laws in Iceland (*LI*: ii. 600–5).

The census of 1703 shows that only 27.8 per cent of women in the fertile age group between 15 and 49 years were married; women, moreover, married late (*Manntalið* 1960: 48–50). The marriage ratio was 'staggeringly low even for a European population' (Hajnal 1965: 137), although delayed marriage was no exception in pre-industrial Europe (Macfarlane 1986). The marriage pattern was related to the possibility of setting up independent households, the composition of which is telling. In the 1703 census some 20 per cent of the 50,358 Icelanders are registered as *vinnufólk* ('servants/labourers'). Another 13 per cent are paupers that were apportioned to households by the parish (cf. Tomasson 1980: 77).

Whatever the reason, we find a ratio of unmarried persons, which is striking—both when compared to Iceland one century later and to the other Nordic countries (see Table 13). Servants and farmhands were

TABLE 13. *Unmarried Persons Aged 20–49 in the Nordic Countries* (thousands)

		Age (men/women)			
		20–9	30–9	40–9	20–49
Iceland	1703	94.1/88.5	53.4/53.6	28.7/41.9	61.6/62.3
Iceland	1801	70.2/67.8	23.0/34.1	10.7/25.7	39.3/45.2
Denmark	1801	78.9/62.1	26.2/18.3	8.9/7.9	40.7/32.7
Norway		73.3/64.5	22.6/26.7	8.7/15.3	38.1/38.6
Sweden		70.3/64.2	21.2/24.7	8.1/13.4	36.4/36.1

Source: Based on Loftur Guttormsson 1983a: 114.

not supposed to marry, nor, for that matter, to reproduce. This was not unique to Iceland, but was a common European experience (Mitterauer and Sieder 1982: 122–3). Others could also be excluded from marital union on grounds of poverty, as we have seen (above, Ch. 3). Only those people who could set up an independent household and could cater for their children were expected to marry and to procreate. In the documents, however, there are occasional hints that this ideology was not strictly observed in practice. Thus in *Búalög* there is a passage about wages, to be *8 alnir fyrir vermann og þá konu, sem hefur barn á brjósti* ('eight ellens for fishermen and for that woman who has a child at her breast' (1915–22: 162, 186, 191, 218)). On the whole, in the eighteenth century, there was a low illegitimacy rate in Iceland when compared to the nineteenth and twentieth centuries (cf. Gísli Gunnarsson 1980a; Tomasson 1976; 1980: 86 ff.). In our period a high illegitimacy rate was not a self-evident consequence of delayed marriage (cf. Goody 1983: 192).

We have very few direct sources on the population structure before 1700, but we can make at least some inferences about household and family structure from the 1703 census. A household was usually centred upon a married couple, and comprised their children and servants, and perhaps one other relative, and a pauper. In 1703, 55.7 per cent of the population lived in households of between four and seven persons; 10.6 per cent lived in smaller households, while 33.7 per cent lived in households of more than eight persons (Loftur Guttormsson 1983a: 98).[12] There is no indication that families with a greater number of grown children had fewer *vinnufólk* (ibid.). The age structure of children and *vinnufólk* is revealing: Table 14 suggests that a good proportion of children left home on their marriage, which usually took place in their late twenties. Joint households comprising two generations of married couples were very rare. The table also suggests that service was one stage in life for many people (ages 15–34), and two stages for others (15–34 and over 40), with years of married life in between, perhaps. 'Life-cycle servants' have been reported from many parts of Europe (Hajnal 1982: 473); in England service seems to have embraced a good many years of childhood as well (Macfarlane 1986: 82 ff.). In Iceland lifetime servants were also of statistical significance and correlated with the low marriage ratio.

There is a logic to the correlation between late marriage and the absence of joint households. Late marriage meant that parents did not survive their children's marriage for very long, in contrast to early age

TABLE 14. *Age-Structure of Children, Domestic Servants, and Farm-hands in 1703* (Total Population 50,358)

Age	Children of household head (total 16,537) (%)	*Vinnufólk* (total 8,953) (%)
0–14	64.2	0.9
15–34	34.3	67.7
35–9	0.8	9.9
over 40	0.6	20.8
Unknown	0.1	0.7

Source: Loftur Guttormsson 1983*a*: 83.

marriage systems which favours two-generational households (Hajnal 1982: 468). Age at marriage is thus a crucial variable in household composition (ibid.: 450).

Households in Iceland were not mainly 'families', as is illustrated by Table 15. We note here that the ratio of servants declined between 1703 and 1729, but this is probably a temporary consequence of the great smallpox epidemic in 1707–9. Otherwise the servant ratio went

TABLE 15. *Persons per 100 Households, Classified by Relationship to Head in 1703 and 1729*

	1703			1729		
	Male	Female	(Total)	Male	Female	(Total)
Married heads	69	69	138	78	73	156
Other heads	17	14	31	14	8	22
Children	100	102	202	111	112	223
Other relatives	11	27	38	5	7	12
Servants	52	66	118	31	61	92
Others (including paupers)	30	57	87	21	42	63
TOTAL	279	335	(614)	260	308	(568)

Source: Hajnal 1982: 485.

on increasing until the late nineteenth century (Guðmundur Jónsson 1981). We also know that during the eighteenth and nineteenth centuries the age of marriage declined (Hajnal 1982). Comparisons with demographic information from other parts of Europe prior to 1700 (which is sparse) makes it reasonable to suggest that for the main part of our period marriage in Iceland was late and at a low ratio, and the typical household was composed of a nuclear family, servants, and dependants.

It has been argued that our ideas of large families in preindustrial Europe are mythical (Mitterauer and Sieder 1982: 24ff.). Detailed local information confirms that in Germany, for instance, the average family in the centuries after the Black Death comprised less than two children (Beuys 1984: 204–5). For Iceland the material is sparse, but we can make some comments about fertility.

In the late sixteenth century Oddur Einarsson wrote that many mothers gave birth to twenty to thirty children 'and I am not talking about the fathers here, who in their 2nd and 3rd marriages get many more' (1971: 85). Two centuries later von Troil notes that 'it is no rare thing to meet with a mother who has had twelve or fifteen children' (1980: 120–1). Eggert Ólafsson echoes this when he says of married couples that they often have ten, twelve, or fifteen children (1772: 451). Successive marriages were probably quite common for both men and women, as we can also infer from the frequent disparity in age between spouses (Tomasson 1980: 77–8). This disparity was due to untimely death, Oddur Einarsson tells. There is no indication that the purpose of marriage was to reach a comfortable widowhood (cf. Macfarlane 1986: 149); households needed the presidency of a married couple. The high mortality rate made successive marriages a logical corollary.

The parish registers from the mid-eighteenth century show that it was not uncommon for a woman to give birth to eight to ten children, or almost one every year in her (relatively late) married life (Loftur Guttormsson 1983a: 136–7; 1983b: 153–4). The 1703 census confirms the pattern of a narrow spacing between births. In spite of this, however, the number of children in the household was relatively small, and the population was stagnant or in decline.

In 1580 Peder Claussøn Friis wrote about the demographic problems of the Icelanders, and attributed these to the Icelanders' aggressive nature. If only they would stop murdering one another in defence of their honour, Iceland would abound in people (Friis 1881: 196). In 1731 Jochumssen explained the continuous demographic crisis as a result of the poverty and bad health of the Icelanders (Jochumssen 1731). Another reason was a high infant mortality rate, which also explains the household composition. It was not until the late nineteenth century that the infant death rate started to decline (Tomasson 1980: 67). During the eighteenth century, when quantitative sources became readily available, the infant mortality rate was about 300 per 1,000 (Loftur Guttormsson 1983*b*: 149; 1983*a*: 147). It may even have been higher, given a probable under-registration of peri-natal mortality and later evidence of a rate approaching 400 (ibid.; Tomasson 1980: 67). A high ratio of still births also seems to have prevailed (Steffensen 1975: 231 ff.).

The infant mortality rate was compounded by a very high overall mortality. Mothers experienced regular loss of their infants and children at a cruel rate. Sigurður Breiðfjörð (1788–1846) gave a picture of this in a poem, *Móðurin við gröfina*, 'the mother at the grave' (*ÍL*: ii. 275). The grief of the mother is implicitly recognized, but a sensation of relief is also noted: now, with the child in the grave, no pain or sickness could ever touch it again.[13] Eggert Ólafsson of the previous generation was less forbearing about Icelandic mothers. He accused them of an unnatural and near deliberate killing of their young. They hardly knew how to give birth any more, he said, and would rather that their infants died instantly.[14] Possibly mother 'love' is no natural instinct, and children may generally have been considered a nuisance (Badinter 1980); even 'childhood' may be a cultural invention (Ariès 1973). All these points have been contested, and it has been argued that in early modern Europe parents both *wanted* their children and enjoyed their company (Pollock 1983). Whatever the 'truth' of these matters, the imputation that Icelandic mothers killed their offspring warrants closer inspection.

Eggert Ólafsson travelled throughout Iceland for some seven years in the mid-eighteenth cntury, in the company of a young physician. Their commission was to describe the state of affairs in this remote corner of the Danish kingdom (*LI*: iii. 70 ff.). Among their results was an explanation of the disastrous infant mortality rate: it was due to the fact that Icelandic mothers did not breast-feed their children (Eggert Ólafsson 1772: 450–3). This also, perhaps, explains the narrow spacing between births (cf. Lithell 1981; Loftur Guttormsson 1983*b*: 152–5).

Of the twelve to fifteen children born to a married couple, only two or three grew up (Eggert Ólafsson 1772: 450–3). Most died immediately after birth or during their first year, because they were given cow's milk and suffered from severe digestive problems. Those who could afford it even gave the infants cream, untreated like the milk (ibid.). In addition to this children were soon given chewed fish or meat diluted with milk, cream, or butter. While it was clear to Eggert Ólafsson and Bjarni Pálsson that this diet virtually killed the infants, the Icelanders saw no connection, and attributed the deaths to external powers beyond their control (ibid.: 452).

The absence of breast-feeding is noted by many eighteenth-century observers. In 1746 Anderson told that children were breast-fed for only eight days, or perhaps fourteen if they were weak (1746: 117). In his attempt to refute Anderson's general description of Iceland, Horrebow actually confirmed the breast-feeding pattern for 'most' of the mothers (1752: 283-4). Children were left on the earth-floor and fed on milk, bread, and fish, and were generally in poor condition (ibid.). Von Troil echoed this (1780: 120) as did Eggers (1786: 176-7). In a late eighteenth-century medical book by Jón Pétursson, mothers are strongly advised to breast-feed (1834: 15). On the whole, there is evidence that from some time in the sixteenth century until well into the nineteenth century, infants in Iceland were not breast-fed (Jónas Jónasson 1961: 263, 311, 332; Steffensen 1975: 216-34; Sigríður Sigurðardóttir 1982; Loftur Guttormsson 1983*b*: 155 ff.). One of the reasons given by contemporary Icelanders was that the practice was unhealthy (Hannes Finnson, cf. Loftur Guttormsson 1983*b*: 155; Helgi Þorláksson 1986). Parallel cases are known from elsewhere, but never, it seems, over such a long period.[15]

The question remains of why Icelandic mothers did not breast-feed their children for several centuries. Perhaps a change in the religious imagery played some role in this. Until the Reformation, the Virgin Mary had a tremendously important position in popular religious practice, and during the purification rite after childbirth, the women would salute Mary in their local church. In European art Mary was often depicted in the act of suckling the infant Jesus (Warner 1978: ch. 13). Her milk was both a sign of 'nature' and of her magical powers (ibid.: 194 ff.). In Iceland, breast-milk was an important ingredient in magical potions, prescribed in the medical books from before the Reformation (Kålund 1907: 365, 394; Larsen 1931: 91). The destruction of the image of Mary (which also occurred elsewhere) may have some correlation to the abandonment of breast-feeding, although it cannot 'explain' it. Another possible factor is found in the fact that while before the Reformation a mother had been considered 'unclean' for forty days after the birth, after the Reformation she could resume work immediately (Helgi Þorláksson 1986). It seems improbable, though, that the domestic work-load should impede lactation.

We may come closer to a partial explanation if we concentrate on the alternative diet: cow's milk, cream, and butter. Horrebow says: 'the mothers never give their children whey but feed them on good cow's milk, into which cream is even poured by some people, so that it becomes fatter and in their opinion better' (1752: 283–4). This is the clue; in comparison with breast milk, cow's was better, and cream the best. Says Eggers: 'Many people believe that they do their children a favour by giving them cream instead of milk; they want them to eat fat' (1786: 77). In this country of farming and of ancient peasant values, the measure of wealth was one of farm produce. Cream and butter were tokens of success, and in all likelihood they became images of the most potent food item in a country stricken by increasing poverty. A verse from the eighteenth century confirms this:

> *Ef þu étr ekki smjer*
> *eða það sem matur er,*
> *dugr allr drepst i þér*
> *danskr Íslendingr*
>
> (Eggert Ólafsson
> 1832*b*: 198.)

(If you do not eat butter, or something else which is food, all doughtiness will be killed in you, Danish Icelander.)

Foreign food-habits were to be avoided, and butter gave strength to both body and soul. When very young children were given solid food like fish, this was mixed with butter, if it was available (Eggers 1786: 77). In doing the best for their children, and in (socially) reproducing the ancient honour-and-butter values, biological reproduction was actually imperilled.

There may have been other factors at work here, including foreign influence (Sigríður Sigurðardóttir 1982: 29; Loftur Guttormsson 1983*b*: 156; Helgi Þorláksson 1986). However, I believe that no explanation can avoid the consideration of a particular Icelandic mentality, expressing itself in a demographically irrational behaviour. The praises offered by the poet Bjarni Gissurarson (1621–1712) to the products of the land testifies to the high evaluation of farming. When he tells how *mjólkurbrunnurinn margar kýr | mettar börnin smáu* ('the well of milk from many cows | satisfies the young children' (*ÍL*: ii. 80)) his testimonial reaches further—into the somewhat sinister reality of infant mortality and the 'un-natural' ways of Icelandic mothers, so greatly deplored by Eggert Ólafsson. Unnatural it may have been, but the absence of breast-feeding was closely tied up with cultural values (cf. Hastrup 1989*a*). Culturally speaking, children were certainly not unwelcome (cf. Helgi Þorláksson 1986); nor was their death generally a relief. Maternal love was keenly felt, as the following brief note in Kjósárannáll shows: *drukknaði barn í Laxá . . . en móðirin missti vitið, og dó skömmu síðar* ('A child drowned in Laxá . . . and the mother lost her senses and died shortly after' (*Ann.*: ii. 426)).

Some children survived of course. On account of poverty, some mothers would occasionally revert to breast milk, and their infants were less likely to die (Eggert Ólafsson 1772: 451). On the other hand, the very poverty which was beneficial in the first few months of life could eventually prove fatal. But how was the new life itself received? There seem to have been few secular rites for welcoming a new child. Sometimes a birth would occasion a social event of beer-drinking and communal feasting; such events seem to have been rare, however, at least when compared to the extensive *barnsöl*-rites in Denmark (Árni Björnsson 1981). *Barnsöl* (lit. 'child's beer') was a women's feast, where the 'midwives' and helpers, as well as the women of the neighbourhood, shared the pleasure of a new life created. Everybody would bring some item of food, and the mutual bonds of community life were thus re-enacted at all births. In Iceland this seems not to have occurred, although a certain amount of mutual coffee-drinking is recorded from the late nineteenth and early twentieth centuries (ibid.: 21–2).

Barnsöl is found also in some earlier sources. When the 'true' ownership to the estate of Vatnsfjörður had to be established in 1475, the document produced tells us how this farm had been given by Björn Þorleifsson to his daughter Solveig at the occasion of her *barnsöl* (*DI*: v. 777). The 'function' of *barnsöl* in this case is to document ownership of a particular estate, which was *publicly* transferred at a social event. As we know, Björn's estate was far from common, and possibly child-birth was always more lavishly celebrated among the prosperous families. At the other end of our period, and possibly also at the opposite end of the social scale, we encounter *barnsöl* as an occasion for excessive drinking of liquor (*brennivín*); this practice was strongly despised and had to be prevented in the future (as seen from 1746; see

LI: ii. 602). In between these two sources, there is little direct evidence of any separate secular social events occurring at the birth of a child.

Baptism was important, however, and would often entail some feasting; it was legally compulsory within five days of birth, or within seven days after 1746 (*AK*: ch. 8; *NGL*: v. 20; *LI*: ii. 606). In winter, and in the more isolated areas, where priests were not at hand, the rite could not always be duly performed. In that case, as in an emergency, parents had to baptize the child themselves (*AK*: ch. 8). The christening rite incorporated the new-born into society; a child could not be registered unless baptized and named. Worse still, children dying before baptism, and in particular those born in secrecy and deliberately killed, could turn into ghost-children, in Iceland known as *útburðir* (Almqvist 1978: 109). If a ghost-child came to haunt a particular place, this could only be stopped by subjecting the ghost-child to the ritual of baptism (this was true anywhere in the West-Nordic area). The naming-rite was essential, and the ghost-child would be baptized Guðrún or Jón (or variations thereof) (ibid.:P 110–11; cf. *AK*: ch. 8). Identity was linked to a name, and without it a child could not even find a proper death.

New-born children were not alone in having to be ritually incorporated into society. Mothers, too, had to go through a rite of incorporation; the ritual 'churching' restored a woman's purity and allowed her back into ordinary (Church) life. Churching was a common practice in both Catholic and Lutheran countries in our period. In Iceland it is first mentioned in 1224, when a distinction between married and unmarried mothers was made (*DI*: i. 448, 460). In 1292 the rite was required to happen between three weeks and one month after birth (*DI*: ii. 280). In 1323 the rite was further elaborated, with unmarried mothers now excluded from the rite altogether (ibid.: 529–30).[16] After the Reformation Danish practice was followed, in accordance with the writings of Peder Palladius.

Some children dying before christening were actually deliberately killed. In ancient times, *barnaútburður* ('disposal of new-born'), was practised, but this ended with the coming of Christianity.[17] It has been suggested that the abandonment of breast-feeding in the seventeenth and eighteenth centuries might be a discrete reintroduction of *barnaútburður* in times of crisis (cf. Helgi Þorláksson 1986: 79). Considering that the children were offered the best of household produce, however, this conclusion can hardly be justified.

The intentional killing of new-born is recorded mainly for children

resulting from incestuous unions. Filtering through even the sparse
prose of the Annals, such events tell their own sad story of women's
fear. In 1695 two cases of father–daughter incest which had resulted in
children were brought before the court. In both cases the (double)
fathers fled, while the mothers were sentenced to drowning, one of
them on account both of incest and child murder (*Ann.*: i. 43). A
lengthier and no less tragic story from about 1630 is told about a young
woman, apparently sick, somewhat disturbed mentally and obviously
pregnant. She came wandering to a certain Ólöf, and denied
vehemently that she was pregnant. She was taken into the house of
Ólöf, but when her time came, she would let no one get near her;
alone, she gave birth to twins, whom she killed; after a few days she
herself died (ibid.: 233; 326; Espolín: v. 48). One of the Annalists, Björn
of Skarðsá, adds: 'may the good God free us from all the Devil's
power', thereby suggesting that evil was involved (*Ann.*: i. 233).

   To conclude this section on reproduction, we can say that as far as
social reproduction was concerned, there was no social system to be
reproduced beyond the household. For biological reproduction, the
recruitment of new members to the household was conditioned by
marriage. The marriage ratio was low, but within the conjugal relationship the fertility rate was high. However, the high fertility rate was
counterbalanced by a very high infant-mortality rate, and a large
number of still-births (Jón Steffensen 1975: 232). The infant-mortality
rate was related to the absence of breast-feeding for much of the post-
Reformation period. Thus, even if married women were constantly
either pregnant or in a state of post-partum impurity, few of their
children would grow up to maturity. Increasing poverty, combined
with an unbroken tradition of honour-and-butter peasant values, must
be our main candidates to explain the continuing stagnation of biological reproduction.

LITERACY

It has been figuratively suggested that a population is created by
numbering, while a 'people' is created by naming (Ardener 1974;
1975*a*). For a people to reproduce, the name has to be constantly
refilled with meaning. The distinctiveness of culture has to be
permanently rumoured, just as the 'social' and the 'human' have to be
differentiated from the non-social and the non-human.

Language and literature are important aspects of this process of re-creation. In this section I shall deal mainly with literature. This will not be a literary history; rather, I try to give an idea of the different kinds of literature, and the matters of literacy, in order to elucidate the range of the literary images. A few words about language are necessary also.

Icelandic has its roots in the common Scandinavian language of Old Norse, with its separate development beginning in the early Middle Ages. In the mid-twelfth century, the *First Grammatical Treatise* distinguished Icelandic from the other Nordic languages, and this was one of the preconditions for an Icelandic ethnic identity (Hastrup 1982). By about 1400, Norwegian and Icelandic probably diverged so much that they were no longer mutually intelligible. This may be inferred from the fact that by 1400 the export of Icelandic books to Norway had stopped (Stefán Karlsson 1979: 17). From then on language and literature were distinctly Icelandic.

Icelandic has been characterized as a language of very slow and small change compared to the other Scandinavian tongues (Haugen 1976: 332–3). This is certainly true for the syntactic and morphological features of language, while the phonology has probably changed a good deal (Hreinn Benediktsson 1964: 63). The continuity in written Icelandic has to some degree masked a discontinuity in the spoken language.

Internally, the development of Icelandic has been noted as astonishingly consistent. Local dialects were little differentiated, and phonetic changes occurred almost instantaneously all over the country (Jón Helgason 1931b: 36–7). It has been suggested that one important factor in this were the migrant fishermen, who linked together widely separated parts of the country (ibid.). In the eighteenth century observers noted some difference in language. Eggert Ólafsson spoke of the pure, old language in the eastern parts, and complained that elsewhere the language was deteriorating, at the sea-shore in particular (1772: 823; 148ff.).[18] The coastal areas were doubtless more influenced by Danish merchants, which may help to explain this. In general, however, Icelandic was conceived of as a variety of Old Norse, which was still perfectly readable for contemporary Icelanders (von Troil 1780: 31–2; Skúli Magnússon 1944a: 21).

The Danish linguist Rasmus Rask, writing about Icelandic in the early nineteenth century, considers language to be the most stable element in the cultural fabric (1817; 1932: i. 21). Nevertheless, he prophesied the complete disappearance of Icelandic, which was under increasing influence from outside, particularly from Danish. As early as the sixteenth century, Icelandic had incorporated many loan-words from Latin, German, and Danish (Westergård-Nielsen 1946), reflecting the major sources of influence—the Church, the Danish administration (the language of which was German for a period), and Danish merchants. When native writers, such as Oddur Einarsson in 1589 (1971: 145) and Arngrimur Jónsson in 1609 (1985: 96), stressed the purity of the old Icelandic language this was only partially correct from a linguistic point of view, but it may have been culturally true. 'Icelandicness' was seen as a distinct quality, and the language in which this distinctiveness could be rumoured was closely connected to Old Norse, in which a celebrated literature was once created and continuously read.

A recent work on the history of Iceland notes that 'Iceland has been uniquely a country of books since the twelfth century' (Sigurður A. Magnússon 1977: 177). Long before printing was invented, the Icelanders made and read books that were handwritten and bound.

Books were one of the consequences of writing, which in Iceland had appeared in the late eleventh century, in the wake of the Church. As Clanchy has recently demonstrated for English material, the transition from memory to written record, or from oral to written forms of transmission, was not made in one leap (Clanchy 1979). It was a gradual process, with a long and peaceful coexistence of oral and literary cultures. The first writings were extensions of speaking; they were a means of shaping voices in letters (Clanchy 1981: 29 ff.). In Iceland, too, there was an intimate relationship between writing and speaking. As I have discussed elsewhere, laws and sagas were for a long time dependent on both modes of transmission (Hastrup 1986d). Written laws were among the first secular writings in Iceland. The decision to write down the laws was made in 1117, until when the lawspeaker had had to memorize and recite the corpus each year at the Althing assembly, according to the constitution of 930. Written laws ultimately made the lawspeaker redundant, and Icelandic society lost the centralized transmission of authority (Hastrup 1986d; see also 1985a: 218 ff.). Writing, in this case, contributed negatively to social reproduction, even though the scribes had only transformed the voice of dictation into letters. They were writers—not authors.[19]

With the sagas, things were different. As a distinct genre, saga writing started about 1200, and with it a truly literary form of expression emerged. The writers of the sagas were truly *authors*; they created a reality of their own, and the text was an end in itself. *Saga* means 'said' and the 'said history' contained *fræði*, or historical knowledge (Meulengracht Sørensen 1977: 155). This literature was composed in silence, but it was composed for recitation, and for reading aloud to an audience of appreciative Icelanders. History had to be said, if not by etymological coercion then at least by cultural prescription; the letters had to be voiced. In both legal codes and sagas, therefore, writing was still closely connected to speaking and hearing. The last sagas were composed in the mid-fourteenth century, but by this time the old sagas had been laboriously and multiply copied by semi-professional scribes; the author had disappeared, and the writer re-emerged. The audience was still there, ready to listen to ancient wisdom.

In the late fourteenth and fifteenth centuries Icelandic society saw an increasing concentration of wealth in a few families. These were the families who could afford to have books written by scribes.[20] It is from this period that the magnificent bound and illuminated books containing several different narratives have been handed down. These books bear witness to a steady interest in the sagas over this period. In the sixteenth century, however, there was a remarkable decline in their reproduction. This may have been connected with the increasing popularity of a new kind of literary expression, namely, that of poetry (Jón Helgason 1931*a*: 158); perhaps more importantly it was connected with the Reformation.

With the Reformation, the spiritual climate became inimical to traditional literature, and there are almost no secular manuscripts from the last part of the sixteenth century. Bishop Guðbrandur Þorláksson (bishop at Hólar, 1571–1627), explicitly denounced the popular reading of 'heathen sagas, *rímur* and *mansöngvar*' (quoted by Jón Helgason 1931*a*: 158). In order to give the people an alternative to these heretical genres, Guðbrandur produced an enormous amount of edifying literature, which he had printed at the See. He attempted to lure Icelanders into homiletic reading by giving his new writings the form of *rímur*, a popular verse-form. His *Vísnabók* of 1612 was not a success, however (Nordal 1937).

In the first half of the seventeenth century, things changed again. A renewed interest in the old stories occurred; at least they were again reproduced and now also collected systematically. Parchment was replaced by paper. Although printing had been introduced, manual reproduction of the narratives by no means stopped, and continued right down to the twentieth century (Springborg 1977: 53). In the first instance, the bishop's effective monopoly of the printing-press blocked the way for secular literature. It is likely also that the tradition of handwriting as such was not so easily dispensed with. It was an integral part of the literary heritage, as administered by a category of more or less professional scribes (cf. Springborg 1969, 1977). The upheaval of literary reproduction in the first part of the seventeenth century was still expressed in handwriting among the ordinary people. Among the learned groups printed books greatly influenced their thinking, and as elsewhere in Europe it was the printed works that accounted for the rapid spread of 'international' ideas (Febvre and Martin 1984).

The Icelandic renaissance in the seventeenth century was to a large extent the result of European humanism, introduced through the renowned Arngrímur Jónsson, who had studied in Copenhagen (Jakob Benediktsson 1957; 1981). He inaugurated a new vision of Icelandic history and made the Icelanders see their literary heritage in a new perspective (Jakob Benediktsson 1957: 78–81). The humanists were literal-minded, and literature was deemed true history.

Some sagas were more popular than others, if we may judge from the number of copies transmitted. Among the most popular was a story like *Grettis saga Ásmundarsonar*, the tale of an outlaw-hero allegedly living in the first part of the eleventh century, whose exploits were probably entrapped in prose in the last part of the thirteenth century (cf. Hastrup 1986a). If the tradition of Grettir, or of any other saga figure, is traced through the centuries it becomes evident that 'tradition' is always translated into a particular historical context. Thus, the manual or printed reproduction of particular texts, be they sagas or something else, is not necessarily a reproduction of their meaning. Meaning is relative to context. Even literal-mindedness was no guarantee of empathic interpretation.

The lawbook, unlike the sagas, was continuously reproduced. To judge from the extant manuscripts, *Jónsbók* was the copyists' favourite. Interestingly, it continued to be copied also in the late sixteenth century, otherwise so poor in secular manuscripts (Springborg 1977: 55). The making of manuscripts to order was a profession; one single scribe is known to have made at least eighteen copies of *Jónsbók* in the 1630s and 1640s (Springborg 1969: 310). The number of lawbooks reproduced testifies to a steady demand. Peder Claussøn Friis, a

Norwegian writing about Iceland in 1580, noted that apart from translations of foreign works 'the Icelanders have the old lawbooks written
in their language' (1881: 191). Even in the most arduous post-
reformatory period, the ancient laws were still very conspicuous
among the writings of the Icelanders. Among the secular works *Jónsbók* is also exceptional in that it was actually *printed* already in the late
sixteenth century, at a time when printed works were otherwise almost
exclusively religious (cf. Halldór Hermansson 1916).

Of the secular literature also the *rímur* deserve separate treatment.
Rímur were a popular form of verse, at least if by 'popular' we refer to
something which a people has made its own (cf. Dronke 1968: 1). The
form was 'invented' about 1400, after the production of the sagas had
stopped (Björn K. Þórólfsson 1934). *Rímur* were a distinct literary
genre, although their motifs were often drawn from old prose
literature, mostly from sagas but also from local folk-tales and fairy-
tales of foreign extraction (Stefán Einarsson 1957: 89). An eighteenth-
century observer characterized the *rímur* as 'sagas turned into popular
poetry to make them stick in the mind' (Eggert Ólafsson 1772: 48).

It has been suggested that the effect of the *rímur* was to preserve

throughout all classes of the population, a feeling for language and rhythm, a
knowledge of the past, an interest in myth and legend, which helped as much
as anything to maintain the continuity of Icelandic literature'. (Craigie
1937: 21.)

It is hard to assess the degree to which this social function was fulfilled
by the *rímur*, rather than by later ideologies, but it is incontestable that
the verses gave voice to old literary motifs and to history.

Poetry was more than *rímur*, however, even if rather non-distinct
until the nineteenth century (ibid.: 23). It was a genre in its own right,
unbounded by the fixed metrical forms of the classical Eddaic poetry
and the younger *rímur*. It emerged gradually during our period. The
oldest known poem is *Lilja* from the fourteenth century, which was an
object of unbroken admiration throughout out period. In poetry the
borderline between religious and secular matters was fluid (Stefán
Einarsson 1957: 188). Poetry apart from the *rímur*, however, need not
greatly concern us here, for it was never truly 'popular' as a genre.
There were individual exceptions, and Hallgrímur Pétursson (1614–
74) deserves mention. He wrote *Passiusálmar* (psalms), which even
today form the bulk of popularly known religious verse in Iceland.

The most important single item in the religious literature was the Bible; after the Reformation the Catechism in principle was known by everyone. The Catechism was edifying in more than one way. In an appendix the general tripartite view of the world was presented. According to Luther, society consisted of a hierarchy of *Ecclesia* (the Church), *politia* (secular political organization), and *oeconomia* (the 'household' as the sum of single households). This world view fitted Icelandic reality to a high degree. A separation of the three spheres had already been effected as the result of transformations taking place in the Middle Ages. Once founded on a unity between religious, secular, and economic virtues, the Church had split itself apart from society during the process of *libertas ecclesiae*. Later, the political offices were no longer in the hands of elected farmers, but fell to foreign administrators. The position of the *bóndi* as head of the household corresponded nicely with Luther's *pater familias*. Generally, therefore, in our period, Icelandic and Lutheran cosmologies fitted together well.

Besides the literary genres already mentioned, a whole series of oral forms existed. The people had their folklore, riddles, legends, and the like, in addition to genealogical knowledge (Jón Helgason 1931a: 17). Folk-tales (*þjóðsögur*) were told and related for centuries (Einar Ó. Sveinsson 1931a). The first systematic collection was made by Jón Árnason (1819–88), within the general European trend of romanticism and nationalism (Hallfreður Örn Eiríksson 1980a, b). The content of the tales is extremely diverse, and spans supernatural forces, prosaic legend, and the origin of place-names.

Fairy-tales of common European stock became popular in the eighteenth century, some of them being subjected to separate Icelandic treatment (Einar Ó. Sveinsson 1931b: 293). Before that, European romance was known in Iceland; this genre had served the interests of the upper class from the thirteenth to the fifteenth centuries in particular, and its successor—the genre of fairy-tales— became popular in the eighteenth and nineteenth centuries (Glauser 1983: 228). Both folk-tales and fairy-tales were significant elements in the literary organization and treatment of reality. Whether realistic or Utopian, literary structures 'are not timeless, ahistorical and auto-nomous, but express concrete experiences and the consciousness of a contemporary time' (Glauser 1983: 233).

This also obtains for folk-literature of a more epigrammatical kind, like proverbs. There was a rich and coherent tradition of these, often integrated with the epic literature.[21] In the proverbs wisdom was transmitted through language from one generation to the next. One proverb says: *því læra börnin málið, að það er fyrir þeim haft* ('Children learn that language which is presented to them') (*ÍM*: 22). Language is one thing, literature another. The question arises whether children and other people of Iceland actually had access to the literature available in the country. This brings us to a consideration of literacy.

An Icelandic scholar has suggested that by the end of the twelfth century at least all the chieftains and bigger *bændur* were able both to read and write (Einar Ó. Sveinsson 1944: 197). Such a statement is open to both debate and definition, but it is possible that to negotiate the often chaotic socio-political reality of the time these categories of people had a special inducement for achieving literacy. They were not necessarily literate in the sense of being learned in Latin, but they were readers of the vernacular (cf. Clanchy 1981).

It is not until the middle of the sixteenth century that we have explicit statements on this issue, however. In 1546 the Danish bishop Peder Palladius wrote about the Icelanders 'that there are few among them who cannot both read and write their mother tongue' (*DI*: xi. 460). A Norwegian observer, Absalon Beyer, corroborates this view in 1567: 'for the Icelanders it is customary to teach their children to read and write, women and men alike, and young boys are encouraged to learn their lawbook by heart' (Storm 1895: 46). We do not know on what kind of evidence such statements rest, and we cannot infer any numbers or percentages from them. It is probably safe, however, to suggest that by comparative Nordic standards the Icelanders were remarkably literate (Loftur Guttormsson 1981: 130–1).

The Reformation entailed a compulsory cathechization, and a minimum of Christian education. Priests were supposed to examine their parishioners, who would have to be at least nominal readers to pass the examination. During the following centuries, however, the decree of domestic discipline had to be repeated and spelled out in detail several times (Loftur Guttormsson 1981). There is thus indirect evidence of a rather slow process towards actual literacy.

A German observer, Daniel Vetter, noted in 1640 that during the long winter nights the Icelanders 'divert themselves with the reading of histories, or other pastimes . . .' (1640: 162). The Icelanders *read*, but the implication is one of reading aloud, and it is hard to assess the actual ability to read and write among the people as a whole. Probably, general literacy in the modern sense was still far away, and the ability to read was something special. Evidence is found in the strangest of connections. Thus, in 1725 a man was wanted on a charge of adultery, and at the Althing his name, his physical characteristics, and his last known route were posted; he was further characterized as 'reading well and writing' (*Aĺ*: xi. 269–70). We might think the ability to read and write to be of no moment in a lawsuit concerning adultery, but apparently these were characteristics that could still help to identify a man.

An ordinance concerning the education of the Icelanders was issued in 1746 (*LI*: ii. 575–6). A parish registration was to follow, and the priests were supposed to note whether the people could 'read books', or could 'read the catechism', or could read at all. There were other gradings, and the scale taken as a whole demonstrates that literacy was not an absolute 'either/or' in eighteenth-century Iceland. A recent analysis of the parish registers made by Loftur Guttormsson from the period 1748 to 1763 has shown that among the oldest group of people (that is, people born 1680–9) a little less than 40 per cent were able to read books. Among the younger age-groups literacy was more widespread, and for those born in 1730–9, almost 60 per cent were 'able to read books'. There is a category for 'poor readers' in the register, and if these are counted as literate, the percentages for the two age-groups are 42 per cent and 83 per cent, respectively (Loftur Guttormsson 1981: 146). These are the first reliable quantitative data on literacy in Iceland, and in spite of their uncertainties (owing to the personal element of the priest having to record facts that may have run counter to his pride and his office), they demonstrate how in all probability literacy increased during the eighteenth century. With the poor readers included there is a near-complete literacy by about 1800.

This quantitative material is supplemented by several qualitative observations, some of which were quoted above. In 1786 a German advocate of Icelandic culture mentions the flourishing reproduction of the sagas, and says that 'the common reading of these old stories, *sögulestur*, is one of the most cherished diversions of the nation' (Eggers 1786: 71). He also notes that in the evenings a boy might read aloud from the saga books, or an entire household might sing *rímur* while they pursued their handicrafts (ibid.). Sir Joseph Banks, travelling in Iceland in the late eighteenth century, states:

in Iceland education is more general than in other countries, and the lower ranks are clearly much better informed than in other parts; in fact the lowest ranks of European society scarcely exist in Iceland. (Quoted Halldór Hermansson 1928: 40.)

In spite of material poverty and economic deprivation, the educational profile was high; as von Troil, writing in 1780, says:

We should . . . form a very wrong judgement of Iceland, to imagine it absorbed in total ignorance and obscurity; on the contrary, I can affirm, that I have found more knowledge among the lower class, than is to be met with in most other places. You will seldom find a peasant who, besides being well instructed in the principles of religion is not also acquainted with the history of the country, which proceed from the frequent reading of their traditional histories (*sagas*) wherein consists their principal amusement. (Von Troil 1780: 170–1.)

He also notes that they have 'better libraries in many parts of Iceland than could have been expected' (ibid.: 171). Foreign observers were clearly impressed by the Icelanders' literary interests. Native observers were perhaps more moderate on the issue. In 1589 Bishop Oddur Einarsson wrote that

at the reception of guests peasants will sometimes produce their sagas and read aloud in clear voices for hours about the deeds of various characters and about distinguished events of old days; sometimes they will sing their old songs in a characteristic tone. (1971: 129.)

Saga reading and the chanting of the *rímur* are still in evidence, but for the native it is associated with special events, such as the arrival of guests—including, one might suppose, foreign travellers.

Eggert Ólafsson, who travelled widely on his native island in the 1750s, also noted the tradition of sagas and *rímur* (regarding the latter as sagas translated into verse form). He goes on to say, however, that

the reading of histories has declined very much in Iceland over the past hundred years. The reason for this is in all likelihood that the highest ranks (*de fornemste*) have far less inclination for this than before. (1772: 47–8.)

Apart from the alleged decline, it is of interest here that Eggert Ólafsson links the interest in literature to the 'higher ranks'.

From quantitative observations on the cost of books alone, one might suspect a divide between élite and popular culture. There was no such divide in Iceland, however; possession of books may have been for the few but access to literature was for all. This was owing to the structural features of Icelandic society. There was no urban culture at all until the nineteenth century; even villages were lacking. Habitations were scattered as single farmsteads. At the farmsteads higher and lower orders lived closely together. Each farmstead or household was a total social universe; landowners, landless labourers, domestic servants, and children shared the social space of the farm. They all lived, worked, and slept in the *baðstofa*, the central room. Any entertainment was directed towards this mixed audience. The entertainment was known by the name *sagnaskemmtun* ('saga entertainment', or 'story telling'), of which there is evidence from the early Middle Ages to the present day (Hermann Pálsson 1962). Not only sagas, but also *rímur*, fables, fairy-tales, and folk-tales were part of the entertainment, as observed by Magnús Stephensen in the late eighteenth century (cf. Loftur Guttormsson 1987*b*: 258). Even if the idyllic picture of communal reading is exaggerated by some observers, there is enough evidence that 'oral tradition and literary transmission are not two separate sources of information' (Schier 1977: 112).

As implied by contemporary observers, sagas were read *aloud*, and the *rímur* were intoned in a high voice. By contrast, the lawbooks were read in silence, and were a primary means of instruction among those who could afford a copy. This was not so much instruction in the laws, as instruction in the art of reading. Once this art was mastered, the 'literate' person could direct his skills towards reading aloud.

The social context of *sagnaskemmtun* was the *kvöldvaka* ('evening wake'), where guests were welcomed as entertainers. Even the *flak-karar* ('vagrants'), who were so unpopular in official legislation, were highly praised guests at the farmsteads; they were often 'not so un-educated and useless as they were poor' (Magnús Gíslason 1977: 45). They had an important function as news-carriers, and they could contribute to the evening pastimes. The *kvöldvaka* was part of the work-rhythm; it was a special time of the day, when indoor activities took over from outdoor life. 'Literary' entertainment may not have been an ever-present accompaniment to handicrafts, but there is, however, little doubt that the tradition of *sagnaskemmtun* was vital to Icelandic society. One of the consequences was a steady reproduction of ancient images of Icelandic history. It has even been suggested that the survival of the isolated Icelanders in the centuries of misery was owed to the sustenance provided by their history, poetry, and literature (Tomasson 1980: 117).

The absence of any divide between élite and popular cultures in Iceland is not just another case of popular culture being everyone's culture, in the sense that it is a second culture for the educated and the only culture for the rest, as was the case in other parts of Europe in the early modern period (Burke 1978: 28). It was a truly shared popular culture, transmitted in the vernacular. There was, indeed, a small minority of learned Icelanders who were versed in Latin, and who produced various treatises in this language. Common to them is their internationalism, and their background in an education abroad. These must be regarded as to some extent outside the world of Icelandic 'popular' culture. In general, however, we can conclude that, owing to the peculiar nature of the Icelandic social structure, everyone had access to tradition, liguistically and physically, even if only a few could pay the actual costs of books (cf. ibid.: 253–4). This shared 'literacy' impressed foreign observers, who made more or less explicit comparisons with other parts of Europe. In contrast to other parts of Europe, where the nobility and the urban centres played a crucial role in the transmission of literary images, in Iceland the *bændur* were never alienated from this. They made books, or had them made (Stefán Karlsson 1970*b*), and in their households these books became part of Icelandic tradition.

It has been argued that 'it is of the *necessary* nature of tradition that it seeks and maintains stability, that it preserves itself' (Lord 1974: 220). The continuity of Icelandic tradition confirms this, and also that its

tenacity springs neither from perverseness, nor from an abstract principle of absolute art, but from a desparately compelling conviction that what the tradition is preserving is the very means of attaining life and happiness. (Ibid.)

Whether this conviction was true or false for Iceland, I will discuss in the concluding section of this chapter.

CONCEPTS OF HUMANITY

Social reproduction is a matter of re-creating the fundamentals of the social system, and reproducing the context of human life. The concepts of humanity, therefore, are of pivotal importance. To end this chapter on morals and letters, we can summarize the findings of the previous sections, and show how morality and literacy interlocked in a particular pattern of social reproduction in Iceland—reflecting particular notions of humanity.

The pattern of landownership, alienating most Icelanders from the land, gradually undermined the medieval kinship system. Neither inheritance nor alliance had any meaning for the majority of the Icelanders. The economic order meant that households rather than *ættir* were the basic units of an atomistic social structure. Marriage was almost inconceivable for the poorer people, and the idea of creating alliances between *ættir*, and thus integrating the kin groups in a wider social order, was beyond imagination.

This particular social experience possibly contributed to the peculiar pattern of socially organizing sexuality in Iceland in this period. The noticeable disregard for rules concerning sexual conduct implies the unimportance of kinship and alliance. The conspicuousness of incestuous relations and the lack of shame, is another remarkable comment upon the development. Sexuality had—to some extent— become a household matter. To engage in incest, and to accept it socially, is to deny one of the foundations of culture and society, which must be based on exchange.[22] If the incest-taboo marks 'the leap from nature to culture', and the constitution of humanity, neglect suggests a reverse movement. We might figuratively regard the Icelanders' negligent observance of rules and taboos as a 'leap back into nature', as it were.

Traditionally, prosperity had been linked to fertility including human fertility. The ancient notion of *ár ok friðr* ('abundance and peace') was a most sincere expression of hope for the future. *Ár* had connotations of the yearly cycle, a rich harvest, and abundance; *friðr* connoted love, love-making, and peace (*LP*: 154; Fritzner 1954: i. 489). The formulaic blessing *til árs ok friðar* thus linked prosperity directly to sexuality (Ström 1954: 30). This conceptual linkage was possibly linked to an old (agricultural) fertility cult of the heathen god Freyr (ibid.). Although in some senses anachronistic in our period, the connections were still clearly felt.

During the early Middle Ages, economic progress and fertility went hand in hand. In the late Middle Ages and throughout our period the negative counterparts of *ár* and *friðr* were operative. Poverty was correlated with restlessness, and with decreasing (social) fertility. Rates of production and reproduction reached a low point in the seventeenth and eighteenth centuries, and were aggravated by a growing sense of the country being gradually laid waste (*LI*: iv. 34–6). Geographically speaking, this may be an exaggeration, but on the conceptual map of Iceland, the *eyðibýli* ('abandoned farms') were abundant (Þorkell Jóhannesson 1928: 87–93; Björn Teitsson and Magnús Stefánsson 1972: 172).

The notion of *eyða* ('to lay waste'), deserves some attention. Diminishing population and general poverty account for some of its momentum, while part of it may be ascribed to the people gradually 'defining themselves out' (Ardener 1974; 1975a). The old proverb *með lǫgum skal land byggja ok ekki með ólǫgum eyða* ('with law shall the country be built and not with unlaw laid waste') points to a near-identification of law and society (Hastrup 1984a; 1985a). In the epoch under discussion here 'un-law' became increasingly prevalent, in the sense that there was an increasing discrepancy between law as text and life as practice.

How do these trends tally with the pattern of literacy? In the sagas old virtues were constantly held up before the Icelanders. As extensions of speaking, the old histories were still 'said', and in consequence heard by everybody. What was once a living history, however, had now become a myth of the past. It had lost its direct bearing on contemporary reality, for free farmers and thralls had long since been replaced by tenants and peasants of various degrees of dependence.

As a myth of the past, the sagas provided a permanent image of the Icelanders in the past tense, as it were. The mirror provided by these stories showed the people that things had changed; but no new literature was created which could have produced a contemporary imagery of moral values, other than the Utopian fairy-tales of general European type. Instead the old cultural models were *re*produced, and the world view was no longer consistent with the world of experience.

The perpetually reproduced lawbook (which was actually read, where the sagas were mainly heard), contained a formal framework of morality, honour, and kinship loyalty. It became increasingly anachronistic, however. It formed the core of Icelandic legislation until the nineteenth century, but during the centuries it was supplemented by innumerable laws, decrees, and ordinances which were never printed for the ordinary people to read, although they might have heard some of them in church. The written laws had once represented a shaping of the law-speaker's voice into letters; this shape became increasingly hollow in our period.

The celebrated books of the country produced a mythological incantation of the past with which the present could not compare, but which was nevertheless the only symbolic contrast to present-day identity. Literature was introspective; literary creativity was an inward movement of continuous self-reflection. Instead of a symbolic exchange with 'others' the Icelanders were mirrored with 'them-selves', in the past tense. This has a parallel in the incestuous relationships which were, ultimately, negations of culture. I contend that there is a significant correlation between cultural deconstruction at this level, and the sonorous repetition of past achievements. In-reading and in-breeding converged.

Social reproduction was also threatened by a failure of biological reproduction which was in part owed to the absence of breast-feeding. We know that children were given cow's milk, cream, and butter instead, all of them items associated with plenty. Cows were the standard of measure of wealth, and in the old stories and in popular *rímur*, butter was used as a metaphor of plenty. To feed the children on this was to give them the best of all possible diets, and so the best chance of survival and prosperity. I have already quoted Eggert Ólafsson, who noted in his report that it never occurred to the Icelanders that their babies died because they were wrongly fed; their deaths were attributed, rather, to external factors, or fate (1772: 452).

Tradition preserved the old images of successful farming life, and associated 'Icelandicness' with the early medieval *bóndi*. Effectively, this meant that contemporary Icelanders defined themselves through fidelity to their own early history. While other peoples invent traditions to match a new historical situation (Hobsbawm and Ranger 1983), the Icelanders reproduced the celebrated images of another epoch to invent themselves. Far from contributing to their survival, this cultural reproduction may have been directly de-structive to their social reproduction. In comparison with the old, 'real' Icelanders, the contemporary people were non-distinct, even invisible. By inventing the Icelanders from past images, the present people was defined out.

The use of the past had repercussions at a more individual level as well. If the 'Icelanders' were defined by their early history, 'man' was defined as the hero of this history. The proud *bóndi* and the 'intensity of courage', which is said to characterize Icelandic literature in general (Ker 1923: 57), were the epitome of manly virtues. Failure to reproduce this standard entailed not only 'un-manliness' but in-humanity. This is aptly illustrated in the seventeenth-century poet Stefán Ólafsson's *Ómenskukvæði* ('Song of Inhumanity'), which laments the condition of contemporary Iceland (Stefán Ólafsson 1885–6: i. 261–78). One of the verses goes thus:

Eg segi þær fréttir
að svo gár þetta
í sveitum nú,
ómenskan sprettur
og álnum flettir
hin öflgu bú
fullrösk að metta
húsgangshjú
er haldin hin rétta
og sanna trú

(I tell you the news that this is so in the countryside now: inhumanity sprouts and cleaves to the marrow the strong household, to feed completely healthy wandering beggars goes for the right and true faith)

In this poem, we get a relatively clear idea of the contours of the semantic field of *ómenska* which I discussed before (cf. above, pp. 78–9). The *bú*, or the household, is under threat, and the idea of individual moral responsibility for one's 'luck' is undermined by the vagrants who beg for their food. This vision of inhumanity had another expression in the sphere of verbal insult. In early medieval Iceland 'un-manliness' was the ultimate defamation (Meulengracht Sørensen 1980), but during our epoch *fulréttisorð* shifted to an accusation for incest—which is also 'inhumanity'.

Use of the concept of *ómenska*, inhumanity, became increasingly frequent during our epoch. In 1720 when the laws were amended, the question was raised whether *ómenskumenn* ('inhuman men') should be allowed to marry (*AÍ*: x. 570). The 'inhumans' were the poor; and in the contemporary vision of the world poverty, idleness, and inhumanity were linked. Only the prosperous *bændur* were true humans. In the sixteenth century the notion of *menskumaður* ('human man') was used by Oddur Einarsson (among others) to distinguish man from spirits and elves (1971: 47; cf. Blöndal 1920–4: 540). This was then a current concept. Through a semantic sliding effect the category *ómenskumaður* ('inhuman man') came, in the seventeenth century, to alienate the poor from human society. The boundary between humans and non-humans had moved far into the community of men. Increasing poverty meant more and more inhumans, who had no particular virtues of the traditional kind. This is true even though Guðmundur Andrésson in his opposition to the *stóridómur* (1564) states that *maðurinn er animal rationale, ein fornufftig skiepna* ('man is a rational animal, a reasonable creature' (Jakob Benediktsson 1948: 16)). Within the species of reason, however, humans and non-humans were two separate cat-egories.

Both the image of 'Icelander' and of 'man' were linked to medieval values which were constantly reproduced in tradition. The very vital-ity of the tradition may have been counter-productive in relation to *social* reproduction, because by old standards the ordinary Icelander was always at risk of being classified as not human at all. If you were so classified, why should you struggle to keep up 'human' standards at the legal level?

The Power of Knowledge

MAGIC, witchcraft, and healing constitute a field of indigenous explanations of individual success or misfortune. It is worth remembering, therefore, that in the social experience of the Icelanders, death and disaster were recurrent phenomena. Demographic crisis, economic stagnation and decline, worsening climate, and unfavourable trade regulations, all contributed to the Icelandic view of the human condition. From 1400 to 1800 catastrophe always lurked in the background, in Iceland as elsewhere in Europe. Whenever disaster struck explanations were called for, and some were found within the field of popular belief.

Popular belief has been a favourite topic in Nordic folklore studies, where it has been studied as an empirical category (Rørbye 1978: 305–6; Kolsrud *et al.* 1978; Rooth 1978). Magical ideas transmitted in popular custom and folk-tale have been regarded as constants of tradition (Lid 1935*b*: 1). Two problems arise out of this; first, 'belief' is no objectively defined category (Needham 1972), second, 'tradition' cannot be held constant in an ever-changing historical context; by definition tradition points to continuity at one level or another, but within a changing context its meaning and significance may shift radically from one period to the next (Chapman 1978; Hastrup 1986*a*). Even within one family of scribes copying the same manuscripts over three generations, we can see how new horizons are incorporated, and the repertoire enlarged (Stefán Karlsson 1970*a*).

My own approach diverges from folklore studies in two ways. First, I regard beliefs merely as a point of entry into Icelandic theories of causation; and 'beliefs' are not an empirical category, because at the empirical level belief cannot be separated from knowledge. Secondly, I interpret popular tradition within the historical context, where it comments upon other domains of life.

Magic, witchcraft, and healing are closely connected concepts in social anthropological discourse. In the Icelandic world they were also intimately linked, and drew upon each other in both theory and practice. In their combination, they provide us with an idea of Icelandic concepts of fate.

MAGIC

It is not easy to define 'magic'. Late-nineteenth-century evolutionist anthropology saw magic as a precursor to religion and, ultimately, science (Tylor 1871), or as a gradually disappearing practice coexisting with both science and religion (Frazer 1922). Characteristically, magic has often been compared to, or contrasted with, religion. In 1950, however, Marcel Mauss formulated a general theory of magic in which he concluded: 'Magic is the domain of pure production, *ex nihilo*. With words and gestures it does what techniques achieve by labour' (Mauss 1972: 141). In the words of Lévi-Strauss, magic is a 'naturalisation des actions humaines', that is, a treatment of certain human actions *as if* they were integral parts of a natural determinism (1962: 292–3). The *as if* is that of the external analyst; from within any system of magical theory the deterministic aspect is rigorous and unquestioned. The naturalization of human action implies that a magical system of thought is self-confirming (Thomas 1971: 767). This means that once the premises are accepted, neither new discoveries nor failures can shake the belief that the system works, because a theory of failure is included. The self-confirming nature of any magical system of thought is one reason for its persistence.

In Iceland magical practice points to a conceptual continuity through centuries. From the Middle Ages and almost to the present day, a continuity of 'belief' shows in the most diverse events. In other words, in this domain of perceived determinism we can identify a structure of *la longue durée*. This is why the discussion of magic precedes the investigation of witchcraft and healing, which are distinct and much more time-bound realizations of the general Icelandic theory of magic.

In the early medieval North, magic and religion were so closely connected that it is hardly possible to speak of separate orders (Ström 1961: 221). With the advent of Christianity in Iceland a distinction was introduced—the ancient heathen and 'magical' practices became, in

principle, outdated and vicious phenomena; 'religion', on the other
hand, was raised to the unique status of a global doctrine. From 1253
on, *Guðs lǫg* ('the law of God', or canon law), was the declared ultimate
frame of reference (*DI*: i. 1). In its capacity as *law*, Christianity came to
refer not only to a theology, but also to a particular kind of society.
Bishop Árni's Christian law of 1275 begins with a declaration of its
social validity: *þat er uphaf lagha várra Islendinga . . . at ver skulum hafa ok
hallda kristilega tru* ('It is the foundation of our, the Icelanders', law . . .
that we shall have and uphold the Christian faith' (*AK*: ch. 1; *NGL*: v.
16)). If we remember the traditional connotations of *vár lög* ('our law'),
which referred to a legal and a geographical as well as to a social space,
this declaration is of no small significance (cf. Hastrup 1981*a*). In consequence, unchristian practices were excluded from the social
domain. The definition of what was 'inside' and what was 'outside' the
law remained in the hands of the Church, at least until the Reformation, and this soon came to be reflected in secular law. According to
Jónsbók, in which Bishop Árni's declaration is repeated (17), the death
penalty or outlawry should follow *fordæðuskap ok spáfarar allar ok útisetur
at vekja troll upp ok fremja heiðni* ('sorcery and all soothsaying and 'out-
sitting' to wake up trolls, and exercising heathenism' (ibid.: 38). Traditional magical practices were, in principle, clearly alienated from
Christian society.

In actual social practice, however, magic and religion remained
closely interwoven in Iceland, and sanctions on heathen magic were
rarely enforced before the Reformation (Páll E. Ólason 1916: 7). In the
Icelandic sources there is evidence of only one person being actually
sentenced to death for sorcery in the pre-Reformation period, and that
was in Greenland. There, in 1407, a man was burnt at the stake after a
court had found him guilty of using magic to get his way with a
woman; she had never recovered mentally and died soon after (Lög-
mannsannáll 1407 (Storm 1888: 288–9)).

Within the Catholic Church itself practices that we might think of
as 'magical' were very prevalent, although holy water, crossings, and
prayers were never classified as such (Ólafur Davíðsson 1940–3: 14).
Apart from this inherently magical element in Christianity, much
traditional pre-Christian magic filtered into the Church (Linderholm
1918: 3–6). The magic power of the Christian 'spells', and of particular
Saints' blessings, had a strong hold among the people.[1] Those wells
which had been blessed by Bishop Guðmundur in the thirteenth
century, were believed to have beneficial and even healing properties

until this century (Ólafur Lárusson 1942). This constant and popular merging of categories perhaps explains why prosecution of magicians was almost unheard of until the Reformation (cf. Eggert Ólafsson 1772: 473). The explicit target of the Reformation was all heresy of previous times, whether of heathen or Catholic origin. The notion of heresy (Danish: *kjetterie ͡ kætteri*) became an all-inclusive category, applicable to any unchristian behaviour ranging from incest to black magic. This time the now politicized Church took its doctrines more seriously. In a large-scale attempt to neutralize social entropy, the double standard of Catholic times, which had separated the clerical from the secular domain, was replaced by a single standard—one against which unsocial or anti-social lapses could be firmly measured (Hastrup 1985*c*: 53–5). Magic was thereby firmly excluded.

Officially, the relationship between magic and religion seems to have been redefined several times. In actual practice, they were usually closely entangled; and for the people involved the distinction probably had little meaning. Paternosters and ancient spells merged in an indigenous theory of causality, which we may identify as magic.

The original term for magic in Iceland was *galdur*. A distinction was made between black and white magic (*svartagaldur* and *hvítagaldur*) but these were not in an even or permanent balance. *Svartagaldur* came gradually to dominate *hvítagaldur*, to the point where the unqualified term *galdur*, by the seventeenth century, was unambiguously associated with black magic. The theory of magic, however, remained constant.

In Old Icelandic *galdr* referred to a song, mainly in the sense of 'charm' or 'spell'. The corresponding verb was *gala*, to 'chant' or to 'cast spells'. This linguistic derivation is an important key to the semantics of magic. It demonstrates the most important instrument of supernatural power in Iceland—words. Words were the means whereby man could produce history *ex nihilo*. Word-actions were represented as physical forces. Thus naturalized and empowered, words encapsulated a force which might be directed towards individuals. In medieval Icelandic literature this is a recurrent theme. For instance, *níð* being a verbal defamation with connotations of sexual perversion (Meulengracht Sørensen 1980), clearly was associated with an age-old concept of magical influence (Almquist 1965). Scaldic poetry was another possible outlet of verbal magic, although it was mainly non-magical (cf. von See 1980: 47ff.). In the provisions of *Grágás*, *níð* and the making of scaldic love verses were offences of the same order, and were both vigorously banned (*Grágás*: i*b*. 183 ff.; ii. 392 ff.). There is no unanimity among literary historians about the origin of scaldic poetry. Opinions have varied between courtly praise and magical practice (Stéfan Einarsson 1957: 44–5), or memorial poetry (Ohlmarks 1944: 198). This discussion shall not detain us here; suffice it to note that praise and scorn, homage and derision, could all be couched in poetry, and clothed in magical words. Words were potentially a means of capturing force, and of directing it towards a specific goal. That was why *skáldskapr* could be dangerous, and why it was connected with *níð*. We know from the sagas that, in spite of the prohibition, love-verses were sometimes made without subsequent sanctions, and this indicates a gradual separation of *skáldskapr*, as a poetic 'genre', from word-magic in general. The evidence of *Jónsbók* sustains this; here *skáldskapr* is not subject to a general prohibition; it is specified as illegal only if used for derision: *Nú kveðr maðr skáldskap til háðungar manni...* ('If a man sings scaldic verse for deriding another man ...')—then he will be prosecuted and fined (*Jónsbók*: 66). It has been suggested about the *skáld* that 'the semantic development must have been from the action to the force lying behind the action and then to the exerter of this force' (Steblin-Kaminskij 1969: 430).[2] Historically this was connected with the rise of conscious authorship (ibid.). The latent power of poetry became a question of will on the part of the scald, rather than of the power of the words themselves. The evidence from *Jónsbók* suggests that this shift of focus had already occurred when the law was made in 1281.

In the earlier literature the notions of scaldic verse and the magical power of words were explicitly linked.[3] In consequence of the development mentioned above, however, by the end of the Middle Ages *skáldskapur* referred to little more than poetry. Magic power henceforward was attributed only to a particular kind of poet—the *krapta-skáld* ('power-scald'). This happened in the fifteenth century, and the *kraptaskáld* was to remain an important feature of popular tradition until the nineteenth century (Almquist 1965: 15 ff.). The emergence of the *kraptaskáld* testifies to an increasing individualization of magical force.[4]

The notions of *kraptr* ('(supernatural) power') and *kraptamaður* ('a man of extraordinary powers'), were not totally foreign to the early medieval literary vocabulary (see, for example, Fritzner 1954: i. 341). The concept of *kraptaskáld* was later in origin, however, and was very much a feature of legend and folk-tale during the period 1400 to 1800 (see, for example, JÁ: i. 447–57; iii. 470–82, *et passim*). A very famous *kraptaskáld* was Jón *lærði* Guðmundsson (*c.*1574–1658). Among his deeds was a successful driving away of a 'Turkish' slave-raider ship, where his only weapon were the words:

> *Hátt ber segl við húna,*
> *hefur strengi knúna,*
> *krullað er hár og krúna,*
> *krotaða hvarmabrúna,*
> *heiðna Tyrkja trúna.*
> *Tapaða get ég frúna.*
> *Séð hef ég risting rúna;*
> *mig rankar til þess núna.*
>
> *Setist að því arður,*
> *ógn og skerjagarður,*
> *stormur og hafís harður.*
> *Hann sé með því barður,*
> *Sem músarhausinn marður,*
> *merjist vonzku arður;*
> *Íslands vega varður,*
> *verði því allur sparður.*
>
> From Sigfús Sigfússon 1922–58; viii.
> 41–2; and cf. Árnason 1954–61: iii.
> 554, 611

'The sail stands high by the mast, with stretched ropes, hair and top are curly, the eyebrows chased, heathen Turkish faith. I could lose my Lady. I have seen runes be carved; I seem to remember now.

Might the plough attack it, the dread and the skerries, storm and hard drift ice. Might he be thrashed by it, crushed like the mousehead, might the wages of evil be fulfilled; might the guardian of Iceland's ways, be spared from all this.)

Up against this, the ship disappeared. In this case the power of the *kraptaskáld* was used for the benefit of society, and to the detriment of the Turks. Something rather similar happened when the target of the *skáld* was an exploitative Danish merchant, although such encounters were more individual (cf. JÁ: i. 452, 539–40; iii. 605–6). One such encounter, which seems to acknowledge the cunning of the merchant at the expense of the *kraptaskáld*, runs:

A man who was a *kraptaskáld*, but who had taken to drink, once came to the trading station where he had often been terribly drunk. He asked the merchant to give him some *brennivín*. 'I will do so', the merchant said, 'if you will sing to death the man I loathe the most.' 'What is his name?' he asked. 'No matter', the merchant replied, 'it just has to be the man I loathe the most, whoever that may be.' He [the *skáld*] then made a lay, after which he dropped dead on the spot; he had himself been the person whom the merchant loathed the most. (JÁ: iii. 482.)

The *kraptaskáld* was clearly a dangerous man, even to himself.

Magical power was not only a feature of the spoken but also of the written word. The first writings in Scandinavia were runic inscriptions, and a close connection between runes and the (origin of) scaldic poetry has been suggested (Olsen 1916*b*). Contesting this, Bæksted has suggested that probably the art of writing in itself was so remarkable an invention that, whatever its form, it would have an aura of extraordinary power (Bæksted 1942: 17–18). 'Runic magic' was a more or less permanent feature of Iceland, even in the seventeenth-century witch trials (Olsen 1933: 105).

Iceland is in fact remarkable for the total absense of runic inscriptions from the early Middle Ages. Although the settlers must have known the runic alphabet of their native Norway, there is no evidence of its use in the Freestate—perhaps because runes in Iceland were carved in wood and not stone. Later, and possibly as a consequence of the Third Grammatical Treatise by Óláfr Þórðarson *hvítaskáld* (*c.*1250), the runes had a renaissance in Iceland in the thirteenth, fourteenth, and fifteenth centuries (Bæksted 1942: 19ff.; Olsen 1933: 104ff.). They were used mainly on tombstones, and their 'content' was Christian; the continuity of form, however, suggests a conceptual linkage between the new runic practice and old traditions of raising memorial 'monuments' (in verse or in stone), at a time when magic, writing, and verse-making were not yet separated (cf. Eggert Ólafsson 1772: 469).

In our period runes were an important feature of magical practice. In the verse by Jón *lærði*, quoted above, we heard of his having 'carved runes' to attain his goal, and generally in the North runes were used as a means of expressing certain formulas of incantation or exorcism, probably well before the Viking Age (Linderholm 1918; Ström 1961: 230–3). *Rún* or *rúna* mean something 'secret' or 'occult', and certainly the runes were used to conceal curses which could not be spoken openly.

In popular belief runes were an important device for directing magical power against people, and knowledge of runes gave access to superhuman power. The first *witch* burnt at the stake in Iceland (1625) was convicted for having in his house a sheet full of runes. Although runic magic at this time was treated very emphatically as an unchristian superstition, it seems, nevertheless, to have continued all through our period (Jónas Jónasson 1961: 400ff.). In 1746 an explicit provision against runic magic appears in the law dealing with domestic discipline. The passage reads: *Skulde og Nogen befindes ved Fisherie eller på andre Steder at have brugt saakaldede Runer og Ristinger, eller anden uchristelig Overtroe* . . . ('If anyone, during fishing or elsewhere should be known to have used so-called runes or carvings, or other unchristian superstition . . .' (*LI*: ii. 617)), then the person in question will be liable to punishment. This passage indicates that runic magic was used in connection with pragmatic matters such as fishing.

Akin to the runes were the *galdrastafir* ('magic staves' or 'signs'), which probably evolved directly from them (Lindquist 1921: 7; cf. Lindquist 1923). Staves worked in conjunction with formulas, which in many ways shared the characteristics of prayers. Although signs of a different kind, staves were not totally disconnected from words. The *galdrastafir* and related formulas were part of the oral tradition of the popular wisdom handed down from one generation to the next (JÁ: i. 423 ff.; Jónas Jónasson 1961: 400–2). In their more elaborate and comprehensive form, staves were also part of a specialist knowledge, and as such often collected in books of magic, of which a few have survived in Iceland (Lindquist 1921: 8–9; Ólafur Davíðsson 1940: 61 ff.).

The traditional centres of learning were also the centres of occult knowledge. The Sees and the schools connected with them seem to have fostered the most powerful magicians. In the seventeenth century the Latin school at Skálholt was virtually inundated with magic (Siglaugur Brynleifsson 1976: 152–67; Jónas Jónasson 1961: 399), and the legendary *Galdra*-Loftur started his career when still a schoolboy at Hólar (JÁ: i. 572–5). The bishops themselves took part in the *kukl* ('magic') in Catholic times. According to legend, Gottskálkur Nikulásson (bishop at Hólar 1498–1520) was the

greatest sorcerer of his time; he took up black magic, unheard of since heathen times, and compiled a book of magic entitled *Rauðskinna* ['Redskin'], a magnificent work in golden lettering. It was written in runic staves, all of them magical. To ensure that the book did not fall into other hands, the bishop took it with him into his grave; that is why his knowledge was never passed on. (JÁ: i. 499.)

According to legend, *Galdra*-Loftur attempted to reclaim the book by conjuring up the bishop from his grave two centuries later; he almost succeeded, but he had forgotten to take into account the human frailty of his assistant, who fainted from fear while holding the bell-rope and so caused the bell to peal, whereupon the bishop disappeared back into his his grave. Loftur only managed to touch a corner of the book (ibid.: 572–5).

Two other magic books were of general notoriety in our period; both were called *Gráskinna* ('Greyskin'), and they were found at the two Latin-schools in the mid-seventeenth century (Ólafur Davíðsson 1940: 62–3). They have been transmitted in fragments (unlike *Rauðskinna* which was transmitted only in popular memory). A few other magical books (*galdrabækur*) were left to posterity; possibly some such books were burnt either in separate book-burnings or with witches who were burnt at the stake (ibid.: 63–4).[5] These few surviving sources are enough to give us some idea of *galdur* in Iceland.

The staves and formulas are many, and illustrate a wide range of concern with magical influence. They were either protective or aggressive. Among the former were staves designed to give protection from all kinds of evil. 'If you wear these staves on you, no one can harm you, no sword or pain, no worm, and no poison in food or drink' (Lindquist 1921: 34). Aggression or violence could be directed against other people; certain 'staves are to be written on a sheet and thrown in the trail of a man's horse; then all his cattle will die if he offends you without reason; hide the stave in the trail' (ibid.: 52). One could also win the love of a woman. To this end a complicated ritual had to be carried out. A hole was dug in the earth-floor where the woman in question often passed, and this was filled with worm's blood; a circle was drawn around the place, where her name and several staves were put; the ritual ended by the reading of a long formula (ibid.: 56–60).

The power of magical spells was taken for granted by the Icelanders of our period, as by people elsewhere in the Nordic countries (Ólafur Davíðsson 1940; Lindquist 1921; Grambo 1979). People were not altogether at the mercy of magic made by others, however; in popular belief one could protect oneself from evil magic of all kinds by wearing a small linen bag containing salt, wheat, and steel. Or, when relieving oneself in the morning, one could suck up a little urine into one's nose; this would afford protection from *galdur* throughout the day (Jónas Jónasson 1961: 402). The theory of magic was eternally self-confirming.[6]

Before the Reformation *galdur* was by no means unknown among the clergy. In 1554 a certain priest was defrocked for having beguiled a young girl to sexual intercourse, by the use of magic spells contained 'in the *galdrabækur* found in his hidings'. He not only lost his living, but was also expelled from the Northern Quarter, and was to have both of his ears cut off if he failed to pay compensation to the girl (and her family) for the dishonour (*DI*: xii. 750–2). Apart from the case from Greenland of 1407, already mentioned, this case of 1554 was the first 'witch-trial' in the Icelandic sources. The absence of court cases between 1407 and 1554 implies that, notwithstanding the formal prohibition in *Jónsbók*, magic was an accepted element in social life until the Reformation; the clergy played no small part in the dissemination of magical knowledge. Conversely, Christian prayers filtered into the magical formulas; they were either mixed up with spells of a different origin, or they worked on their own account. The Lord's Prayer (paternoster) in Latin was for a long period after the Reformation generally looked upon as a powerful formula of conjuration by the common men (Jónas Jónasson 1961: 403).

We can suppose that the formulaic Christian prayers, and to some extent also the 'Godspells', caught the ear of the Icelanders, trained as they were by tradition to listen to verse and to clothe their view of the world in this form. Magical formulas in Iceland were characterized by a duel nature: they were evidence of a common Christian transmission of formulas, both oral and written; and at the same time they testify to a specific literary aspiration of maintaining a separate Norse metric form, deriving from Nordic antiquity (Ohrt 1935: 87).

The most prominent vehicle of magic or *galdur* in Iceland was unquestionably the *word*, spoken or written. The magical genres were poetry, runes, staves, and prayers, each with their individual saliency yet closely interconnected. To visualize their internal relationship, we may represent them as in Figure 4. Words were accessible to everyone, and potentially any Icelander could practise magic. There was a limit to this in practice, however, since only those words that were uttered out of *knowledge* were powerful. The native term for a person versed in magic of some kind was *fjölkyngi* ('of much knowledge'). As we shall see, the witches burnt at the stake in the seventeenth century were almost invariably sentenced for *galdur* and/or *fjölkyngi*. The notion of *kunnáttumaður* ('man of knowledge'), had similar connotations. The category was used for a man who 'knew a thing or two' almost up to the present day (Jónas Jónasson 1961: 398). The boundary

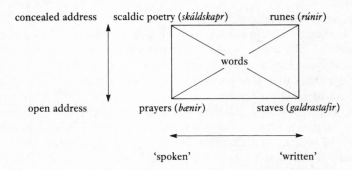

FIG. 4. *Magic Words: A Structure of Transformation*

between wisdom and magic, understood as a theory of causality, is difficult to draw in most instances. Certainly, in Iceland, the categories of worldly and occult knowledge were confounded. The See-schools that were centres of learning were also centres of *galdrar* and *kukl* ('magic').

If words were the principal instrument of magic, knowledge was its ultimate source. Theoretically, anyone could learn, and conceptually individual force and will were seen as important motors of the local history. Magical knowledge was linked to particular kinds of knowledgeable men, administering the four magical genres discussed above. The magicians may be grouped according to a similar scheme (see Figure 5). At a general level the position of any individual in the social system was partly defined by his relationship to 'knowledge' and his ability to muster the forces of nature. From a consideration

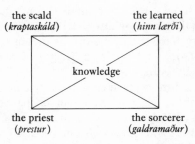

FIG. 5. *Classification of Magicians*

of magic alone, we might suspect that causality, in Icelandic cosmology, was individualized.[7]

The belief in individual fate-making was also related to ancient
notions of spirituality. When the first missionaries needed a word in
Icelandic to translate the Christian concept 'soul', they found none
suitable; they therefore borrowed the word *sawl* from Old English,
and constructed the Icelandic *sál* (*sála*) (*IED*: 516–17; de Vries 1977:
460). The *sál* of the Icelanders was thus a distinctly Christian term.
Any comparable Norse concept was clearly of pre-Christian content
(Mundal 1974: 43–4; Falk 1926). Such a concept was *hugr*, referring to
a unity of man's non-material aspects (Ström 1961: 205; *KL*: vii. 34).
Hugr was both 'thought' and 'mind', and was believed to be able to
liberate itself from the body and to wander about on its own (ibid.).

Originally the concept of *hugr* may have been related to the idea of
fetches, *fylgjur*, being people's counterparts. In early Icelandic
literature *fylgjur* (lit.: 'followers') play an important role as dramatis
personae, whose entry upon the scene augurs some future event
(Mundal 1974; cf. also Hermann 1903: 80–3). This literary tradition
might have contributed to a (renewed?) popular belief in fetches
(Mundal 1974: 23).[8] Mutual influence between written and oral
literature was a common element in the Icelandic tradition (Einar Ó.
Sveinsson 1931a: 194). Although possibly a *literary* product in early
Iceland, *fylgjur* were an important element in the oral tradition of our
period (Árnason 1954–61: i. 340ff.). The presence of the fetches was
believed to give form to particular dreams, which were then interpreted as auguries (Kelchner 1935: 17ff.). The idea of dreams as omens
of the future has been one of the most persistent elements in the
popular culture of Iceland (cf. Hallfreður Ö. Eiríksson 1972; Erlendur
Haraldsson 1978). Dreams concerned fate; they tended to foretell the
more sinister events of life, although they might equally help a fisherman to seek out the best fishing grounds (Lúðvík Kristjánsson 1986:
323ff.). Generally, dreams were interpreted as counsels for action; for
eighteenth-century Jón Steingrímsson, the dream counsel was given
by the good Lord (1945: 104), but in earlier times it seems to have been
conceptually related to the wanderings of the *hugr*.

When the *hugr* left the body, it could take on a material shape of its
own, thereby enabling the individual to change shape (*hamr*). A
person who could change his shape was *hamrammr* (Ström 1961: 205).
This concept had roots in pre-Christian Icelandic culture, and was
semantically related to a comprehensive (literary) imagery of more or

less overlapping concepts.[9] If nothing else, this imagery testifies to an element of shamanism always present in medieval Icelandic culture (Buchholz 1971; cf. Jón Hnefill Aðalsteinsson 1978*b*).

A final concept relating directly to the vision of humanity and fate should be mentioned. This is the concept of *hamingja* ('fortune'), the content of which has been subject to some controversy. Falk maintains that *hamingja* derives from *ham-gengja*, and thus originally referred to someone going about in another 'skin' (*hamr*) (1926: 171). He classifies it with the traditional Norse concepts of soul, and while this interpretation has largely been accepted by later scholars, it has also been amplified with reference to other Old Norse concepts. *Hamr* ('slough' or 'skin') may refer to the outer 'shape' of the soul, but it also has a more concrete reference—the caul of the new-born. To be born with a caul was a sign of luck, and *hamingja* came to refer to a personal measure of 'luck', sometimes associated also with a personal guardian spirit (de Vries 1956–7: i. 224). Thus the idea of *hamingja* was a particular Norse concept of 'fortune' (Ström 1961: 204; Sydow 1935: 102).

Within its associative field *hamingja* has been seen as more or less identical to *fylgja*, either through a semantic conflation of 'skin' and 'fetch' (Turville-Petre 1964: 230), or because the two concepts were essentially of the same nature, and both related to destiny—personal and social. Hermann suggests that *fylgja* was the guardian spirit of the kingroup, while *hamingja* was personal (ibid.). The opposite view has also been argued, however, making the *fylgja* the personal guardian spirit, and interpreting *hamingja* as the spirit of the (female) ancestors, guarding the kin group (Mundal 1974: 90–1; Turville-Petre 1964: 230).

There is some controversy about the proper interpretation of 'fortune words' (*gæfa*, *gipta*, *hamingja*) in Old Icelandic literature; I do not propose to enter this debate, but will instead cite Hallberg, who is of the opinion that we are faced with a pre-Christian concept of fate (Hallberg 1973). He singles out *hamingja* as of distinct profile; it is characterized by 'a touch of personification', being almost a spirit in its own right (Hallberg 1973: 153). Analysing the frequency of appearance, Hallberg found that *hamingja* gradually became less frequent (ibid.: 149–52). Transmitted mainly as a literary motif, the concept of *hamingja* (and related concepts of fortune) remained part of the Icelandic tradition for centuries. The idea of a personal measure of fortune or luck seems to have been a persistent element in Icelandic culture; it was an accepted fact that some people would be *gæfumenn* ('men of luck') and others not, and references to this personal 'quality' are found throughout our period. Some kin groups were more favoured by history than others, and with no theories of class struggle, the concept of *hamingja* served the purpose of explaining the individual and familial destinies. The *literary motif* of 'fortune' of the High Middle Ages was transformed into a *popular concept* of personal fortune. This concept made man the object of his destiny, rather than its subject.

Supernatural powers also existed outside of man, and a brief investigation into some of them will be appropriate before we leave the general field of magic. We have already quoted a passage from *Jónsbók*, containing provisions against heathen practices. Such practices were, for example, bewitching (*fordæðuskapr*), soothsaying or divination (*spáfarar*), and the invocation of spirits (*útiseta at vekja upp tröll*). Of these, bewitching was related to man's personal powers, that is, to his ability to use his occult knowledge. The second, divination, bridged the gap between man's internal powers and such external powers as he might invoke. When auguries were given in dreams, the power of divination was human in nature and related to the idea of individual fetches; auguries, however, might also be sought from outside. By the act of *útiseta* ('sitting out'), it was possible to invoke supernatural beings for the purpose of divination. In legal terminology this practice would be covered by the notion of *sitja úti til fróðleiks* ('to sit out for wisdom', or 'knowledge') (cf. *DI*: i. 243). Again, 'knowledge' is the goal, and 'sitting out' is merely a means to this end. 'Sitting out for knowledge' was a transformation of the ancient shamanistic idea, but it was also part of the popular tradition of our period. This is evidenced, for example, by *Skíðaríma*, a popular rhyme of the fifteenth century, to which I have already referred. This rhyme continued to be repeated right down to the nineteenth century. In *Skíðaríma*, Þórr and Skíði meet a certain Ölmóðr, and ask him to tell their fortunes; he is able to do so because he is 'sitting out' to seek knowledge when they meet him (*Skíðaríma*, v. 56 (Finnur Jónsson 1905–22: i. 19)).

Sitting out for wisdom was in a sense turning one's back on society and seeking contact with the supernatural beings of the 'other' world. This is clear from the notion of *útiseta at vekja upp tröll* ('sitting out to wake up trolls'). At the time, the trolls referred to were part of the pre-Christian mythology, and they were associated with the *landvættir* ('guardian spirits of the land'). A contemporary elaboration made on the provision against *útiseta* in *Jónsbók* demonstrates this association between the trolls and the *landvættir*. In 1281 it was decreed that it was illegal to *vekja upp troll eða landvættir i fossum eða haugum* ('to wake up trolls or landspirits in the waterfalls or in the mounds' (*DI*: ii. 224)). The reality of these beings was not in question, nor was man's ability to arouse them; it was simply illegal to do so. When heathen imagery was being increasingly suppressed (and as the Christian idea of the resurrection was presumably gaining hold), the 'waking up of the spirits' came to be associated with the 'raising of the dead'. Well before 'the age of witchcraft' (that is, the seventeenth century), the supernatural beings that could be invoked by the sorcerers were associated with the ghosts of the dead, or *draugar* and *afturgangar* (Ólafur Davíðsson 1940–3: 14; Siglaugur Brynleifsson 1976: 104). Whether they were *landvættir* or ghosts, the conjured spirits rose from the earth; they were associated with a 'below', in contrast to the (Christian) Heaven, 'above'.

To approach the spirits of the nether world, or to acquire the powers of the dead, the Icelanders would sometimes disinter the bones of dead persons and keep them as magical instruments, efficacious for divination and healing purposes. How common this was is difficult to judge, but in 1609 the king (Christian IV) issued a strong prohibition of so ungodly a practice (*LI*: i. 172). Nevertheless, the magical power of bones was not forgotten, and in 1714 the Danish monarch had again to remind the Icelanders of the law of 1609, with reference to a particular case (ibid.: 697–8). In this case the culprit was pardoned on the grounds of his senility, and on the whole the tone of the resolution is far less heated than that of a hundred years previously. The century of superstition and of zealous prosecution was over.

The dead were in general very powerful inhabitants of 'the wild'.[10] 'Superstition' regarding the dead had a very strong hold in Icelandic popular belief (Jónas Jónasson 1961: 420). Ghosts, *draugar* and *afturgangar*, played an important role in the folk-tales; they seem to have been a feature mainly of early medieval and of post-Reformation concepts of reality, and to have been of less moment in Catholic times (Einar Ó. Sveinsson 1940: 166–71). Contrary to the explicit wish to weed out heresy and superstition, the Reformation apparently brought about some degree of revitalization of 'heathen' motifs, including the ghosts (cf. Eggert Ólafsson 1772: 574). This may, however, also be due to a change in official sentiments about superstition, and consequently to a change in the source material (Einar Ó. Sveinsson 1940: 75 ff.). The *draugar* and *afturgangar* were not the only inhabitants of 'the wild'. There were also the *útburðir* ('ghost-children'), for instance. We will deal in more detail with the 'wild' space in the next chapter. For the moment, we can simply note that the inhabitants of the world beyond society were apt for magical work.

The magical discourse linked the individual Icelander with history in a relatively direct fashion. The naturalization of human action was founded in age-old notions of human nature, of the power of any individual to appropriate the forces of nature. By means of wisdom and with the use of words, everyone was a potential magician; anyone could influence the course of things. Counter to this ran the idea that individuals had different 'lucks', and that they were under influence from different destinies or inborn possibilities.

Common to both ideas of influence was the individual focus. Both, moreover, derived their deterministic power from a dual classification of the world. There was an inside, social, and visible world, alongside an outside, non-social, and invisible world. The powers of the invisible world could be appropriated through *fróðleikur* or wisdom. With words and knowledge people could cause history.

WITCHCRAFT

Witchcraft is a theory of misfortune. It is a specific variant of the general magical theory of causation. In witchcraft the magical intervention into history is directed against individuals or their property. In Iceland 'witches' did not emerge until the seventeenth century, if by witches we mean people who were actually convicted of witchcraft.

Although clearly witchcraft was in some senses a continuation of ancient magical concepts, its emergence as a distinct category in Iceland resulted from external influence. European ideas were of great impact upon the interpretation of misfortune in the seventeenth century. The aim of this section is to demonstrate how witchcraft in Iceland was a time-bound realization of a general theory of magic, and to show how *galdur* changed meaning in a shifting European context.

In Icelandic seventeenth-century society catastrophe had become an ever-present accompaniment to life. Under these circumstances it is not surprising that the Icelanders should search for evil forces causing their misfortune, nor that, given their ancient Icelandic theories about human causation, such forces were personalized rather than naturalized. What is more surprising, perhaps, is the limited number of witchcraft trials, with only some 120 known from the period.[11] The numbers are slightly uncertain, mainly because the vocabulary of the witch-trials primarily derived from the age-old language of black magic, and only secondarily from international demonology. Thus, the case reported from 1554, when a priest was defrocked and exiled for having seduced a young girl by means of magic spells contained in *galdrabækur* ('books of magic') (cf. Ch. 6 and *DI*: xii. 750–2), may or may not be classified as a witch-trial. In this case, as in later trials, the accusation was one of *galdur*. Apart from such liminal cases we have reports, of some 120 witch-trials from 1604 to 1720. Of these, twenty-two sent the witch to the stake. The first person to suffer this fate was sentenced in 1625, the last in 1685.

The trials were not evenly distributed over this period. From 1625 many years were to lapse until the next fire was lit in 1654; as Fitjaannáll has it: *það haust lét Þorleifur Kortsson sýslumaður í Strandasýslu . . . brenna 3 galdramenn . . .* ('that autumn the sheriff Þorleifur Kortsson in Strandasýsla let three witches burn' (*Ann.*: ii. 174)). The sheriff repeated the act in the spring of 1656, when two *galdramenn* were burnt (ibid.: 179). After this, there was a lapse until 1667, when one more person died in the flames. The annals are not equally extensive on this case; in Kjósárannál, for instance, it is just mentioned, that *það sumar var brenndur galdramaður af Vestfjörðum á alþingi* ('that summer a *galdramaður* from the Westfiords was burnt at the Althing') (ibid.: 445). By contrast, Fitjaannáll also supplies the information that the victim had admitted that a girl had died from his magic, and that he had thought evil about a certain priest who later died in great pain (ibid.: 211). Shortly after, the fires resumed, and from 1669 to 1685 fifteen individuals were sentenced to the stake. The uneven distribution in time is matched by an uneven distribution in space; there is a remarkable concentration of cases in the Westfiords (north-west Iceland). Both of these factors are related to the ruling of particular local sheriffs (*sýslumenn*), and they give us a first hint of the accidental nature of witchcraft accusations.

Iceland was part of the Danish kingdom and in the seventeenth and eighteenth centuries little Icelandic autonomy was left. Royal decrees were simply announced at the Althing, which no longer had a proper legislative function. The Reformation, moreover, had taken from the Icelanders the right to define their own ways of dealing with sexuality and religion. After the *stóridómur* (1564; cf. above, Ch. 6) local sheriffs, who were appointed by the Danish rulers, had to take action in all cases of 'heresy' and bring them to the court (*LI*: i. 84–9). This provided the administrative precondition for the dealings with witch-craft of any particular *sýslumaður*. Some of these were more zealous than others, and took immediate local action against witchcraft. Until 1686 Icelandic courts could of themselves sentence people to death and execute them, but in 1686 it was decreed that all death sentences had to be referred to the High Court in Copenhagen. This decree, in all probability, was instrumental to the termination of the witch-craze in Iceland.

One remarkable feature of Icelandic witchcraft is that, of the 120 trials, only ten concerned women, and among the twenty-two witches killed only one was a woman. During the period one more woman was smothered and thrown in the river for witchcraft (and one more man was hanged, another decapitated), but given the nature of such 'atypical' sentences it is uncertain whether these should be regarded as proper witch-trials. This is not only a matter of definition for the analyst; for the people in seventeenth-century Iceland there may also have been a serious problem of how to deal with 'traditional' instances of *galdur*, without contaminating the cases with European derived notions. Generally, death sentences were rather common in Iceland in the seventeenth century, for both men and women. Concerning witch-craft in particular we note, that in contrast to other European countries, including England and Scandinavia, the typical witch in Iceland was male.

Iceland was like England and Scandinavia in another respect, how-ever. The root of the charge was always found in *maleficium* (cf. Monter 1983: 29). Concrete harm done to people or animals was the trigger for an accusation; association with the Devil was secondary and mainly entered into the proceedings as part of the judges' general vocabulary of evil and heresy. The idea of the Sabbath was entirely absent in Iceland. Thus, to the ordinary Icelander, the witch frenzy of the seventeenth century was more a revitalization of ancient 'arts of sorcery' (Eggert Ólafsson 1772: 473) than a product of any modern demonology.

Early modern Europe was much afflicted by witch prosecutions (Ankarloo and Henningsen 1989); although a unified evil from the point of view of the Church, witchcraft was realized in a variety of forms, corresponding to local cultures (see, for example, Le Roy Ladurie 1978; Macfarlane 1970*a*; Alver 1971; Henningsen 1980). While Satan always lurked in the background, he was variously perceived, and there is as much divergence as unity in the European witch-prosecutions of these dark centuries. In 1487, however, some coherence was created by *Malleus Maleficarum*, written by Heinrich Institor Krämer and Jakob Sprenger, German inquisitors. Witches had been executed before this, but *Malleus Maleficarum* established the rule of more systematic prosecution. The book seems to have been in great demand, being published twenty-nine times between 1487 and 1669; in about 1625 an administrator in the Westfiords brought its rule to Icelandic soil, thus paving the way for the 120 witch-trials that were to take place in Iceland before the end of the seventeenth century.

Oddur Einarsson (whom I have already frequently cited) also wrote, in the late sixteenth century, of the Icelanders' belief in spirits of various kinds. He maintained that delusions of Satan were probably of less moment in Iceland than in various other countries, where Hell also had a more conspicuous position (Oddur Einarsson 1971: 48–9). It is ironical that in these other countries, many people of the sixteenth and seventeenth centuries seriously believed that Hell was situated inside Mount Hekla, an Icelandic volcano which had always been shrouded in mystery. Oddur Einarsson was aware of this, and felt compelled to state that he did not believe that Hekla contained Hell (ibid.). Like his compatriot Arngrímur Jónsson, Oddur Einarsson was anxious to correct what he felt to be an unfavourable external impression of Iceland. In spite of Oddur Einarsson's attempt to rehabilitate Hekla, however, it remained associated with Hell-fire for centuries. In Icelandic cartography of the period and well into the eighteenth century, Hekla looms large on both Icelandic and foreign maps, often appearing as the central feature of the island (see Nørlund 1944; Haraldur Sigurðsson 1971–8).

The menace of Hekla, as experienced by the Icelanders, seems to have been of a more natural order. Yet 'one would not put it past them to have been superstitious and to have believed in demonic powers altogether', as von Troil observed, in a delightful understatement (1780: 89). Even the reverend Oddur Einarsson firmly believed in diverse spirits, and generally the clerics shared the views of the 'people' in these matters (Thoroddsen 1892–1904: ii. 20ff.; Páll E. Ólason 1916: 8–10).

The annals provide evidence that more visions, apparitions, and natural auguries were experienced during the sixteenth and seventeenth centuries than ever before. We should, however, remember that this period was also the heyday of annalist writing. One example from the annals will illustrate some of the characteristic elements. In 1637 a certain Jón Þorvaldsson was subject to much misfortune.

Then somebody dreamt that a ghost which had been aroused in the East was destroying him. This explanation was received sympathetically, as it had already been heard that a man had been killed by a ghost at Eyjafjall, and that another man had been caught by a female ghost and dragged up a mountain where his clothes were torn off on Christmas night. He was later found, witless and nearly dead. (Espolín: vi. 87.)

In such a case, completely disconnected events and hearsays could combine to form a single coherent explanation of a person's economic misfortune. The next step (not in fact taken in this case of 1637) would consist in discovering who had been responsible for arousing the ghost. The notion of *vekja upp* ('to wake up'), made it possible to seek a human culprit.

Man the sorcerer could become man the victim. With a changing historical context, the wise man in touch with the wild was open to accusations of witchcraft. The first person to die at the stake for witchcraft was a certain Jón Rögnvaldsson in 1625. The year had been full of misfortune; the winter—called *Svellavetur* ('the winter swollen with ice')—had been unusually cold and there had been great losses of livestock; *dó allt kvikfjé manna víðast um Ísland, sem ekki hafði hey* ('in many parts of Iceland, men lost all their livestock, because they had no hay') (*Ann.*: ii. 104). On top of that there was an outbreak of plague costing many lives (Thoroddsen 1916–17: 67–8). At Munkaþverá the *sýslumaður* Magnús Björnsson learned that ghosts had caused a boy to fall ill, and horses to die. Magnús Björnsson had been educated in Copenhagen and Hamburg, and had become acquainted with *Malleus Malificarum*. In the case of the sick boy, the *malificium* was beyond questioning, but the *galdramaður* still had to be identified; the tacit assumption was that ghosts worked on behalf of such a man. We do not know why, but the bewitched boy pointed to Jón Rögnvaldsson as the offender; he took God as his witness (Þorsteinn M. Jónsson 1957: 9–10; Ólafur Davíðsson 1940: 109).

The sheriff seized Jón and searched his dwellings. There, a sheet of runes was found, which Jón admitted to having made. The general opinion was then that Jón was *fjölkunnugur* ('of much knowledge') (Espolín: vi. 27–8). Jón's brother, Þorvaldr, was a well-known scald, but even his testimony about Jón's simple-mindedness could not prevent Jón from being accused of *fjölkyngi*. The sheriff needed no further proof than the runes and the boy's oath, and was convinced that Jón worked with Satan himself. Since he was familiar with *Malleus*, he knew that such things had to be dealt with accordingly and without further prosecution. Normally, all cases of any gravity had to be put before the court at the Althing; Jón Rögnvaldsson, however, was condemned locally, and sent to the stake. What is more, the case never seems to have been published at the Althing; it is, at least, absent from the records. The most detailed record of it is found in the annal written by Björn á Skarðsá. He notes succinctly: *Brenndur til dauðs í Eyjafirði eptir dómi Jón Rögnvaldsson ur Svarfaðardal fyrir fjölkyngishátt. Hann hafði uppvakið einn dauðan, hver að sótti að einum pilti á Urðum, drap þar hesta og gerði aðrar skráveifur* ('Jón Rögnvaldsson from Svarfaðardalur was burnt to death in Eyafjörður after conviction for witchcraft. He had woken up a deceased person who had attacked a boy at Urðir and killed horses and played other malevolent tricks' (*Ann.*: i. 221).

We note that the annalist takes the accusation for witchcraft at face value. Jón's scald brother was less sure of the case. In a poem he laments the loss, and says that even if Jón had practised *galdur* it was hardly willed. Jón did not have the necessary power (*vald*); he was much too simple-minded (*einfaldur*) (Espolín: vi. 28). The scald sensed a paradox there, but apparently the officials did not.

It will be recalled that there was a legal institution of *tylftareiður* ('judgement by twelve lay persons') which in most cases could be used for acquittal. If twelve men were prepared to swear to one's innocence, the accusations would be dropped. When the second witch-process came up in 1629, the accused witch was given the possibility of acquittal by *tylftareiður*. The accused was unable to find twelve people in his home district who were prepared to swear to his innocence, but finally he succeeded in his paternal home district (Sjávarborgarannáll (*Ann.*: i. iv. 256). Others were later to have a similar good fortune. In 1630 a royal decree about witchcraft (passed in Denmark 1617) was enforced in Iceland, and sustains the impression of an increasing tension in these matters (*AÍ*: v. 188–9). It was not until 1654 that the next fire was made, however. Three men were burnt for witchcraft within a few days at the same place, victims of another zealous *sýslumaður*, Þorleifur Kortsson in Strandasýsla (Sigfús H. Andrésson 1957). The producer of the annal Sjávarborgarannáll explained the burnings by noting that the entire area was haunted by 'ghost-devils' (*Ann.*: iv. 293). The author of Seiluannáll corroborates this in his own way by mentioning atrocious Devil's charges; he adds that

The Power of Knowledge

only one of the men had shown remorse (ibid.: i. 305). Apparently the Devil had become a more 'popular' figure than before. This may be owed to the fact that a couple of Icelandic writings about the Devil's workings had appeared. The first was written in 1627 by Guðmundur Einarsson, prompted by the occult practices of Jón lærði Guðmundsson, the *kraptaskáld* and wise man. This work has an elaborate title (part of which is *lítil hugrás yfir svik og vélrædi djöfulsnins* ('Some Reflections on the Deceit and Contrivance of the Devil'), and is perhaps best characterized as a linking of the Lutheran demonology with ancient practices of *galdrar* in Iceland (Thoroddsen 1892: 43–6).

The second Icelandic demonology, *Character Bestiae*, written by Páll Björnsson, *c.*1630, was a truly international piece of scholarship. Páll Björnsson referred extensively to *Malleus Maleficarum* among other works, and *galdur* is directly defined as Satanic learning (*djöflalærdómur*) (ibid.: 49–50). Other writings appeared in the 1650s and 1670s (ibid.: 50–1) corresponding in time with the two most serious waves of witch-hunts. Demonology, however, was generally an élite preoccupation, and was little referred to in the court cases, although the Devil was spoken of with increasing frequency. Witches rarely admitted association with the Devil, even though they were often accused of it. There is no sign that Icelandic witches ever thought of themselves as a collectivity, or as a Satanic community as elsewhere in Europe (Cohn 1975: 102).

A singular character during this period of witchcraft was Jón lærði ('the learned') Guðmundsson (*c.*1574–1658), who was known as *málari*, *tannsmiðir*, *skáld*, *fræðimaður* ('painter, toothsmith, scald, scholar') (*IÆ*: iii. 127). His power as a scald was forcefully expressed in his own *Fjandafæla* (1611), which was popularly considered the most powerful magical poem in Iceland.[12] Jón lærði's story shall be retold here for the insight it provides into the spiritual climate of the period.

In a long autobiographical poem, *Fjölmóður*, Jón lærði recounts his life history (*SSÍ*: v. 31–85). This *æviðrápa* ('life-song') neatly complements the legends and tales of more or less obscure events associated with his name. A gifted son of educated parents, Jón was sent to the school at Skálholt, and apparently did well there. A solid clerical career awaited the man of whom it has been said that he was one of 'the most gifted men of the period' (Halldór Hermannsson 1924: iii). He was a keen genealogist, although mainly preoccupied with establishing his own distinguished ancestry (Hannes Þorsteinsson 1902). Jón was also one of the first Icelanders to compile a natural history of

Iceland (Halldór Hermannsson 1924), and there is no doubt that Jón, although autodidact, was learned enough to deserve the nickname, *lærði*.

Jón *lærði* was also skilled in a different field, however. While living on the island of Ólafsey in Breiðafjörður with his wife (who was also known to be *fjölkunnug* (Espolín: v. 136)), Jón succeeded in exorcizing a ghost (*Fjölmóður*: v. 41 ff.). Perhaps this frightened the people of the island; at any rate, they persuaded him to leave. At the same time another ghost was haunting the neighbouring district of Snæfellsness and causing much trouble to the people. Exorcism had been tried without success, and so appeal was made to Jón *lærði*. Jón, by means of magic songs, conjured the ghost to rest. These songs, the so-called *Snæfjallavísur*, have been preserved, and—with *Fjandafæla*—are among the most forceful magic poetry in Iceland. In a late nineteenth-century edition the first song from the last group of *Snæfjallavísur* runs as follows:

> *Far niður, fýla,*
> *fjandans limur og grýla;*
> *skal þig jörð skýla*
> *en skeytin aursíla;*
> *þú skalt eymdir ýla*
> *og ofan eptir stýla,*
> *vesall, snauður víla;*
> *þig villi óheilla bríla.*
>
> *Bind eg þig til basta,*
> *bróðir steinkasta,*
> *lygifaðir lasta,*
> *laminn í eymd hasta;*
> *ligg þú í fjötri fasta*
> *um fjögur þúsund rasta;*
> *þar skal bistur brasta*
> *í bölmóð heitasta.*
>
> *Sný eg að þér bandi,*
> *snauður djöfuls andi,*
> *biturlegum brandi*
> *þig bannfærandi;*
> *gleipnir grandi*
> *gegnmyrjandi;*
> *þau atkvæðin standi*
> *óbifandi.*
>
> Jon Guðmundsson
> 1895: 22–3

(Go down, monster, devil's scum and witch; may the earth hide you and tie you in mud, you shall howl in pain and go downwards, poor, wretched, to lament, might the smell of disaster bewilder you. / I bind you to bands, brother of stoneheaps, lying father of vices, bound to hurry in misery; lie you in tight chains four thousand miles down; there you shall grimly scrape through the hottest of pains. / I turn bands against you, you poor devil's spirit, a biting sword, that puts you in ban, may the chain destroy you, crushing you to the last bone, may these incantations stand unshakeably.)

When the magical songs had been sung by Jón, '*kom þá fullgódur friður á eftir*', absolute peace was restored, according to his own account (*Fjölmoður*: v. 47; *SSÍ*: v. 37). Jón *lærði* won great fame for this, 'but such fame cut both ways in the period of witchcraft trials' (Halldór Hermannsson 1924: v). Apart from the event itself, Jón's exorcism is of interest because it shows that individuals were able to conjure ghosts to rest as well as to raise them.

As for Jón *lærði*, an event of 1615 which took place in the Westfiords was to be decisive in his career. In that year the legendary *spánver-javígin* ('the killing of the Spaniards'), was the rather sinister outcome of an encounter between Basque whalers and the local populace. The whalers had frequented the coast for some years in succession, but had now taken to piracy and the local sheriff gathered some men to fight them off. A veritable slaughter of the Spaniards ensued, and thirty-one of them were killed (Espolín 1943: v. 136). Jón's part in this event is far from clear, but it seems to have been the reason for his being sent wandering again (Halldór Hermannsson 1924: pp. vii–x).

From his own account of the incident it is obvious that Jón had become well acquainted with the foreigners, or at least with a certain Martein who possessed magical powers (see Jónas Kristjánsson 1950). Martein's power was such, that even after his death (by drowning, as he was pursued into the fiord), his *galdrakropp* ('sorcerer's body') caused the storm to subside (ibid.: 25). This was very frightening, and tension rose. Because of his acquaintance with the Spaniards Jón *lærði* reacted critically to the official vendetta, and in consequence he was accused of having volunteered information to the pirates as to where and whom to plunder. The *sýslumaður* was not without insight in the art of magic (*seiður*), as acknowledged by Jón (*Fjölmóður*: v. 177; *SSÍ*: v. 3, 56; cf. also Espolín: v. 137). A fight between them might easily get out of control, and Jón fled to Snæfellsnes to avoid the fate of the whalers. At the Althing in 1615 and 1616 the case of the killings was heard; they were legitimized because the pirates were retrospectively

outlawed (*Áí*: iv. 309–23). No mention was made of Jón, now apparently living peacefully in Snæfellsnes. Rumours began, however, that
he was keeping a kind of school there, instructing young fishermen in
occult subjects (Halldór Hermannsson 1924: p. x). Prompted by these
rumours Guðmundur Einarsson, the local dean, composed a strong
condemnation of witchcraft in general and of Jón's magical songs
Snæfjallavísur in particular (Thoroddsen 1892–1904: ii. 43–6). In this
piece, commonly known as *Hugrás* (and referred to above, p. 218),
Guðmundur Einarsson linked the Devil and the ancient practices of
galdrar in Iceland, as a united heresy. The work of the *kraptaskáld*, in
particular, was condemned. Jón *lærði*'s position became very difficult
and once again he was obliged to flee the region.

A few years later Jón's son, the priest Guðmundur, accused the
governor-general's representative of having sought improper relations
with his (Guðmundur Jónsson's) wife. To get revenge, the representative accused both Guðmundur *and* his father of witchcraft, and now
Jón could no longer escape the courts. The case was brought before
the Althing in 1631 and both father and son were sentenced; Jón was
outlawed, Guðmundur defrocked. Both sentences were really a kind of
excommunication for having fraternized with the powers of darkness.

According to the court verdict, Jón *lærði* was sentenced not only for
his well-known exorcisms (which after all had benefited the local
communities), but also for having *nokkur blöð* ('some sheets') of secret
knowledge, arranged in over thirty chapters, and dealing with a
composite mass of black magic, healing, and the calming of storms
(*Áí*: v. 483–4). While the law of God would immediately have
demanded the death penalty, the 'civil code' of the kingdom (as
expressed in a royal letter of 1630, ibid.: 188–9), which was referred to
in the verdict, allowed of a more merciful punishment: loss of property
and expatriation (*skulu hafa fyrirfarið sinni búslóð og rýma öll vor ríki, lönd
og furstadæmi*). Translated into the Icelandic reality, the sentence
passed on Jón was *útlægð* ('outlawry') (ibid.: 485). In 1635 his outlawry
was publicly announced at the Althing and Jón had to flee (ibid.: 376).
He succeeded in getting passage to Copenhagen in the summer of
1636, and there he was able to persuade some influential person that
he had not had a fair trial. The governor-general received a royal letter
instructing him to appoint a new court to deal with the case again.
Thus at the Althing assembly of 1637 Jón faced a new group of twelve
judges; they confirmed the earlier verdict, and Jón once more had to
leave the country (ibid.: 482–3). A new problem arose, however,

because in his destitute state Jón was without means to pay for his passage abroad, and no public funds were available for such things. He was, therefore, allowed to retire to obscurity in the Eastfiords, where he lived until his death in 1658, and where most of his works were written.

I have elaborated on Jón *lærði*'s case because of its exemplary qualities. Jón's career as a *galdramaður* shows us how traditional means of exorcism, used for the benefit of people and gratefully acknowledged, could suddenly be translated into witchcraft. Under particular circumstances and due to a series of accidents, entirely external to the case itself, the work of the *kraptaskáld* was deemed black magic, and the *galdramaður* convicted as a witch. At another level Jón's case is instructive because it shows us how the *fjölkyngi* was a source of admiration and fear. Jón *lærði*, in particular, had an ambiguous position. He drew on all poles in the system of magical powers (as established in the previous section). He had a clerical education, he was learned in natural science, he was a skilled exorcist, and certainly a distinguished *kraptaskáld*. At a certain time, a multifaceted learning like Jón's could be fatal. It became easy to turn too much knowledge into a trap in which to catch the knowing.

If we compare the cases of Jón Rögnvaldsson and Jón *lærði* Guðmundsson, the sentences inflicted on them (in 1625 and 1631(–7) respectively) appear disproportionate. Jón Rögnvaldsson was sentenced to death on the testimony of one young boy, and on the evidence of one sheet of runes found in his house. Such runes could have been part of the household's medical library, copied by Jón himself. He was burnt at the stake, with nobody lifting a finger to prevent it. Jón *lærði*, on the other hand, was truly *fjölkunnugur*; he had used his powers publicly, he had even taught others, or so his judgement averred (*AÍ*: v. 482). But he was first only exiled, and then allowed a place of retreat in the Eastfiords.

The lack of proportion requires some reflections. First, at the level of events, the different fates of the two witches were doubtless in part due to their falling into the hands of different administrators, who held different opinions on the relative seriousness of the crime of *galdur*. The two administrators, moreover, used the law differently, one judging by the law of God and according to the procedure of *Malleus Maleficarum*, without referral of the case to the Althing, and the other judging by a Danish royal letter, and using the traditional court functions of the Althing. On another dimension, however, the difference in judgement can be referred to a structural paradox. By all accounts, Jón Rögnvaldsson was probably a rather simple-minded person, yet he was charged with *fjölkunnugur*, with great and secret knowledge. Partly because he had no such knowledge, he was defenceless against the charge. By contrast, Jón *lærði* was famous on account of his success in exorcism, and he truly was *fjölkunnugur*, by any standard. This meant that he was able to defend himself, and to call upon personal acquaintance with influential persons in Copenhagen. So the witless was burnt at the stake for possessing secret knowledge, while the learned escaped because of his openly recognized powers. Under these particular historical circumstances, the notion of *fjölkyngi* seems to have been turned inside out; the less one actually *knew*, the less were one's chances of being acquitted if one was charged with witchcraft.

Among the more spectacular witchcraft trials was one in 1656, which resulted in two burnings. The case is famous because the victim of the witchcraft, Jón Magnússon, wrote an elaborate account of his adversities in his *Píslarsaga* ('passion story'). *Píslarsaga síra Jóns Magnússonar* is autobiographical, but it is also an important cultural document about witchcraft in general (Nordal 1967).

In 1655 *síra* Jón was stricken by a strange (mental) illness. The Devil haunted him while he was carrying out some of his priestly functions at Kirkjuból (*Píslarsaga* 1967: 40ff.). His household began to experience strange incidents; one of the farmhands was struck dumb by the Devil's spirit while he was out fishing (ibid.: 63–4). Similar devilry continued, and *síra* Jón fulminated against it from the pulpit. After a time he came to the conclusion that his illness, and the more general acts of evil, were caused by two of his parishioners who were bewitching him. He had first seen the Devil at their farmstead. So persuaded, he went to the *sýslumaður*, and persuaded him too. The case was brought before the local court.

The two parishioners, father and son, were charged with *fjölkyngi og galdragjörningur* ('witchcraft and magic work'). In the proceedings of the court the offences are listed point by point. They fall roughly into three categories, and apply more or less equally to both Jón Jónsson *eldri* (the father) and Jón Jónsson *yngri* (the son). First, they had both embodied the Devil. Second, they possessed *galdrabækur* and *galdrastafir*, both of which were found in their houses. Third, Jón senior had inflicted harm to livestock, while Jón junior had attempted to seduce an unwilling girl by means of love-magic (*rúnir*).

Father and son were found guilty of association with the Devil, of the possession of books of the Black Art, and of the offensive application of this art. In the first place, Jón senior admitted to having possessed a *galdrabók*, and Jón junior acknowledged the presence of *galdrablöð* ('sheets'); upon further probing Jón senior admitted having cast spells upon a cow, and having willed the priest's weakness. He did not directly testify to the association with the Devil. Jón junior did so, however. In an attempt to cure one of his calves, which the Devil had pestered, he had used an old magical device, *Solomons insigli*. The Devil had appeared before him the following night, and demanded an explanation. To this Jón had answered 'Fye upon you, you shall not deceive me'. Later the same night the Devil had moved a cow from the mountains to demonstrate his power. Jón junior also admitted the lesser charges.

In order to judge the sentence, all possible legal documents were consulted. It was generally argued that the Lord had urged people to fight against witchcraft; several passages from the Bible were quoted to this effect. Second, *Jónsbók* (of 1281) was quoted for its prohibition of witchcrat, soothsaying, and 'sitting out', which I discussed earlier. Third, the royal decree of 1617 (made law in Iceland in 1630) was invoked; this decree introduced the death penalty for witchcraft. Fourth, it was argued that all Christian laws, even old Icelandic ones, demanded burning as the only proper penalty for so ungodly a crime. The conclusion was clear; father and son were sentenced to the stake. They were executed in 1656, after which the case was publicized at the Althing where 'all the God-fearing and justice-loving judges thought it right' (*Aĺ*: vi. 384).

For father and son this was the end, but the sufferings of *síra* Jón continued. The Devil reappeared, and the egregious Jón soon convinced himself that Þuríður Jónsdottir (daughter and sister of the two witches already disposed of) was bewitching him. He produced endless evidence of her evils. The girl, however, was allowed to clear herself by *tylftareiður*. Þuríður and her family in turn sued *síra* Jón for damages, which he was obliged to pay; he forfeited most of his property (ibid.: 384). After this, Jón sat down to write his *Píslarsaga*, with the double aim of justifying himself, and of accusing the administrators of inadequate ruling and lenient practice.

Leniency, indeed, often seems to have characterized witchcraft trials in Iceland. After *síra* Jón's case they continued in the Westfiords, but only a limited number of cases ended with fire, most of which were concentrated in the 1670s. We need look at only one more case in 1679, the only one in Iceland in which a woman was burnt.

The most comprehensive source on the matter is the contemporary *Mælifellsannáll*, in which the annalist states:

Þuríður Ólafsdóttir and her son Jón were burnt in the Westfiords; they were accused of magical practices (*galdur*); the woman had spent all her life in *Skagafjörður* [in the Northern Quarter], and never been up to *galdur*. Like other poor people she had gone westwards in the spring of 1677 together with her son Jón, of whom little is known, except that he was also without any reputation for *galdur*. Her son is reported as saying that she had traversed all the waterfalls of the Northlands without horse or ferry, by means of *galdur*, and she must then have been in possession of magical powers. His lies were believed and later they were both arrested and burnt, what he thought would not happen. (*Ann.*: i. 550.)

In another annal (Eyrarannáll) it is said, 'two relatives from the Northlands, Þuríður and her son Jón Þórðarson, were burnt for having caused illness to Helga Halldórsdóttir in Selárdalur' (ibid.: iii. 310). Helga was the wife of the rural dean, and since she fell ill shortly after the arrival of the two strangers, they were obvious scapegoats. In 1678 their fate seemed almost 'natural' to the people of the Westfiords. On the basis of coincidence alone, Þuríður and Jón were burnt without ever having admitted anything at all.

Although a woman this time died in the flames, we are nevertheless a long way from the idea of the Black Sabbath, or of a possible sexual relationship with the Devil. The rumour of the witch flying over the waters may tie in with broomsticks, but no direct reference was ever made to any such thing.

To end this discussion of Icelandic witchcraft, I will try to put it in a European perspective. The Icelandic witch-trials of the seventeenth century have a number of features in common with witch-trials elsewhere in Europe. Like Basque witchcraft, they show signs of 'a temporary syncretism of the witch-beliefs of the common people with those of the more specialized or educated classes' (Henningsen 1980: 391). Like English witchcraft, the Icelandic cases demonstrate a 'solitary pattern' (Macfarlane 1970a). The witches are lone figures, caught in a web of suspicion arising out of age-old categories and translated by local officials into modern Satanic notions. This interpretation of popular belief as Satan-worship is a widespread feature of the European witch-craze (Cohn 1970: 11).

The root of the accusations was always found in a concrete instance of *maleficium*, and in this respect Iceland was much like other

Northern European protestant nations (Monter 1983: 29; Thomas 1971: 531). The common people were concerned about individual damage or misfortune, while the rulers waged war against Evil at a much more abstract level. Satan was an apt metaphor for Evil in this sense. Generally, he belonged in a learned discourse—a discourse, that is, of Latin or international schooling. The *sýslumaður* or the priest who had been educated abroad was more likely to refer to Satan, than were local 'men of knowledge'. Popular notions of *galdur* and *maleficium* merge with foreign learning in the case of Jón Magnússon, whose *Píslarsaga* documents the syncretism at the autobiographical level.

The similarities between Icelandic and other manifestations of the witch-craze are not surprising, given the overall integration of Iceland into the European religious community. The political status of the island as part of the Danish kingdom made Iceland an immediate object for any new moral standards or legislation emanating from Copenhagen. After the Reformation, a single moral standard replaced the double standard of Catholic times, when clerical and secular judgement had rarely been consistent with one another.

Just as monotheism is a prerequisite of the unequivocal identification of Evil (Cohn 1970: 4), so one single moral standard is a precondition for the identification of 'heresy' (at least in the broad sense of the term used in the *stóridómur* (1564) for instance). Thus, the Reformation in Iceland entailed a sharpening of categories of right and wrong. This meant that everything falling outside or between these categories was a potential (conceptual) danger to the social order (Douglas 1966). This was the historical precondition of witch-craft in seventeenth-century Iceland. *Galdur* and *fjölkyngi* were no longer tolerated.

Fjölkyngi was not only occult knowledge and unchristian; it was also associated with forces living and ruling beyond society. 'Outside' the boundaries of the social were ghosts, trolls, and spirits, which could be invoked to harm people, by men who possessed adequate knowledge. The equation between *galdur* and the 'outside', made *galdur* a prominent target for rulers who wanted to clean 'wild' elements from the categories of 'the social'. This is part, at least, of the structural explanation of the witch-trials in seventeenth-century Iceland.

There is no ready functional explanation, it seems. While perhaps providing some relief of tension at the individual level, there are no indications that witch-beliefs upheld old conventions of village life, as reported from England (Thomas 1970: 68). The clash between old ideas of neighbourliness and mutual support, and new social necessities and public responsibility, may have precipitated witchcraft accusations in England (Macfarlane 1970a; 1970b; Thomas 1970; 1971), but there is no such evidence from Iceland. In England, two essential features were a necessary background to allegations of witchcraft—the occurrence of a personal misfortune, and an awareness on the victim's part of having neglected or refused a traditional social obligation (Thomas 1970: 63). In such a situation, the victim of misfortune played the primary active part in witchcraft; the suspect need give no direct evidence of malevolence. Most witches in England were elderly women of low social status; from the point of view of the local community they were more or less anomalous social persons.

In Iceland the social historical circumstances were different. There were no local communities of the village kind, and partly because of the generally very poor conditions of living there was little idea of neighbourliness—apart from the compulsion to house paupers. Most families barely managed to survive on their own on the scattered farmsteads. The *hreppur*, which was the smallest administrative unit, shared the responsibility for the paupers (*ómagar*), and taxes were levied on individual farmers to meet this demand. Poor relief, therefore, had long been public in Iceland. What is more, with scattered habitation it was difficult to locate 'outsiders' in relation to a geographical centre. We know that the poor Þuríður, who was burnt at the stake in 1679 together with her son, came from the Northlands and was conceived of as a stranger. Generally, however, Icelandic witches were neither outcasts nor strangers. They were ordinary men; some of them well-to-do.

The common word for witch in Iceland was *galdramaður*, denoting a *man*. Prior to the seventeenth century, this category covered any man of magical skills; in the seventeenth century, however, it came to be associated with 'witches', people who used their powers to the detriment of others. *Galdrakona* ('*galdra*-woman') was a little-used term, correlating with the scarce representation of women in the *galdramál* ('witch-trials'). A few female witches were referred to by derivations of their proper name, like Galdra-Manga (Margrét Þórðardóttir), who was the woman smothered for witchcraft (see JÁ: i. 517–20).

The masculine gender of the generic term for witch in Iceland is logically and historically connected with the fact that, ever since the introduction of Christianity, *frœði* or *fróðleikur* ('wisdom') had been associated with men. The *kunáttumaður* had no female counterpart.[13] Women were thus less visible than men as an embodiment of magical knowledge. Men were the wise ones, and the ones in touch with the 'outside' (cf. Hastrup 1985*a*). The ancient shamanistic notions, including the notion of possible contact with the evil forces of the uncontrolled 'outside', provided the cultural precondition for the social acknowledgement of witchcraft in the European, demonical, sense.

Similarly, the traditional concept of *galdur* was very easily translated into new ideas of *maleficium*. Within local cultural categories *galdur* was a means of inflicting harm upon other persons, through an act of will. The main vehicle of *maleficium* were words, spoken or written, sung or carved. Everyone had access to words, and many formulas and magical staves were in popular use for various purposes of healing and protection. Potentially, words might wage war, within a discourse from which nobody could fully escape. In consequence, anyone was open to accusations of witchcraft. Misfortune was explained by retrospective reference to malevolent acts, which had usually not been noticed as such when they occurred. 'Proof' was then found in a sheet of runes, or in a tale about having flown above waters. Finally, the court procedures and the sentence itself firmly classified the alleged *maleficium* as Satan's work.

The general Icelandic theory of magic, in which anyone could appropriate the forces of nature, and influence it by their will, was turned inside out. The individual was now caught, unwillingly and unknowingly, in accusations that were self-confirming to the extreme and over which he or she had no control at all. In this context as in so many others, the powers of definition slipped out of the Icelanders' hands.

HEALING

Healing refers to a medical practice which is directed towards restoration rather than curing. Restoration is social and psychological as well as physiological; thus, healing strategies are part of a comprehensive social and semantic system in relation to which illnesses are classified and bestowed with meaning for ordinary people.[14] Like magic, 'healing' rests on an appropriation of the forces of causation.

In Iceland there was a close interrelationship between magic and healing both in theory and in practice, as we find from even the earliest evidence. In an Eddaic poem from the early Middle Ages—which continued to be reproduced until well after the Reformation—we find the following verses:

> *Bjargrúnar skalt kunna,*
> *ef bjarga vilt*
> *ok leysa kind frá konum,*
> *á lófum þær skal rísta*
> *ok of liðu spenna*
> *ok biðja þá dísir duga.*
>
> *Limrúnar skalt kunna,*
> *ef vilt læknir vesa*
> *ok kunna sár at séa,*
> *á berki skal þær rista*
> *ok á barri viðar,*
> *þeims lúta austr limar.*
>
> *Sigrdrífumál*, vv. 8 and 10
> (Finnur Jónsson 1932: 251)

(Birth-runes learn, if help thou wilt lend, the babe from the mother to bring; on thy palms shall write them, and round thy joints, and ask the fates to aid. / Branch-runes learn, if a healer wouldst be, and cure for wounds would work; on the bark shalt thou write, and on trees that bee, with boughs to the eastward bent (trans. Bellows 1969: 392–3)).

Whether for midwifery or for the healing of wounds, runes were a necessary instrument. There was never any great difference between a *læknir* ('healer'), and a *galdramaður*. Jón *lærði*'s teaching at Snæfellsnes has been interpreted as a kind of medical training, for instance (Páll E. Ólason 1916: 20). At the trial, Jón was charged with having possessed magical books, containing both conjuring and healing formulas. Unfortunately these books have been lost, but to judge from the court report they drew on all kinds of knowledge.

Books or writings of a specifically medical content are found in Iceland from the thirteenth century and onwards, but only a handful have been transmitted from the period before the Reformation.[15] The pre-Reformation medical works display a high degree of unity; they are more or less directly copied from the Dane Henrik Harpestræng's medical book, often via a Norwegian copy. Henrik Harpestræng (d. 1244) was a healer of the Salernian medical school, founded on the

doctrine of the four cardinal fluids of man, fluids which corresponded
to the four cardinal elements in the world (air, water, fire, and earth).
The four cardinal fluids were blood, phlegm, yellow bile, and black
bile, and their internal balance decided the health of man. Different
qualities were attributed to the fluids: blood was hot and moist (like
air), phlegm was cold and moist (like water), yellow bile was hot and
dry (like fire), and black bile was cold and dry (like earth). These
qualities formed two separate dimensions, as in Figure 6. Sickness was
due to a displacement of the balance between these elements, and
healing was a matter of restoring the balance through a 'replacing of
the lack and a removing of the superfluous' (*KL*: xi. 80).

	hot	cold
moist	blood	phlegm
	(air)	(water)
dry	yellow bile	black bile
	(fire)	(earth)

FIG. 6. *The Salernian Scheme*

In Iceland, this general medical philosophy was introduced through
the aforementioned medical books, listing medicines to be used for
restoration. The medicines were compounded mainly of herbs, but
also of other natural products such as honey, minerals, and milk.
Herbs were classified according to their relative hotness and coldness,
and to relative moistness or dryness. In theory each of these
dimensions had four grades, but in practice few medicines were so
tightly specified. A few examples from the fifteenth-century Icelandic
Medical Miscellany will illustrate the principle:

Allium is garlic. It is hot and dry in the fourth degree. If one eats it or rubs one-self with it, that helps for the sting of vipers and of intestinal worms ... (Larsen 1931: 142).

Athenum is dill, hot and dry in the second degree. If a wet-nurse drinks broth of dill, she gets sufficient milk in her breast. It is also good for diarrhoea ... (ibid.: 145).

Atriplex is orach. It is cold in the first degree and wet in the second. It loosens the bowels ... (ibid.: 145).

Borago is a herb, hot and wet in the first degree. It is good for pains in the heart. If one drinks it with wine, one becomes gay. But if it is boiled with honey and sugar and is drunk so, it helps the chest and gives relief from what is harmful ... (ibid.: 147).[16]

This kind of medicine was part of a learned, more or less international tradition. Of the herbs mentioned, some were alien to the Icelanders, while items like honey and wine would be known but hardly accessible to most people. Thus, it is difficult to estimate the penetration of the specific Salernian medical knowledge, even if we know herbs had been widely used in healing in Iceland ever since the Middle Ages. In the sagas we get glimpses of skilled persons, women in particular, who treated wounds with herbs.[17] Medical prescriptions were also found in the magical books, sometimes to act against bewitchment. An example of this is found in the sixteenth-century magical book, published by Lindquist (1921): if one had bewitched a person to incapability of digestion by means of magical staves, this could be neutralized by treating him with 'hot milk and dry Album Grecum'; this, it added, was also very effective against diarrhoea (Lindquist 1921: 50–1). Magic and medicine were two sides of the same coin, and the healing qual-ities of particular herbs were also described outside the medical books of the learned tradition, which was largely in the hands of the Church, in Iceland as elsewhere. This was related to the clerical 'monopoly' on education, as well as to its (increasing) dominance in dealing with human weaknesses of all kinds.

After the Reformation medical books and manuscripts of many kinds abounded (Thoroddsen 1892–1904: ii. 55–61; cf. Loftur Guttormsson 1987a: 35). All sorts of medical knowledge, of herb-medicine, and of household remedies, point to a popular healing prac-tice of great vitality. Among the books were translations of foreign works like that of Henrik Smith from the Danish, which appeared in Icelandic in 1696. Henrik Smith (or Smid) (c.1495–1563) was trained in

Germany, and his education, like his writings, was diverse. It was
through his medical books, in particular, that he was to be remembered, however (Brade 1976: 13). Essentially, he shared the medical
philosophical background of the thirteenth-century Henrik Harpestræng mentioned above. Partly due to the Church monopoly, medical
knowledge had developed very little since the Salernians, although the
beginnings of an experimental medicine can be found in the teachings
of Leonardo da Vinci (1452–1519) and Paracelsus (1493–1541). However, these new trends had not penetrated to the popular medicine of
the Nordic countries in the sixteenth and seventeenth centuries,
although they were later to do so (Bø 1973: 16–17). Henrik Smith in his
Lægebog ('Medical book' (1577)) (which was a collection of six lesser
books on specific themes) largely reproduced the principles of the
humoral pathology of the Salernian school. These principles were
also found in contemporary German medical books, parts of which
were translated by Henrik Smith and incorporated into his more comprehensive works. With the Icelandic translation of this work a somewhat outdated medical philosophy was thus generously reproduced.[18]

A diversified popular medical literature appeared in the seventeenth and eighteenth centuries alongside the learned works. According to Jónas Jónasson most of the works were *gamlar kærlingabækur, sem
ekkert vit var í* ('old crone's books, without sense at all'), while the true
medical books were never accessible to the common people (1961:
312–13, 318ff.). The complex medicines of earlier centuries were
replaced by simple one-herb antidotes, and more 'meaningless' magic
filtered into the healing practices (ibid.: 319). Matthias Jochumssen,
travelling in Iceland between 1729 and 1731, stated bluntly that
'medicine is not used in the country' (1977: 9), and a few decades later
Eggert Ólafsson noted how medical herbs had fallen into disuse (1772:
452). A counter-measure to this forgetting of traditional knowledge
was Jón Pétursson's *Lækningabók fyrir almúga* ('Medical Book for the
Common People'), which appeared in 1834, following his more
learned medical treatises (1767; 1791). Some primitive 'medicines'
seem to have been part of a continuing tradition, however. For
instance, with colds and 'chest-diseases', it was common to drink
blood-mixed herb-tea, to eat juniper berries, or to drink a juniper
extraction (Jónas Jónasson 1961: 325).[19]

Medical literature is one thing, practice another. Until the end of
the eighteenth century the learned medical tradition was largely
administered by the clergy, while other healers practised popular

medicine. From the beginning of our period, the *bartskerar* ('barbers') had a prominent position as all-purpose physicians and wound-healers. They appear in Icelandic sources from the thirteenth century (Blöndal and Vilmundur Jónsson 1970: 18ff.). Like the word itself, the first *bartskerar* were of German origin. They came to Iceland on fishing or merchant vessels, staying in the country for the summer, and like other foreigners they had to leave again before winter. In summertime, when the trading ports were busy, a *bartskeri* in Iceland could make a lucrative living, since other professional healers were absent. A verdict passed at the Althing in 1526 provides an illustration of this; maximum prices for healing services were fixed according to a scale of relative severity of the sickness (*DI*: ix. 363). In spite of a tendency to overcharge, the *bartskerar* were nevertheless valued as healers, and were much in demand even beyond summer-time. They were allowed to winter in Iceland by a decree of 1545, although an individual *bartskeri* had to have the permission of the local sheriff, which was given only on condition that he was *landzmǫnnum til gagns og goda* ('of use and good to the people of the country' (*LI*: i. 63; *DI*: xi. 427). The general permission for *bartskerar* to winter in Iceland was indirectly restated in 1551, when the (Danish) king made a treaty with the Hamburg merchants. In this treaty the general prohibition on foreign wintering was confirmed, exempting '*bartskerar, drengir að lære mál eða skipbrotsmenn*' ('barbers, young men learning the language, and the shipwrecked' (*DI*: xii. 213). The *bartskerar* fulfilled an important function in Icelandic society, and some of them had more or less permanent positions in the households of leading persons. In Skarðsáannáll in 1619 it was noted, for instance, that the *bartskeri* of the governor-general had drowned (*Ann.*: i. 211; cf. *AÍ*: iv. 479), and there are many similar references (see Blöndal and Vilmundur Jónsson 1970: 20).

The emergence of 'personal' *bartskerar*, from the short-term free enterprise of the first German healers, reflects a major change in the order of trade in general. In 1602 the Danish trade monopoly was introduced, banning all non-Danish ships from the Icelandic calling-places. This meant that the supply of German *bartskerar* dried up. During the seventeenth century, foreign healers were gradually replaced by local ones, and they assumed a different position in Icelandic society from the one occupied by the German *bartskerar*. The original *bartskerar* had been their own masters, and earned their entire living from their profession. The Icelandic healers, however, either affiliated themselves to a particular (rich) household, or were part-time healers with their main living in farming. The *bartskerar* remained important healers in Iceland; before trained physicians appeared in the country during the nineteenth century they were one of the only sources for treatment. The autobiographer Jón Steingríms-son, living in the eighteenth century, tells how he had his broken leg cured by a *bartskeri* as a child (1945: 23).

It was not until 1760 that a trained physician came to practise in Iceland—about the same time as in the other Nordic countries (Loftur Guttormsson 1987*a*: 29). In that year the office of *landphysicus* (*land-læknir*) was institutionalized by a royal decree (*LI*: iii. 384–5). The first to hold the office was Bjarni Pálsson, who had travelled about the island with Eggert Ólafsson in the 1750s to supply information on the state of health of the Icelanders. A specific law gave detailed instruc-tions to the *landphysicus* (ibid.: 409–16). The *landphysicus* was obliged, for example, to treat poor people for nothing, while charging the richer ones according to their wealth (ibid.). He also had to prepare the appointment of physicians in each quarter. In 1766 the first two such physicians were installed, and midwifery was introduced by the same decree (*LI*: ii. 547–9). This professionalization was correlated with other trends of the Enlightenment (Loftur Guttormsson 1987*a*: 33–6).

'Hospitals' had been established at an early stage. The first ones appeared in the fourteenth century, and were meant for retired priests who were unable to support themselves (see *KL*: vi. 692–3). They were thus nursing-homes rather than hospitals, and they played only a small role in Icelandic society, where they were 'forgotten' during the fifteenth century. When, in 1555, hospitals (*spítali*) reappear in the sources, the previous ones are not mentioned at all. With the *Bessastaðasampykt* of 1555, it was decided to establish four hospitals in Iceland, one for each quarter (*LI*: i. 72; *DI*: xiii. 55). These were mainly intended as shelters for lepers, rather than places for curing diseases. In 1589 Oddur Einarsson complained that 'hospitals' were non-existent in Iceland, although they would reduce infectious diseases (1971: 86), and it was in fact not until 1651 that the hospitals decreed in 1555 were established. In 1651 a supplementary decree allowed four royal estates to be turned into hospitals for lepers and the disabled (*LI*: i. 242; Eggert Ólafsson 1772: 325). In the years to follow more detailed specifications about the financing and administration of these hospitals appeared, and there is reason to believe that by and by they began to function according to their design, continuing to do so for the remainder of our period; a 'disorderly' element of society was thereby removed (cf. Foucault 1961). In 1746 a new tax, *spítalafiskur* ('hospital fish'), was introduced to contribute to the upkeep of the hospitals. On a specific day of the year, varying according to locality, one part of all fish caught was to go to the hospital (*LI*: ii. 585); this law remained in force throughout our period (cf., for instance, Skúli Magnússon 1944*a*: 88).

The general state of health in Iceland from 1400 to 1800 was poor, even according to contemporary standards. The death rate was high and life-expectancy low. In 1589 Oddur Einarsson reported all sorts of diseases, spreading rapidly because people were unaware of the nature of the infection, and continued ordinary social intercourse (1971: 86). If anyone withdrew from social intercourse from fear of disease, common people called him superstitious and an unbeliever, since he clearly did not acknowledge the fact that God was the only master of his fate, and would keep him in good health for as long as it pleased him (ibid.). There is clearly a discrepancy between the learned and the popular vision of sickness, and while Bishop Oddur Einarsson regretted that there was no physician on the island (ibid.), the people in general were prepared to trust themselves to the hands of God.

In 1640 Daniel Vetter described the state of the Icelanders as miserable, mainly because they lacked necessities such as salt, wood, beer, wine, fruit, and garden produce (1931: 173). Surprisingly, he also noted that the healthy air made certain diseases, like rheumatism and plague, unknown in Iceland (ibid.: 174). A century later, Mathias Jochumssen tried to understand why the population in Iceland had declined. No wars could explain it, he knew, and although many people drowned at sea while fishing, the numbers were not remarkable (1977: 7–8). He quoted the Icelanders for their own reference to plagues and smallpox epidemics (neither of which was endemic to Iceland in contrast to continental Europe), and although he felt that this popular explanation had a certain truth, he nevertheless sought an answer beyond the infectious diseases. He found, finally, that the main reason for the bad health of the Icelanders was 'an unusually poor standard of living, and rotten food' (ibid.: 9). In general this entailed many deficiency symptoms, such as scurvy and widespread stopping of women's periods (ibid.: 23). Quite apart from malnutrition, the Icelanders also suffered from their way of living; Jochumssen relates how poor footwear, for example, resulted in permanently wet feet, which caused consumption (ibid.: 20–1).

Children's diseases, plagues, smallpox, and diseases of the respiratory organs and digestive system were also common in Iceland between 1400 and 1800, as has been extensively documented (Sigurjón Jónsson 1944). Of children's diseases, measles was particularly serious. The first evidence of measles dates from 1644, when several annalists noted the advent of a new *sótt* ('illness'), called *messling* by the Danes (see *Ann.*: i. 270, for instance). Not only the name but also the disease (which was thenceforward referred to as *mislingasótt*), seem to have come from Denmark: *kom út með Dönskum á Eyrarbakka* ('It came with the Danes to Eyrarbakki' (ibid.: iii. 203)). The Danish trade monopoly was not only in material goods! Deaths from measles were numerous in 1644, but already by the third epidemic in 1694, the effects were less fatal, according to Fitjaannáll (ibid.: ii. 309). Measles often recurred, but it seems that the Icelandic population quite quickly built up a certain resistance to it (cf. Sigurjón Jónsson 1944: 52–7).

Long before the Danish colonial order had imposed itself on the state of health of the Icelanders, they had been integrated into the global order of infectious disease through other foreign merchants. The Black Death, 1402–4, was the first catastrophe of the kind to hit Iceland, which thus unified it with the rest of the world through disease (cf. Le Roy Ladurie 1981 *b*). First-hand evidence of the plague (*plágan mikla* ('the great plague')) is sparse, while a little more information about the later plague (*plágan síðari*) of 1494–5 is available (Sigurjón Jónsson 1944: 11–29; Siglaugur Brynleifsson 1970; Steffensen 1975: 320–40; Kristín Bjarnadóttir 1986). Apart from these two clear instances of plague, a number of recurrent *drepsóttir* ('killerdiseases') were noted by the annalists all through the period, the nature of which is hard to determine exactly. In the popular view, plague was caused by supernatural agents. We know, from elsewhere in Europe, that the plague was linked to notions of an avenging God, and this was probably true in Iceland as well. Soul's gifts (cf. above, p. 95) became very numerous at the time of the Black Death (Espolín: i. 124); in 1403, for example, Halldórr Loptsson bequeathed his estate to Church and convent, fearing the *grimmradauði* ('the awful death') (*DI*: iii. 684–8).

The plague was not only linked to the Christian world view, but was also conceptually linked to ancient notions of sorcery (Siglaugur Brynleifsson 1970: 144). Fitjaannáll noted of the later plague of 1494–5, that *sú plága er sagt komið hafi ur bláu klæði, sem út hafi komið í Hvalfirði, (en sumir segja í Hafnarfirði við Fornubúðir). Og þegar hún kom upp fyrst úr klæðinu, hafi hún verið sem fugl at sjá, og úr því sem reykur upp í loptið* ('That plague is said to have emerged from a blue cloth, which had come to Hvalfjörður (but some say Hafnarfjörður at the old booths). And when it first came out of the cloth, it looked like a bird, and later like smoke in the air' (*Ann.*: ii. 27).

A naturalistic explanation of this has been suggested, to the effect that the merchant bringing the plague to Iceland from England had blue cloth among his merchandise, in which a rat had hidden; when the rat scurried ashore people might have mistaken it for a bird (Siglaugur Brynleifsson 1970: 127). The semantics of the situation, however, warrant closer inspection. The 'blue cloth' seems to have carried a rich semantic load, whether or not it was part of any English-man's cargo. Whenever the Black Death was mentioned, so was the blue cloth (cf., for example, *Biskupa-annálar Jóns Egilssonar*, *SSÍ*: i. 43). We know that the colour blue (*blá*) had special connotations in medieval Iceland. It was used as a generalized term for 'black' or dark, and in composite terms it was used as an amplifier; it was also the colour of sorrow and of sinister augury.[20] Thus the 'blue cloth' was no coincidence, and can be read as 'Black Death' translated into the traditional Icelandic imagery. As far as the bird is concerned, it seems futile to reduce this to an error of perception. From ancient times, birds appearing under particular circumstances had been interpreted as the *fylgjur* of the persons involved in the event; the plague was often depicted as personified death in the oral tradition (see, for example, JÁ: i. 308–10; ii. 101). The bird, therefore, is readily interpreted as the *fylgja* or augury of the anthropomorphized plague.

Learned medicine explained the plague in a different way. In *Henrik Smiths Lægebog* (1577: iv) we find a full treatment of the subject. The causes of plague (*pestilenze*) were, first, the evil influence of specific stars; second, evil vapour and smoke stemming from the earth where poisoned animals or dead bodies lay murdered and unburied (although 'it may also come from where the buried lie' (Smith 1577: iv. 1)). The first of these causes is wholly supernatural, and relates directly to the prevailing ideas of external influence; the second cause suggests an incipient knowledge of infectious sources. This know-ledge was not developed until later, and we note that the image of the 'smoke', part of the popular account of the advent of the plague in Iceland in 1402, was still part of learned vocabulary some 200 years later. *Henrik Smiths Lægebog* was translated into Icelandic in 1696, and it appears that the image of the plague was consistent throughout our period. The tradition of this illness included the idea that the country had been laid waste by plague, at least twice (1402–4 and 1494–5) (Eggert Ólafsson 1772: 688; Þorkell Jóhannesson 1928). Plague was always treated as *externally* caused.

Another infectious disease from which Iceland suffered was smallpox (*bólusótt*). Space does not permit of full detail here (for which, see Sigurjón Jónsson 1944: 29–49; Steffensen 1975: 275–319), and a few general remarks must suffice to situate smallpox in the field of disease in Iceland. Smallpox occurs in the sources from the thirteenth century onwards, and it was a killer, as the records show. Unlike the plague, however, smallpox never seems to have been interpreted as personified death, or as the vengeance of God. We know that the epidemic of 1707 (taking place after the first population census of 1703) killed approximately one-third of the population (that is about 15,000 people). Even in the eyes of contemporary observers, smallpox seemed to have had a less random course than the plague, and the annalists (indirectly) acknowledged the inoculatory effect of earlier epidemics. In Setbergsannáll, for instance, we learn of the smallpox epidemic of 1430 called *mikla bóla* ('big') that '*þessi sótt tók alla þá, sem ekki fengu þá fyrri bólu*' ('This *sótt* took all those who had not had the preceding one') (that is, of 1378) (*Ann.*: iv. 43). Remarks of this kind, which recur throughout our period, testify to a general awareness that resistance was obtained through inoculation, and that certain age-groups were more exposed to infection than others. In the late eighteenth century, this popular knowledge was put into dramatic effect. One person, on his own initiative, sent smallpox infected pus by post across the country, so that his father could inoculate his younger siblings. This started a local epidemic, and intensified the debate about smallpox inoculation, which was new in the medical world at the time (Vilmundur Jónsson 1969: 77–91).

Diseases were not all of them epidemic, or imposed on the Icelanders from outside. Life in Iceland was difficult, and all kinds of respiratory and digestive diseases flourished (see Sigurjón Jónsson 1944). Malnutrition or *hungursóttir* (lit.: 'hunger diseases') were a common experience. As elsewhere in Europe, famine recurred so insistently and for so long that it became incorporated into man's biological regime (Braudel 1981: 73). This contributed significantly to the repeated demographic 'crises' in Europe until about 1800 (Flinn 1981). On the sub-arctic margins of the European system, the Icelanders were particularly vulnerable. In our 400-year period, at least 85 years were noted by annalists and others as having particularly high numbers of deaths from starvation, attributed to a variety of factors such as cold, poor crops, poor fish-catches, and so forth (Steffensen 1975: 399–417; cf. Thoroddsen 1916–17; Finnsson 1970; and *Ann.*: i–iv, *passim*). The sources clearly indicate a concentration of misery at the turn of the seventeenth century, with several successive years of severe famine.

Hungursóttir ('hunger diseases'), were a significant consequence of nutritional deficiency. Among them was scurvy, of which 'leprosy' was classified as a particularly severe kind (Jón Pétursson 1767; Eggert Ólafsson 1772: 323–4; Skúli Magnússon 1944*a*: 20; Steffensen 1975: 342–8). 'Leprosy' was considered incurable, and seventeenth-century lepers were isolated in hospitals, although this was not always the case (*LI*: i. 237; Eggert Ólafsson 1772: 820–1). An interesting glimpse of the popular image of leprosy is given by Mathias Jochumssen, who reported in the 1730s that it was non-contagious, and considered to be innate; lepers, in his view, lived as long as anyone else (1977: 23).

In 1796 the Reverend Bishop Hannes Finnsson published a history of population decrease from hunger in Iceland from the tenth century until his day. In the Introduction to this history, he compared the 'sword of hunger' to the weapons of war which had recently caused so much misery in Europe. There was the difference, however, that while war spared women and children, hunger spared no one. What is more,

it kills after prolonged suffering, it entails a host of sicknesses, it carries off cattle and livestock, so that distress continues long after the hunger has abated, and what is no less important: it brings about robbery and stealing, while it lasts, and later virtue and government are replaced by a self-willedness which burns a long time after, not to speak of the hunger-plague which has often either been kindled by lean years or started since (Finnsson 1970: 1).

These observations, from the end of our period, are a precise acknowledgement of hunger as 'a total social fact' (Le Roy Ladurie 1981*a*: 18–19). The wretchedness which hunger entailed in Iceland almost exceeds the limits of our modern imagination: a father killed his own son who, drawn by hunger, had stolen some food out of the household provisions (Vallholtsannáll 1662; *Ann.*: i. 360).

Skin diseases were extremely common, as noted by Oddur Einarsson in 1589 (1971: 86; cf. also Jochumssen 1977: 22). Scabies was as common as colds and coughs, and it appears that people were unwilling to administer any cure for the scabies, since it was believed to function as a kind of purification of the body, letting evil out through the skin (Jónas Jónasson 1961: 312). This idea of letting out evil had been part of the philosophy of healing from the Middle Ages. Since time immemorial two cures had been prescribed: blood-letting and sweating (ibid.: 313). Blood-letting was done by the *bartskerar*, or the *blóðtökumenn*, who were not all of them equally skilful (ibid.: 315).

To end this discussion of healing and health in Iceland, I shall refer to von Troil who wrote in 1780 that 'the climate of the country and the purity of the air, contribute very much to make the Icelanders strong and healthy, though their food and way of life frequently produce the contrary effect' (von Troil 1780: 119–20). We have already dealt with both the food and the way of life as features of the poor state of health in Iceland. In addition to the specific Icelandic circumstances, the people also suffered from more general pre-modern problems. Women were to a large extent victims of their bodies, as elsewhere in Europe (Shorter 1984), and death in childbed was not uncommon.[21] Men, by contrast, were victims of their tasks at sea in particular. 'The way of life' produced a collective experience of untimely death— including suicide (cf. Sigurjón Jónsson 1944).

Illnesses contributed to the same trend. In Iceland, they were essentially of two 'kinds': *infectious diseases* originating 'outside' Iceland, integrating it into a global order of disease, and *deficiency diseases*, related to internal poverty. The infectious diseaes (plague, smallpox, measles, and the like) were 'incurable', yet a gradual resistance occurred for measles and an inoculatory effect was noted for smallpox. 'Infection', however, was not at all a clear concept. The diseases quite clearly were 'passed on'; they were conceived of as 'immaterial' and their causes were sought outside humanity in evil air, dangerous smokes, malicious spirits, and so forth (cf. also Tillhagen 1977: 18–22). The airy nature of the plague was sometimes personified, with the image of the bird-*fylgja* providing a conceptual link between man and the immaterial world.

Besides these 'external' illnesses, the 'internal' diseases played an equally important role in real life. These were colds, coughs, rheumatism, digestive diseases, and they were treated by various kinds of medicine. In general, cures were found in herbs and formulaic wisdom, forming a more or less coherent tradition based on the Salernian philosophy. Popular antidotes often had learned justifications; the mixture of blood and tea taken for a cold throughout the period, for example, is prescribed in an Icelandic 'Book of Simples' from the fifteenth century which is explicitly Salernian (Larsen 1931: 74). Learned and popular medicine formed a coherent whole in Iceland, even if they expressed different degrees of literacy, as it were.[22] 'Popular' medicine had its own rationality (cf. Tillhagen 1977: 18).

The greater the temporal distance to the Salernians the more did this rationality become 'diluted'. The eighteenth-century reports from Iceland are unanimous in their declarations about a very sparse or even absent use of medicine. When the first physician was appointed in the late eighteenth century, a modern medical science finally replaced the classical scheme, and a redressment of health and medicine began.

The semantics of illness in Iceland must be understood within the context of the general state of health and social life. Given the high risks of life and the recurrent problems of famine and malnutrition, illness became a steady companion in any household. As technology and economy declined, it became increasingly difficult to avert misery, and people neglected whatever medical knowledge they had had before. The Icelanders failed to connect important parts of their experience—as we saw also for the absence of breast-feeding, and the dying of infants—and, in consequence, they became increasingly fatalistic. Internally consistent, perhaps, the semantics of illness in Iceland externalized cause and left it to a fate that could not be neutralized.

CONCEPTS OF FATE

In Old Norse cosmology two different concepts of fate intermingled (Ström 1961: 200–4). One concept gave to any individual a certain measure of life; it was impersonal in the sense that one's measure was more or less accidentally defined, and administered by the three Norns, guarding the *Urðarbrunnr* ('the well of fate'); whence the designation *skǫp norna* ('Norn-destiny') (Strömbäck 1970: 204). The second concept of fate was more personal; it was an innate quality of 'fortune'. This was the *hamingja* and the *gæfa* of the individual, that is one's personal giftedness to exploit, or even to avoid, the larger destiny.

These two concepts are not immediately valid in our period, although a notion of *hamingja* is found. Nevertheless, they disclose a feature of general valency, namely a co-existence of an external and an internal determination of the course of life. This opposition is at co-variance with the opposition between an impersonal and a personal force. Ever since the beginnings of history the cosmology of the Icelanders contained two fundamental concepts of causality. One posited the Icelander under influence from external forces; the other made him of influence upon his own destiny.

In magic, these concepts met. Magical theory and practice were founded in a concept of man's dual nature; one aspect of man was visible, and more or less gifted with words and knowledge, which could act immediately upon the world. Another aspect of man was invisible, and could separate from this world to seek force 'outside' society. 'Sitting out for wisdom' was a means of assuming external powers, of darkness or of light. Man was both an object and a subject of destiny.

With the Reformation the innate magical force, the personal gift, changed in meaning. Wisdom, in the old sense of the term was alienated from the social, and deemed to be heresy under the new religious cosmology. This externalization of ancient magical knowledge eventually resulted in the witch-trials of the seventeenth century. Although relatively few, these trials were a conspicuous new element in the social experience of the Icelanders. They were an experience which confirmed one part of the deterministic system at the expense of the other. External forces now made man an object of a destiny defined by others. Internal powers and *fjölkyngi* were inefficient and undesirable in the redefined socio-religious context. Before, wisdom had granted man a position as subject in relation to history; now, experience told the opposite tale, and left the Icelanders out of control.

In the field of healing there was a similar trend. From a medical practice which included herb-medicines, the healing system deteriorated. The cause of sickness was externalized, and even the repairing of the effects was gradually given up. Here, too, man saw himself as an object of a destiny, which was defined by powers that were beyond his control.

A cosmology is a theory of space and of the contours and coherence of the world. It contains a particular view of man's position in the world. In Iceland, there was at least one consistent feature in the cosmological structure which we may identify as belonging to *la longue durée*. This was a conceptual opposition between 'inside' and 'outside', associated with the opposition between 'the social' and 'the wild'. Man could mediate this opposition; he could sit out for wisdom (cf. Hastrup 1985*a*: ch. 5). After the Reformation, however, the frontiers gradually froze. The wild became associated with evil, evil with the Devil, and the Devil with anything asocial. Heretics could now be defined and prosecuted. The Icelanders were transformed into objects by external powers—comprising God, the Devil, the Danish king, and the local sheriffs who judged ancient practices of *galdur* and healing spells by new external standards.

Causality, on the other hand, contains a theory of time and of the course of history. It also includes a vision of man's powers to determine history. Another long-term feature of the Icelandic world view was an idea of a man being able to naturalize physical force, and to affect history as the subject of his own fate. He was also, however, always an object of a destiny determined by others. The Norns lost their grip upon the imagination of the Icelanders, but God and the secular authorities provided a ready replacement. In social experience, the object side of the theory of causality became increasingly enforced, while the subject side dwindled.

The long-term structures of cosmology and causality remained dualistic throughout out period, but the balance tipped. In the spatial dimension the 'outside' became increasingly uncontrolled, and in the temporal dimension man came under upsurging external influence. This left the Icelanders with little potency, and no legitimate power to cause.

The experience of impotence was amplified in all social domains, as we saw in Part II. The inability to counter exogenous force is poetically expressed by Eggert Ólafsson in his *Búnaðarbálkur*, wherein he complains that his fellow countrymen had lost hold on their own fate. He was part of the Enlightenment, as it came to Iceland in the late eighteenth century. Effectively, the Enlightenment meant a revival of the long-subjugated idea that man could influence his own fate. This time, the source of influence was not ancient wisdom, but new and enlightened knowledge.

The Environment

AN environment can only be defined relative to something else whose environment it is. In this chapter we are still dealing with the human condition, and the environment under consideration is that of the Icelandic people, as seen from their point of view. Although the Icelanders lived in a space which obviously had certain objective physical characteristics, these did not in themselves constitute the environment; they were, rather, conceptually moulded by people, who thus defined the significant qualities of their space.

It is in this sense that nature is part of the human condition. Nature is mediated by culture, and people react to it according to a particular conceptual system (Lévi-Strauss 1974: 15–16; Hastrup 1989c). The objective facts of nature are transformed into a set of ideas about natural conditions, which in turn affect the total eco-social system (Bateson 1972: 504–5). Culture not only defines and appropriates nature, but may also recondition the conditions (Boon 1982: 114). Ideas about nature need not be static, and in Iceland it seems that the Enlightenment introduced new ideas, which were gradually to entail a reconditioning.

Throughout our period, however, certain concepts about the environment prevailed, which were conditional to Icelandic society. It is into these concepts that we shall enquire here, an enquiry that will take us through the animal world, the hidden dimension, and into natural science. Each of these domains was an important part of the environment of the Icelanders. In the final section concepts of nature will be discussed in relation to the economic order, and the circle of investigation will be closed.

A few introductory words about the temporal and spatial referents of the Icelanders are necessary. In an earlier work on medieval Iceland I showed how the social space was created by the first few generations of settlers (Hastrup 1985 a). The settlers arrived on an empty island, and their creation was of immense proportions, also as far as the environment was concerned. Time and space were socialized, named, and historicized, in ways which marked the physical space by culture for generations to come.

Concerning time, the basic division of the year into summer and winter persisted until this day. From the inception of the legal calendar in Iceland, recurrent events such as the annual meeting of the Althing were fixed in time by counting 'weeks of summer' (cf. Hastrup 1985 a: 19 ff.). Although changes had occurred in the political structure, the legal calendar was still relevant in many respects throughout our period. Apart from the meeting of the Althing, which of itself was a time-indicator (cf. *Jónsbók*: 32), the *fardagar* ('parting days'), were still very important. These were dates of contract between landlord and tenant, and between farmer and servant; they were defined thus: *Fimtidagr viku er vi vikur eru af sumri er hinn fyrsti fardagr* . . . ('Thursday of that week when six weeks of summer have passed, is the first parting day . . .' (*Jónsbók*: 136)). In a cyclical social order like that of Iceland (cf. above, Ch. 4), the recurrent *fardagar* were a major time referent.

The calendrical structure was much more than a measurement of time, however; it was also an indication of the relative position of various economic activities, as reflected in 'month' names like *heyannir*, hay-time. This particular economic time-indication was to remain crucial, while the medieval 'months' were probably not of general use in our period (if ever).[1] Von Troil noted 'the computation of time among the Icelanders is not determined according to the course of the sun, but by their work' (1780: 117). Johann Anderson, by contrast, claimed that the Icelanders knew nothing at all about time-reckoning, but adjusted themselves to ebb and flow of the sea and to the sun when it was visible (Anderson 1746: 126).

Von Troil is not only more generous towards the Icelanders but probably also more accurate in his supply of details of the Icelandic time-reckoning. He said, for instance, that although the Icelanders had four different seasons 'like us', they counted only two: summer and winter (von Troil 1780: 117). These two seasons were divided into twelve months which had names of a common European origin, 'but in ancient records, and among the lower class of people', they were called:

1. *Midsvetrar*   ('mid-winter')
2. *Föstugangs m.*   ('month of fast')

3. *Iafndaegra m.*	('month of equinox')
4. *Sumar m.*	('summer month')
5. *Fardaga m.*	('parting-day month')
6. *Nöttleysu m.*	('months without nights')
7. *Midsumar m.*	('mid-summer months')
8. *Heyanna m.*	('month of hay-harvest')
9. *Adratta m.*	('month of seining')
10. *Slaatrunar m.*	('month of slaughtering')
11. *Ridtidar m.*	('month of breeding')
12. *Skammdeigis m.*	('month of short days')

(von Troil 1780: 117–18)

The list is composed of names referring either to economic activities or to physical features. I shall not go into details of the month names, merely note that as far as the 'lower class' was concerned, it appears that the old principles for socializing time still predominated over the Christian calendar in the late eighteenth century.

From the beginning of our period, Icelandic space was extensively marked by cultures. As the environment of social action, space is always structured by humans (Harré 1978). Despite the inconspicuous houses, which were built like nature from earth, stone, and turf, and the thinly scattered population, the landscape was rich in meaning. Place-names were important, but also the movements between various places were semantically creative. The concept of orientation provides evidence of this (Haugen 1957; Hastrup 1985a: 51 ff.). Distances, also, were humanized and measured according to human movement. Von Troil noted that distances were measured in *thingmannaleid* 'that is, as far as a man, who is travelling to a place where justice is administered, can go in one day' (1780: 56). Such measurements may seem imprecise to us, because obviously they cover vastly differing mileages, but they are precise from the relevant point of view: that of human movement in the varied landscape of Iceland.

The point at issue here is that the physical environment and the basic dimensions of time and space do not form an objective framework of culture. Evidently, it sets some limits, but the human mind does not remain inactive in relation to the environment. It is conceptually transformed, and strategies for coping with it are designed accordingly just as the 'natural resources' are.

Even climate (see above, Ch. 2), which is commonly seen as an independent variable in history, is not an objective cause in cultural terms. Ways of socially adapting to climatic conditions form an important and integrated part of this 'cause'. As 'environment', nature is incorporated into a larger field of cultural concepts.

In Icelandic the word *náttúra*, a loan-word from Latin *natura*, was of currency since the Middle Ages. Fritzner attributes three different meanings to it. First, it refers to nature as the ultimate and objective conditions of human life; second, it refers to a natural 'quality', 'peculiarity', or 'ability'; third, it refers to a supernatural being or 'power' (Fritzner 1954: ii. 791–2; see also *IED*: 449). The multiple reference of *náttúra* provides us with a semantic key to the present chapter. The first section will deal with some natural 'qualities' or 'peculiarities' of the environment. The next will deal with the 'super-natural' dimension of the landscape. The last will revert to the first of Fritzner's meanings, and deal with nature as the ultimate (and allegedly objective) conditions of human life.

My concern is to show how the Icelanders were permanently engaged in drawing a boundary between themselves and their environment. This boundary was also a boundary between the inside and the outside, or between the controlled and the uncontrolled space.

THE ANIMAL WORLD

Studies of animal classification have been popular in social anthropology since Lévi-Strauss made the observation that animals are good to think with (1962). The animal world mirrors the human world, in the sense that various ideas and values are projected on to the animals and then read back into the human condition. A recent study of changing attitudes towards animals in England during the period 1500 to 1800 demonstrates how these attitudes reflect changes of a much more fundamental kind (Thomas 1983). In the English case we detect a radical—although gradual—shift in the idea of nature: from being something man had to put up with, nature became something man could tame and dominate. In the same period, the boundary between man and animal was drawn more firmly and tightly: the farmers moved the animals out of their houses, and into separate stables (ibid.: 40). The attitudes towards nature and especially the theme of domestication reflected new modes of thinking about *social* subordination as well. Thus, even if thought with animals, humans provided the sound-board in the orchestration of natural classification.

Iceland was not caught in the same web of industrial and capitalist development as England, and there seems to be no major shift in the popular image of nature until the nineteenth century. The point is, however, that whatever the projections from the human to the animal world in the first place, the animals talk back to us (Löfgren 1985: 207). Far from being a static structure of classification, the animal world is a counterpart to a human dialogue.

Animals can be classified according to various major criteria. Edibility and utility are two, the distinction between tame and wild is a third one (Thomas 1983: 53 ff.). Conceptually, the latter is relatively more abstract than the others, but it had a concrete manifestation in Iceland, where there was a clear distinction between domesticated and wild animals. According to Oddur Einarsson in 1589, the domesticated or tame animals were cows, sheep, horses, goats, pigs, dogs, and cats (1971: 97–102). As discussed previously (Ch. 3, above), pigs were soon to disappear completely, and goats were of limited currency. They were found only in the few remaining woodlands; they were extremely useful, because they gave much milk and had a fine skin (ibid.: 101). In 1638 Gísli Oddsson lists horses, cows, sheep, and goats as the important domesticated animals (1942: 96). It is noteworthy that no fowl are mentioned. In 1772 Eggert Ólafsson remarked that previously tame birds like geese had been common, but that these were now completely absent (1772: 59, 202).

Cows and sheep remained the pillars of the Icelandic economy, but they occupied different positions in the image of the animal world. Both were domesticated, edible, and useful, but they were dissimilar in relation to the human world. Cows belonged entirely to the domesticated sphere. Like women they belonged *inside* the social, and were classified as female (Hastrup 1985a). In popular imagery, cows were human to the point where they might speak in human language, either on New Year's Night or on Twelfth Night. At midnight one cow would start by saying *mál er að mæla* ('we have to talk'); any human present would soon be deliberately confused by the cows, so that only a few sentences of the cow-talk would be remembered (JÁ: i. 609).

By contrast, sheep only partially belonged to the human world. Some were milked, and the entire flock was kept on the farmstead during winter, but during summer the sheep 'went wild'. They crossed the boundary between inside and outside, just as the men did during the autumn round-up. The sheep were more 'male' than the cows (Hastrup 1985b). The association between the sheep and the 'supernatural' outside is testified to by Gísli Oddsson, for instance, who in 1638 noted that some ewes give birth to lambs without intervention of rams. Whenever rams entered a particular place, they were immediately killed, probably by 'elves or "hidden people" or their "hidden sheep-puppies", which have sometimes appeared in the shape of a hunting dog or a fox' (Gísli Oddsson 1942: 96). The implication is that the hidden people, the subterranean inhabitants of the outside, wanted the sheep for themselves.

Deformed lambs were also blamed on the hidden people (ibid.). In the eighteenth century Eggert Ólafsson relates: 'The superstitious peasants still blame the hidden people and other ghosts for the birth of monsters but reasonable people know better' (1772: 196). Reasonable people knew it as a result of environmental forces of a different kind; where the sheep graze at the sea-shore, for instance, 'there are many insects, fish and birds, which together with the emanation in the air could evoke several strange beings in the imagination of a sheep, carrying a lamb' (ibid.).

Horses were an object of much pride. They were perceived as strong, so strong that they could carry two barrels of iron, beer, or butter at the same time. Other horses were mainly used for riding, and while men could only mount one at a time, the entire lot would follow (Oddur Einarsson 1971: 101). They went loose but stuck to the human world when required and had a sense of internal 'community'. Half a century later, Gísli Oddsson also praised the Icelandic horses, whose wit and running capability foreigners 'like the British and the Danes' found almost supernatural (1942: 97). Just as the sheep were connected to the outside, so also the horses struck a note of the wild.

'Tamed' horses had a more wild cousin in the *nikur*, or 'water-horse'. The *nikur*, or *nikurhestur* ('-horse'), was a sometimes ill-willed water-spirit, who might appear in various shapes (Gísli Oddsson 1942: 69). Those who had investigated the matter, sometimes had seen glistening ore at the bottom of the water from which the *nikur* emerged (ibid.). A puzzle to the scholar and Bishop Gísli, it was nevertheless as real to him as to his flock.

The *nikur* lived in running waters as well as lakes, and had even been observed in the sea around the island Grímsey, to the north of Iceland. A *nikur* was predominantly light-grey, and mixed with ordinary horses. Most tales about the *nikur* tell how it lured people on to its back, and then rode straight into the water, under pretence of helping them cross the river (for example, JÁ: i. 129–32). In a sense, the *nikur* gave a name to a very real danger. In 1772 the 'enlightened' Eggert Ólafsson contended that the *nikur* was fiction, thus testifying to a new scientific rationality; he admitted, however, that the *nikur* was still real for the ordinary people (55).

Wild mammals were few. The largest one was the fox, *refur* or *melrakki*, which in Iceland was endowed with slyness, and was closely associated with the dangers of the outside (Haraldur Ólafsson 1987). It was considered a serious threat against livestock. In the Freestate white fox-skin could be used as a means of payment, the value of a fox-skin being equal to a sheepskin (*Grágás*: i*b*. 141, 192). Fox-hunting (*melrakkaveiðar*) was unrestricted, even on another's property: *Melrakki er á hvers manns jǫrðu úheilagr* (*Jónsbók*: 192; cf. *Grágás*: ii. 507). In 1680 *melrakkaveiðar* was made a compulsory task, when a law was issued to the effect that each *bóndi* in possession of six or more sheep had to kill two young or one old fox per year, failing which he would face a fine of 3 *álnir* (or more, in case of late payment) (*LI*: i. 379). Clearly, the *melrakki* was seen as a malignant element of the Icelandic natural environment, which man should strive to destroy.

The same applied to the polar bears which occasionally appeared in Iceland, coming on drift-ice from Greenland. *Bjǫrn er úheilagr á hvers manns jǫrðu, ok á sá bjǫrn er fyrstr kemr banasári á* ('a bear is nowhere sanctified, and belongs to the man who gives the mortal wound' (*Jónsbók*: 192)). This passage points to the bear normally being hunted by a collectivity of people, while belonging to the individual who first inflicted the mortal wound on it. With contemporary weapons, a group of men had to encircle the bear in order to get within spearing distance. In Skarðsárannáll of 1518 there is an elaborate story of a bear-hunt, which demonstrates both the real danger which the bear represented, and the cunning and strength required of the bear-hunters (*Ann.*: i. 82–3; Espólín: iii. 50–1). A polar bear had landed in Skagafjörður on the north coast, where it immediately killed six people, all of them women and children. A local 'hunter' of renown organized a hunt, and fourteen men set out, weapons in hand, to bring down the beast. They chased it for a whole day on land and out into the fiord, where finally it received its death blow from an axe. Polar bears were not particularly common in Iceland, but those that did drift ashore played a memorable role.[2]

The story of 1518 referred to here is of further interest because it links the hunter Ketill's success in the bear-chase with his great skills in shark-catching. Shark (*hákarl*) was much praised as food, and it was said of Ketill that he was *aflamaður mikill* ('a great provisioner'), who had succeeded in catching eighty, even ninety, sharks in one spring season. With this renown in the domain of *veiðar* ('hunting'), it was Ketill, of course, who could bring down the monstrous polar bear. This points to the close conceptual connection between wild nature and the sea-resources.

Polar foxes and bears were not the only inhabitants of the wilderness, but they played an important role in the Icelandic imagery of the hostile environment. They were hunted by the Icelanders in their own interest, as it were. By contrast, falcons were hunted and caught in the interest of the king and only by royal privilege (*LI*: i. 177, *et passim* (1614); cf. Skúli Magnússon 1944*a*: 69, 82–3). The external ruling embraced nature too. This was also exemplified when in the eighteenth century the king decreed that hares and reindeer be imported to Iceland for the sake of hunting (*LI*: iv. 637 (1782); v. 61–2 (1784)). The project had little success, however.

Among the other inhabitants of the conceptual wilderness were many species of wild birds. In 1589 Oddur Einarsson lists some thirty kinds, and seems to know them well (1971: 102ff.). The king of the birds was the eagle, which occasionally took lambs and even children. The raven was wicked, and occasionally attacked and killed horses. The birds were classified as either sea- or land-birds, and Oddur Einarsson related how the migratory birds arriving at Reykjanes on exactly the same day every year were so exhausted from the flight that one could catch them by hand (ibid.: 106). The Icelanders did not do this, however, because in this as in other matters they saw a divine right (ibid.). Only later, when the birds were dispersed over the island would men hunt them.

Some sea-birds provided feathers and down,[3] others were hunted for meat, and eggs were collected from the nesting sites on the cliffs. The now extinct *geirfugl*, the great auk, deserves particular mention. According to Oddur Einarsson it almost had no wings and was unable to fly. It was an enormous bird, and when hunters went out for *geirfuglar*, these would confront the men in great flocks and run them down unless the men succeeded in killing a few birds in the front-line, which would then discourage the rest (ibid.: 106–7).

Gísli Oddsson (1638) and Jón *lærði* Guðmundsson (*c.*1640) also listed the birds they knew. Gísli praised the ingenuity of nature, which allowed the grouse to change colour, and thus to adapt to the natural conditions of summer and winter (Gísli Oddsson 1638; Jónas Rafnar

1942: 84). Jón *lærði* told of a bird, *hrijsehuislann* (the nature of which remains obscure), which lived in the woods, and was used by the old doctors for healing (Jón Guðmudsson 1640; Halldór Hermansson 1924: 20). Other birds had different powers: *giæs og alpt hafa skadligann anda, ef þeirra frijsingar koma á men* ('geese and swans have a pernicious spirit if their breathing hits men' (ibid.)).

In the popular tradition, some birds had a special image. Most tales were about the eagle (*örn*) or raven (*hrafn*) who were mighty or sly. The eagle's power could be transferred to humans: if someone wanted to divine or to 'see' for others, for example, he could take a feather from the left wing of the eagle and place it under his pillow. Thus he would acquire the eagle's exceptional sight. And if a young child drank milk through a straw made from an eagle's feather he would acquire an exceptional memory (JÁ: i. 613). The raven had the nickname *augnavargur*, 'eyes' wolf', because of its taste for the eyes of animal carcasses (ibid.). It is interesting that the notion of *vargur* ('wolf') was used, since this was also the label orginally given to outlaws (cf. Hastrup 1985*a*). The fox, too, would occasionally be so designated, and on the conceptual level there seems to be an association between raven, fox, and outlaw.

Birds had a world of their own, but they also had definite relations to man, either economic or conceptual. The world of birds was not wholly inaccessible to man, because there was a way of understanding their language.

To understand birds' language wise men have discovered a means—to take a tongue from a merlin, which is blue, and put it into honey for two days and three nights; if it is then placed under the tongue, then the bearer will understand the birds' language. (JÁ: i. 611.)

One had to be careful, however, because the merlin was noxious (ibid.).

Unlike the cows who spoke human language, the birds had a separate language. The cows could confuse humans *not* to understand, while men could use their own ingenuity to understand birds. By certain means and at a certain risk, the outside could be accessible and temporarily conquered.

Risk was also part of the appropriation of the sea resources. The Icelanders had extensive knowledge of fish and other deep-sea beings, not all of which are known to science. It has been suggested that the aquatic environment is alien to man because of the strange behaviour of the water objects (Hewes 1948: 238). The closed or hidden world of the fish thus represents an entirely different world from the humans'. Although it is probably true that fish are rarely used as metaphors for the social because there are few obvious points of resemblance (Kleivan 1984: 889), this does not preclude a vivid imagination of the life below the surface. Certainly, this was a feature of Icelandic thinking.

The *sæbúar* ('water-dwellers'), embraced all kinds of fish, whale, seals, and supernatural beings, many of which had a strong grip on the Icelandic imagination (Ólafur Davíðsson 1900; Lúðvík Kristjánsson 1986). In a recent work, Gísli Pálsson has shown that 'thinking with fish' in Iceland was related to the position of fish as a resouce in a specific historical and technological environment (Gísli Pálsson 1987). In a period like the one from 1400 to 1800 the technological skills remained largely unchanged, and so did probably the idea of fish.

No clear boundary was drawn between fish and other sea-beings. Not only whales and seals but also a great variety of other beings were classified with the fish. Some whales were wicked and assumed fantastic proportions, like the *stökkull* ('jumper') or 'horse-whale' (Oddur Einarsson 1971: 116; Jón Guðmundsson 1924: 80). The *stökkull* was almost blindfold by flaps of skin hanging down over his eyes. The only way he could lift these flaps was by jumping out of the water; when in the air, he could see and identify what was floating on the surface—and which he would then proceed to sink (ibid.; Ólafur Davíðsson 1900: 318–19). Almost as dangerous to man was the *loðsilungur* ('hairy trout'), allegedly created by giants and demons. Men become deadly sick or die from those hairy trouts ...' (Jón Guðmundsson 1924: 9).

There were also sea-people. 'Latin-speaking people call them either *tritóna* or *sýrenur*, but in our language the males are called *marbendill*, and the female *margýgur*' (Gísli Oddsson 1942: 71). Seamen and mermaids had become rare when Gísli Oddsson wrote his work, but he found it documented that in 1586 such beings were seen in south Iceland (ibid.). Mermaids could be fatal to the fishermen, and *hafstrambur* were always so. They were female beings who emerged upright from the sea, and dragged sailors out of their boats in order to eat them (ibid.). By contrast, the similar but much smaller being, *mjaldur*, was very useful; wherever he was seen at sea, the catch was abundant (ibid.: 72).

The Icelanders knew a large animal world, which they incorporated in their conceptual universe together with imported foreign bestiaries with pictures of elephants and other strange creatures (cf. Hermannsson 1938). A few general points are clear. The animal world was primarily divided into domesticated and wild spheres. Cows, sheep, and horses were domesticated, but stood in different positions in relation to man. The wild animals were of differing utility and edibility. Birds and fish comprised both edible and inedible species; they represented an environment which could be partially exploited. Some wild animals were just wild, like the sly fox or the malign polar bear.

The animal world may be arranged in the scheme illustrated by Figure 7, inspired by Lévi-Strauss 1962 (cf. Hastrup 1985*b*: 58). Cows and sheep were related metonymically to the human world; they both belonged to social farming. The cows were always close to home and were more or less 'human'; they spoke human language, for instance. The sheep were non-human in the sense that they crossed the boundary between inside and outside at regular intervals.

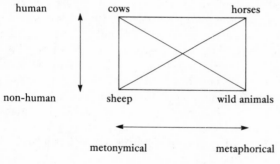

F IG. 7. *Classification of Animals*

Horses belonged to a separate space; they were tamed yet left more or less wild and out-of-doors for the entire year. They had both will and character, and I have here designated them as metaphorical humans. They were not edible but certainy utile, and endowed with both physical strength and a power of orientation in the wilderness which man had to traverse on horseback.

Wild animals, and especially the bear and the fox, were metaphorical non-humans. They belonged to a distinct series and were not part of the human world. Rather they affronted society, and people might kill them.

This scheme of classification demonstrates how animals were good to think with in Iceland. It does not exhaust the issue, but serves as a preliminary result of our visit to the animal world.

THE HIDDEN DIMENSION

The fish took us to the invisible space of the waters, where the boundaries of the animal world were fluid. Partial invisibility is also a keynote in the present section, where I shall deal with the hidden dimension of the landscape. On closer inspection we realize that the Icelandic landscape was always inhabited by invisible beings, and for the modern observer they would seem supernatural or unreal. This is a consequence of our having been educated in the Western visualist tradition, where veracity and visibility have been equated (Hastrup 1986c). But in the world of the Icelanders the hidden dimension was as real as anything. Even today, the ethnographer may experience this empirical unreality of the Icelandic landscape (Hastrup 1987b).

In the early medieval sources we find references to *landvættir* ('land spirits'), and in the sagas there are occasional references to spirits of other kinds, as well as monsters and ghosts.[4] Although it is difficult to get a systematic picture of the hidden realm in this period, there is much evidence of powers emanating from 'outside', some of which took human shape while others were more abstract.

The powers of the 'beyond' were also at work in our period. We dealt with some of them in connection with magic (see Ch. 7), and saw how these powers could be appropriated by man and directed towards his own goals. Some elements of the outside could not be controlled, however. Among these were the various anthropomorphic beings which animated the social landscape and formed the more or less hidden dimension of the environment.

There were four main categories of such beings which I shall deal with in turn: *útilegumenn* ('out-lying men'), ghosts and apparitions, trolls and other monsters, and finally the *huldufólk* ('hidden people'). There is a rich and varied folk tradition concerning these.[5] In the following I present a generalized picture of each of these categories.

The *útilegumenn* were originally of society. They were men (or occasionally women) who had left the social and, so to speak, gone wild. In the early Middle Ages they were primarily outlaws, or *skógarmenn*, who had committed a crime and been sentenced to outlawry. Because law and society were one, the outlaws merged with the wild (Hastrup 1985*a*: ch. 5; 1981*a*). When the law ceased to be the defining feature of Icelandic society (Hastrup 1984*a*), outlawry disappeared as punishment, and the *skógarmenn* evanesced. They were conceptually replaced by the *útilegumenn* ('out-lying men'). Originally, the term *útilegumaðr* in Old Norse referred to a man who had chosen to leave human company, and only later was it to become associated with criminal behaviour. This semantic shift had occurred by the time *Jóns-bók* was made. Thus, in the chapter on *níðingsverk* ('felony'), where all the capital offences are listed, it is stated that men must pay with their life for theft (*þýfska*) and *útilega*, whether they have robbed a ship or persons inland (*Jónsbók*: 38). The implication is that the *útilegumaður* was a robber, who had set himself outside the social.

In our period, the *útilegumannasögur* (tales about the *útilegumenn*) were extremely popular. They were numerous, elaborate, and widely circulated. Although the element of crime was an important feature of the category, the *útilegumenn* were not unequivocally associated with evil. What they were always associated with was the outside, a field of great semantic richness. Like Grettir the Strong, the famous outlaw-hero from the eleventh century, the *útilegumenn* were also endowed with legendary strength and with a capacity for survival which made them heroic in the eyes of men (Hastrup 1986*a*).

Many place-names derive from *útilegumenn* who lived in places beyond society. The place-names are explained in various folk-tales like the following:

Oddkelsver is connected to a certain Oddkell, of whom it is said that he had *lagzt út* [been lying out] with his sister by whom he had children. He had killed the children born to them 'out' there by drowning them in Oddkelsós by Odd-kelsalda. It was said that the housecarls of the bishop at Skálholt found him when they were visiting Tjarnarver, at Sóleyjarhöfðavað. They saw smoke in the *ver* at Oddkelsalda.[6] Oddkell maintained he had found his sheep there and had not stolen them, but the housecarls killed him, nevertheless. Others say that some travellers whom he had attempted to rob, had killed him and 'cairned' him at the *ver*. (JÁ: ii. 163–4.)

Besides explaining the origin of particular place-names, this tale also reveals other significant themes. First, the motive for leaving society was an incestuous relationship, and the killing of the babies heightened the offence. The outlaw couple lived like other humans from sheep, but in the eyes of the housecarls such sheep must of necessity be stolen; the housecarls feel themselves, therefore, entitled to kill Oddkell. In the alternative ending, Oddkell is a thief, who is not only killed but 'cairned'. The heaping of stones upon a body was the strongest possible contrast to a proper burial. Even in death, the *útilegumaður* remained outside.

There is an abundance of tales about *útilegumenn* who robbed farmers. Not only sheep and wealth, but also daughters and wives, were at risk. Some of these legends take us to poetical places, and the *útilegumenn* prove to be both loving and gentle (for example, ibid.: 201–3). Characteristically, they lived in hidden places, to which the entrance was eternally shrouded in mist. Many *útilegumenn* were *fjölkunnugir* ('of much knowledge'), who could enchant people into following them, and could control the mists (ibid.: 189). That was how they contrived to remain hidden in their valleys. Most were lonely wanderers, but sometimes they had built a kind of society of outlaws; in the legends there are sheriffs, farmers, and sometimes even priests, in the community of *útilegumenn*. They seem to form a mirror-image of human society; like other mirrors, however, this one also both reflected and distorted reality.

One distortion was the recurrent image of plenty in the hidden valleys of the outlyers. This theme was a literary motif already in the saga of Grettir the Strong where Þórisdalur was the place of his plenty (cf. Hastrup 1986*a*: 301 ff.). It is much more than a literary motif, however. We note the theme again and again in the folk-tales, *þjóðsögur*, and in scientific treatises on Iceland from the seventeenth century the hidden valleys are described as a geographical fact. Jón *lærði* Guðmundsson devoted an entire work to this topic, and others went along with the implicit view of a hidden source of wealth somewhere beyond the horizon of society.[7]

Although the *útilegumenn* were renowned for the nuisance they caused, their theft of sheep, and for the threat they posed to travellers, they had an ambiguous position in the mind of the Icelanders.[8] Few *útilegumenn* illustrate this ambiguity as well as Fjalla-Eyvindur, whose heroism matched that of Grettir, his predecessor by some seven centuries (cf. Hastrup 1986*a*). The tale is too long to tell, but the point of the story is that Fjalla-Eyvindur survived his outlying for twenty years (JÁ: ii. 237–45). After twenty years *útilegumenn* were freed from the ban and redeemed sacrosanct (*friðhelgir*). There was a way back to the inside; if the *útilegumenn* were strong and smart enough, society welcomed them back.

In many ways the *útilegumenn* represent not only the hidden parts of the landscape, but also the hidden dimensions of human life. They upset order; they steal and withdraw; they are incestuous and asocial; they live in plenty and on their own. They are alienated from society, and yet they have a strong hold on the imagination of the Icelanders; dreams repressed in the real social world could be allowed to flourish in this 'alternative space'.

Draugar ('ghosts'), were of two major kinds. *Afturgöngur* ('revenants'), were dead people who could not find rest either because they had committed suicide or because they had not been properly baptized or buried. *Uppvakningar* ('raised from the dead'), were ghosts that had been conjured back to 'life' by magicians. Among the revenants were the *útburðir*, the infants that were disposed of in secrecy. These would sometimes sing their mothers to insanity (ibid.: i. 218), but were not harmful to others.

Many tales concerned drowned men, who appeared before their beloved women, and addressed them in verse-form. This was often how the women learnt about the death of their loved ones. One young woman was very shaken by the experience and asked someone to help her prevent the man from returning. The door was locked against him. The following night, however, the woman dreamt that the man was standing at her window and reproaching her for shutting him out. Then he spoke the following lines:

> *Vér höfum fengið sæng i sjó*
> *sviptir öllu grandi;*
> *höfum þó á himni ró*
> *hæstan guð prísandi.*
>
> JÁ: i. 224

('We have got a bed in sea divested of all destruction; thus we have rest in heaven praising the highest god.')

After hearing this the girl rushed out to take her own life; but others caught her, however, and she recovered. The apparition never came again.

Other dead people who could not find rest were those who had been ill-tempered when living and had offended many. Rich misers suffered similarly, and after death would often return to their hidden wealth. Sometimes this happened to the unexpected profit of a third party. Generally, *afturgöngur* could fall in love, they could hate, and they could tease and trouble the living; whatever the relationship they were for the most part relatively harmless.

By contrast, the *uppvakningar* ('ghosts') or *sendingar* ('messengers') brought evil. They were raised from the dead by *fjölkyngismenn* ('men of much knowledge'), who used them for their own purposes (for example, ibid.: 304–7). The youthful dead seem to have been preferred for this purpose, and during the raising there was a particular formulaic style of question and answer between the wizard and the ghost. It was important that the wizard should conjure the ghost back to the grave again, otherwise it would haunt him and his descendants for nine generations. The *uppvakningur* was often talked about as *óhreinn andi* ('unclean spirit'), and magical devices were needed to cleanse the human environment of their presence. A recital of the fourteenth-century religious poem *Lilja* was one powerful means among others to avert the 'evil messenger'.[9] Recitation of the gospels would also serve (for example, ibid.: 307).

Galdrastafir ('magical staves'), were also used as protective devices. In popular wisdom the *ægishjálmur* ('Ægir's helmet'), offered absolute protection (see Fig. 8). It was cast in lead, and printed on to the forehead between the eyebrows. When one said *Ægishjálm er ég ber milli brúna mér* . . . ('the *ægishjálmur* which I bear between my brows . . .') victory over evil was certain (ibid.: 438).

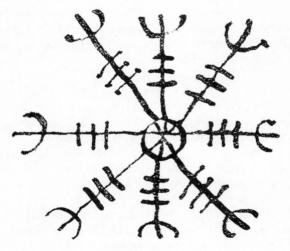

FIG. 8. *Ægir's Helmet*

In some cases the spirits were sent to kill, or to claim some object or other. There are also cases of a more humorous kind, however. On one occasion, for example, some seamen found themselves without tobacco, and woke up a dead man and sent him north to find some, which he eventually did, not without difficulty (ibid.: i. 332–3). *Sendingar* were also said to have been used against the Black Death, but only with little success.

The main features of the *draugar* are already clear. They were more or less human, and in the case of *uppvakningar* they also worked on behalf of humans. Their 'work', or their power, derived from an only partially controlled environment. Formulas and rituals were no guarantee of safety, and even the wizards might suffer from the attacks of their ghosts, if they were not sufficiently knowledgeable. One sorcerer's apprentice, for example, unwittingly conjured up his own mother. She was not at all pleased with her son, and wrestled with him; finally she spat in his eye, leaving him wall-eyed (ibid.: 321). The scene of a man wrestling with his own dead mother is a powerful symbol of the relationship between humans and *draugar*, and we can leave man and ghost locked in their combat.

Trolls, *tröll*, were a manifest feature of the landscape. Plenty of place-names indicate that they were a conspicuous element in the environment since the Middle Ages. Trölladyngja, Tröllakirkja, Tröllaskógur, and so forth are reminders of the ubiquity of trolls. They are also expressions of one of the main features of the giant beings; they were not supposed to move about in daylight, and if they did, they were turned to stone. So it is that many of the great stones or single-standing rocks in Iceland were regarded as petrified trolls.

The Icelanders had many names for the trolls, such as *bergbúar* ('rock-dwellers'), *jötnar* ('giants'), *þussar*, *risar*, *skessur*, and *gýgjur* (the last two being female). They lived among the rocks and in caves, and made occasional inroads into the human world. They stole sheep, and could empty a lake of fish with a curse. Not all of them were mischievous, however, and even those that were seemed very vulnerable to the ringing of church bells, which could also turn them to stone or make them disappear.

Tales about trolls tended to be local, and featured beings living at particular named places. One folk-tale is related to a particular farm, Hvoll in Borgarfjörður, which was rich in cattle and servants, and where the *bóndi* disappeared one Christmas night. He was never found again, and at *fardagar* ('parting-days') it was decided that one of the farm-hands should take his place and remain for another year. It so happened that the farm-hand disappeared the following Christmas, and the housewife decided to move away from the farm during winter. She had a dream, then, that a poor-looking woman came to her and asked for milk to give to her infants, since the farm had four cows while she herself had no milk. She also said that she knew that the husband and the farm-hand had been abducted by a *skessa* (a female troll) who had given birth some years ago, and who wanted to feed her young on human meat every Christmas. If the woman had her milk she would help the housewife to avert this latent threat. When the housewife woke up she set milk for the dream-woman as she had been told to, and continued to do so through the winter. Close to Christmas, the housewife again dreamt of the woman, who thanked her for the milk, and told that now her own cow had calved she was no longer in need of the farm's milk. She revealed herself to be a *huldukona* ('a woman of the hidden people') and gave the housewife advice as how to out- wit the *skessa*, who would come for her at Christmas night (JÁ: i. 148–51).

The point of citing this tale—which ended happily with the neutral- ization of the *skessa*—is to show how in Icelandic imagery, trolls and hidden people belonged to the same 'hidden' space. They were not equal, however; hidden people were humanized—feeding their infants milk, and helping people in return for their charity—while trolls were de-humanized—feeding their infants human flesh, and offending people.

Trolls might revenge offences against them. Thus, once upon a time in Fljótshlíð, eighteen men went looking for sheep in the mountains, and sat down to rest in a cave (*hellir*). They discovered a trollwoman there, as old as the hills, and all, with one exception, started mocking her. The trollwoman cursed them and let *drépsótt* ('killer disease', 'plague') kill them all, sparing the friendly one. Since that time the cave has been called Sóttarhellir ('the cave of disease') (ibid.: 176). Trolls, and events concerning them, are one way among many in which history was mapped on to nature, in the form of place- names.

Trolls lived in nature, but they were not without a desire to fraternize with men. In Fnjóskadalur a shepherd was once caught by a lonely *skessa*, who wanted a man about the house; she showed kindness to him, but he wanted to escape, and did so (ibid.: 180–1).

Other *menskir menn* ('human humans') were less fortunate. One group of *vermenn* (migratory 'fishermen'), on their way to the southern fishing-places, was caught in bad weather and sought refuge in a cave. To pass the time the fishermen decided to sing, and fell to discussing which tune to choose, Andrarímur or Hallgrímssálmar. From the bottom of the cave a voice was heard suggesting the former. So they intoned the (secular) Andrarímur. When this was finished, a voice said: 'Now I am pleased, but my wife is not, she wants to hear the Hallgrímsrímur.' So they sang the psalm as well, after which the voice said: 'Now my wife is happy, but I am not.' Eventually the *vermenn* were offered porridge to eat and when they woke up the following day, the sky was clear and they could continue their journey. When they reached inhabited areas they learnt that the wife of the troll was a woman abducted from the valley (ibid.: 186). She, apparently, had been caught for good.

To summarize, trolls were part of the environment in a very literal sense. They personified the rocks and stones, and inhabited the clefts and caves in the mountains. They were generally gargantuan creatures, strong but not very clever. Bestowed with certain human features, they were nevertheless not human, and not of human origin; they did not generally live in families. Most of them were single, although they might occasionally take a spouse, or give birth to young. The tales tell us little about their way of life; they seem to live by nature itself most of the time.

One category of beings remains to be discussed. They are the *huldufólk*, the 'hidden people'. *Huldufólk* were a kind of elf, and as such had much in common with elves known from other parts of Europe. In the early Middle Ages the Icelandic notion of *álfar* testified to this connection. In place-names referring to supernatural beings and spirits of all kinds, *álfar* are predominant (Bjarni Einarsson 1967). In our period the most common name for elves is *huldufólk* (*huldumaður* ('-man'), and *huldukona* ('-woman')); these terms were first recorded in the fourteenth century, and seem to have caught on quickly. In the oral tradition and legends of the Icelanders, the *huldufólk* play a prominent part.

There were two versions of their origin. According to one, the hidden people were descended from those of Eve's children that she had not shown to God because they were still unwashed. God discovered her treachery and said *það sem á að vera hulið fyrir mér skal vera hulið fyrir mönnum* ('That which has to be hidden from me, shall also be hidden from men') (JÁ: i. 7). According to the other myth of origin, the Devil raised a revolt in Heaven, and he and all who fought for him were driven into outer darkness. Those dwellers of Heaven, who turned and looked after him, were likewise expelled. Those who were neither for him nor against him, and were not members of either party, were driven down to Earth, where it was decreed that they should live in knolls, hills, and rocks, and be called elves or hidden people (ibid.). In both versions the elves, while occupying the same topographical space as man, are doomed to remaining 'hidden'.

The *huldufólk* lived like humans. They had farms, families, and tended their livestock. They could show themselves to humans if they chose, and occasionally did so. Many hidden women, for instance, could not give birth without human assistance. There are many tales about *huldumenn* fetching visible women to help their wives in childbirth (JÁ: *passim*).

Love was a recurrent theme in the encounter between visible and hidden people. Male elves made determined efforts to seduce solitary shepherdesses on mountain pastures. This was a common element in Norwegian and Swedish tales, but in these the amorous attempt was almost always foiled. In Iceland the encounter often resulted in deep love between the two, or in a child (cf. Oddur Einarsson 1971: 48).

In a characteristic tale the foster-daughter of a priest falls deeply in love with a *huldumaður* at the summer shieling. She bears him a son, whom she leaves with the man. When later she is forced to marry somebody else, she goes on yearning for her secret lover. During a tale-telling session with her mother-in-law she relates her story—disguised as a tale about somebody else. However, a slip of the tongue betrays her, and when she is found dead in the arms of a stranger who had passed by the farm in company with a young man, everyone knows that the stranger must be her former lover and that the young man is her son. They had died from the grief of their forced separation (JÁ: i. 63–6).

The tale gives a vivid impression of the love between a *huldumaður* and a woman, and of its context. At one level the context is the shieling; the woman has left the fenced inside and become 'game' in the men's wild, where also the *huldumenn* roam. At another level, the social context of foster-fathers and arranged marriages, of sheep-rearing, hay-making, and spinning gives an impression of a prefigured order, from which the life of the shieling offered an escape. We also note that the story itself has a scene of story-telling, so very important a part of the context of tradition in Iceland. Through the telling of stories, images of the hidden people were re-created. Events continued to confirm these images, and no one doubted their reality. The number of legends about the *huldufólk*, and their position in living memory even today, testify to their enduring grip on the Icelandic imagination.

The power of the hidden people was very much a function of their human-like qualities. All they lacked for full humanity was one vital part—a soul. Jón Guðmundsson, in his *Fjandafæla* (cf. above, Ch. 7) of the mid-seventeenth century, says about elves:

> *Hafa þeir bæði heyrn og mál,*
> *hold og blóð með skinni;*
> *vantar ei nema sjálfa sál,*
> *sá er hluturinn minni.*
>
> (JÁ: i. 4; Strömbäck
> 1931: 70)

('They have both hearing and speech, flesh and blood with skin, they want nothing but the soul, which is the lesser part.')

We are now in a position to bring together our information about the four categories of *útilegumenn*, *draugar*, *tröll*, and *huldufólk*. These were all part of the hidden dimension of the Icelandic environment, but their position within it differed from one category to another.

The *útilegumenn* lived in another place, in the mountain wastelands or in hidden valleys. They were topographically separated from the humans. *Draugar*, on the other hand, were topographically independent; they were raised from the small topographic slots of their graves, and were then able to move about the entire space. *Tröll* were part of the topography of the mountains. They *were* rocks and stones, and they lived in the caves of far-away areas. They were visible expressions of a topographic otherness: the wilderness beyond the boundary of the cultivated world. By contrast, the *huldufólk* were invisible but the ubiquitous inhabitants of the proximate space. They lived in the knolls and rocks in the immediate neighbourhood of the farmsteads, that is, in those small points where the wild broke through the cultivated surface.

These topographical differences were paralleled by different conceptual relationships to the *menskir menn* ('the human humans') with whom the hidden folk were implicitly compared. Once again, as for the animals, we can establish a structure, allowing us to indicate transformations in two dimensions (see Fig. 9). The *útilegumenn* were metonymical humans. They were *men*, and they were of society. By an act of their own they had set themselves apart from decent people but they were still serially related to them. *Draugar* were metonymical non-humans. They were *of* the human world, but as apparitions they were no longer quite human. *Huldufólk* were metaphorical humans. They lived *like* real people but in a space of their own. They mirrored human society, yet in a distinct world. The *tröll* formed their own series as well, but did not live like people. They were metaphorical non-humans.

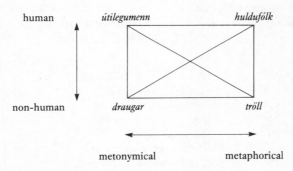

FIG. 9. *Inhabitants of the Wilderness*

The conceptual positions occupied by these creatures of the environment gave them different possibilities for intrusion on the human world, as we have seen. What we have also seen, I hope, is that every step the Icelander took in the landscape was informed by his knowledge of the hidden dimension.

THE NATURAL SCIENCE

In early modern Europe a new kind of science dawned, including a science of nature. It was spurred by the humanists whose will to understand the world in non-religious terms laid the foundations for modern science (Mandrou 1978). Iceland was on the margins of European culture, but it certainly had its own humanist intellectuals.

266 The Environment

There was also a genuine and early native interest in describing and classifying the features of the Icelandic natural environment.

The aim of the present section is to present the proto-scientific view of nature, as held by learned Icelanders of the sixteenth, seventeenth, and eighteenth centuries. Sources from the fifteenth century are meagre, although we can infer a certain view of nature as a mighty opponent to culture from the annals.

Nature, as such, is mentioned occasionally in the sagas, but only when an integral part of a story (Stefán Einarsson 1957: 134). The exception, perhaps, is Arngrímur Abbot's *Guðmundar saga*, which opens with a brief natural description of Iceland.[10] In the fourteenth-century poem, *Lilja* ('The Lily'), which as we have seen remained popular in spite of its Catholic origin and religious bent, refers to the miraculous event of the Virgin birth, when even nature was stricken by wonder, and acknowledged God's superior power:

> *Loftin öll af ljósi fyllast,*
> *Legir á grundu stóðu ok undrast,*
> *Kúguð sjálf svo nærri nógu*
> *Náttúran sér ekki mátti.*
> *Giftist öndin guðdóms krafti*
> *Góð, ok huldist Maríu blóði;*
> *Glaðrar dvelst í júngfrúr iðrum*
> *Ein persóna þrennrar greinar.*

Lilja, v. 31.

('With glorious light all heavens fill, and wonderstruck all waters still their course on earth. In powerless way self-nature all prostrated lay. The soul, wed to the power of God, was shrouded in good Mary's blood; in the favoured Virgin's womb doth lie He who is One in Trinity.')[11]

The first true natural history of Iceland, however, was Oddur Einarsson's *Qualisqunque* (1589), which devoted several chapters to nature. It opened with an attempt to locate the position of Iceland, as his son Gísli was to do in his work of 1638. Neither of them seem to be aware of the map produced by Bishop Guðbrandur Þorláksson some time before 1585 (see Fig. 10 and cf. Fig. 1). The Hólar bishop had succeeded in determining the position of Iceland with tolerable accuracy, and his map was included in Orthelius' comprehensive world atlas (Halldór Hermannsson 1926; Nørlund 1944; Haraldur Sigurðsson 1971–8).

Among the subjects treated by Oddur Einarsson were those of

FIG. 10. *Guðbrandur Þorláksson's Map of Iceland*
Reproduced by permission of The British Library

drift-ice and glaciers; he claimed that glaciers were growing (1971: 36), giving us eyewitness of the approach of the little Ice Age.[12] Other subjects were rocks that were inhabited by hidden people; and lakes inhabited by monsters. In contemporary experience, glaciers and hidden people were equally real. There was no sharp distinction between the natural and the supernatural environment of the people.

A similar conflation is found in Gísli Oddsson's work on the nature of Iceland. He actually devoted two works to this topic, which supplemented each other, *Annalium in Islandia farrago* (1637) and *De Mirabilibus Islandiae* (1638) (Halldór Hermannsson 1917: p. vi).[13] Both dealt with what Gísli Oddsson called *mirabilia Islandiae*: 'The wonders of Iceland.' In *Annalium* the wonders were recorded in chronological sequence from 1106 to 1637, in a historical record of occurrences. In contrast *De mirabilibus* is a synchronic description of the nature of the island. For Gísli nature unfolded in both time and space.

Annalium dealt with extraordinary events such as floods, volcanic eruptions, apparitions, disasters, and the like. It has been shown that the occurrences listed from 1106 to 1402 were copied from older annals; the rest were an original compilation (Halldór Hermannsson 1917: p. vii). Many events are recorded from Gísli's own observations during his lifetime (b. 1593). In his postscript he emphasized that he had only included events that he considered true, and that were supported by authority (ibid.: 27). Irrespective of their 'reality', the events of nature depicted in *Annalium* are a mighty force—external to society—which momentarily might turn order into chaos.

De mirabilibus has a spatial referent, and the nature depicted is more a geography than a history. The first chapter deals with the position of Iceland; the second with the polar ice around the island. There then follows a description of meteors and other similar phenomena, which were associated with catastrophes like earthquakes and volcanic eruptions. We are then introduced to sea-monsters, after which we move on to whales and fishes, after which there are chapters on birds, insects, and mammals. Chapters on mountain caves and their hidden inhabitants finally lead to a series of chapters on the Icelandic people and their ways of life. Gísli Oddsson's geography is apparently organized in a conceptual model of concentric circles, with people living in the innermost circle which is the only completely controlled space.

This theme of the domesticated versus the untamed space is also prevalent in the works on Icelandic nature by Jón *lærði* Guðmundsson and Jón Eggertsson. About 1640 Jón *lærði* wrote *Um Íslands aðskiljan-*

legar náttúrur ('About the peculiar nature of Iceland').[14] This was as far as we know, the first natural history written in the vernacular. In some ways it supplemented the work of Gísli Oddsson. Gísli had a fuller description of the country and of its animals and plants. Jón *lærði* had an elaborate description of the smaller islands around Iceland, and a remarkable chapter on whales. Both dealt with monsters and fabulous animals, and both had a firm conviction of the mineral wealth of the country. Their landscape inevitably contained hidden riches.

The sea also contained a marvellous resource in the whales. From his own observations, and probably from his acquaintance with Basque whalers, Jón *lærði* was very knowledgeable about the whales. He told of the various species, their size, habits, and general nature. Of the *hvítingur* or *miallur* he says, for instance, that it is so inquisitive and wise, that once it boarded a ship where the men were asleep; when they woke up one of them clubbed it and it disappeared. Others warned him that the *miallur* would seek revenge, and he fled to the mountains and stayed there for a full eighteen years, after which he went back to the sea on the assumption that the whale had died. On his first fishing-trip the *miallur* emerged, however, and dragged him down into the deep, never to be seen again (Jón Guðmundsson 1924: 7). Again, we note how 'scientific' knowledge was not separate from popular tradition.

Local knowledge was supplemented by foreign sources. One source to which Jón *lærði* refers is the *Speculum Regale* or *Konungs skuggsjá*, a thirteenth-century Norwegian Treatise.[15] Jón adds his own knowledge, however. One example will illustrate this process of fusion between ideas of nature, it is the rather interesting example of the walrus.

In the Viking Age, walrus was hunted in the far northern parts of Norway under the name of *hrosshvalr* ('horse-whale'). When *Konungs skuggsjá* was written the *hrosshvalr* was thought of as a fabulous creature; the decline of walrus-hunting had transformed the animal into an element in popular folk-tale (Nordgård 1920: 112). Meanwhile, a new word for walrus had become predominant in Norway, namely *rostungr*. The description in *Konungs skuggsjá* leaves no doubt about the identity of the *rostungr*. Thus, in the course of time, the walrus had been split into two categories: the (fabulous) *hrosshvalr* and the *rostungr*.

Jón Guðmundsson was partly aware of this, saying of the *rostungr* that 'some call it *rosmhvalur*' (1924: 13–14). The drawing which accompanies the information clearly depicts a walrus, which he set apart as a distinct species. However, in his list of whales he includes the *hrosshvalur*, with the alternative name *stöckull* ('jumper') (ibid.: 8), a creature which, as we have seen, was extremely dangerous to men. Jón referred to *Konungs skuggsjá* as one source for this. The fabulous walrus had by this time achieved autonomous existence, which was confirmed in many fishermen's tales about the assaults of the 'jumper', right down to the present century (Gísli Pálsson 1987).[16]

These representations of the walrus are interesting for a variety of reasons. They show how Jón *lærði* meticulously compared his own knowledge with traditional authorities like *Konungs skuggsjá*. Further, they demonstrate how particular categories could become hollow, only to become refilled with new meaning. The walrus was defined out of the category of *hrosshvalur*, which was then occupied by the legendary 'jumper'; in a changing context, the environment is open to redefinition.

Jón *lærði* wrote another treatise on plants and their healing capacities,[17] showing how inconspicuous grasses could be put to good use, and how Icelandic aridity could be made to serve social ends. Parts of the landscape which were left unexploited were also potentially useful. In his treatise on 'hidden places and covered valleys in Iceland', Jón *lærði* described and substantiated the existence of a hidden space of living.[18] It was a space where so far only the 'outsiders' lived, but he seemed convinced that the hidden places could be useful also to ordinary people, if only they could find their way into them. The space was already defined; it only waited for discovery.

Jón Eggertsson (*c.*1643–80) voiced a similar belief in hidden possibilities, in his own treatise on the nature and conditions of Iceland.[19] He observed that the climate was cold and bad, and the grazing sparse, with cattle often starving to death, or dying from intestinal maggots; fishing, too, was difficult. In his opinion, however, the main reason for the grim conditions of the country was the inhabitants' own neglect and sloth; even where good grazing and fishing were found the Icelanders let these go to waste (Jón Eggertsson 1650: fo. 3). They threw away part of the cod, and held certain other perfectly valuable species too cheap to eat (ibid.: 4). The general impression was of the Icelandic people disregarding nature's gifts. Among these gifts were an unknown number of hidden valleys. In connection with his description of Þórisdalur, the hidden valley of Grettir the Strong, he said how difficult it was to find because 'the master of nature' had covered it with a roof of rock. This was also the reason why no snow destroyed the grass there (ibid.: 14).

Both Jón *lærði* and Jón Eggertsson saw nature as extremely potent. It caused history and contained miraculous spaces. By an appropriation of the hidden treasures, the Icelanders would find a real resource for social wealth which so far only belonged in their dreams of another world, another life in Iceland.

A century later, the Enlightenment reached Iceland. On behalf of the Danish king, Eggert Ólafsson and Bjarni Pálsson travelled about the island in the 1750s, and produced an extensive report in 1776, from which I have often quoted. Their works were much influenced by the educational context of Copenhagen. 'Science' and 'research' had replaced 'belief' and 'rumour'. Nature was still an object of general concern, but the scope was local, and every main district was meticulously described in terms of geography, soil, rivers and lakes, thermal springs, flora, people, economy, and so forth. Empirical knowledge had replaced the speculative world of the seventeenth century.[20]

In one matter, however, the two enlightened travellers corroborated their predecessors: nature in Iceland was an imperfectly appropriated resource. Farming and fishing could be vastly improved—and the Icelandic conditions reconditioned—if the Icelanders would only exploit nature instead of allowing it to exploit them. The same general message is found in other late-eighteenth-century writers, Ólafur Olavius (1780) and Skúli Magnússon (1785; 1786)—each from their own point of view—also engaged themselves in the re-education of the Icelanders. It was some time before new ideas of 'improvement' caught hold of the people, but by the end of the eighteenth century ideas of nature were certainly changing. The environment changed accordingly if only very gradually.

To conclude about the natural science, we note how the learned Icelanders acknowledged a natural duality. Once it beacme an object of separate treatment nature was conceived of as both power and resource. As power, it introduced movement, disorder, and external threats into the lives of people. From outside it created history; like everything else belonging to the outside it was uncontrollable and often hostile to humans.

As a resource, nature was an object of actual and potential appropriation. The potential was not always established by fact but belonged to the mirror-world of the observers. Hidden valleys, mineral wealth, and self-confident Icelanders were part of their wistful thinking. While the idea of expanding resources was present already in Jón Eggertsson's seventeenth-century treatise on Icelandic nature, it still belonged to the pre-Enlightenment world. In contrast to the late eighteenth-century reformers, Jón Eggertsson and his contemporaries (and their precursors) lived in an animate world. The mechanical view on nature was still alien to seventeenth-century Icelanders; to them nature was an organic whole of inanimate and animate elements. And one could not exploit the former without due reference to the latter.

The wild could *not* be controlled, even if some of it could be tamed and put into use. The environment was loaded with a life of its own, which it took more than a few Enlightenment reformers to kill.

CONCEPTS OF NATURE

The nature of Iceland always fascinated travellers. The meeting of the oppositions of fire and ice made a powerful impression on foreigners, and it was easy for them to believe that Hell was situated in Mount Hekla. We have seen how learned Icelanders tried to rid themselves of this image. The bishop at Hólar, Guðbrandur Þorláksson (1542–1627), urged both Oddur Einarsson and Arngrímur Jónsson to refute the unflattering notion that Hell was in Iceland. Oddur's 'answer' was *Qualisqunque* of 1589 presenting the first 'scientific' view of the Icelandic nature.

Arngrímur Jónsson, a renowned humanist, made his *Brevis Commentarius de Islandia* in 1593, which was explicitly directed against the distorted images of Iceland held by foreigners.[21] The tone of his writing was, therefore, polemical rather than 'scientific'. His first work did not succeed in breaking down the foreigners' image, and in the early seventeenth century he again refuted the works of Blefken and Fabricius on Iceland (Jakob Benediktsson 1957: 33 ff.). Arngrímur's work was not primarily concerned with the natural environment, but it bore witness to problems that the external world posed to the Icelanders. These were not only a matter of misrepresentation by foreigners, but also of self-definition. In the late sixteenth and early seventeenth centuries this problem became an issue among learned Icelanders. To perceive themselves clearly, they had not only to draw boundaries around their 'Icelandicness', but also to define its content. At one level the content was contrasted to that of other European cultures, and its distinctness was published in Latin for a European audience. At another level, culture had to be continually bound off from nature, and here we are in a more popular field of Icelandic self-understanding.

We have seen how the Icelandic environment was popularly conceived of as having its own life. The natural and the supernatural merged, as did the visible and the invisible dimensions of the wilderness. The dimensions of nature were independent of religion; the landscape was entirely secular and loaded with creatures, that had nothing to do with Christianity. The result of the social reproduction of natural categories was a view of nature as both animate and inanimate. In the spatial or atemporal dimension, nature comprised both life and resources, visible or hidden. In the temporal dimension, nature was no changeless frame. Irrespective of the objective long-term fluctuations which may just be perceptible within a span of four hundred years, nature had its own history in the eyes of the successive generations of Icelanders. The events of nature were historicized and linked to each other, such as meteors being precursors of earthquakes, and to the history of man. Short-term fluctuations would affect the economic conditions, and increasingly so. The annals demonstrate this very fully.

The history of nature also resulted in the naming of particular winters, that were thereby incorporated into the man-made universe of time indications. Here quality took precedence over chronology (cf. Alver 1970). A famous example is *hvítivetur* ('the white winter') of 1633/4, which struck particularly hard. Its repercussion in the life-history of *síra* Jón Jónsson (*gamli*) at least, was immense. In the early seventeenth century *síra* Jón chanted:

> *Níu á eg börn og nitján kyr,*
> *nær fimm hundruð sauði,*
> *sjö og tuttugu söðladyr,*
> *Svo er háttað auði.*

(Hannes Þorsteinsson
1924–7: 378)

('I have nine children and nineteen cows, close to five hundred sheep, twenty-seven saddle-animals, such is fortune shaped.')

After *hvítivetur* he was forced to revise his poem:

> *Níu á eg börn og níu kyr,*
> *Nærri fimmtíu sauði,*
> *Sex eru eptir sööladyr,*
> *svo er háttað auði*

(ibid.)

('I have nine children and nine cows, close to fifty sheep, six saddle-animals remain, such is fortune shaped.')

The poems speak for themselves and illustrate the historical dimension of nature in a pre-modern society—where the environment had a particular meaning.

'Environment' is relative to a particular social system. In Iceland, the economic and social order was founded in farming and fishing, and we may now reconsider these modes of livelihood in relation to the prevailing concepts of nature. Generally speaking, farming is based on a principle of *harvest* while fishing is a kind of *hunt*. Harvesting depends on sowing and investment of labour in a long-term perspective, while hunting is independent of last year's relative success. Farming, therefore, requires planning and social organization: fishing, by contrast, is based on an instantaneous relation between man and his prey. The contrast may seem trite, but in Iceland it had socially important implications.

Farming and fishing had unequal positions in the economic order of the Icelanders, as we have seen (Ch. 3). They also held different positions in the Icelandic conceptual world, where boundaries between the social and the wild, between culture and nature, were continually redrawn. Farming was incorporated into the social; it was part of the very definition of Icelandic culture. Fishing, on the other hand, was excluded; apart from brief interludes in the fourteenth and fifteenth centuries, fishing was associated with the non-social, the wild.

Farming represented nature domesticated; fishing took place in the untamed wilderness. Logically, we may represent them as in Figure 11. The relationship between the social system and farming is one of inclusion; farming is a defining feature of the entire social context. Between the social system and the 'environment' there was a relationship of exclusion, that was part of the mutual definition. *Veiðar* took place in this environment, and was thereby externalized from the

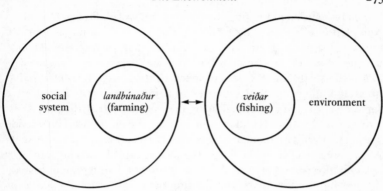

FIG. 11. *Farming and Fishing in Relation to the Social System*

social system. Evidently, this placed farming and fishing in different strategic positions. Both soil and sea were 'natural' resources, but not equally so.

The social inside was defined as domesticated, controlled, and settled. The outside was untamed, uncontrolled, and moving. To fish was to engage temporarily in an appropriation of the wild, but this was, as we have seen, a dangerous activity. By stepping into the wild, the Icelanders became vulnerable to forces beyond their control, whether these were jumper-whales, polar bears, or *útilegumenn*. 'The gifts of nature' were not readily given to the people by the inhabitants of the wild; rather they had to be wrested from them, under threat of revenge.

When hard times came, and when nature struck deep into the experience of the Icelanders, they reacted by concentrating their efforts on the social—on farming. In a short-term perspective, fishing was often turned to as a weapon against starvation. In the long term, however, in the perspective of four centuries, the more 'nature' shook history, the more nature *moved*, the more dangerous and inaccessible the environment felt. As a consequence the hunters returned home.

In his critical poem, *Búnaðarbálkur*, Eggert Ólafsson made a similar point; he says: *hungur kjósandi í hvílu að þola, heldr en veiða smádýrin* ('They chose to endure hunger in their beds, rather than to hunt small animals' (Eggert Ólafsson 1832a: 32)). His enlightened eye saw many unexploited resources, where the ordinary Icelander perceived only a hostile and ever-encroaching natural environment.

We are justified in arguing that the natural world, for the Icelander, expanded into and took over parts of the social. The 'movements' of nature accumulated to such an extent that counter-movements became more or less impossible. We have seen how saeters disappeared, shrinking the social space. Later, even the fences disintegrated, allowing nature to creep far into the domesticated area. Barns disappeared as well, allowing the rain to destroy the hay. Tufts sprouted in the infields and erosion spoiled the outfields. The outside encroached itself on to the inside from all directions; from above, from below, and from across the fence, the wild approached. The boundary between the social system and the environment disintegrated. Instead of renewing the boundary and fighting back, the Icelanders concentrated their social energy in the centre of the social: the *bú*. Nature could not be averted, but culture could at least be protected.

We shall return to this in the discussion of causes and effects in Icelandic history. Here we can draw the preliminary conclusion, that due to the particular concepts of nature, the 'natural history' gradually changed the human condition on Iceland. It was not until after the Enlightenment, and well into the nineteenth century, that culture was able to recondition these conditions.

IV

IMPLICATIONS

9

Analytical Results

IN the preceding chapters I have drawn a picture of Icelandic history over four hundred years. The analysis concerned both a society and a period. Neither in theory nor in practice can time and space be separated, for it is in the course of history that a society reveals itself (Dumont 1957: 21). In that sense, I have provided only a rather straightforward analysis of an empirical reality, unfolding in both time and space. My account differs from most anthropological analyses only in its long-term perspective, a perspective which in turn allows me to draw more substantial conclusions about Icelandic culture than might otherwise have been possible. History provides us with a privileged experimental situation (cf. Evans-Pritchard 1950; 1964: 147).

My conclusions are both analytical and theoretical, and I have chosen to deal with them under the general heading of 'implications'. The choice of term indicates that the results are *implied* by the empirical evidence, which remains the fundamental source of anthropological thinking.

The theoretical range of the implications is partly related to the specific nature of the island. Iceland is sufficiently small and well-described for us to approach the historical matter *in toto*, even though I would not claim to have read all extant documents from the period. Furthermore, Iceland has been sufficiently isolated in the North Atlantic to allow a separation of internal and external factors in its development. It is a privileged case for writing a total history, a history written from its own centre. In other words, Iceland provides an important basis for writing a history in *n* dimensions (Braudel 1980: 131). In the present context, the dimensions dealt with are named 'society', 'Uchronia', and 'culture'.

'Society' is an empirical category, and in the section so named I sum up the results of my investigation into the actual development of

Icelandic society during four hundred years. The scope is empirical and serves as a necessary background for the following sections. It shows some generalized trends in history, and also serves to help identify some diachronic patterns of change.

'Uchronia' represents an ever-living dream of another time.[1] As a temporal counterpart of Utopia, the concept gives us a clue to the Icelanders' vision of their reality. We go beyond the empirical with this concept, for it was not part of the contemporary vocabulary. Yet it is established with reference to the empirical, and its potentiality as an explanatory device is based in the Icelanders' own self-understanding at the time.

'Culture' is the final dimension to be investigated here. It is an analytical implication of the Icelandic world of experience. It embraces society and Uchronia because it constitutes the implicational space, which gives logic to both the social experience and the collective representations of a lost time. The discussion of Icelandic 'culture' allows us to see the constistency in the pattern of social change and transition from 1400 to 1800.

SOCIETY: CONTEMPORARY EXPERIENCE

Society is an empirical category; albeit usually identified only in space it also unfolds in time. My analysis of Icelandic society has covered a period of four hundred years, and has addressed a wide variety of themes. I shall sum up briefly what we now know about this society, and what were the experiences and conditions of the Icelanders.

The social experience was primarily shaped by the household, which framed the life of every single individual. The household was not only the smallest social unit it was also the most pertinent in the Icelandic vision of the world. It was the main unit of both production and consumption. It was society writ small, and concretized in the landscape.

By and large the Icelanders had a 'domestic mode of production' (Sahlins 1974), which appeared to be persistently underproductive. Underproduction was not, in this case, a choice made by an affluent society, in order to allow itself more leisure time (of which ethnography has given us many examples). It was, rather, a more or less unconscious strategy of a people whose primary capital was their history. This history was written by the structurally dominant *bændur*, and from the analysis there is a definite feeling that whatever resources the Icelanders had, they did not exploit these optimally. In their case, 'underproduction' was almost fatal.

We saw how the range of environmental exploitation shrank during the period. Grain-cropping and ploughing first disappeared, then the use of summer shielings. Barns were largely abandoned, and the fences around the infields disintegrated. By the end of our period, the Icelandic farming pattern was one of simple sheep-rearing and hay-growing. Production had become far less intensive than previously. The yield diminished accordingly, and the margin for survival decreased. Lean years became more frequent, and hunger was an integral part of the social experience.

It must be emphasized that although climate and other natural phenomena certainly played some part in this, they were not in any way final causes. Small variations in average temperature and pre-cipitation need not be catastrophic by themselves, but they have the potential to be so if they are not met with proper social measures.

Icelandic domestic organization favoured farming at the expense of fishing. Steps were continually taken to make fishing less attractive to the people. Laws were passed on behalf of the landowners, who were short of labour, that made full-time fishing illegal. Fishing could only be undertaken on a part-time basis, and all 'fishermen'—who are mentioned as a specific category of people only once, in the early fifteenth century—had to register at a farm. They were thus trans-formed into ordinary *vinnumenn*, farm-hands, and subsumed under the prevailing household structure.

Fishing was to remain a part-time enterprise. During the peak season migrations from the northern and eastern to the southern and western areas of the country were part of the Icelandic experience. Fish, moreover, remained an important means of exchange in this country without monetary systems. Even so, empirical evidence shows how technological innovation was repressed and the coefficient of utilization in steady decrease. In the fourteenth and fifteenth centuries the Icelanders were fishing on an 'international' scale; from the sixteenth century onwards, however, they were alienating themselves from former standards. While foreigners exploited the sea around Iceland, the local people gazed at them from small offshore rowing boats.

Generally, the economic order was 'archaic' and centred around the household, or *bú*. The autonomy of households was rigorously maintained; it subordinated the autonomy of individuals, who by law and by definition were included into the *bú*. The social structure was atomistic; there was no integrative mechanism above the household. In spite of the formal framework provided by national law, the experience (and the ideology) of the Icelanders was one of autonomous and self-sufficient households, only loosely connected by mechanical solidarity.

The pattern of landownership was complex. From being an innate right of every (kins-) man, access to land had become a privilege of the few. We saw that only about half of the land was privately owned, while Church and Crown owned the other half in shifting proportions. Of the privately owned land most was in the hands of a small group of very wealthy farmers, while much the greater part of the Icelanders were either smallholders or tenants.

Although Icelandic society was not feudal, there was a definite pattern of hierarchy. This was correlated to a cosmological model of concentric circles. The closer one was to the centre of the *bú*, the more 'noble' and 'clean' one was. The people of the periphery, whether they were fishermen, day labourers, or foreigners, were 'ignoble' and conceptually dangerous.

The cosmological model defined Icelandicness and humanity in terms of the 'inside', featuring permanence and social order. The pattern of landownership implied that more and more people were alienated from the inside. The experience of many Icelanders was one of mobility and disorder. An increasing impoverishment of the population sent ever more people on the move, which ultimately defined them out of the social order and made them merge with the wild.

The Icelandic world could not accommodate the unsettled; social reproduction remained a household matter.

In the domain of foreign relations the social experience was largely one of double standards. In matters of constitution, Church, and commerce there was a manifest discrepancy between an internal and an external standard. Iceland was certainly part of a larger order of reproduction, but local autonomy was maintained in many matters. Englobed by royal (Danish) concerns at one level, the Icelanders nevertheless preserved their own standards. The annual Althing assembly was a means to this end, although its power to define Icelandic standards became increasingly hollow.

In matters of religion, the Icelanders also sustained a degree of independence, which was annoying to the higher levels in the hierarchy of the Church. Besides simple neglect of the commandments even by the clerics, the local Icelandic definition of spiritual needs incorporated many non-Christian phenomena. There was often a discrepancy between secular and clerical standards, leaving room for varying interpretations of right and wrong. The Icelanders reacted by sticking with their own household standards. Although increasingly integrated into the political order of Copenhagen and definitely englobed by European Christendom, the Icelanders continually stressed their autonomy in social practice.

Commercial patterns also integrated the Icelanders into a non-local order. They were dependent on foreign imports and were permanently engaged in the exchange of goods. Yet again, two standards prevailed. Internally, exchange had the character of barter and had its own standard of relative pricing. Externally, exchange was a real trade, and pricing was co-variant with the development of markets outside Iceland.

One consequence of the two standards prevailing in all the domains of foreign relationships was the coexistence of two separate histories. The outside history largely integrated Iceland in the developing capitalist civilization of Modern Europe; the inside history resisted modernity, and stressed the necessity of household autonomy in an archaic social structure. The ruling order in Iceland from 1400 to 1800 must be understood in relation to the contemporary experience of having to negotiate these two histories.

From social experience we moved on to the human condition, that is the conditions set for and by humans living in Icelandic society. Here, we found evidence that social reproduction was threatened. Investigation into matters of sexuality, reproduction, and literacy demonstrated a gradual breakdown of the social system. The social organization of sexuality disintegrated—at least by the legal standard set. Kinship and alliance became immaterial for the greater proportion of the population, and the infringement of the incest taboo was one of the consequences.

Biological reproduction was also in only a very fragile balance. The marriage ratio was low, and although marital fertility was high, the population was 'controlled' at a level which only barely achieved self-replacement, and which failed even to do this in the seventeenth and early eighteenth centuries. The demographic structure of the first complete census of 1703 shows a population in decline.

We know some of the reasons for this. Starvation and risky trades made the general life-expectancy short. In addition to that, a remarkably high infant mortality rate negated the fertility of Icelandic women. Because children were generally not breast-fed for more than a week or two, a great proportion died from digestive diseases. Children were fed on cow's milk, cream, and butter—signs of wealth since time immemorial.

At quite a different level, the old images of Iceland were continuously reproduced. A high degree of literacy and of literary interest, combined with the structure of the household, meant that most Icelanders were familiar with the old stories. There was no great divide between élite and popular cultures; no urban centres existed, and no feudal lords set themselves apart from their servants. Even the wealthiest among the Icelanders lived in modest farmsteads, where masters and servants shared the same social space. Literature was for reading aloud, and few could escape at least some knowledge of the past glory of Iceland.

These widely differing aspects of 'reproduction' meant that a growing proportion of Icelanders felt incapable of meeting what they regarded as Icelandic cultural standards. Many became 'non-human', according to their own definitions.

Investigation into the magical power of knowledge took us through the domains of magic, witchcraft, and healing. Old theories of causation were translated into new realities. A fundamental proposition remained: man was able to influence his own history by appropriating the forces of 'the outside'. In magic the principal means for this was found in words, and the ultimate source was knowledge. Every Icelander, within this scheme, was a potential magician.

When the witch-craze hit Iceland, this potential led over twenty persons to the stake. Witchcraft accusations transformed some people from subjects to objects of history. The outside order impinged itself most unhappily on the witches.

Among the targets of zealous administrators were the ancient healing formulas that were part of popular wisdom. Healing practices originally included herb-medicines based in the Salernian principles; over the years, however, this ancient knowledge was forgotten, leaving only a minimal knowledge of antidotes, magic runes, and formulas. In the Icelandic experience, illness was 'incurable' to an increasing degree.

Concepts of fate were gradually displaced. Originally there had been some balance between a concept of man as a maker of his own fate and a concept of predestiny. The balance, however, gradually moved to favour the idea of predestiny. Experience made the Icelanders increasingly fatalistic because the 'outside' forces became even more difficult to appropriate.

In the final chapter on the human condition in Iceland I analysed the constituents of the environment. The animal world was shown to be organized in a scheme of classification which related the various species to the human world. The visible beings of the environment had some more or less invisible counterparts in the hidden dimension. These also stood in distinct relationships to humans, who specified the characteristics of the non-human world themselves. The investigation into the proto-scientific views on nature left a vivid impression of nature being both animate and inanimate, and comprising secret resources.

Having encircled the environment this way, we were in a position to reconsider farming and fishing as two modes of exploitation of natural resources. The conspicuous asymmetry between the two modes of livelihood was correlated with their different positions in relation to the social system and the environment. Farming was part of the social; fishing was alienated from it, and counter-specified as wild.

In their attempt to fight off the wild at all levels, the Icelanders put much effort into the maintenance of the boundary between the social and the wild. But nature could not be entirely averted, and culture was only moderately protected, by these efforts.

So much for the recollection of the essentials of the preceding chapters. The recollection was made at the level of *society*, that is at the empirical level where *history* sums up the facts of succession in the course of time.

Specifying the general trends (or 'diachronic rules') in this history we saw a stress upon the autonomy of the household, a concentration of labour in farming at the expense of fishing, and a distinctive valuation of settled life at the expense of mobility. By drawing the boundary between the social and the wild at an ever-smaller distance from the centre, however, more and more people were alienated from the social. Destiny became a natural fact, with which the Icelanders could not cope.

UCHRONIA: REALITY IN PAST TENSE

Uchronia is nowhere in time. If Utopia is a parallel universe, Uchronia is a separate history. It is a history out of time, so to speak. In Iceland, Uchronic visions were part of the collective representations of the world, and as such they deeply influenced the response of the society to its own history.

With modernity, a new vision of history as linear growth emerged in Europe. In contrast to the old view of a qualitatively defined time-space, the new chronology and linearity implied that any stage in history was temporary. They also indirectly sustained the idea that history could not go absolutely wrong; it had its own directional logic. We know that Iceland resisted modernity until very recently, and the development of Icelandic society teaches us that the vision of history as linear growth was alien to the Icelanders. Even in modern Europe this vision remained élitist for a long time; it alienated the rank and file from history in more ways than one.

The conceptual discrepancy between two views of history, if not actually between two histories, makes room for Uchronic imagination on the part of the people. Where this is found, and certainly where it achieves the proportions of the Icelandic case, it reveals a feeling of incapacity to influence actual history. It also points, however, to a failure on the part of the dominant historical discourse to incorporate the experience of ordinary people. The gap between the two histories leaves people in a void.

In Iceland, this observation is acutely relevant. With no experience of a progressive history, the Icelanders knew that history *could* go wrong; the kind of misery it entailed had no logic. In the fight between fire and ice, between the hot and the cold conditions of history, the Icelanders retreated to an imaginary time when history was 'right'. This gave rise to Uchronic visions which were at odds with present social experiences. Uchronia had its own reality, of course, but from the point of view of the modern analyst, this reality was hypothetical.

We cannot ask contemporary Icelanders about their imaginations, but we can infer them from a wide range of historical evidence. Uchronia, as the vision of another 'time', connects otherwise disconnected elements, and adds a level of comprehension to our historical narrative. The history out of time entertained by the Icelandic imagination was informed by their view of the past. The past was over, yet in narrative form it was continuously reproduced and invoked by the Icelanders, in the search for meaning in the void between two histories. In the recasting of the old myths of creation and of the past virtues of man and society, the Icelanders were perpetually confronted with an ideal world nowhere in time.

In a previous chapter I argued that while other peoples invent traditions to match a new historical situation, the Icelanders reproduced the images of the past to invent themselves (Ch. 6). This implied a distinctly 'non-modern' pattern of reaction to the actual historical situation. The Icelanders did not live in the past, but neither did they put the Middle Ages into action. Uchronia informed their ways of coping with the demands of the present.

In the collective representations of the right history, there was a strong emphasis on the Icelander as *bóndi* ('farmer'). Early Icelandic literature featured the *bóndi* as a mythical representative of 'freedom'—individual and collective (cf. Weber 1981). Iceland was colonized by farmers, and Icelandic society was defined by settlements. Since then, Icelandicness had been associated with settled farming life. The externalization of the fisheries was a consequence of this. Whenever a shortage of labour was perceived, the reaction was one of immediate withdrawal to the farmstead.

In fact, this pattern of reaction was so pertinent that it identifies an a priori relationship. It will be recalled how two pawns in the same column on the chessboard immediately signal that one of them had taken an opposing piece in a previous move. This supposition holds a priori, given the rules of the game. Similarly for the laws and rules enforcing compulsory farm-work on the landless population. We know immediately that it must have been preceded by (a feeling of) labour shortage—even when we have no other evidence of a demographic problem. Given the 'rules'—induced from empirical evidence—we know that this is so.

The recasting of the past was a constant reminder that the *bú* ('household') was the proper frame of social life, and that it ought to be self-sufficient. Wealth was measured in farm-produce, and the honour of the *bóndi* was related not only to his ascribed position but also his achieved status as a successful farmer. In this image there was little symbolic space for cotters, day-labourers, and foreign merchants.

Social reproduction in Uchronia was entirely a household matter. In Iceland, from 1400 to 1800, this had an unusual corollary in the breaking down of the social organization based on exchange.

Numerically, incestuous relations may have concerned only a minority of the population, but the extremely low marriage ratio confirms the general impression of a society with very little exchange between the units. Poverty was one reason for this, but we can also read it as a consequence of more and more people being alienated from the social, and thus becoming inhuman by their own standards. Inhumans do not engage in exchange. It was not poverty and misery of themselves that generated the peculiar marriage pattern; it was, rather, the fact that poor people were reclassified as 'inhuman'.

Regarding the sexes, the trends of social change also had certain noticeable implications. Maleness had always implied occasional leaps into the wild, which could thereby be temporarily conquered. In *veiðar* and in sheep round-ups, men left the fenced and protected social world and moved out into the uncontrolled wilderness. In the course of our period, however, the wilderness approached the door-step, and man no longer entertained the idea of being able to tame it. Moving out into the wild no longer served the purpose of attaining masculinity, it was only a means of survival. The mythical reality which favoured settlement at the expense of mobility made the vagrants of the wild an outcast category.

Even the women, who had always had their say in social matters *innan stokks* ('indoors'), concentrated their efforts on ensuring the survival of the *bú*. They left the shielings, and concentrated on the completely domesticated sphere of milk cattle and young children. The honour of the women, and their main contribution to household wealth, were connected to milk-production. Their infants became victims of the honour and butter complex.

The Uchronic imagination was concurrently sustained by the invocation of the past. Because the Icelanders had no 'real' others to identify 'themselves' against, the mirror-image of themselves in the past tense had major social consequences. Living in the imaginary world of Uchronia, the Icelanders had no symbolic exchange with others, and no way of obtaining a position from which they could see 'themselves' as they really were and perceive their situation in 'realistic' terms. They lacked a contemporary comparative reality, against which they could define their own 'culture' (cf. Boon 1982). Paradoxically, this meant that the present escaped them; they felt this, and as a consequence they stuck even more firmly to Uchronia, which at least preserved a sense of injustice in the existing world.

I maintain that the Icelandic Uchronia was shaped by the medieval world view, as continuously reproduced in the literature. One of the most important features of this world view was the concentric cosmological model (Hastrup 1981*a*; 1987*c*). The mythological opposition between Miðgarðr and Útgarðr was repeated at many levels of society. As far as the humans were concerned, the original model included all humans in the centre, while non-humans were exiled to the outer circle (see Figure. 12).

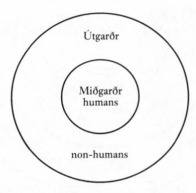

FIG. 12. *The Concentric Model of the World in Early Medieval Cosmology*

In the course of events the clear-cut distinction between these two categories became increasingly blurred. The composition of the population became more complex, and while all settlers by definition had been free and independent farmers, their descendants displayed all degrees of dependence. The concentric model of the world persisted, however, and it remained an organizing principle of the social categories—firmly distinguishing between the 'inside' and the 'outside'.

In fact, more and more people came to live outside the ideal household-structure that was part of Uchronia (see Figure 13). The cosmological model still had its centre in the *bú*, and the social was defined by the inner circle. As a consequence, more and real people merged with the category of non-humans, or *ómenskir menn*. History had 'gone wrong', and had produced more and more non-human beings; Icelandicness was continually defined by the narrow circle of settled farmers in control of their lands and lives.

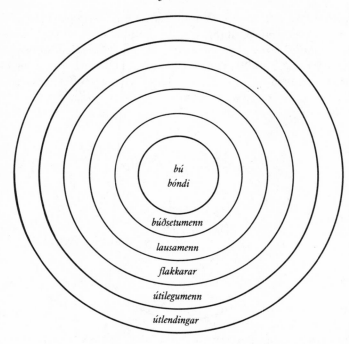

FIG. 13. *The Concentric Model of Social Categories in our Period*

The split between the historical and the Uchronic realities placed
the Icelanders in a kind of an inverse 'prophetic condition' (Ardener
1975*b*; 1989*b*; cf. Hastrup 1989*e*). The prophetic condition is a condition of both structures and individuals finding themselves between
two worlds. Prophets do not predict the future, because that would
have to be in terms of the present. Rather, they foretell a reality before
it has been accommodated in the collective representations and in
language. Prophets, therefore, have to create a new language which in
turn helps define the new reality.

The Icelanders also found themselves between two worlds. They
lived between two histories, or between history and Uchronia. Rather
than defining a new reality and shaping it in language, they defined
their present in terms of a past of which only the language remained
real. They lived in a 'post-phetic' condition.

Prophets are situated in the 'old' world but give voice to a new one.

Often the voice of prophecy is not heard; it is incomprehensible beforehand, trivial afterwards. When the new world has become a commonplace the prophet's voice cannot be distinguished from general speech. When the new world fails to happen, or when it remains latent for an extensive period, prophets may not be registered at all. When the epistemological gap between the worlds is too great, the structural condition is not in favour of prophecy. Prophets may, then, be discarded along with other anomalies of the social.

In the Icelandic case we experience the paradox inherent in the inverse position: reality itself was discarded as anomalous because it no longer fitted the old language. Creative effort was directed towards a recollection and a continuation of 'proper' history, at the expense of a comprehension of present realities.

Uchronia represented a structured world nowhere in time which strongly contrasted with the experiential space. Uchronia was a dream about the primordial, 'cold', society—about the timeless history when man was fully human.

CULTURE: ECCENTRICITY

Culture is the implicational space of the world to which people owe their experience of coherence and meaning in individual actions. In this section we shall seek to identify the Icelandic culture from 1400 to 1800; as a result of anthropological analysis, this culture gives consistency to the disparate realities of society and Uchronia. As a culture in time, the Icelandic mentality lends coherence to history.

In the preceding chapters we have seen how a growing proportion of the Icelandic space was taken over by nature. It will be recalled that the fences disintegrated, and that the wilderness expanded into the inner social space. Nature was a resource, but it was also a threat—of change, of movement, and of disaster. And it encroached relentlessly. One of the consequences of this was a decreasing area of domesticated nature. The socially controlled circle narrowed down to the centre itself. From this narrow viewpoint not only nature but also the larger part of history were beyond control.

'History' itself became split into two: an external uncontrolled succession of movements, and an internal repetition of values traditional. The repetition owed its force to the reproduction of past images in a discourse which mirrored the negativities inherent in the contemporary Icelandic world. With no symbolic exchange with real others the Icelanders could engage in no relationship of identification other than with themselves in the past tense. In a sense they became 'others' themselves. As such they were alienated from the larger history—and ultimately from their own present.

This alienation was correlated with a particular pattern of event-registration. It will be recalled that social 'events' are happenings which are registered as significant according to a particular cultural scheme. This scheme is constantly subjected to risk by social action; even reproduction may eventually entail transformation. In Iceland it was the other way round; the scheme persisted. The Uchronic vision was intimately linked to the reproduction of the past—in voice and in action. The literary image of the free *bóndi* was proudly read out to everyone, and the image was confirmed in action by the Althing's decisions to concentrate energy in the reproduction of the *bú* and to destroy the *búðir*. Due to the conscious reproduction of an outdated cultural scheme, actions became anachronistic, and contemporary happenings failed to register as events. In contrast to the event-richness of the past—as collectively memorized in history—the present was event-poor (cf. Ardener 1989*a*).

Some spaces or some periods always seem to generate more social events than others. This is not solely and not even primarily a mensurational feature, but more importantly a feature of registration. For events to be registered as such, they have to be significant from the point of view of the world as defining (Ardener 1978). The Icelandic world of our period did not single out many happenings as significant social events. The social space was event-poor; movement, change, and innovation were relegated to a non-social space where 'events' did not register.

We may conclude, then, that in the period from 1400 to 1800 Iceland was in a state of event-poverty. By comparison to the event-richness of the previous period, the present reality was marked by absences. While the Icelanders certainly *had* a history during the event-poor centuries, they did not *produce* it. Poverty was both material and symbolic. The two levels merged in the experience of the people.

Event-richness is a feature of space, and it is identified in the synchronic dimension. In the diachronic dimension, relative event-richness is transformed to relative historical density (Ardener 1989*a*). In the representation of history, historical density is a measure of the relative memorability of particular events. For events to be memorized and to become part of 'history' they must have been experienced as significant. This apparently self-evident point covers a profound truth: the structuring of history, or the selective memory, is not solely imposed retrospectively. Contemporary event-registration always serves as the baseline for the trace of experience left in history.

For Iceland this implies that the event-rich period of the early and high Middle Ages was matched by a historical density in this period. This contrasts with the unmarked later periods. The continuous attention paid to past events made the present seem insignificant. The comparative historical density of the past also made the present look like not history at all. The reproduction of culture impeded the production of history.[2]

How can we explain the implied 'cultural inertia' of Iceland. Vehement attachment to the past and its traditions does not necessarily entail a social deconstruction of the kind we have witnessed here.[3] We must, therefore, briefly consider the particular nature of Icelandic historical tradition.

First of all we note that no conceptual distinction between history and fiction was made. The notion of *saga* denoted everything that was 'said' of history; as such, it contained its own complete claim to truth (cf. Hastrup 1986*b*). When the main corpus of sagas was written in the late twelfth and thirteenth centuries, their object was to tell Icelandic history. Although they were certainly literary products, they were perceived as history proper. This was also true for the reconstruction of the ninth- and tenth-century events and characters in the *íslendingasögur* ('The Family-Sagas'). In this particular kind of saga, dealing with the distant pre-Christian period, the past is re-created in the shape of a *Freiheits-mythos* (Weber 1981). In the thirteenth-century historical context of increasing political dependence, the *íslendingasögur* maintained an image of an original *free* state. In the stories it was told how the Icelanders-to-be had emigrated from Norway due to the tyranny of Harald Fairhair. This tradition sustained an image of an original leaning towards independence, which had become antithetical to thirteenth-century reality.

The entire literary activity of the thirteenth century may be read as a more or less explicit attempt to raise the local consciousness of the Icelandic achievements in the *terra nova* (Schier 1975). From the perspective of the imminent surrender to Norway, *terra nova* was the location of the original free state of the Icelanders, inhabited by the noble descendants of the *landnámsmenn*. The 'noble heathen' was the

Icelander *par excellence* (Lönnroth 1969). Even then, Iceland already belonged to two worlds (Hastrup 1984*a*).

In many respects the original free state, as it was remembered, was an optical illusion created by the thirteenth-century authors of the Icelandic sagas (ibid.: 250–1). It became definitional to the social identity of the Icelanders, however, because it was created in opposition to an actual external ruling by symbolic 'others'. Any world, or culture, is a separate definition space (cf. Ardener 1975*b*), but 'separateness' requires at least one other comparable space in order to be conceivable.

I argue, then, that the remarkable tenacity of the old literature and its image of the Icelander is owed to the particular historical context which created it in the first place—and which at the same time created 'Iceland' as a separate world. In this way, the power structure in the social system of which Iceland was part (in spite of itself), worked itself into the self-definition of the Icelanders. It continued to do so during the period from 1400 to 1800, because the only clear image that the Icelanders had of 'themselves' belonged to a time of alleged autonomy and local statesmanship. History had become myth.[4]

If 'culture', generally, encompasses the existentially unique in the conceptually familiar (Sahlins 1985: 146), this had a particular truth in Iceland. The strength of the conceptual scheme actually entailed a failure to register the uniqueness of present existential conditions. In other words, while 'culture' is an organization of current situations in terms of the past (ibid.: 155), in Iceland the 'current situation' hardly registered, because the 'terms of the past' were so strong.

The strength of the traditional language entrapped the Icelanders in a state of refracted vision. Their world view was focused in another time, on another history, and culture became increasingly eccentric.

We are now approaching the point where we can identify the condition which ultimately terminated an epoch for the Icelanders. The inherent refraction in their view of themselves relegated nature, wilderness, fishing, and mobility to an uncontrolled non-social space. This attitude alienated the Icelanders from their own actual history—a history so full of fish and movement. It also, and very importantly, implied that change itself became 'unhistorical'. The diachronic 'rules' for change meant that social energy was concentrated in an ever-smaller circle, and that fully human conditions were attained by ever fewer people. Causes were externalized from the inside controlled world to the outside uncontrolled space due to the increasing eccentricity of Icelandic culture—an eccentricity that amounted to a panchronic feature.

The externalization of cause was correlated with a particular social experience. As a result, 'real' history remained beyond human control. This is what 'checkmated' the Icelanders, and why it was so difficult for Icelandic culture to recondition its own conditions.

Theoretical Reflections

ANY theory in anthropology is informed by the empirical, and all 'evidence' is marked by theoretical assumptions. Once data have become evidence they are evidence of something external to themselves. To discuss the theoretical implications of a history like the one I have tried to write is, therefore, to unfold an argument which was already inherent in the presentation.

Like culture, the theoretical order is virtual rather than empirical; in the territory of knowledge it is *potentia* rather than *presentia* (cf. Sahlins 1985: 153). To perceive the potency of Icelandic history the theoretical argument must be presented in some form, however, and that is the purpose of the present chapter. The mode of presentation will be rather general, but the multitude of particular instances from Icelandic history still form the mirror for my theoretical reflections. I have chosen two separate theoretical themes: first, I will discuss causation in the world; secondly, I will discuss the nature of anthropological history.

TOWARDS A THEORY OF CAUSATION

History is movement and change. That is why we perceive it at all. In 'cold' societies bathing in the liquid of history there is no sense of movement, and consequently no production of history (Lévi-Strauss 1961; cf. above, Ch. 5). In Iceland, we have seen how people took 'age' to be a hallmark of authenticity, not in the sense of a distant past, but of an eternal present. In one sense the Icelanders refuted history, as change; while in another sense they were caught by historical currents they could not control at all.

The awareness of a past, and hence of history, derives from two distinct experiences: of antiquity and decay (Lowenthal 1985: 125). Antiquity implies a sense of age, decay of material change. Both were integral elements in the Icelandic awareness of the past. The Icelanders lived between two histories, an indigenous one that was age, permanence, and authenticity, and an external one entailing decay, movement, and extraneousness.

In the collective representations of the Icelanders these two histories were not connected. For the analyst, it is clear that the nature of the decay was correlated with a view of permanence that was unwarranted by almost any standard. This immediately leads to a recognition of different kinds of causalities, which must be explained here. Once we are dealing with change and movement, the question of cause is implicit and demands an answer. Since anthropology abandoned the natural analogies and the idea of 'laws', we have realized that any theory of causation is marked by culture. Invoking David Hume, Mary Douglas reminded us that causality is no more than a construction upon past experience (Douglas 1975: 276). This provides a pertinent starting-point for the present thoughts.

Causality is a relationship between cause and effect, and although relations cannot normally be seen, causality is an empirical matter. In human society this implies that causality is part of the cultural scheme, and is based on local social experience. We catch fewer fish and experience hunger, and we induce that the former causes the latter. Icelandic notions of causality at this level of empirical knowledge were implicit in the discussions of the Icelandic world. We still have to unfold it, however, if we want to get beyond the experiential and reach the implicational level of understanding—where we may discuss *causation* as distinct from causality.

The proposition that ideas of causality are based in social experience implies that they are part of the collective representations. From the moment that the causal relation has been collectively stated by the group it becomes independent of every individual consciousness (Durkheim 1976: 442). Causality is identified from a world in which experience and definition merge, and where the individual and the collective are continuous with one another. We know this from the shaman: 'Quesalid n'est pas devenu un grand sorcier parce qu'il guérissait ses malades, il guérissait ses malades parce qu'il était devenu un grand sorcier' (Lévi-Strauss 1958: 198). Like the famous shaman, history also offers a kind of performance to the audience, in which success or failure to reproduce the social system cannot be measured by external standards, but are eternally subjected to a social consensus. The self-affirming nature of magical thought (cf. above, Ch. 7), also applies to historical thought in any society.

The point is that in any discussion of causality in the human world, collective representations play an all-important part. In Iceland, the representations of causality were tied to the rules for diachronic change which I discussed earlier. 'Rules' are recurrent relationships between elements of the social, and while they are not of themselves 'causes', the fact of their recurrency of necessity informs the notions of causality. Calling home the fishermen to compulsory farm-work again and again correlated with a popular experience of the cause of agricultural decay to be found in the excessive interest in fishing. Stressing the unnaturalness of any geographical mobility that was not defined as a journey between two farms was correlated with a perception of vagrants as a cause of social problems. Burning witches implied a final refutation of their innocence, and witchcraft could be identified as the cause of particular misfortunes. In the Icelandic representations of causality, the collective experience of particular social reactions to certain historical circumstances were prominent. In that sense the social system was self-affirming; experienced 'simultaneities' were defined as 'causalities'.

In the course of time this had some important consequences. We have seen how the Icelanders originally believed themselves capable of influencing history by means of magic, and how they would attempt to heal illnesses by herbs or formulas. In the course of history their experience tended to belie this, and the idea of human causation faded, giving way to ideas of external and largely uncontrollable causes of all changes. In social experience, nature and foreign merchants, mobility and vagrants were causal agents *external* to Icelandic culture. As experience continually emphasized this, the local representations of causality became increasingly focused on external forces, leaving the internal and system-specific reasons for change in the realm of silence.

Icelandic culture traditionally determined the representations of cause as either external or internal. When culture shrank, so to speak, more and more causes were externalized—and socially defined as beyond influence. Culture and causality were linked to a degree which made an ever-diminishing part of cosmos under control.

Cosmology always informs our ideas of causality, even when we leave the 'real' world and move into the world of scholarly explanations. A cosmology is a theory of space and structure, while causality involves time and process. They are not opposites but mutually defining. In scholarship the dominating world view has been mechanistic for the past five centuries, representing cosmos in terms of still lesser parts at the expense of the whole (cf. Merchant 1980). The European consciousness moved from humanism to science as modernity approached (cf. Mandrou 1978). Indeed, modernity was largely defined in terms of the scientific discoveries.

Causality has been represented in similar mechanistic terms. One event caused the other; causes and effects were endlessly connected in the course of time. In the present position the basic assumptions of this particular cosmology are seriously questioned (Lyotard 1984). The questioning is owed partly to the fact that history itself has undermined the mechanistic ideas of progress and gradual emancipation through knowledge. If nothing else, the present condition implies that historical thought is no longer as self-affirmative as it used to be. This gives room for renewed reflections on, among other things, causation.

Concern with causation is not new in the science of history, where it has had the distinct shape of a 'temporal causation' (Rabb 1982: 331). This implies that historians have established contexts by making connections in time—rather than connections in space. The latter would link particular events to culture and cosmology.[1] Given the *post eventum* character of historiography (Leff 1969: 26), causal connections are made from events to antecedent phenomena—whence 'temporal causation'. The result is that antecedents in general have been treated as causes. Evidently this seems to make way for a process of infinite regress, but historians have attempted to punctuate the process and to identify *the* relevant antecedent in many cases. In other words, historians have tended to elevate their own representations of causality to a general theory of causation. The inquisitor, however, is but a partial observer (cf. Rosaldo 1986), and his identification of causes on a single-stranded time-scale is a 'modern' refraction inherent in all historical writing. In an illustrative example Marc Bloch shows how 'causes' are extrapolated from all the necessary antecedents, not by their being most necessary, but by their being most recent, least permanent, and most exceptional in the general order of things; they also seem to be those antecedents that could most easily have been avoided (Bloch 1954: 191). The problem is that in historical scholarship 'the most constant and general antecedents remain merely implicit' (ibid.).

The shortcomings of the idea of temporal causation is owed to the fact that history is not only a series of events but also the links between them, as Evans-Pritchard has already noted (1964: 174). The empirical order of events and their succession must be understood with reference to an implicational space, which is not unlike the 'implicate order' of modern physics (Bohm 1986).[2] The 'explicate' order of events reveals an implicate order, which is unbroken wholeness in constant motion (ibid.: 152). The event is culture made manifest. Like the implicate order, culture escapes the Cartesian co-ordinates. If movement is not—or not only—what happens to a spatially defined entity from one point in time to the next, history cannot be 'represented' by reference to the temporal dimension alone. We realize, therefore, that 'temporal causation' is just one particular representation of causality. *Causation* is a different matter when movement is redefined as successive manifestations in space of a non-empirical order. In the human world this kind of movement represents that kind of history which *all* societies have—in spite of our classifying them as societies with or without history. We 'read' the history in the series of events, which are crystallized expressions of culture, and if the crystals remain comparatively similar for an extended period we have tended to classify the societies as 'without history'—which is an epistemological fallacy. All societies have histories of equal length, dating back to their beginnings.

They are not equal in other respects, though. Some societies *produce* history, others do not. We have seen how Europe produced a kind of history to which Iceland could not accommodate because the Icelanders had a timeless vision of history. This is why in Iceland movement appeared to be induced from outside.

To the series of events studied by empirically oriented historians,[3] who have established links of temporal causation between them, we may now add two more levels of history: the implicate order of culture, and the movement by which it 'explicates' itself. Both are causes of actual chains of events.

Culture, which is not an entity or a thing but a world of relationships, connects the events of the empirical order in a non-arbitrary pattern. In that sense the whole and its internal logic determines the particular events. In turn, the explicit forms may induce changes in the implicate order: culture is put at risk in action. The 'order' is neither permanent nor absolute in the human world.

All worlds are moving—at different speeds and under different risks. They all have 'histories' by the simple fact that new people are born and add their own life and human creativity to the world. There is a fundamental continuity between the space and the individuals that constitute it: they are both defined by the space and the defining consciousness of that space (Ardener 1987*a*: 39). That is why the cultural order is never reducible to a mechanical world of laws and rules, and why there is a latent schism between 'the cultural order as constituted in society and as lived by the people' (Sahlins 1985: p. ix).

Historical movement cannot be explained solely by reference to different degrees of inventiveness or creativity on the part of the people, however. The distinct temporalities of particular societies are owed also to their inherent structural propensities. Lévi-Strauss has argued, for example, that ('hot') societies based on social difference have a greater potential for producing history than have ('cold') egalitarian societies (Lévi-Strauss 1961).

In Iceland from 1400 to 1800 society was involved in two different histories. From the internal perspective, 'history' was timeless and 'cold'; it had become a myth which was not concerned so much with the succession of events as with the moral significance of situations (cf. Evans-Pritchard 1964: 179). The 'moral' significance was defined by Uchronia. From an external perspective 'history' was progressive and 'hot'; the succession of events reflected Iceland's involvement in a larger order of social reproduction, which was based on social difference and gradually entailed 'modernity' in Europe.

The discrepancy between these two 'histories' made the Icelanders externalize change. The magnitude of the schism between the cultural order as *constituted* in society and as *lived* by the people in Iceland entailed a particular representation of causality; moreover, it caused a particular history—of disintegration.

Cause, then, must be identified with reference to a combination of empirical and implicational orders. From this perspective, temporal causation is a poor metaphor for the connections in history, or the links *of* history. A theory of causation in the world cannot reduce history to time. It explodes in culture.

THE ANTHROPOLOGY OF HISTORY

There has been a distinctive trend in anthropology as far as 'history' is concerned.[4] In the 1950s history was invoked in order to save

anthropology from natural science. Thus Evans-Pritchard stated that
fundamentally 'social anthropology is a kind of historiography' (1964:
152). Later, within the same British tradition 'history' became an
object of analysis. The focus was on history *and* social anthropology.
The value of history for anthropology was in the amount of factual
material available from an extended period (Lewis 1968: p. xxiv). The
present work might perhaps be taken as a confirmation of this.

In the 1980s the conjunctive *and* no longer exhausted the relationship between history and anthropology. We have reached a point
where an anthropology *of* history may crystallize (Sahlins 1983). The
factual material serves the explicit purpose of tracing change and of
exploding the concept of history by the anthropological concept of
culture (ibid.: 534; and Sahlins 1985: 72). There is no longer any
perception of 'opposition' between culture and history, or between
structure and event. They are mutually defining. In my own words,
these categories are adjective to one another (cf. Introduction , p. 2
above).

In the preceding pages we have experienced how Icelandic history
from 1400 to 1800 was grounded in structure, being the systematic
ordering of contingent circumstances; however, the Icelandic structure itself proved to be 'historical' (cf. Sahlins on Hawaii, 1985: 144).
Within the panchronic frame, structure has an internal diachrony,
consisting in the changing relations between general categories (ibid.:
p. xv). In so far as mentality is structure—or a culture in time—we can
reformulate the analytical results of this work in terms of changing
relations between key-categories in the Icelandic world. Previously,
settler, farmer, household head, independence, honour, and butter
had defined the 'human' in Iceland. As categories were twisted and the
equations between them undermined by history, the essence of
Icelandicness was no longer realized. It was maintained only in the
mental category of humanity—alienating the majority of people.

Reality is a process of becoming, and history may be seen as the
movement by which the implicate order explicates itself. The analytical task of anthropology then becomes one of making the reverse
movement: turning history backwards until the explicate events
condense in the implicate order. In this analytical process we leave
temporal causation for a much more complex vision of causality. In
turn that allows us to explain the 'virtual particles' of culture, those
fragmented realities which exist only for an instant and which seem to
be caused by nothing and deriving from the void.[5] In the experiential

space of the world we sense such instants, and although they are gone before we get hold of our notebooks, we *know* them to be real—and to contain a condensed information of the 'nothing' beyond the Cartesian space.

We should be careful here not to reify a new opposition between the explicate and the implicate, the empirical and the virtual. It is all part of the same whole. Wholeness is testified to not only in analysis and logic but also in the historical realization of synchronicities, apparently accidental simultaneities between events. They need not be accidental, if we accept that there are other causal connections than the ones we may trace in time and space.

The idea of doing an anthropology of history is to establish the context of causation, synchronicity, and historical density.[6] It is from the perspective of culture that history and mentality become connected.

The anthropological perspective also allows us to see man as both object and subject of history—at least in theory. In the Icelandic case, he ceased to see himself as subject, and he therefore became object of an ever-more malevolent destiny. In social experience the Icelander knew history to form his life through a series of external agents. The old wisdom of Icelandic magical logic had taught the Icelander that all blessing and all suffering had a cause and that causality was essentially moral (Wax 1969: 52). This wisdom made the Icelanders live in a partly anachronistic world. Although the people felt objects of history, because their experience proved that it could not be redirected, we must maintain that even they were also subjects in history. We have already noted the continuity between the social space and the individuals (Ardener 1987a: 39), and we realize that people do become authors of their own concepts by the fact of their being responsible for their own actions (Sahlins 1985: 152). People are naturally 'cultural'. Although they are born into a culture, they also take responsibility for whatever culture has made them. Powerlessness may be part of experience, but in the human world, it is never an absolute truth. Humanity is a self-announcing species; one of the expressions of the self-defining capacity of the human world is a continual process of redefinition (Crick 1976: 168).

The Icelanders failed to put their concepts at risk; they gave up on the process of redefinition, which experience otherwise would have seemed to provoke. By an accumulation of accidents they had become prisoners of the *longue durée*. Anthropology teaches us that such prisons may explode in the course of individual action.

An anthropology of history is not only an analysis of a particular period in time, it is also a study of the dynamics of history in general. To achieve this we have to approach a period like we would approach a culture, with no preconceived notions. Relativism is the first and necessary step to comprehend 'other times'. We must realize, though, that there is no contradiction between realism and objectivism.[7] We now know that relativization is our only mode of objectivization (Ardener 1987a: 40). Once again, anthropology dissolves the ossified oppositions of Western epistemology.

Thus, to do an anthropology of history is simply to do anthropology. That is all I can claim to have done in the present work.

Conclusion

Territory of Knowledge

THE concept of reality in anthropology dissolves the old oppositions between mind and matter, statics and dynamics, structure and event (Ardener 1982; Sahlins 1985; Hastrup 1987*d*). This is primarily owed to the well-established method of field-work. In field-work we have experienced the virtual order of other worlds, and when we have seen things happen or witnessed events, we have *sensed* a reality beyond the visible order (Hastrup 1986*c*; 1987*d*). In order to mediate the separate reality, we have to write it, however, and we must acknowledge ethnographic comprehension as a creation of ethnographic writing (Clifford 1986*b*; 158).[1] Anthropological knowledge crystallizes from the meeting between two different implicational spaces: the 'other' culture and our own world of scholarship.

Knowledge is no longer seen as a result of discovery, but as a consequence of a process of creation. Discovery and definition merge (Hastrup 1987*d*). The knowledge of Icelandic history between 1400 and 1800 which we may have achieved in the course of the preceding pages is neither absolutely objective nor in any way final. It is a suggestion about one possible way of comprehending the world of the Icelanders.

Writing cultures produces them in the sense that words and textual presentation in general shape a particular perception of reality. I have already noted, and there is a general agreement in recent critical anthropological reflections, that we can never adequately *represent* the other—nor, for that matter, ourselves.[2] Imprisoning worlds in words transforms them in often obscure ways.

I want to make the point here that the aim of anthropology is perhaps best not seen as representation at all. Whatever the scope of particular analyses, we must re-create reality in a different form to let it speak for itself (Hastrup 1986*c*: 13). We cannot fully represent the multifaceted Icelandic reality over a period of four hundred years, containing some 35,000 to 50,000 people's lives over twelve to fifteen generations, but we can re-create it in a form which makes it speak for itself. In other words, while we have to abandon any idea of a straight-forward representation of the other world, we may still evoke it (cf. Tyler 1986).

In the mechanistic world view and under positivist ruling in anthropology, representation was not a problem. The empirical order, with which *l'ancien régime* in anthropology was concerned, appeared to lend itself easily to description. With the acknowledgement of culture as an implicational space rather than an empirical entity anthropologists have realized that descriptions—thin or thick—are only means to the end of evocation.[3] This, in turn, forms the basis for a comprehensive science of man, where the 'facts of succession' and the 'facts of repetition' are reintegrated.

In this work I have attempted to evoke an Icelandic reality, which is fascinating for its separateness. Although anthropology tends to cement the inherent exaggeration of cultures (Boon 1982; Hastrup 1985*d*), just as history tends to exaggerate the difference between periods (Lowenthal 1985: p. xvii), Icelandic 'distinctness' is not solely the result of my own imagination of otherness. Admittedly, the process of recovering the deeper motivations and meanings inherent in Ice-landic culture, and of dragging the latent out of the manifest, requires a degree of imagination which entails questions of plausibility and proof (Rabb 1982: 319). Yet, in a non-positivist anthropology plaus-ibility is the only 'proof' we can expect. The separateness of the Icelandic world is plausible from my analysis, I believe. I have evoked their world partly in my own vocabulary, but the Icelanders have had their say as well.

No wars over national boundaries between separate armies were ever fought in Iceland, while elsewhere in Europe such wars often generated historical change at many levels. In Iceland, the principal battlefield was not on national boundaries, but on the symbolic boundaries of Icelandic culture. There was an eternal war between separate histories going on in Iceland, and that was the major 'differ-ence' in the Icelandic experience.

It was not until the nineteenth-century nationalist movement that this difference was formulated in terms of a separate national identity and a quest for sovereignty, but certainly the Icelanders lived in a world of their own long before that. In many ways this world was and still is a 'remote area' (Ardener 1987*a*). As such it begins to attract the interest of anthropologists—discovering yet another island, and using the discovery for expanding the territory of knowledge.

Anthropology is part of itself; any statement about culture is also a statement about anthropology (Crick 1982: 307). In a similar way history is always its own conclusion. Yet history is also always prefatory to something else—either another history or another set of reflections.

I offer this work as a preface to further thinking on Icelandic history. Like the old Icelanders we sometimes have to 'sit out for wisdom', and our journey to the remote island of anthropology may make us wiser also about history in general. While knowledge is time-bound and culture-bound, *sagesse* is part of human nature—according to Montaigne—and thus extends far beyond pages of written words.[4] Montaigne's motto was '*Que sais-je?*' ('what do I know?'), and I should like to end with this question, confident that there will always be more knowledge to pursue and more wisdom to gain.

NOTES

Introduction: Island of Anthropology

1. See Hastrup (1989*f*) for a more detailed discussion.
2. A recent conference on 'The Anthropology of Iceland' held at Univ. of Iowa, USA, May 1987, confirms the pattern. Among the twenty or so anthropologists present who had a professional interest in Iceland, at least half of them were archaeologists or historians. See Paul Durrenberger and Gísli Pálsson 1989.
3. I use the notion of 'historiography' here in contradistinction to 'history', in order to separate the science of the past from the past itself (Atkinson 1978: 9).
4. In anthropology there is an increasing awareness of the extent to which we 'write' other cultures (Clifford and Marcus 1986), and how ethnography transforms reality from life to text (Ardener 1985). The discerned truth about other cultures and other times therefore remains partial (Clifford 1986*a*).

Chapter 1

1. The model has been elaborated in Hastrup 1988*b*.
2. It is important to note that in general *diachrony* not only refers to actual moves or changes but also and even more importantly to the rules for change (Saussure 1974; Ardener 1971*b*).

Chapter 2

1. The distinction between 'emic' and 'etic' I owe to Pike (1967). 'Etic' refers to an external objective standard, while 'emic' refers to an internal, system-specific, standard.
2. The settlements have been extensively described by Foote and Wilson (1970). Among the most recent works on the Viking expansion in general is Sawyer (1982).
3. *Adam af Bremen, De hamburgske ærkebispers historie og Nordens beskrivelse* (Henrichsen 1968: 285–6).
4. '*Sagði þat ósannligt at Ísland þjónaði eigi undir einn konung sem ǫll ǫnnur lǫnd i verǫldu.*' *Hákonar saga Hákonarsonar*, *Flateyjarbók* (Guðbrandur Vigfússon and Unger 1868: 172).

5. In Hastrup (1985*a*) I discussed the contradiction between the horizontal and vertical models of social organization in Iceland, and the increasing predominance of the vertical principle during the twelfth and thirteenth centuries. This was connected with changes in notions of property (189–200).

6. The point is that any social system can be viewed at different levels of reproduction (cf. Friedman 1982).

7. The Almanac is published by Hið íslenzka þjóðvinafélag, under the auspices of Univ. of Iceland. I am using the 1982 edn. here, but the chronological table has been constant since last century, when the Almanac was first published.

8. For a comprehensive picture of Icelandic intellectual life during the Reformation period, see Páll Eggert Ólason 1919–26. Loftur Guttormsson draws attention to the fact that the Reformation entailed a change in popular culture, because the reformers wanted to abolish the popular interest in 'heathen stories' and replace it with edifying literature (Loftur Guttormsson 1981: 127).

Chapter 3

1. *Laxdœla saga*.Einar Ó. Sveinsson, ed. 1934.

2. This tradition belongs to the thirteenth century and finds its major expressions in *Heimskringla* (Bjarni Aðalbjarnarson 1941–5); *Haralds saga ins Hárfagra* (ibid.); and *Óláfs saga Tryggvasonar en mesta* (Ólafur Halldórsson 1958–61).

3. *Landnámabók*, ÍF. i.

4. More details on the scale of values can be found in Chs. 4 and 5.

5. See e.g. Hastrup (1985*a*).

6. See *KL*: xvi. 578 and Hastrup (1985*a*: 193 ff.).

7. Marshall Sahlins has coined the concept of 'the domestic mode of production' where the household is to the tribal economy what the manor is to the medieval economy. Although Icelandic society was not 'tribal', its economy displayed an important feature of the domestic mode of production, namely, its noticeable underproduction in relation to existing economic capacities (Sahlins 1974: 41 ff.). This will be substantiated below.

8. Provisions against *flakkarar* ('vagrants') are found in numerous sources. See below, Ch. 4, for more details.

9. This was also a distinction between 'culture' and 'nature' (cf. Hastrup 1981*a*; 1985*a*; 1985*d*).

10. The social structure was actually more complex than the normative sources might lead us to believe. There was a certain structure of exploitation which imposed taxes and land rent on the households of crofters, for instance. Thus, the *bú* described here mainly refers to the *lögbýli* as an

actually self-contained unit, incorporating one or more crofters. The household composition will be further dealt with in the next chapter.

11. *Búalög*, i-xvi, Reykjavík 1915–33.

12. It is significant that Espolín, writing an indigenous history of Iceland in the early nineteenth century, should note that both clerical and secular authorities and the peasantry (*almuga*) assented to this rule (Espolín: ii. 113).

13. The 'dryness' of the croft might also refer to the absence of any milk produce, which was essential for farming proper. See below.

14. The distinction between intentional and implicational meaning is from Hanson (1975).

15. *Guðmundar saga* is found in several versions. The one used here was written by Arngrímur Brandsson c.1350, with the aim of promoting Guðmundur's saintly status. In the present context, this saga is of interest mainly for its brief introductory description of Iceland.

16. Oddur Einarsson (1559–1630) is known as the first manuscript collector in Iceland (Stefán Einarsson 1957: 179), and he may have known *Guðmundar saga*. Oddur was taught, and later became bishop (1589) at the northern See at Hólar, where Guðmundur had also been bishop (1203–37). It is, then, possible that Oddur is reproducing Arngrímur's point about grain-growing in the south, but it seems unlikely that he should volunteer the statement that it was 'of much use' to the people, unless he had some direct knowledge of it.

17. Jón Eggertsson, *Adskilligt om Islands Beschafenhed og Wilkor*, fo. 6. This is an unpublished mid-seventeenth-century manuscript, now included in the Thott collection (no. 1738) in the Royal Library in Copenhagen, and to which folio references are given.

18. The passage from *Þorgils saga ok Hafliða* goes: *Á Reykjahólum varu svá góðir landskostir í þenna tíma, at þar váru aldri ófrævír akranir. En þat var jafnan vani, at þar var nytt mjöl haft til beinabótar ok ágætis at þeirri veizlu, ok var gildit at Óláfsmessu hvert sumar* (*Sturlunga saga* 1946: i. 27).

19. Konrad Maurer, *Reise nach Island* 1858. This is an upublished manuscript, located at the Institut für nordische Philologie und germanische Altertumskunde der Universität München. Pagination is given from the typed version of the manuscript. For access to this I am grateful to Prof. Kurt Schier, Munich, and to Deutscher akademischer Austauschdienst, who made my stay in Munich possible.

20. Iceland was divided into quarters by a constitutional amendment of c.965. The quadripartition remained of social and conceptual importance in spite of its legal insignificance.

21. I am grateful to Stefán Karlsson of Stofnun Árna Magnússonar á Íslandi for drawing my attention to this unpublished diploma. *AM* refers to the Arnamagnean Collection of manuscripts.

22. For a complete enumeration of *veiðistöðvar* in Iceland during the centuries see Lúðvík Kristjánsson (1982: 29–84).

23. Lúðvík Kristjánsson has made an extensive study of the technology of boat-building in Iceland, where all details about the workmanship and skills can be found (1982: 85–364).

24. For detailed descriptions of fish-processing see Horrebow (1752: 194–207; 1966: 146–53); Eggert Ólafsson (1772: 345–7); Skúli Magnússon (1944a: 64–6).

25. For editions of *Skíðaríma* see Finnur Jónsson (1905–22: 10–42) and Homan (1975).

26. *Ómenska* literally means inhumanity, but in ordinary speech it also signified laziness or passivity. Until recently a current expression was *liggja i léti og ómensku* ('to be idle and inhuman'). The semantic field around *ómenska* thus indicates that humans had to be hard-working to be humans at all. Cf. discussion in Ch. 6.

Chapter 4

1. This will be elaborated in Ch. 6.

2. Ólafur Lárusson has traced the history of the farm Skarð in detail, and shows how this particular farm was passed on (through men or women) within the kin group for eight centuries (Ólafur Lárusson 1925).

3. The *óðal*-chapter commences thus: *Ef maðr selr jorð sína við verði, þá skal hann bjóða með vitnum hinum nánustum frændum sínum fyrst at kaupa eptir jǫfnu verði, þeim þó er fé hefir til* (*Jónsbók*: 126n.).

4. See e.g. Espolín's Introduction to the second volume of his *Árbækur* for an eighteenth-century Icelandic appraisal of this moral decline.

5. In Skarðsárannáll (*Ann.*: i. 71) and in Espolín (ii. 105) the year is said to be 1484. The stories about Björn, Ólöf, and their kinsmen have been told in some detail by Arnór Sigurjónsson (1975).

6. In some manuscripts of *Jónsbók*, a clause is added to the general rules of inheritance stating that in case the parents married after they had had children 'the oldest illegitimate son would inherit the *höfuðból* after the father' (Magnús Már Lárusson 1970: 46). The matter was far from clear even then, because apparently the children were not actually reclassified as legitimate.

7. In 1220 a *máldagi* ('inventory') for the church of Saurbær refers to landowners, *leiglendingar* and *hiábuðar menn* (*DI*: i. 402). This last term, which is probably the earliest concept for *hjáleigur*, conveys the significant information of the *hjáleiga* being conceived of as a *búð* ('temporary abode') in contrast to a *bú*.

8. For a discussion of this see Hastrup (1985a: ch. 8).

9. The process of consolidation which the Church went through in this early period has been dealt with in detail in Hastrup (1985a: ch. 7). There one can also find a discussion of the process of Christianization in general and its impact upon history and culture.

10. *Staðamál* derives from *staður*, lit. 'place' or locus, i.e. the church farm, and *mál* ('case' or 'discussion').
11. For a detailed account of the king's acquisition of land at the Reformation see Páll E. Ólason (1919–26: ii. 5 ff.).
12. *Crymogæa* was a treatise on Icelandic history made by Arngrímur Jónsson in 1609, influenced by European humanism (Jakob Benediktsson 1985). Written in Latin, it was mainly directed towards a European audience.

Chapter 5

1. Cf. Hørby (1980).
2. The quarters of 965 were not only judicial units, but more importantly they also gradually became the major units in the semantics of orientation (Hastrup 1985a: ch. 2). They remain so even today, where the geography of the island is largely conceived of in terms of this quadripartition.
3. Cf. Ch. 4 n. 12 above.
4. A detailed account of the history of local government is found in Lýður Björnsson (1972–9).
5. In my work on the Icelandic Freestate I discussed the fact that the Icelanders primarily orientated themselves towards 'centres' rather than boundaries (Hastrup 1985a: *passim*).
6. In a recent study of rural cultures in the British Isles it has been shown how people 'belong' to their local area, even when deeply integrated into a larger order (Cohen 1982).
7. *Íslendingabók* (Jakob Benediktsson 1968). See also Strömbäck 1975 and Jón Hnefill Aðalsteinsson (1978*b*).
8. *Biskop Arnes Kristenret, Norges Gamle love* (*AK*, *NGL*: v.).
9. Skáld-Sveinn (*c.*1460–*c.*1530) actually gives a very detailed and critical account of the Icelandic conditions around the turn of the fifteenth century. The social differentiation, the individual interpretation of the laws, and the excessive drinking of the rich are all themes in the poem, which almost amounts to an ethnographical satire (*Kvæðasafn* (Jón Þorkelson 1922–7): 238–44; Nordal 1924: 3–8).
10. For an elaborate account of Guðbrandur Þorláksson's life and work, see Páll Eggert Ólason (1919–26: iii. 424–753).
11. *Píningsdómur um verzlum* (*LI*: i. 41–3). For later references to this rule, see e.g. *AÍ*: vii. 475, 589–90, concerning 1679 and 1682 respectively. See also *Historia Ecclesiastica Islandiæ* (Finnur Jónsson: ii. 245 and Espólín: ii. 113).
12. An early history of Icelandic trade, focusing on the monopoly (1602–1787) and describing in detail the various companies and their dealings, is found in Aðils (1971, 1st edn. 1919). Björn Þorsteinsson (1970) deals with 'The English Age', as does Finnur Magnússon (1833). Recently two other scholars have devoted themselves to Icelandic trade: Gelsinger (1981) deals with the Middle Ages and Gísli Gunnarsson (1983) is concerned

thin?

with the period of the monopoly. The latter in particular provides a stimulating analysis of the interrelationship between external trade and internal socio-economic conditions.

13. See e.g. Þorkell Jóhannesson (1933); Arnór Sigurjónsson (1930: 176); Gísli Gunnarsson (1983).

14. The distinction between 'hot' and 'cold' societies was made by Lévi-Strauss (1961: 37ff.), who used it to describe the difference between civilized and primitive societies. The former are based on inequality and use it as energy to promote history. In the process, disorder or entropy is generated. Primitive societies are democratic and produce neither history nor entropy. Although 'democracy' may be an unwarranted term for the Icelandic conditions prior to capitalization, there was certainly always a striving towards individual autonomy.

Chapter 6

1. Cf. Clanchy (1981: 29), quoting a medieval scholar.

2. An introduction to Icelandic scaldic poetry is given by Turville-Petre (1976).

3. Jón Helgason is very doubtful about Loftur *ríki* being the author (1953: 166), while the editor of the two latest published versions, Jón Þorkelsson, takes it for granted (1922–7: 8).

4. Cf. also *DI*: v. 45–6 concerning 1450.

5. I shall deal with impotence as a reason for divorce later when considering marriage. There is no evidence that in Iceland impotence was interpreted as a result of evil magic, as it was in sixteenth-century France (cf. Le Roy Ladurie 1974*b*).

6. For a discussion of the application of corporal punishment, see Páll Sigurðsson (1971: 9–89). For a comparative analysis of the death penalty in the Scandinavian countries, see Ström (1942). From his analysis it appears that drowning was an exclusively female form of execution, while hanging was exclusively male, and beheading applicable to both sexes (ibid.: 115–88). In Iceland the distinction by sex was rigorously maintained. No traces are left from the decapitations of men, but at the Althing site, the *drekningarhýlar* ('drowning pool') still reminds us of the fate of numerous women from our period.

7. It is interesting to note here that incest was depicted as both a religious and a secular crime—hence the division of property between Church and Crown. We also note how both of these institutions could acquit the culprits on their own account. This clearly gave rise to many conflicts between the two standards of value.

8. An elaborate tale of sibling-incest is *Systkinin frá Viðivallagerði*. The story is set in the last part of the seventeenth century, and provides a fine

illustration of the humane view of such cases, as held also by priests. The tale is printed in *Gríma*, xx (1945).

9. In a document from 1488 (seven years after the establishment of her rights in the confiscated estate), Bjarni's wife gave away in *fjörðungsgjöf* and *tíundargjöf* part of her property at Hvassafell, with the consent of Bjarni (*DI*: vi. 640–1).

10. It is the exchange of spouses which necessitates 'society' as an organizational system above the nuclear family (Lévi-Strauss 1949). In general, real and symbolic exchange is the *sine qua non* of 'the social' (Mauss 1950; cf. Hastrup and Elsass 1988). We know of incest from a variety of societies, where it has been *regulated* and clearly demarcated as exceptional. I refer to *ESS*, s.v. Incest, for a summary.

11. We have no statistical evidence of this. Indirectly, however, the number of farms falling into waste, the recurrent notices in the annals about mass extinctions due to catastrophes of various kinds, and the seventeenth- and eighteenth-century reports testify to an increasing demographic 'problem'. In legislation (1774) this was also acknowledged, and reasons of illness, hygiene, bad food, wasteland, and other things were given (*LI*: iv. 34ff.). Possibly the Icelandic population was recovering in the sixteenth century from the Black Death and the 'later plague' (1494–5); Oddur Einarsson mentions hordes of people roaming about the country (1589; 1971: 85), but this observation is probably best interpreted as a qualitative statement about a poverty-stricken populace, rather than a quantitative measure.

12. Cf. also Tables 9 and 11 in Ch. 4.

13. To give the gist of the poem, I shall quote the first verse: *Kæri barn mitt, korríró| kúrðu vært og sof nú lengi.| Vekja þig af vænní ró,| verkjatök né meinsemd engi.|* ('My dear child, *korríró*, crouch you calmly and do sleep long, no pain or sickness can now wake you up from the blissful peace) (*ÍL*: ii. 275).

14. In contrast to the unsentimental report of 1772, Eggert Ólafsson's 'Búnaðarbálkur' (1832a) is very emotional. The sufferings of his people, recorded by the level-headed emissary of the Danish king, had made a strong impression on Eggert's feelings, which he allowed himself to express in this poem.

15. See e.g. Knodel and van de Walle (1967); Lithell (1981).

16. Actually the decree distinguishes between the polluted categories as either concubines, adulterers, or 'those who have had children by their affines or kinsmen'. Later decrees followed similar patterns (*DI*: ii. 530).

17. There are references to this practice in the sagas, and we know that it was legal to set out the infants before they had been named. However infrequent this might have been the conceptual connection between 'disposed infants' and 'ghost-children' was strong and persistent, as testified by the word *útburður* for both. See Einar Ó. Sveinsson (1940: 168); Sydow (1935: 113); Almqvist (1978); Pentikäinen (1968); cf. also *JÁ: passim*.

18. This need not be a linguistic fact; it is, rather, an ideological statement. Even today, scholars of the Icelandic language consider the fishing population to be bad Icelandic speakers by comparison with the farmers (Gísli Pálsson 1979). •
19. The contrast between writer and author is from Barthes (1982: 185–93). I have dealt more extensively with it in Hastrup (1987*b*).
20. The cost of books has been discussed extensively by Lönnroth (1964: 45–51). On the basis of inventories and other original documents he concludes that books were not within the reach of ordinary people. In 1490 a certain Björn Guðnason bought his father a lawbook for five hundreds, i.e. the price of five milking cows (*DI*: vii. 154). The book has been identified as *Skarðsbók*, one of the most famous Icelandic books, written in 1363 (Lönnroth 1964: 48). The important thing to note is that the value of books was generally measured in 'hundreds'.

Sigurður Nordal actually takes an opposite point of view, suggesting that books were relatively accessible to ordinary peasants, both because they had much calf-skin for the parchment, and because they had time to make books (Nordal 1954). Solrún Jensdóttir has made a study of books owned by ordinary people in the eighteenth century (1975–6).
21. Proverbs embedded in medieval Icelandic literature have been anthologized by Finnur Jónsson (1914). Proverbs from MS AM 604 (4to) were published by Kålund (1886). In the seventeenth century Peder Syv (1631–1702) published a number of Icelandic proverbs as an appendix to the Danish collection (Syv 1682). At about the same time an Icelander, Jón Rúgman (1636–79), collected a fair number of Icelandic sayings and proverbs, but they were not published until this century (Rúgman 1927–8). The first Icelandic edition of proverbs to appear in print was made by Guðmundur Jónsson, and printed in Copenhagen in 1830 on behalf of the then very active Icelandic literary society.
22. The idea that distant marriage enlarges the range of social relations was entertained already by the Church Fathers, who recognized that out-marriage multiplied social relations and prevented villages from becoming closed communities (Goody 1983: 57).

Chapter 7

1. The word *guðspjall* ('gospel'), provides an interesting example of the mixing of categories taking place in early Christendom. The word was borrowed from OE 'godspell' via English missionaries. 'The true etymological sense, however, was lost, probably because the root vowel had become short in England by the time that the word was transplanted to Iceland, so that *guðspjall* was understood to mean not *good spell* but *God's spell*' (*IED*: 219–20; cf. de Vries 1977: 193).
2. The point made by Steblin-Kaminskij is based on a consideration of

etymologies. In spite of this distinct origin it has a general bearing on my point about the change in the meaning of *skáldskapr*.

3. Magic was not a prime feature of *skáldskapr*, though, but it seems to have been a latent quality. Thus in *Njáls saga* it is said of a particular woman that she is *skáldkona og orðgifr* ('scaldwoman and word-gifted'), and the context leaves no doubt as to her supernatural powers (Einar Ó. Sveinsson 1954, *ÍF*: xii. 87). Today *skáldkona* refers to any woman-poet (cf. Guðrún P. Helgadóttir 1961–3).

4. Another illustration to this is provided by the ON concept of *varðlokur* ('ward-closers'), referred to in *Eiríks saga Rauða* (Storm 1891: 16). This term, which refers to a particular incantation, is cognate with Scottish *warlock*, referring to a wizard (Olsen 1916a: 19). Historically, a conflation between the song and the sorcerer occurred. This was possible because both 'enclosed' the spirits (ibid.).

5. In post-Reformation Iceland, real bonfires made of heretical books were probably very few. Jón *lærði* Guðmundsson tells of a series of such fires having taken place at the convent of Helgafell 1623–4, and this is the only known evidence according to Halldór Hermannsson (1922: xvi–xvii).

6. A very common stave for general protection against evil and enemies was the *Ægishjálmur*. See below, p. 259.

7. A complementary conclusion is reached by Rosalie Wax, who states that for the Icelanders causality was essentially moral (Wax 1969: 52). We shall return to this in Ch. 10.

8. It has been a matter of controversy whether the fetch was related to the afterbirth, since both were named *fylgja*. The connection has been established by Turville-Petre (1940: 54), but wholly dismissed by Sydow (1935: 158 n. 20).

9. The changing of shape from man to animal was part of this imagery. Only one manifestation of this seems to have been more than a literary motif and truly an element of popular belief in the Nordic countries, namely, that of the werewolf (Sydow 1935: 120). This has been read as a central European literary motif transposed on to the Norse ideas of *hamrammr*, i.e. the shamanistic practice related to the changing of shape by the human 'counterpart' (Strömbäck 1943–4; 1970: 257).

10. The conceptual opposition between 'the social' and 'the wild' has been developed by Ardener (1972), and applied by myself to medieval Icelandic society (Hastrup 1981a; 1985a; ch. 5).

11. General sources on the seventeenth-century Icelandic witch-trials are Thoroddsen (1892–1904: ii); Ólafur Davíðsson (1940–3); Siglaugur Brynleifsson (1976); Páll Eggert Ólason (1916). In a separate article I have analysed the witch-trials in a general European perspective (Hastrup 1989g).

12. *Fjandafæla* has been transcribed and edited by Einar Gunnar Pétursson, who generously allowed me to study the as yet unpublished manuscript during my stay at Stofnun Árna Magnússonar á Íslandi.

13. In the Viking Ages, women were the ones who practised *seiðr* ('magic')
    (Strömbäck 1935), but generally they seem to have lost touch with the
    external powers during the Middle Ages.
14. The distinction between disease and illness has become common in
    medical anthropology. 'Disease' refers to the specialist's model, while 'ill-
    ness' contains the patient's model, including a social and semantic com-
    ponent making the state meaningful; the distinction corresponds to a
    distinction between curing and healing (see Kleinman 1980; Young 1982).
15. The oldest manuscript is AM 655, xxx (4to) from the thirteenth century.
    Next comes AM 194 (8to) from 1387 (Kålund 1908), which has a close
    parallel in AM 434 a (12mo) from the eighteenth century (Kålund 1907).
    Related, yet more elaborate, is the manuscript from the Royal Irish
    Academy 23 D 43, from the fifteenth century (Larsen 1931).
16. The translations are by the editor of the Miscellany, Henning Larsen.
17. For references, see *KL*: *Kirurgi*.
18. New possibilities for Icelanders to go to Copenhagen for higher education
    had been created in the post-Reformation humanistic spirit, and it was in
    this context that Henrik Smith was translated. At the University of Copen-
    hagen the natural and medical sciences were increasingly important
    subjects, and from this university impulses at all levels of culture kept fil-
    tering into Iceland.
19. In a recent publication of traditional Icelandic herb-medicine, juniper is
    still listed as an efficient drug against colds (Björn L. Jónsson 1973: 34).
20. Thus, for example, a *blámaður* (lit.: 'blue man') was a 'black', *bláfátækur*
    (lit.: 'blue poor') was 'extremely poor', *falda blá* ('to cover the head in blue')
    equals 'to dress in sorrow'. Whenever death had to be augured in the liter-
    ature a man in a 'blue cloak' would appear (cf. *IED*: 68; Fritzner 1954: i.
    147; *LP*: 51, 52).
21. Childbearing was a risky business, but it was a risk to which only a
    minority of women were exposed, given the low marriage ratio. Complica-
    tions were part of the collective experience, however, and delivery must
    have been faced with foreboding (cf. Shorter 1984: 69 ff.). Also cases of
    miraculous survival from extremely complicated births became widely
    known, and were noted by annalists (see e.g. *Ann.*: i. 82 (1517); ibid.: ii. 656
    (1731)).
22. This also seems to have been the case in Norway in the same period,
    where it was practically impossible to make any firm distinction between
    popular and learned medicine in terms of different rationalities (Bø 1973:
    7–171). However, during the eighteenth and nineteenth centuries, medical
    practice became a matter of controversy between the peasants and the
    growing class of public servants, the latter wishing to 'take over' the issue
    by means of legislation against 'wise' men and women (ibid.). In Iceland
    this was true only to a lesser degree because the social order was different;
    the public 'servants' were themselves peasants (farmers) because no urban

culture had yet established itself (cf. Loftur Guttormsson 1987*a*: 33–5). Also, the category of 'professional lay healers' (*kloge koner* in Scandinavia) was insignificant in Iceland.

Chapter 8

1. See the present author's discussion of the Icelandic 'months' (Hastrup 1985*a*: 29 ff.).
2. Gísli Oddsson maintains that they were not rare at all (1638; 1942: 57), and Jón Eggertsson (*c.*1650: fo. 3) speaks of the 'many bears of Iceland' being greatly damaging to both men and cattle. Writing in the mid-seventeenth century these two observers were witnesses to an increasing number of hard winters, and drift-ice would be more common by then. Oddur Einarsson (1589) has an extensive chapter on the irregularity of drift-ice (1971: 34–5).
3. In his unpublished travel account from 1858 Konrad Maurer gives a very elaborate description of the eiderdown collection (1858: 272–86; page ref. is given to the typed manuscript located at Univ. of Munich). Probably the details were much the same in our period.
4. For an outline of the supernatural themes in the early Icelandic literature, see the motif-index made by Boberg (1966).
5. A main source of knowledge about these creatures is Jón Árnason's six-volume collection of *Íslenzkar þjóðsögur* (1954–61). This was compiled in the nineteenth century, but represents an older oral tradition.
6. *Ver* may refer to either a fishing place, or to a grassy plot which is like an oasis in an uninhabited area (Blöndal 1920–4: 925).
7. We return to that in the section on the natural science below.
8. See *JÁ: passim*.
9. On *Lilja*, see n. 11 below, and cf. above, Ch. 5.
10. *Guðmundar saga* (*Biskupa sögur*, i (1858)) was written *c.*1350.
11. *Lilja* has appeared in a number of editions, and is still a very popular poem. Many religious poems were written in the fourteenth and fifteenth centuries, but *Lilja* was among the few to survive the Reformation. In a somewhat 'cleaned' up version it was even included in Guðbrandur Þorláksson's *Vísnabók* of 1612. The edition quoted here is the one made by Eirík Magnússon (1870); he also made the English translation.
12. In the 1971 Icelandic translation of *Qualisqungue*, Sigurður Þórarinsson comments on the actual scientific value of Oddur's observations (1971: 18–25).
13. They have been published by Halldór Hermannsson (1917) in the original Latin. An Icelandic translation has been published under the name of *Annálabrot* and *Undur Íslands* by Jónas Rafnar (1942).
14. Halldór Hermannsson reaches the conclusion that the work must have been written between 1640 and 1644 (1924: xxiii).

Notes 319

15. *Speculum Regale. Konungs-skuggsjá. Konge-speilet* (Keyser, Munch, and Unger 1848). The editors date the piece to the late twelfth century, although modern research suggests that the 1250s are more likely (Schreiner 1953).

16. To complicate matters, Oddur Einarsson (1589) refers to *hrosshvalir* and *springhvalir* ('jump-whale') as two separate species of whales, quite distinct from the walrus. The *hrosshvalir* derives its name from its mane of 30–40 ellens length. It is wicked and dangerous, but in a quite different way from the jumper (Oddur Einarsson 1971: 114–15).

17. An extract is pulished by Halldór Hermannsson (1924) as an appendix to the Natural History. See also Steindór Steindórsson (1981: 29), and cf. above, Ch. 7 on healing.

18. The treatise has been published by Bjarni Einarsson (1955). The authorship has been questioned by Einar G. Pétursson (1971), who suggests that Jón Eggertsson is the actual author. They were contemporaries, and doubtless Jón Eggertsson knew about Jón *lærði*'s work (Bjarni Einarsson 1955: lxi).

19. Jón Eggertsson (*c*.1650), *Adtskilligt om Islands Beschafenhed og Wilkor*, written in the mid-seventeenth century, is unpublished. It is found in MS Thott no. 1738 (in Copenhagen) and in a copy made by Páll Eggert Ólason Lbs. 1437 (4to) (in Reykjavík). Folio references are to the Thott MS.

20. For a discussion of Eggert Ólafsson's achievements as a natural scientist see Steindór Steindórsson (1981: 41–81).

21. Jakob Benediktsson (1957). *Brevis* was spurred mainly by the appearance of the work in Low German by Gories Peerse 'whose account abounds with misunderstandings and exaggerations and testifies to a sublime contempt for the peculiar island people' (Jakob Benediktsson 1943: p. ix).

Chapter 9

1. My use of this term was inspired by a paper by Alessandro Portelli on 'Uchronic Dreams: Workers' Memory and "Wrong" Versions of History', presented to the Sixth International Oral History Conference, Oxford, 11–13 Sept. 1987. I have reconstructed the concept and its implications from my lecture notes.

2. The point could be made that for the Icelanders culture *was* history, and vice versa. Precisely because they had not accepted the 'modern' view of progressive history, there was no split between the spatial and the temporal dimensions of their world. This was part of the medieval heritage (Gurevich 1985). Significantly, Nordal (1942: 40) asserts that his book *Íslenzk menning* ('Icelandic culture'), might as well have been called *Veraldarsaga Íslendinga* ('The Icelanders' World-History')!

3. The deconstruction in many ways looks like an achieved helplessness and a symptom of what could be called a collective depression. This cultural

psychological analogy has been developed in Hastrup (1988*a*), where I treat it as a case of self-destruction. This is not to say that it was either willed or conscious, only that it was a reactive process. In the present context I shall leave the notion of deconstruction as it stands.

4. The notion of myth as used here does not imply that what is said is not true. It is rather a designation of a particular genre of historical representation (Hastrup 1987*e*). It serves the purpose, also, to identify the time-referent of the traditional Icelandic 'history-story' which was essentially non-linear and 'timeless' (ibid.). Further, myth 'is not concerned so much with a succession of events as with the moral significance of situations' (Evans-Pritchard 1961; 1964: 179). This is very much the case of the sagas.

Chapter 10

1. The Annales school, and the concern about mentality in general, is a symptom of a change in this respect.
2. It will be understood that my reference to David Bohm is heuristic, and should not be taken as an indication of my reclassifying anthropology as a 'natural science' in the old sense. Bohm's *Wholeness and the Implicate Order* has been translated into Danish, and references are given to the Danish version (Bohm 1986).
3. In Ch. 1 I defined history as the empirical series of events. That is of course how we may *read* history at all. But in the world of historians, the empirical is a much more definitive quality of their object. Says Rabb of history: 'it can be distinguished from the commitments of other social sciences in its insistence on empirical evidence from appropriate times and places' (Rabb 1982: 331). Anthropology too is concerned with the empirical—but its 'evidence' may also be implicational.
4. I have dealt with this in Hastrup (1985*a*: 1–7). For a more elaborate discussion see Gaunt (1982).
5. The 'virtual particles' described by modern physics could not be accommodated in the Cartesian co-ordinates, because they are only 'nearly-real' (Ravn 1987: 9).
6. The notion of historical density is from Ardener (1987*b*), cf. Ch. 9.
7. See Bernstein 1983 for a philosophical treatment of this opposition.

Conclusion

1. For further discussion of anthropological writing, see, for instance, Clifford and Marcus (1986), and Hastrup (1989*d*).
2. See ref. n. 1 above. Further discussion is found in Fabian (1983); Marcus and Fisher (1986); and in Strathern (1987).
3. The notion of 'thick description' is from Geertz (1983: 3–30). It is essentially a metaphor for pursuing ethnography.

4. Montaigne developed his ideas in the *Essais*, which have been studied by the Romance scholar Andreas Blinkenberg (1970; on *sagesse* see p. 267 in particular). Andreas Blinkenberg was my grandfather, and until his death in 1982 at the age of 89 our long conversations contributed much to my perception of humanistic scholarship. I take this opportunity to acknowledge my hidden debt to a much-loved grandfather.

REFERENCES

AÐALBJARNARSON, BJARNI (ed.) (1941–5) *Heimskringla*, i–iii. Íslenzk fornrit, 27–8. Reykjavík: Hið íslenzka fornritafélag.

AÐALSTEINSSON, JÓN HNEFILL (1978a) *Hugmyndasaga*. *Frá sögnum til siðaskipta*. Reykjavík: Iðunn.

—— (1978b) *Under the Cloak. The Acceptance of Christianity in Iceland with Particular Reference to the Religious Attitudes Prevailing at the Time*. Studia Ethnologia Upsaliensia, 4. Uppsala: Acta Universitatis Upsaliensis.

ADAM OF BREMEN (1968) *De hamburgske ærkebispers historie og Nordens beskrivelse*. Transl. C. L. Henrichsen, 2nd edn. Copenhagen: Rosenkilde og Bagger.

AÐILS, JÓN J. (1971) *Einokunarverzlun Dana á Íslandi 1602–1787*. 1st edn. 1919. 2nd edn. Reykjavík: Heimskringla.

ÁGUSTSSON, HÖRÐUR (1968) 'Islandsk byggeskik i fortiden'. *Islandsk Byggedag*. 10.

AHLMAN, H. W. (1937). 'Vatnajökull. Scientific Results of the Swedish–Icelandic Investigations 1936–37'. *Geografiska Annaler 1937*, 19.

ALMQVIST, BO (1965) *Norrön niddiktning. Traditionshistoriska studier i versmagi*, i. Uppsala: Nordiska texter och undersökningar, 21.

—— (1974) *Norrön niddiktning. Traditionshistoriska studier i versmagi*, ii. Uppsala: Nordiska texter och undersökninger, 23.

—— (1978) 'Norske utburdsägner i västerled'. In *Tradisjon og samfund*. Oslo: Universitetsforlaget. Kolsrud, *et al.* (eds.).

Alþingisbækur Íslands. (1912–82), i–xv. *Acta comitiorum generalium islandiæ*. Reykjavík: Sögufélagið.

ALVER, BRYNJULF (1970) *Dag og Merke. Folkelig tidsrekning og merkedagstradition*. Oslo: Universitetsforlaget.

ALVER, BENTE GULLVEIG (1971) *Heksetro og Trolddom. Et studie i norsk heksevæsen*. Oslo: Universitetsforlaget.

ANDERSEN, RAOUL (ed.) (1979) *North Atlantic Maritime Cultures: Anthropological Essays on Changing Adaptations*. Paris: Mouton.

ANDERSON, JOHANN (1746) *Nachtrichten von Island*. Hamburg: G. C. Grund.

ANDERSON, PERRY (1974a) *Passages from Antiquity to Feudalism*. London: New Left Books.

—— (1974b) *Lineages of the Absolutist State*. London: New Left Books.

ANDRÉSSON, GUÐMUNDUR (1948) *Deilurit* (1564), ed. Jacob Benediktsson. Íslenzk rit siðari alda, 2. Copenhagen: Hið íslenzka fræðafélag.

References   323

ANDRÉSSON, SIGFÚS H. (1957) 'Þorleifur lögmaður Kortsson'. *Skírnir*, 131, pp. 152–71.

ANKARLOO, B. and HENNINGSEN, G. (eds.) (1989) *Early Modern European Witchcraft. Centres and Peripheries*. Oxford: OUP.

ANON. (1945). 'Systkinin frá Viðavallagerði'. *Gríma*, 20.

APPLEBY, ANDREW B. (1981) 'Epidemics and Famine in the Little Ice Age'. In *Climate and History*, ed. R. I. Rotberg and T. K. Rabb. Princeton, NJ: Princeton Univ. Press.

ARDENER, EDWIN (1970) 'Witchcraft, Economics, and the Continuity of Belief'. In *Witchcraft Confessions and Accusations*, ed. M. Douglas. ASA Monographs, 9. London: Tavistock.

—— (1971a) 'Introductory Essay: Social Anthropology and Language'. In *Social Anthropology and Language*, ed. E. Ardener. ASA Monographs, 10. London: Tavistock.

—— (1971b) 'Social Anthropology and the Historicity of Historical Linguistics'. In *Social Anthropology and Language*, ed. E. Ardener. ASA Monographs, 10. London: Tavistock.

—— (1972) 'Belief and the Problem of Women'. In *The Interpretation of Ritual*, ed. J. Lafontaine. London: Tavistock.

—— (1974) 'Social Anthropology and Population'. In *Population and its Problems: A Plain Man's Guide*, ed. H. B. Parry. Oxford: Clarendon Press.

—— (1975a) 'Language, Ethnicity and Population'. In *Studies in Social Anthropology: Essays in Memory of E. E. Evans-Pritchard*, eds. J. Beattie and R. G. Lienhardt. Oxford: Clarendon Press.

—— (1975b) 'The Voice of Prophecy. Some Further Problems in the Analysis of Events'. The Munro Lecture. Edinburgh: Institute of Social Anthropology. (Repr. Ardener 1989b.)

—— (1978) 'Some Outstanding Problems in the Analysis of Events'. In *Yearbook of Symbolic Anthropology*, ed. E. Schwimmer, i. London: Hurst.

—— (1982) 'Social Anthropology, Language, and Reality'. In *Semantic Anthropology*, ed. D. Parkin. ASA Monographs, 22. London: Academic Press.

—— (1985) 'Social Anthropology and the Decline of Modernism'. In *Reason and Morality*, ed. J. Overing. ASA Monographs, 24. London: Tavistock.

—— (1987) 'Remote Areas: Some Theoretical Considerations'. In *Anthropology at Home*, ed. A. Jackson. ASA Monographs, 25. London: Tavistock.

—— (1989b) *The Voice of Prophecy and other Essays*, ed. Malcolm Chapman. Oxford: Blackwell.

—— (1989a) 'The Construction of History: "Evidence of Creation"'. In *History and Ethnicity*, ed. E. Tonkin, M. McDonald, and M. Chapman. ASA Monographs, 29. London: Routledge.

ARIÈS, PHILIPPE (1973) *L'Enfant et la vie familiale sous l'ancien régime*. Paris: Seuil.

Árna saga byskups (1948). In *Byskupa sögur*, Guðni Jónsson, i. Reykjavík: Íslendingasagnaútgáfan.

ÁRNASON, JÓN (1954–61) *Íslenzkar þjóðsögur og ævintýri*, i–vi. 2nd edn.,

324 References

ed. Árni Böðvarsson and Bjarni Vilhjálmsson. Reykjavík: Bókaútgáfan Þjóðsaga.

ARNÓRSSON, EINAR (1949) *Alþingi og frelsisbaráttan 1845–1874*. Reykjavík: Alþingissögunefnd gaf út.

ASAD, TALAL (1987) 'Are there Histories of Peoples without Europe? A Review Article'. *Comparative Studies in Society and History*, 29, pp. 594–607.

ATKINSON, RONALD F. (1978) *Knowledge and Explanation in History: An Introduction to the Philosophy of History*. London: Macmillan.

BADINTER, ELISABETH (1980) *L'Amour en plus*. Paris: Flammarion.

BAILEY, ANNE M. (1985) 'The Making of History. Dialectics of Temporality and Structure in Modern French Social Theory'. *Critique of Anthropology*, 5.

BARBUT, C. (1970) 'On the Word Structure in Mathematics'. In *Structuralism. A Reader*, ed. M. Lane. New York: Basic Books.

BARTHES, R. (1982) 'Authors and Writers'. In *A Barthes Reader*, ed. S. Sontag. London: Jonathan Cape.

BATESON, GREGORY (1972) *Steps to an Ecology of Mind*. New York: Ballantine.

BELLOWS, HENRY A. (1969) *The Poetic Edda*. New York: Biblo and Tannen.

BENEDIKTSSON, HREINN (1964) 'Íslenzkt mál að fornu og nýju'. In *Íslenzkt mál*, ed. Halldór Halldórsson. Reykjavík: Almenna bókafélagið.

—— (ed.) (1972) *The First Grammatical Treatise*. Publications in Linguistics, 1. Reykjavík: Univ. of Iceland.

BENEDIKTSSON, JAKOB (ed.) (1939) *Gísli Magnússon (Vísi-Gísli). Ævisaga, ritgerðir, bréf*. Safn fræðafélagsins, 11. Copenhagen and Reykjavík: Hið íslenzka fræðafélag.

—— (ed.) (1943) *Two Treatises on Iceland from the Seventeenth Century*. Bibliotheca Arnamagnæana, 3. Copenhagen: Munksgård.

—— (ed.) (1948) *Guðmundur Andrésson: Deilurit*. Íslenzk rit síðari alda, 2. Copenhagen: Hið íslenzka fræðafélag.

—— (1957) *Arngrímur Jónsson and his Works*. Copenhagen: Munksgård.

—— (ed.) (1968) *Íslendingabók, Landnámabók*. Íslenzk fornrit, 1. Reykjavík: Hið íslenzka fornritafélag.

—— (1974) 'Markmið Landnámabókar'. *Skírnir*, 148. (Repr. Benediktsson 1987.)

—— (1981) 'Den vågnende interesse for sagalitteraturen på Island i 1600-tallet'. *Maal og Minne*, 3–4.

—— (ed.) (1985) Arngrímur Jónsson, *Crymogæa. Þættir úr sögu Íslands (1609)*. Reykjavík: Sögufélagið.

—— (1987) *Lærdómslistir. Afmælisrit 20. júlí 1987*. Reykjavík: Mál og menning/ Stofnun Árna Magnússonar.

BERLIN, KNUD (1909) *Islands Statsretlige Stilling efter Fristatstidens Ophør*. Copenhagen: Brødrene Salomonsens boghandel.

BERNSTEIN, R. J. (1983) *Beyond Objectivism and Relativism*. Oxford: Blackwell.

BEUYS, BARBARA (1984) *Familienleben in Deutschland. Neue Bilder aus der deutschen Vergangenheit*. Hamburg: Rowohlt.

Biskupa sögur. (1858–8), i–ii. Copenhagen: Hið Íslenzka bókmenntafélag.

BJARNADÓTTIR, KRISTÍN (1986) 'Drepsóttir á 15. öld'. *Sagnir*, 7, pp. 57–64.

BJØRN, CLAUS (1981) *Bonde, Heremand, Konge. Bonden i 1700-tallets Danmark*. Copenhagen: Gyldendal.

BJÖRNSSON, ÁRNI (1981) 'Barnsöl og sængurbiti'. In *Afmæliskveðja til Halldórs Halldórssonar 13 juli 1981*, ed. Guðrún Kvaran, Gunnlaugur Ingólfsson, and Svavar Sigmundsson. Reykjavík: Íslenska málfræðifélagið.

BJÖRNSSON, BJÖRN (1971) *The Lutheran Doctrine of Marriage in Modern Icelandic Society*. Oslo: Universitetsforlaget.

BJÖRNSSON, LÝÐUR (1972–9) *Saga sveitarstjórnar á Íslandi*, i–ii. Reykjavík: Almenna Bókafelagið.

—— (1973) *Íslandssaga 1550–1830. Frá siðaskiptum til sjálfstæðisbaráttu*. Reykjavík: Bókaverzlun Sigfúsar Eymundssonar.

BLEFKEN, DITHMAR (1946) *Islandia*. (Trans. into Icelandic.) In Sigurður Grímsson (ed.), *Glöggt er gests augað. Úrval ferðasagna um Ísland*. Reykjavík: Menningar og fræðslusamband alþýðu.

BLINKENBERG, ANDREAS (1970) *Montaigne*. Copenhagen: Gyldendal.

BLOCH, MARC (1954) *The Historian's Craft*. Manchester: Manchester Univ. Press.

—— (1965) *Feudal Society*, i–ii. London: Routledge & Kegan Paul.

BLÖNDAL, LÁRUS H. and JÓNSSON, VILMUNDUR (1970) *Læknar á Íslandi*, i. 2nd edn. Reykjavík: Ísafold.

BLÖNDAL, SIGFÚS (1920–4) *Íslensk-Dönsk Orðabók*. Reykjavík: Gutenberg.

BOBERG, INGER M. (1966) *Motif-Index of Early Icelandic Literature*. Bibliotheca Arnamagnæana, 27. Copenhagen: Munksgård.

BOHM, DAVID (1986) *Helhed og den indfoldede orden*. Trans. Jeppe Christensen. Århus: Ask.

BOON, JAMES A. (1982) *Other Tribes Other Scribes. Symbolic Anthropology in the Comparative Study of Cultures, Histories, Religions and Texts*. Cambridge: Cambridge Univ. Press.

BOSERUP, ESTHER (1965) *The Conditions of Agricultural Growth*. London: Allen & Unwin.

—— (1982) *Population and Technology*. Oxford: Blackwell.

BRADE, ANNE-ELISABETH (1976) 'Efterskrift'. *Henrik Smiths lægebog*. Copenhagen: Rosenkilde og Bagger.

BRAUDEL, FERNAND (1976) *The Mediterranean and the Mediterranean World in the Age of Philip II*. London: Fontana/Collins.

—— (1980) *On History*. Chicago, Ill.: Univ. of Chicago Press.

—— (1981) *The Structures of Everyday Life. Civilization and Capitalism 15th–18th Century*, i. Trans. Siân Reynolds. London: Collins.

—— (1982) *The Wheels of Commerce. Civilization and Capitalism 15th–18th Century*, ii. Trans. Siân Reynolds. London: Collins.

—— (1984) *The Perspective of the World. Civilization and Capitalism 15th–18th Century*, iii. Trans. Siân Reynolds. London: Collins.

326   *References*

BREDSDORFF, THOMAS (1971) *Kaos og Kærlighed. En studie i islændingesagaens livsbillede*. Copenhagen: Gyldendals uglebøger.

BRIEM, ÓLAFUR (1959) *Útilegumenn og auðar tóftir*. Reykjavík: Bókútgáfa Menningarsjóðs.

BRUHN, OLE (1985) 'Tradition og litteraritet i tidlig islandsk middelalder, set it europæisk belysning.' Thesis: Aarhus Univ.

BRUUN, DANIEL (1928) 'Fortidsminder og nutidshjem på Island'. Copenhagen: Gyldendal.

BRYNLEIFSSON, SIGLAUGUR (1970) *Svarti-Dauði*. Reykjavík: Mál og menning.

—— (1976) *Galdrar og brennudómar*. Reykjavík: Mál og menning.

Búalög (1915–33) *Búalög um verðlag og allskonar venjur i viðskiptum og búskap á Íslandi*, i–iii. Reykjavík: Sögufélagið.

BUCHHOLZ, PETER (1971) 'Shamanism—the Testimony of Old Icelandic Literary Tradition'. *Mediaeval Scandinavia*, 4.

BUGGE, SOPHUS (ed.) (1867) *Sæmundar Edda hins fróða*. Christiania: O. T Mallings Forlagsboghandel (Norrøn Fornkvæði).

BURGUIÈRE, ANDRÉ (1982) 'The Fate of the History of *Mentalités* in the *Annales*'. *Comparative Studies in Society and History*, 24, pp. 424–37.

BURKE, PETER (1978) *Popular Culture in Early Modern Europe*. London: Temple Smith.

—— (1980) 'Fernand Braudel'. *The Historian at Work*, ed. John Cannon. London: George Allen & Unwin.

—— (1986) 'Strengths and Weaknesses of the History of Mentalities'. *History of European Ideas*, 7/5, pp. 439–51.

BÆKSTED, ANDERS (1942) *Islands Runeindskrifter*. Bibliotheca Arnamagnæana, 2. Copenhagen: Munksgård.

BØ, OLAV (1973) *Folkemedisin og lærd medisin. Norsk medisinsk hverdag på 1800-talet*. Oslo: Det Norske Samlaget.

CARPENTIER, ELISABETH (1962) 'Autour de la peste noire: Famines et épidémie dans l'histoire du XIVᵉ siècle'. *Annales*, 17/6.

CHAPMAN, MALCOLM (1978) *The Gaelic Vision in Scottish Culture*. London: Croom-Helm.

CLANCHY, M. T. (1979) *From Memory to Written Record 1066–1307*. London: E. Arnold.

——(1981) 'Literate and Illiterate; Hearing and Seeing: England 1066–1307'. In *Literary and Social Development in the West: A Reader*, ed. H. D. Graff. Cambridge: Cambridge Univ. Press.

CLARK, Sir GEORGE (1966) *Early Modern Europe from about 1420–1720*. 2nd edn. Oxford: OUP.

CLIFFORD, JAMES (1986a) 'Introduction: Partial Truths'. In *Writing Culture: The Poetics and Politics of Ethnography*, ed. J. Clifford and G. E. Marcus. Berkeley, Calif., Los Angeles, Calif., and London: Univ. of California Press.

—— (1986b) 'On Ethnographic Self-Fashioning: Conrad and Malinowski'. In *Reconstructing Individualism: Autonomy, Individuality, and Self in Western*

Thought, ed. T. Heller, M. Sosna, and D. Wellberg. Stanford, Calif.: Stanford Univ. Press.

—— and MARCUS, G. E. (eds.) (1986) *Writing Culture. The Poetics and Politics of Ethnography*. Berkeley, Calif., Los Angeles, Calif., and London: Univ. of California Press.

COHEN, ANTHONY (ed.) (1982) *Belonging. Identity and Social Organization in British Rural Culture*. Manchester: Manchester Univ. Press.

COHN, NORMAN (1970) 'The Myth of Satan and his Human Servants'. In *Witchcraft Confessions and Accusations*, ed. M. Douglas. ASA Monographs, 9. London: Tavistock.

—— (1975) *Europe's Inner Demons*. New York: Basic Books.

CRAIGIE, WILLIAM (1937) *The Art of Poetry in Iceland*. Oxford: Clarendon Press.

CRICK, MALCOLM (1976) *Explorations in Language and Meaning. Towards a Semantic Anthropology*. London: Malaby Press.

—— (1982) 'Anthropology of Knowledge'. *Annual Review of Anthropology*, 11.

CURTIUS, ERNST ROBERT (1953) *European Literature and the Latin Middle Ages*. (Trans. from the German by W. R. Trask). London: Routledge & Kegan Paul.

CUSHING, D. H. (1975) *Marine Ecology and Fisheries*. Cambridge: Cambridge University Press.

DANSGAARD, W., JOHNSEN, S. J., MOLLER, J., and LANGWAY, C. (1969) 'One Thousand Centuries of Climatic Record from Camp Century on the Greenland Ice Sheet'. *Science*, 17.

DAVÍÐSSON, ÓLAFUR (1900) 'Folklore of Icelandic Fishes'. *The Scottish Review*, 36/72.

—— (1940–3) *Galdur og galdramál á Íslandi*. Reykjavík: Sögufélagið (Sögurit xx).

—— (1949) 'Íslenzkar kynjaverur í sjó og vötnum'. *Þjóðlífsmyndir*, ed. G. Guðmundsson. Reykjavík: Iðunn.

DAVIS, RALPH (1973) *The Rise of the Atlantic Economies*. London: Weidenfeld and Nicolson.

DOUGLAS, MARY (1966) *Purity and Danger. An Analysis of Concepts of Pollution and Taboo*. London: Routledge & Kegan Paul.

—— (1975a) 'Self-evidence'. In *Implicit Meanings: Essays in Anthropology by Mary Douglas*. London: Routledge & Kegan Paul.

—— (1975b) *Implicit Meanings: Essays in Anthropology by Mary Douglas*. London: Routledge & Kegan Paul.

DRONKE, PETER (1968) *Medieval Latin and the Rise of European Love-Lyric*. 2 vols. 2nd edn. Oxford: Clarendon Press.

DUMONT, LOUIS (1957) 'For a Sociology of India'. *Contributions to Indian Sociology*, 1.

DURKHEIM, ÉMILE (1933) *The Division of Labour*. Trans. G. Simpson. New York: Macmillan.

—— *The Elementary Forms of Religious Life*. Trans. J. W. Swain. London: George Allen & Unwin.

DURRENBERGER, P. and PÁLSSON, GÍSLI (eds.) (1989) *The Anthropology of Iceland*. Iowa: Iowa Univ. Press.

DYRVIK, STÅLE, *et al.* (1979) *Norsk Økonomisk Historie 1500–1970*. i. *1500–1850*. Bergen, Oslo, and Tromsö: Universitetsforlaget.

EGGERS, C. U. D. (1786) *Philosophische Schilderung der Gegenwärtigen Verfassung von Island*. Altona: J. D. U. Eckhardt.

EGGERTSSON, JÓN (*c.*1650) 'Adtskilligt om Islands Beschafenhed og Wilkor'. The Thott Collection no. 1738. Unpub. 4to manuscript. Royal Library of Copenhagen. Copy in Landsbókasafn Íslands, no. 1437.

EGILSSON, ÓLAF (1969) *Reisubók séra Ólafs Egilssonar (1628)*, ed. Sverrir Kristjánsson. Reykjavík: Almenna bókafélagið.

EINARSSON, BJARNI (1966) *Munnmælasögur 17. aldar*. Íslenzk rit síðari alda, 6. Reykjavík: Hið íslenzka fræðafélag.

—— (1967) 'Vættatrú og nokkur íslenzk örnefni'. Reykjavík: Árbók hins íslenzka fornleifafélags.

EINARSSON, ODDUR (1971) *Íslandslýsing. Qualiscunque descriptio Islandiae* (1589). Trans. Sveinn Pálsson and with Introductions by Jakob Benediktsson and Sigurður Þórarinsson. Reykjavík: Bókutgáfa Menningarsjóðs.

EINARSSON, ÓLAFUR (1957–8) 'Ættlera-aldarháttur'. *Íslenzkt ljóðasafn*, i.

EINARSSON, STEFÁN (1957) *A History of Icelandic Literature*. Baltimore, Md.: Johns Hopkins Press.

Eiriks saga rauða. (1891), ed. Gustav Storm. Copenhagen: Samfund til udgivelse af gammel nordisk litteratur.

EIRÍKSSON, HALLFREÐUR ÖRN (1972) 'Lifsatriði og draumar'. *Súlur. Norðlenzkt Timarit*.

—— (1980*a*) 'Þjóðsagnasöfnun og Þjóðfrelsishreyfing'. *Gripla*, 4.

—— (1980*b*) 'Folkminnenas roll i den litteräre renässansen på Island under 1800–talet'. *Tradisjon*, 10.

ELIAS, NORBERT (1978) *The History of Manners: The Civilizing Process*, i. Trans. Edmund Jephcott. Oxford: Blackwell.

—— (1982) *State Formation and Civilization: The Civilizing Process*, ii. Trans. Edmund Jephcott. Oxford: Blackwell.

Encyclopedia of the Social Sciences. (1963), ed. L. David. London and New York: Macmillan and Free Press.

EVANS-PRITCHARD, E. E. (1950) 'Social Anthropology: Past and Present'. *Man*, 198. (Repr. in Evans.Pritchard 1964).

—— (1961) 'Anthropology and History'. Manchester: Manchester Univ. Press. (Repr. in Evans-Pritchard 1964).

—— (1964) *Social Anthropology and Other Essays*. New York: Free Press.

EYÞÓRSSON, JÓN (1935) 'On the Variations of Glaciers in Iceland'. *Geografiska Annaler*.

—— (1949) 'Temperature Variations in Iceland'. *Geografiska Annaler*.

FABIAN, JOHANNES (1983) *Time and the Other. How Anthropology Makes its Object*. New York: Columbia Univ. Press.

References 329

FABRICIUS, DAVID (1890) *Van Isslandt unde Grönlandt eine korrt beschryuinge uth warhafften Scribenten mit ulyte colligeret unde in eine richtige ordnung vorfathet*. Gedrucht im Jahr 1616. Bremen: Karl Taunen.

FALK, HJALMAR (1926) 'Sjælen' i hedentroen'. *Maal og Minne, 1926*.

FEBVRE, LUCIEN and MARTIN, H.-J. (1984) *The Coming of the Book: The Impact of Printing 1450–1800*. London: Verso.

FERNANDEZ, JAMES W. (1986) *Persuasions and Performances. The Play of Tropes in Culture*. Bloomington: Indiana Univ. Press.

FINNSSON, HANNES (1785) *Um Barna-Dauða á Íslandi*. Copenhagen: Rit lærdomslistafélagsins, 5.

—— (1970) *Mannfækkun af hallærum* (1796), ed. Jón Eyþórsson and Jóhannes Nordal. Rit lærdomslistafélagsins. Reykjavík: Almenna bókfélagið.

First Grammatical Treatise. (1972), ed. Hreinn Benediktsson. Publications in Linguistics, 1. Reykjavík: Institute of Nordic Linguistics, Univ. of Iceland.

Fjölmóður. In *Ævidrápa Jóns lærða Guðmundssonar*, ed. and with Introduction by Páll E. Ólason. *Safn til sögu Íslands og islenzkra bókmennta að fornu og nýju*, v.

FLANDRIN, JEAN-LOUIS (1985) 'Sex in Married Life in the Early Middle Ages: The Church's Teaching and Behavioural Reality'. In *Western Sexuality. Practice and Precept in Past and Present Times*, ed. P. Ariès and A. Bégin. Oxford: Blackwell.

FLINN, MICHAEL W. (1981) *The European Demographic System 1500–1820*. Brighton: Harvester Press.

FOOTE, PETER and WILSON, DAVID (1970) *The Viking Achievement: The Society and Culture of Early Medieval Scandinavia*. London: Sidgwick & Jackson.

FOUCAULT, M. (1961) *Histoire de la Folie*. Paris: Plon.

—— (1985) 'The Battle for Chastity'. In *Western Sexuality. Practice and Precept in Past and Present Times*, ed. P. Ariès and A. Bégin. Oxford: Blackwell.

FOX, ROBIN (1985) 'The Condition of Sexual Evolution'. In *Western Sexuality. Practice and Precept in Past and Present Times*, ed. P. Ariès and A. Bégin. Oxford: Blackwell.

FRANK, ANDRE GUNDER (1978) *World Accumulation 1492–1789*. London: Macmillan.

FRAZER, JAMES G. (1922) *The Golden Bough. A Study in Magic and Religion*. London: Macmillan.

FRIEDMAN, JONATHAN (1982) 'Catastrophe and Continuity in Social Evolution'. In *Theory and Explanation in Archaeology*, ed. C. Renfrew *et al.* London: Academic Press.

FRIIS, PEDER CLAUSSØN (1881) *Samlede skrifter*, ed. G. Storm. Kristiania: Den Norske Historiske Forening.

FRITZNER, JOHAN (1883–96) *Ordbog over det gamle norske Sprog*, i–iii. Kristiania: Den norske Forlagsforening.

GAUNT, DAVID (1982) *Memoir on History and Anthropology*. Stockholm: Council for Research in the Humanities and Social Sciences.

GEERTZ, CLIFFORD (1983) *The Interpretation of Cultures*. New York: Basic Books.

GELSINGER, BRUCE E. (1981) *Icelandic Enterprise. Commerce and Economy in the Middle Ages*. Columbia, SC: Univ. of South Carolina Press.

GÍSLASON, MAGNÚS (1977) *Kvällsvaka. En isländsk kulturtradition belyst genom studier i bondebefolkningens vardagsliv och miljö under senare hälften av 1800–tallet och början av 1900–tallet*. Uppsala: Acta Universitas Upsaliensis.

GLAUSER, JÜRG (1983) *Isländische Märchensagas. Studien zum Prosaliteratur in Spätmittelalterliche Island*. Beiträge zum nordischen Philologie, 12. Basel: Helbing & Lichtenbahn.

GODELIER, MAURICE (1975) 'Modes of Production, Kinship, and Demographic Structures'. In *Marxist Analysis and Social Anthropology*, ed. M. Bloch. ASA Studies, 2. London: Malaby Press.

—— (1987) 'Introduction: The Analysis of Transition Processes'. *International Social Science Journal*, 114.

GOODY, JACK (1983) *The Development of the Family and Marriage in Europe*. Cambridge: Cambridge Univ. Press.

GRAMBO, RONALD (1979) *Norske Trollformler og magiske Ritualer*. Oslo: Universitetsforlaget.

GRÍMSSON, SIGURÐUR (ed.) (1946) *Glöggt er gests augað. Úrval ferðasagna um Ísland*. Reykjavík: Menningar og fræðslusamband alþýðu.

Guðmundar saga. (1858) *Biskupa sögur*, iii. Copenhagen: Hið íslenzka bókmenntafélag.

GUÐMUNDSSON, GUNNAR F. (1981) *Eignarhald á afréttum og almenningi. Sögulegt yfirlit*. Reykjavík: Sagnfræðistofnun.

GUÐMUNDSSON, JÓN (1895). 'Snæfjallavísur'. *Huld*, 5.

—— (1916) Fjölmóður. Ævidrápa Jóns lærða Guðmundssonar, ed. Páll E. Ólason. *SSÍ* 5, pp. 1–85.

—— (1950) *Spánverjavígin 1615*, ed. Jónas Kristjánsson.

—— (1924) *Ein stutt undirrietting um islands adskilianlegar náttúrur. c.*1640, ed. Halldór Hermannsson. Islandica, 15.

GUÐMUNDSSON, VALTÝR (1889) *Privatboligen på Island i sagatiden samt delvis i det øvrige Norden*. Copenhagen: Høst og Søn.

GUNNARSSON, GÍSLI (1980*a*) *Fertility and Nuptiality in Iceland's Demographic History*. Lund: Meddelande från Ekonomisk-Historiska Institutionen, Lunds Universitet, 12.

—— (1980*b*) *A Study of Causal Relations in Climate and History. With an Emphasis on the Icelandic Experience*. Lund: Meddelande från Ekonomisk-Historiska Institutionen, Lunds Universitet, 17.

—— (1980*c*) 'Landskuld í mjöli og verð þess frá 15. til 18. aldar'. *Saga*, 18, pp. 31–48.

—— (1983) *Monopoly Trade and Economic Stagnation. Studies in the Foreign Trade of Iceland 1602–1787*. Lund: Studentlitteratur. Skrifter udgivet af Ekonomisk-historiska föreningen i Lund, 38.

GUREVICH, A. YA. (1977) 'Representations of Property during the High Middle Ages'. *Economy and Society*, 6/1.

References 331

GUREVICH, A. J. (1985) *Categories of Medieval Culture*. Trans. G. L. Campbell. London: Routledge & Kegan Paul.

GUSTAFSSON, HARALD (1985) *Mellan Kung och Allmoge—Ämbetsmän och Inflytande på 1700-talets Island*. Stockholm: Alqvist och Wiksell.

GUTTORMSSON, LOFTUR (1981) 'Island. Læsefærdighed og folkeuddannelse 1540–1800'. *Läskunninghet och Folkbildning före Folkskoleväsendet*. Mötesrapport: Historikermøtet Jyvaskylä.

—— (1983a) *Bernska, ungdómur og uppeldí á Einveldisöld*. Reykjavík: Ritsafn sagnfræðistofnunar, 10.

—— (1983b) 'Barnaeldi, ungbarnaðauði og viðkoma á Íslandi 1750–1860'. *Athöfn og Orð. Afmælisrit helgað Matthíasi Jónassyni*. Reykjavík: Mál og menning.

—— (1987a) *Uppeldi á upplýsingaröld. Um hugmyndir lærdómsmanna og hátterni alþýðu*. Ritröð kennaraháskóla Íslands og Iðunnar. Reykjavík: Iðunn.

—— (1987b) 'Bókmenning á upplýsingaröld. Upplýsing i stríð við alþýðumenningu.' In *Gefið og þegið. Afmælisrit til heiðurs Brodda Jóhannessyni sjötuguru*, ed. Þuríður Kristjánsdóttir. Reykjavík: Iðunn.

HAJNAL, JOHN (1965) 'European Marriage Patterns in Perspective'. In *Population in History. Essays in Historical Demography*, ed. D. V. Glass and D. E. C. Eversly. London: Edward Arnold.

—— (1982) 'Two Kinds of Preindustrial Household Formation System'. *Population and Development Review*, 8.

Hákonar saga Hákonarsonar. (1868) *Flateyjarbók*, ed. Guðbrandur Vigfússon and C. R. Unger. Norsk historisk kildeskriftfonds skrifter, 4. Oslo: P. T. Malling.

HALLBERG, PETER (1973) 'The Concept of *Gipta-gæfa-hamingja* in Old Norse Literature'. Proceedings of the First International Saga Conference, Univ. of Edinburgh, 1971. London: Viking Society for Northern Research.

—— (1974) *De islandske sagaer*. Copenhagen: Gyldendal.

HALLDÓRSSON, ÓLAFUR (1904) 'Indledning' (Introduction). In *Jónsbók, Korg Magnus Hakonssons Lovbog for Island. Vedtaget på Altinget 1281*, ed. Ólafur Halldórson. Copenhagen: S. L. Möllers bogtrykkeri.

—— (ed.) (1958–61) *Óláfs saga Tryggvassonar en mesta*, i–ii. Editiones Arnamagnæana, Ser. A. Copenhagen: Munksgård.

HANSON, F. ALLAN (1975) *Meaning in Culture*. London: Routledge & Kegan Paul.

—— (1983) 'Syntagmatic Structures: How the Maori's Make Sense of History'. *Semiotica*. 46.

HARALDSSON, ERLENDUR (1978) *Þessa heims og annars. Könnun á dulrænni reynslu Íslendinga, trúarviðhorfum og þjóðtrú*. Reykjavík: Saga.

HARRÉ, ROM (1978) 'Architectonic Man: On the Structuring of Lived Experience'. In *Structure, Consciousness and History*, ed. R. M. Brown and S. M. Lyman. Cambridge: Cambridge Univ. Press.

HARRISON, G. A. and BOYCE, A. J. (1972) 'Introduction: The Framework of

Population Studies'. In *The Structure of Human Populations*, ed. G. A. Harrison and A. J. Boyce. Oxford: Clarendon Press.

HASTRUP, K. (1979) 'Classification and Demography in Medieval Iceland'. *Ethnos*, 3–4.

—— (1981*a*) 'Cosmology and Society in Medieval Iceland'. *Ethnologica Scandinavica*, 1981.

—— (1981*b*) 'Kinship in Medieval Iceland'. *Folk*, 23.

—— (1981*c*) 'Creating a Nation: Nationalist Trends in Eighteenth and Nineteenth Century Iceland'. Proceedings from the IUEAS intercongress, Amsterdam. (Repr. in id. *Island of Anthropology*, Odense, 1989: Odense Univ. Press).

—— (1982) 'Establishing an Ethnicity. The Emergence of the "Icelanders" in the Early Middle Ages'. In *Semantic Anthropology*, ed. D. Parkin. ASA Monographs, 22. London: Academic Press.

—— (1983) 'Kulturelle kategorier som naturlige ressourcer: Exempler fra Islands historie'. In *Samhälle och Ekosystem—om tolkningsproblem i antropologi och arkeologi*, ed. A. Hjort. Stockholm: Forskningrådsnämden.

—— (1984*a*) 'Defining a Society. The Icelandic Freestate between Two Worlds'. *Scandinavian Studies*, 56/3.

—— (1984*b*) 'Finding Oneself in History'. Proceedings from the Conference on 'Nationalism and Identity'. University of Copenhagen. (Repr. in id. *Island of Anthropology*, Odense, 1989: Odense Univ. Press).

—— (1985*a*) *Culture and History in Medieval Iceland. An Anthropological Analysis of Structure and Change*. Oxford: Clarendon Press.

—— (1985*b*) 'Male and Female in Icelandic Culture'. *Folk*, 27.

—— (1985*c*) 'Entropisk elegi. Kristendommen og den sociale uorden på Island efter år 1000'. *Stofskifte*, 12. (English trans.: 'Tristes Entropiques. Christianity and Social Disorder in Iceland'. In id. *Island of Anthropology*, Odense, 1989: Odense Univ. Press).

—— (1985*d*) 'Anthropology and the Exaggeration of Culture. A Review Article'. *Ethnos*, 50/3–4.

—— (1985*e*) 'Literacy and Morality: Cultural Deconstruction in Iceland 1400–1800'. Proceedings from the Conference 'From Orality to Literacy and Back'. University of Copenhagen. (Repr. in id. *Island of Anthropology*, Odense, 1989: Odense Univ. Press).

—— (1985*c*) 'Hinsides videnskaben om det konkrete. Antropologiske reflektioner over "stammer", "stater" og andre metaforer'. *Fortid og Nutid*, 2.

—— (1986*a*) 'Tracing Tradition. An Anthropological Perspective on *Grettis saga Ásmundarsonar*'. In *Structure and Meaning. New Approaches to Old Norse Literature*, ed. G. W. Weber, J. Lindow, and L. Lönnroth. Odense 1985: Odense University Press.

—— (1986*b*) 'Text and Context. Continuity and Change in Medieval Icelandic History as "Said" and "Laid Down"'. In *Continuity and Change. A Symposium*, ed. E. Vestergård. Odense: Odense Univ. Press.

—— (1986c) 'Veracity and Visibility. The Problem of Authenticity in Anthropology'. *Folk*, 28.

—— (1987a) 'Fieldwork among Friends. Ethnographic Exchange within the Northern Civilisation'. In *Anthropology at Home*, ed. A. Jackson. ASA Monographs, 25. London: Tavistock.

—— (1987b) 'The Challenge of the Unreal'. *Culture and History*, 1.

—— (1987c) 'Studying a Remote Island. Inside and Outside Icelandic Culture'. Proceedings from the Conference on 'The Anthropology of Iceland'. University of Iowa. (Repr. in id. *Island of Anthropology*, Odense, 1989: Odense Univ. Press).

—— (1987d) 'The Reality of Anthropology'. *Ethnos*, 52/3–4.

—— (1987e) 'Presenting the Past. Reflections on Myth and History'. *Folk*, 29.

—— (1988a) 'Selvdestruktion. Et islandsk eksempel på kollektiv afvikling'. *Psyke og Logos*, 6.

—— (1988b) 'Indenfor historiens rammer. En antropologisk diskussion af "tidsrum" og "tekster"'. In *Fra Stamme til Stat*, ed. P. Mortensen. Aarhus: Aarhus Univ. Press.

—— (1989a) 'A Question of Reason. Breastfeeding "taboos" in Iceland and their Implications.' In *The Anthropology of Breastfeeding*, ed. Vanessa Maher. Oxford: Berg (in press).

—— (1989b) 'Saeters in Iceland 900–1600. An Anthropological Analysis of Economy and Cosmology.' *Acta Borealia*, 6/1.

—— (1989c) 'Nature as historical space.' *Folk*, 31.

—— (1989d) 'Writing Ethnography: State of the Art.' In *Anthropology and Autobiography*, ed. H. Callaway and J. Okely. ASA Monographs, 31. London: Routledge.

—— (1989e) 'The Prophetic Condition'. In E. Ardener, *The Voice of Prophecy and Other Essays*, ed. M. Chapman. Oxford: Blackwell.

—— (1989f) *Island of Anthropology. Studies of Icelandic Past and Present*. Odense: Odense Univ. Press.

—— (1989g) 'Witchcraft in Seventeenth Century Iceland'. In *Early Modern European Witchcraft: Centres and Peripheries*, ed. B. Ankarloo and G. Henningsen. Oxford: OUP.

—— and ELSASS, P. (1988) 'Incest i tværkulturel belysning'. *Nordisk Sexologi*, 6.

—— and MEULENGRACHT SØRENSEN, P. (eds.) (1987) *Tradition og Historieskrivning. Kilderne til Nordens ældste historie*. Aarhus: Aarhus Univ. Press.

Háttalykill. (Loftur Guttormsson) (1922–7). In *Kvæðasafn*, ed. Jón Þorkelsson. Reykjavík: Hið íslenzka bókmenntafélag.

HAUGEN, EINAR (1957) 'The Semantics of Icelandic Orientation'. *Word*, 13/3.

—— (1976) *The Scandinavian Languages. An Introduction to their History*. London: Faber & Faber.

HELGADÓTTIR, GUÐRUN, P. (1961–3) *Skáldkonur fyrri alda*, i–ii. Akureyrí: Kvöldvökuútgáfan.

HELGASON, JÓN (1931a) 'Isländsk Litteratur under 1500-talets senare hälft'.

334   *References*

Island. Bilder från gammal och ny tid. Stockholm: Skrifter utgivna av samfundet Sverige-Island, 1.

HELGASON JÓN (1931b) 'Från Oddur Gottskálksson till Fjölnir. Tre hundra års isländsk språkutveckling'. *Island. Bilder från gammal och ny tid.* Stockholm: Skrifter utgivna av samfundet Sverige-Island, 1.

—— (1953) 'Norges og Islands digtning'. *Norrøn litteraturhistorie.* Nordisk kultur, 8B. Stockholm, Oslo, and Copenhagen: Albert Bonniers förlag *et al.*

HENNINGSEN, GUSTAV (1980) *The Witches' Advocate. Basque Witchcraft and the Spanish Inquisition.* Reno: Univ. of Nevada Press.

HENRICHSEN, C. L. (ed.) (1968) *Adam af Bremen: De Hamburgske ærkebispers historie og Nordens beskrivelse.* Trans. C. L. Henrichsen. 2nd edn. Copenhagen: Rosenkilde og Bagger.

HERMANN, PAUL (1903) *Nordische Mythologie in Gemeinverständlichen Darstellung.* Leipzig: Wilhelm Engelmann.

HERMANNSSON, HALLDÓR (ed.) (1916) *Icelandic Books of the Sixteenth Century.* New York: Islandica, 9.

—— (1917) *'Annalium in Islandia farrago' and 'De mirabilibus Islandiae' by Gísli Oddsson, Bishop of Skálholt.* New York: Islandica, 10.

—— (1922) *Icelandic Books of the Seventeenth Century 1601–1700.* New York: Islandica, 14.

—— (1924) *Jón Guðmundsson and his Natural History of Iceland.* New York: Islandica, 15.

—— (1926) *Two Cartographers.* New York: Islandica, 17.

—— (1928) *Sir Joseph Banks and Iceland.* New York: Islandica, 18.

—— (1931) *The Cartography of Iceland.* New York: Islandica, 21.

—— (1938) *The Icelandic Physiologus.* (Facsimile edn. with Introduction). New York: Islandica, 27.

HEWES, G. W. (1948) 'The rubric "Fishing and Fisheries"'. *American Anthropologist,* 50.

HITZLER, E. (1979) *Sel—Untersuchungen zur Geschichte des isländischen Sennwesens seit der Landnahmezeit.* Oslo: Universitetsforlaget.

HOBSBAWN, ERIC J. and RANGER, T. (eds.) (1983) *The Invention of Tradition.* Cambridge: Cambridge Univ. Press.

HOLLIS, MARTIN (1985) 'Of Masks and Men'. *The Category of the Person. Anthropology, Philosophy, History,* eds. M. Carrithers, S. Collins, and S. Lukes. Cambridge: Cambridge Univ. Press.

HOMAN, THEO (1975) *Skíðaríma. An Inquiry into the Written and Printed Texts, References and Commentaries. With an Edition and an English Translation.* Amsterdamer publikationen zur sprache und literatur, 20. Amsterdam: Rodopi NV.

HORREBOW, NIELS (1752) *Tilforladelige Efterretninger om Island.* Copenhagen.

—— (1966) *Frásagnir um Ísland.* Trans. Steindór Steindórsson. Reykjavík: Bókfellsúfgáfan.

HUNTINGTON, E. (1915) *Civilisation and Climate.* New Haven, Conn.: 1915.

HØRBY, KAJ (1980) 'Tiden fra 1340 til 1523'. *Danmarks Historie*, ii, ed. A. E. Christensen, *et al.* Copenhagen: Gyldendal.

JAEGLÉ, PIERRE and ROUBAUD, PIERRE (1987) 'Les Lois des processus: aspect scientifique et aspect historique'. *La Pensée*, 257, pp. 37–51.

JENSDÓTTIR, SÓLRÚN (1975–6) 'Books Owned by Ordinary People in Iceland 1750–1830'. *Saga-Book of the Viking Society for Northern Research*, 19.

JENSEN, JØRGEN (1979) *Dansk Socialhistorie*, i. *Oldtidens samfund. Tiden indtil år 800*. Copenhagen: Gyldendal.

JOCHUMSSEN, MATHIAS (1977) *Anmerkninger ofver Island og dessen indbyggere. Inberetning eftr reser på Island i årene 1729–31*, ed. O. Vasstveit. Skrifter, 5. Oslo: Universitetsbiblioteket.

JÓHANNESSON, ÞORKELL (1928) *Lýðir og landshagir*, i. Reykjavík: Almenna bókafélagið.

— (1933) *Die Stellung der freien Arbeiter in Island bis zur Mitte des 16. Jahrhunderts*. Reykjavík: E. P. Briem; Copenhagen: Levin og Munksgård.

JÓNASSON, JÓNAS (1961) *Íslenzkir þjóðhættir*. 3rd edn. Reykjavík: Ísafold.

JÓNSSON, ARNGRÍMUR (1593) *Brevis commentarivs de Islandia 1593*. (Formáli eftir Jacob Benediktsson, with an English Summary). Reykjavík 1968: Íslenzk rit í frumgerð, 2.

— (1609) *Crymogæa. Þættir úr sögu Íslands*, (ed. and trans. Jakob Benediktsson). Reykjavík: Sögufélagið.

JÓNSSON, BJÖRN L. (1973) *Íslenskar lækninga- og drykkjarjurtir*. Reykjavík: Rit Náttúrulækningafélags Íslands, 13.

JÓNSSON, FINNUR (1772–8) *Historia Ecclesiastica Islandiæ*, i–iv. Copenhagen.

JÓNSSON, FINNUR (ed.) (1905–22) *Rímnasafn. Samling af de ældste Islandske rimer*, i–ii. Copenhagen: Samfund til udgivelse af gammel nordisk litteratur.

— (1907–15) 'Bæjanöfn á Íslandi'. *Safn til sögu Íslands og íslenzkra bókmennta að fornu og nýju*, iv.

— (1914) 'Oldislandske ordsprog og talemåder'. *Arkiv för Nordisk Filologi*, 30.

— (1932a) 'Om Háttalykill, der tillægges Loptr Gutthormsson'. *Arkiv för Nordisk Filologi*, 48.

— (1932b) *De gamle Eddadigte*. Copenhagen: G. E. C. Gads Forlag.

JÓNSSON, GUÐMUNDUR (1830) *Safn af íslenzkum orðskviðum, fornmælum, heilræðum, snilliyrðum, sannmælum og málsgreinum*. Copenhagen: Hið íslenzka bókmenntafélag.

JÓNSSON, GUÐMUNDUR (1981) *Vinnuhjú á 19. öld*. Reykjavík: Ritsafn Sagnfræðistofnunar.

JÓNSSON, SIGURJÓN (1944) *Sóttarfar og sjúkdómar á Íslandi 1400–1800*. Reykjavík: Hið íslenzka bókmenntafélag.

JÓNSSON, VILMUNDUR (1969) *Lækningar og saga. Tíu ritgerðir*. Reykjavík: Bokútgafa Menningarsjóðs.

JÓNSSON, ÞORSTEINN M. (1957) *Brennan á Melaeyrum 1625*. Akureyri: Bókforlag Þorsteins M. Jónssonar.

KARLSSON, STEFÁN (1970a) 'Halldór Guðmundsson, norðlenzkur maður'. *Opuscula*, 4. Copenhagen: Munksgård. (Bibliotheca Arnamagnæana, 30).
—— (1970b) 'Ritun Reykjarfjarðarbókar. Excursus: Bókagerð bænda'. *Opuscula*, 4. Copenhagen: Munksgård. (Bibliotheca Arnamagnæana, 30).
—— (1979) 'Íslandsk bogeksport til Norge i middelalderen'. *Maal og Minne*, 1–2, pp. 1–17.
KELCHNER, GEORGIA D. (1935) *Dreams in Old Norse Literature and their Affinities in Folklore*. Cambridge: Cambridge Univ. Press.
KER, W. P. (1923) *The Dark Ages*. Edinburgh and London: William Blackwood.
KEYSER, R., MUNCH, P. A., and UNGER, C. R. (eds.) (1848) *Speculum Regale. Konnungs-Skuggsjá. Konge-speilet*. Christiania: Carl C. Werner.
KJARTANSSON, ÞORGEIR (1982) 'Stóridómur. Nokkur orð um siðferðishugsjónir Páls Stigssonar'. *Sagnir*, 3.
KLEINMAN, ARTHUR (1980) *Patients and Healers in the Context of Culture. An Exploration of the Borderland between Anthropology, Medicine and Psychiatry*. Berkeley, Calif.: Univ. of California Press.
KLEIVAN, INGE (1984) 'The Fish World as a Metaphorical Eskimo Society'. In *Studies in Ethnology, Cultural Ecology and Folklore*, i–ii, ed. B. Gunda. Budapest: Akadémiae Kiadó.
KNODEL, J. and VAN DE WALLE, E. (1967) 'Breast Feeding, Fertility and Mortality'. *Demography*, 14.
KNUDSEN, ANNE (1989) *En Ø i Historien. Korsika. Historisk Antropologi 1730–1914*. Copenhagen: Basilisk.
KOLSRUD, KNUT, HODNE, B., GRAMBO, R., and SWANG, A. (eds.) (1978) *Tradisjon og samfund. Festskrift til Olav Bø på 60-års dagen, 19 May 1978*. Oslo: Universitetsforlaget.
Konungs Skuggsjá. (1920) *Speculum Regale*, ed. Finnur Jónsson. Copenhagen: Det Kongelige Nordiske Oldskriftselskab.
Kormáks saga. (1939), ed. Einar Ól. Sveinsson. Íslenzk fornrit, 8. Reykjavík: Hið íslenzka fornritafélag.
Kristinna þáttr Árna Þorlákssonar. (1895). *Norges Gamle Love*, V. Christiania: Det Norske Historiske Kildeskriftfond.
KRISTJÁNSSON, JÓNAS (ed.) (1950) *Spánverjavígin 1615. Sönn frásaga eftir Jón Guðmundsson lærða og Víkinga Rímur*. Íslensk rit síðari alda, 4. Copenhagen: Hið íslenzka fræðafélag.
KRISTJÁNSSON, LÚÐVÍK (1980) *Íslenzkir sjávarhættir*, i. Reykjavík: Menningarsjóður.
—— (1982) *Íslenzkir sjávarhættir*, ii. Reykjavík: Menningarsjóður.
—— (1983) *Íslenzkir sjávarhættir*, iii. Reykjavík: Menningarsjóður.
—— (1985) *Íslenzkir sjávarhættir*, iv. Reykjavík: Menningarsjóður.
—— (1986) *Íslenzkir sjávarhættir*, v. Reykjavík: Menningarsjóður.
KRISTJÁNSSON, SVERRIR (ed.) (1969) *Reisubók síra Ólafs Egilssonar*. Reykjavík: Almenna bókafélagið.

Kvæðasafn. (1922–7) *Eptir nafngreinda íslenzka menn frá miðöld*, ed. Jón Þorkelson. Reykjavík: Hið íslenzka bókmenntafélag.

KÅLUND, KRISTIAN (1886) *Islandske ordsprog fra AM 604, 4to*. Småstykker, 7. Copenhagen: Samfund til udgivelse af gammel Nordisk litteratur.

—— (ed.) (1907) *Lækningabók íslenzk. Den islandske lægebog. Cod. Arnam. 434a, 12mo*. Copenhagen: Det Kongelige Danske Videnskabernes Selskab's Skrifter, 6. række, Historisk Filologisk Afdeling, 6.

—— (ed.) (1908) *Alfræði Íslenzk. Islandsk encyklopedisk litteratur*, i. Cod. mbr. Am: 194, 8vo. Copenhagen: Samfund til udgivelse af gammel nordisk litteratur.

LACAPRA, DOMINICK (1985) *History and Criticism*. Ithaca, NY and London: Cornell Univ. Press.

LAMB, H. H. (1966) *The Changing Climate*. London: Methuen.

—— (1972) *Climate: Present, Past and Future*, i. *Fundamentals and Climate Now*. London: Methuen.

—— (1977) *Climate: Present, Past and Future*, ii. *Climatic History and the Future*. London: Methuen.

LARSEN, HENNING (ed.) (1931) *An old Icelandic Medical Miscellany*. Trans. with Introduction by H. Larsen. Oslo: Det Norske Videnskabsakademi.

LÁRUSSON, BJÖRN (1967) *The Old Icelandic Land Registers*. Lund: Gleerup.

LÁRUSSON, MAGNÚS MÁR (1970) *Á höfuðbólum landsins. Saga*, 9. Reykjavík.

LÁRUSSON, ÓLAFUR (1925) Elzta óðal á Íslandi'. *Iðunn*, 1925. (Repr. Lárusson 1944).

—— (1929) 'Úr byggðarsögu Íslands'. *Vaka*, 1929. (Repr. Lárusson 1944).

—— (1936) 'Island'. In *Befolkningen i Oldtiden*, ed. H. Shetelig. Nordisk Kultur, I. Copenhagen, Stockholm, and Oslo: Albert Bonniers Förlag *et al.*

—— (1942) 'Guðmundur góði í þjóðtrú Íslendinga'. *Skírnir*, 1942. (Repr. Lárusson 1944).

—— (1944) *Byggð og saga*. Reykjavík: Ísafold.

Laxdæla saga (1934), ed. Einar Ó. Sveinsson. Íslenzk fornrit, 5. Reykjavík: Hið íslenzka fornritafélag.

LEDANOIS, E. (1938) *L'Atlantique, histoire et vie d'un océan*. Paris.

LEFF, GORDON (1969) *History and Social Theory*. London: Merlin Press.

LEGOFF, JAQUES (1974) 'Les Mentalités. Une histoire ambigue'. *Faire de l'histoire*, 3. Paris: Gallimard.

—— (ed.) (1978) *La Nouvelle Histoire*. Paris: Retz.

LE ROY LADURIE, E. (1970) 'Pour une histoire de l'environment. La part du climat'. *Annales*, 1970.

—— (1972) *Times of Feast, Times of Famine: A History of Climate since the Year 1000*. London: Allen & Unwin.

—— (1974a) *The Peasants of Languedoc*. Trans. John Day. Urbana, Ill.: Univ. of Illinois Press.

—— (1974b) 'The Aiguillette: Castration by Magic'. *Europe*, Mar. 1974. (Repr. Ladurie 1981a).

—— (1978) *Montaillou: Village Occitan de 1294 à 1324*. Paris: Gallimard.

LE ROY LADURIE (1979) *The Territory of the Historian*. Trans. Ben Reynolds and Siân Reynolds. Chicago, Ill.: Univ. of Chicago Press.

—— (1981*a*) *The Mind and Method of the Historian*. Trans. Ben Reynolds and Siân Reynolds. Chicago, Ill.: Univ. of Chicago Press.

—— (1981*b*) 'A Concept: The Unification of the Globe by Disease (Fourteenth to Seventeenth Centuries). In *The Mind and Method of the Historian*. Trans. Ben Reynolds and Siân Reynolds. Chicago, Ill.: Univ. of Chicago Press.

LÉVI-STRAUSS, CLAUDE (1949) *Les Structures Élementaires de la Parenté*. Paris: Presses Universitaires de France.

—— (1958) *Anthropologie Structurale*. Paris: Plon.

—— (1960) 'Le champ d'anthropologie'. *Anthropologie Structurale Deux*. Paris: Plon.

—— (1961) *Entretiens avec Claude Lévi-Strauss*, ed. C. Charbonnier. Paris: 10: 18.

—— (1962) *La Pensée Sauvage*. Paris: Plon.

—— (1967) *Structural Anthropology*. New York: Doubleday.

—— (1974) Structuralism and Ecology. *Social Science Information*, 12/1.

LEWIS, I. M. (ed.) (1968) *History and Social Anthropology*. ASA Monographs, 7. London: Tavistock.

LID, NIELS (1935*a*) 'Folketru'. *Nordisk Kultur*, 19.

—— (1935*b*) 'Indledning. Magiske fyrestellingar og bruk. *Nordisk Kultur*, 19.

—— (1937) 'Til Varulvens Historie'. *Saga och Sed*, 1937.

Lilja (The Lily) (1870), ed. Eiríkr Magnússon. London: Williams & Norgate.

LÍNDAL, SIGURÐUR (1973) 'Retshistorie og Politik. Om Islands Statsretslige stilling 1262–1662'. *Tidsskrift for rettsvitenskap*, 86.

LINDERHOLM, EMANUEL (1918) *Nordisk magi. Studier i nordisk religions- og kyrkohistorie*. Svenska landsmål och svenskt folkeliv, 20. Stockholm.

LINDQUIST, NAT. (ed.) (1921) *En Isländsk Svartkonstbok från 1500-tallet*. Uppsala: Appelberg/Längmanska Kulturfonden.

LINDQUIST, IVAR (1923) *Galdrar. De gamla germanska trollsångernas stil undersökt i samband med en svensk runinskrift från folkvandringstiden*. Gothenburg: Elanders boktrykning.

LITHELL, V. B. (1981) 'Breast-Feeding Habits and their Relations to Infant Mortality and Marital Fertility'. *Journal of Family History*, 6/2.

LORD, ALBERT B. (1974) *The Singer of Tales*. New York: Atheneum.

LOWENTHAL, DAVID (1985) *The Past is a Foreign Country*. Cambridge: Cambridge Univ. Press.

LUKES, STEVEN (1975) *Émile Durkheim. His Life and Work*. Harmondsworth: Penguin.

LYOTARD, JEAN-FRANÇOIS (1984) *The Postmodern Condition: A Report on Knowledge*. Trans. G. Gennington and Brian Massunin. Minneapolis, Minn.: Univ. of Minnesota Press.

LÖFGREN, ORVAR (1985) 'Our Friends in Nature. Class and Animal Symbolism'. *Ethnos*, 50/3–4.

LÖNNROTH, LARS (1964) *Tesen om de två kulturerna. Kritiska studier i den isländska*

sagaskrivningens sociale förutsättningar. *Scripta Islandica*. Isländska sällskapets årsbok, 15.
—— (1969) 'The Noble Heathen. A Theme in the Sagas'. *Scandinavian Studies*, 41/1.
MacFarlane, Alan (1970a) *Witchcraft in Tudor and Stuart England*. London: Routledge & Kegan Paul.
—— (1970b) *Witchcraft in Tudor and Stuart Essex*. In *Witchcraft Confessions and Accusations*, ed. M. Douglas. ASA Monographs, 9. London: Tavistock.
—— (1978) 'Modes of Reproduction'. In *Population and Development*, ed. G. Hawthorn. London: Cass.
—— (1986) *Marriage and Love in England 1300–1840*. Oxford: Blackwell.
Magnus, Olaus (1976) *Historia om de nordiska folken. (Books 1–22)*, i–iv. Stockholm: Gidlunds.
Magnússon, Árni and Vídalín, Páll (1913–43) *Jarðabók Íslands*, i–xi. Copenhagen: Hið íslenzka fræðafélag.
Magnússon, Eiríkr (ed.) (1870) *Lilja (The Lily)*. *An Icelandic Religious Poem of the Fourteenth Century by Eysteinn Ásgrímsson*. London: Williams & Norgate.
Magnússon, Finnur (1833) 'Om de Engelske's Handel og Færd på Island i det 15de Aarhundrede, især med hensyn til Columbus's formeentlige Reise dertil i Aaret 1477, og hans Beretninger desangående'. *Nordisk Tidsskrift for Oldkyndighed*, ii. Copenhagen.
Magnússon, Finnur (1986) 'The Hidden Class: The Emergence of a Maritime Working Class in Iceland'. *Ethnologia Scandinavica*, 1986.
Magnússon, Gísli (1647) *Consignatio Instituti seu Rationes*, ed. and trans. Jakob Benediktsson. Safn fræðafélagsins, 11. Copenhagen and Reykjavík: Hið íslenzka fræðafélag.
Magnússon, Sigurður A. (1977) *Northern Sphinx. Iceland and the Icelanders from the Settlement to the Present*. London: Hurst & Co.
Magnússon, Skúli (1784) *Sveita-bóndi*. Copenhagen: Rit lærdómslistafélagsins, 4.
—— (1944a) *Beskrivelse af Gullbringu og Kjósar sýslur* (1785), ed. Jón Helgason. Bibliotheca Arnamagnæana, 4. Copenhagen: Munksgård.
—— (1944b) *Forsøg til en kort beskrivelse af Island* (1786), ed. Jón Helgason. Bibliotheca Arnamagnæana, 5. Copenhagen: Munksgård.
Mandrou, Robert (1978) *From Humanism to Science 1480–1700*. Harmondsworth: Pelican.
Manntalið. (1960) Population Census 1703. Reykjavík: Statistics of Iceland, ii, no. 21.
Marcus, G. E. and Fischer, M. M. J. (1986) *Anthropology as Cultural Critique*. Chicago, Ill.: Univ. of Chicago Press.
Maurer, Konrad (1858) *Reise nach Island*. Unpub. MS. Univer. of Munich.
—— (1874) *Island vor seinen ersten Entdeckung bis zum Untergange des Freistaats*. Munich: Christian Kaiser.
—— (1968a) 'Island und das dänishe Grundgesetz' (1856). In 'Zur politischen

geschichte Islands. Gesammelte aufsätze'. New edn. Aalen: Scientia Verlag, pp. 1–32.

MAURER, KONRAD (1968b) 'Zur politischen geschichte Islands. Gesammelte aufsätze' (1880). New edn. Aalen: Scientia Verlag.

MAUSS, MARCEL (1950) Essai sur le don. Paris: Presses Universitaires de France.

—— (1972) A General Theory of Magic. Trans. R. Brain. London: Routledge & Kegan Paul.

MEULENGRACHT SØRENSEN, PREBEN (1977) Saga og Samfund. Copenhagen: Berlingske.

—— (1980) Norrønt Nid. Odense 1980: Odense Universitetsforlag. (English trans. by Joan Turville-Petre, The Unmanly Man. Concepts of Sexual Defamation in Early Northern Society. Odense 1983: Odense Univ. Press.)

MERCHANT, CAROLYN (1980) The Death of Nature. Women, Ecology and the Scientific Revolution. San Francisco, Calif.: Harper & Row.

MITTERAUER, MICHAEL and SIEDER, REINHARD (1982) The European Family. Oxford: Blackwell.

MONTER, WILLIAM (1983) Ritual, Myth and Magic in Early Modern Europe. Brighton: Harvester Press.

MUNDAL, ELSE (1974) Fylgjemotiva i Norrøn Litteratur. Oslo: Universitetsforlaget.

NEEDHAM, RODNEY (1971) 'Remarks on the Analysis of Kinship and Marriage'. In Rethinking Kinship and Marriage, ed. R. Needham. ASA Monographs, 11. London: Tavistock.

—— (1972) Belief, Language, and Experience. Oxford: Blackwell.

NORDAL, SIGURÐUR (1924) Íslenzk Lestrarbók 1400–1900. Reykjavík: Bókaverslun Sigfúsar Eymundssonar.

—— (ed.) (1937) Biskop Gudbrands Vísnabók. Monumenta Typographica Islandica, 5. Copenhagen: Munksgård.

—— (1942) Íslenzk menning. Reykjavík: Mál og menning.

—— (1954) 'Tid och kalvskinn'. Scripta Islandica, 5.

—— (ed.) (1967) 'Trúarlif Síra Jóns Magnússonar'. Píslarsaga. Reykjavík: Almenna bókafélagið.

NORDGÅRD, O. (1920) Forklaringer til de viktigste av Kongespeilets dyrenavne', ed. Finnur Jónsson. Konungs Skuggsjá, 1920.

NØRLUND, N. E. (1944) Islands Kortlægning. En historisk fremstilling. Geodætisk Instituts Publikationer, 7. Copenhagen: Munksgård.

ODDSSON, GÍSLI (1942) Undur Íslands (De Mirabilibus Islandiae) (1638). In Íslenzk annálabrot og Undur Íslands, ed. Jónas Rafnar. Akureyrí: Þorsteinn M. Jónsson.

OHLMARKS, ÅKE (1944) 'Till frågan om den fornnordiske skaldediktningens ursprung'. Arkiv för Nordisk Filologi, 57.

OHRT, F. (1935) 'Trylleformler'. Nordisk Kultur, 19.

ÓLAFSSON, EGGERT (1772) Reise igiennem Island. Sorø: Det Kongelige Videnskabsakademi.

—— (1832*a*) 'Búnaðarbálkur'. *Kvæði Eggerts Ólafssonar*. Íslenzk kvæðabok, i. Copenhagen.

—— (1832*b*) *Kvæði Eggerts Ólafssonar*. Íslenzk kvæðabók, i. Copenhagen.

ÓLAFSSON, HARALDUR (1987) 'The Hunter and the Hunted. A Study in the Survival of Traditional Culture'. Paper Presented to the Conference 'The Anthropology of Iceland', Univ. of Iowa, May 1987.

ÓLAFSSON, STEFÁN (1885–6) *Kvæði*, i–ii. Copenhagen: Hið íslenzka bókmenntafélag.

ÓLASON, PÁLL EGGERT (ed.) (1916) *Fjölmóður. Ævidrápa Jóns lærða Guðmundssonar*. Safn til sögu Íslands og íslenzkra bókmennta að fornu og nýju, v. Reykjavík: Hið íslenzka bókmenntafélag.

—— (1919–26) *Menn og menntir siðskiptaaldarinnar á Íslandi*, i–iv. Reykjavík: Bókaverzlun guðm. Gamalíelsonar Bókaverzlun Ársæls Árnasonar.

OLAVIUS, O. (1780) *Oeconomisk Reise igiennem Island*. Copenhagen: Gyldendals Forlag.

OLRIK, HANS (1968) *Danske Helgeners Levned*, i–ii. 2nd edn. Copenhagen: Rosenkilde og Bagger.

ÓLSEN, BJÖRN M. (1910) 'Um skattbændatal 1311 og manntal á Íslandi'. *Safn til sögu Íslands og íslenzkra bókmennta að fornu og nýju*, iv. Reykjavík: Hið íslenzka bókmentafélag.

OLSEN, MAGNÚS (1916*a*) 'Varðlokur. Et bidrag til kundskap om gammelnorsk trolddom'. *Maal og Minne*, 1, pp. 1–21.

—— (1916*b*) 'Trollruner'. *Edda*, 1916.

—— (1933) 'De norröne runeinnskrifter'. *Nordisk Kultur*, 6.

PÁLSSON, GÍSLI (1979) 'Vont mál og vond málfræði'. *Skírnir*, 153, pp. 157–201.

—— (1982) 'Representations and Reality: Cognitive Models and Social Relations among the Fishermen of Sandgerði, Iceland'. Unpub. Ph.D. thesis, Univ. of Manchester.

—— (1987) 'The Idea of Fish: Land and Sea in the Icelandic World View'. In *Signifying Animals*, ed. Roy Willis. London: Unwin Hyman.

PÁLSSON, HERMANN (1962) *Sagnaskemmtan Íslendinga*. Reykjavík: Mál og Menning.

PEERSE, GORIES (1946) *Um Iislandt* (1561). In Sigurður Grímsson (ed.), *Glöggt er gests augað. Úrval ferðasagna um Ísland*. Reykjavík: Menningar og fræðslusamband alþýðu.

PENTIKÄINEN, JUKA (1968) *The Nordic Dead-Child Tradition. Nordic Dead-Child Beings. A Study in Comparative Religion*. Communications No. 202. Helsinki: Academia Scientarium Fennica.

PÉTURSSON, EINAR GUNNAR (1971) 'Rit eignuð Jóni lærða í Munnmælasögum 17. aldar'. *Afmælisrit til Steingríms J. Þorsteinssonar prófessors, 2. júlí 1971*. Reykjavík.

PÉTURSSON, HALLGRÍMUR (1887–90) *Sálmar og kvæði*, i–ii. Reykjavík: Sigurður Kristjánsson.

PÉTURSSON, JÓN (1767) *Den saakaldede Islandske Skiørbug*. Sorøe 1767.

PÉTURSSON, JÓN (1791) *Um orsakir til sjúkdoma á Íslandi, yfirhöfuð.* Copenhagen: Rit lærdomslistafélagsins, 11.

—— (1834) *Lækningabók fyrir almuga.* Copenhagen: Rit lærdomslistafélagsins.

PIKE, KENNETH L. (1967) *Language in Relation to a Unified Theory of the Structure of Human Behavior.* The Hague: Mouton.

Píslarsaga síra Jóns Magnússonar. (1967), ed. Sigurður Nordal. Reykjavík: Almenna bókafélagið.

POLLOCK, LINDA A. (1983) *Forgotten Children. Parent–Child Relations from 1500 to 1900.* Cambridge: Cambridge Univ. Press.

PORTELLI, ALESSANDRO (1987) 'Uchronic Dreams: Workers' Memory and "Wrong" Versions of History'. Paper Given at the Sixth International Oral History Conference, Oxford, 11–13 Sept. 1987.

POUILLON, JEAN (1977) Plus c'est la même chose, plus ça change. *Nouvelle Revue de Psychanalyse*, 15.

RABB, THEODORE K. (1982) 'Coherence, Synthesis, and Quality in History'. In *The New History. The 1980s and Beyond*, ed. T. K. Rabb and R. I. Rotberg. Studies in Interdisciplinary History. Princeton, NJ: Princeton Univ. Press.

RAFNAR, JÓNAS (ed.) (1942) Gísli Oddsson. *Undur Islands (De Mirabilibus Islandiae)* (1638). *Íslenzk annálabrot og Undur Íslands.* Akureyrí: Þorsteinn M. Jónsson.

RAFNSSON, SVEINBJÖRN (1974) *Studier i Landnámabók. Kritiske bidrag til den Isländska fristatstidens historia.* Bibliotheca Historica Lundensis, 31. Lund: Gleerup.

RASK, RASMUS (1932) 'Det gamle Nordiske eller Islandske sprogs Oprindelse' (1817). *Udvalgte Afhandlinger*, 1.

—— (1932–5) *Udvalgte Afhandlinger*, i–iii, ed. Louis Hjelmslev and Holger Pedersen. Det danske sprog- og litteraturselskab. Copenhagen: Clevin og Munksgård.

RAVN, IB (1987) 'Den indfoldede orden. En indføring i David Bohms fortolkning af kvantemekanikken'. *Paradigma*, 1/3.

ROOTH, ANNA BIRGITTA (1976) *Folkelig diktning. Form og teknik*, 3rd edn. Lund: Studentlitteratur.

—— (ed.) (1978) *Folkdikt och folktro.* Lund: Liber Läromedel.

ROSALDO, RENATO (1976) 'From the Door of his Tent'. In *Writing Culture. The Poetics and Politics of Ethnography*, ed. J. Clifford and G. E. Marcus. Berkeley, Calif.: Univ. of California Press.

RÚGMANN, JÓNAS (1927–8) *Jónas Rúgmans samling of isländska talesätt.* Uppsala.

RØRBYE, BIRGITTE (1978) 'Folketroen som begreb og forskningsfelt'. In *Tradisjon og samfund. Festkrift til Olav Bø på 60-års dagen, 19 May 1978*, ed. K. Kolsrud, B. Hodne, R. Grambo, and A.Swang. Oslo: Universitetsforlaget.

SAHLINS, MARSHALL D. (1974) *Stone Age Economics.* London: Tavistock.

—— (1981) *Historical Metaphors and Mythical Realities. Structure in the Early History of the Sandwich Islands Kingdom.* Ann Arbor, Mich.: Univ. of Michigan Press.

—— (1983) 'Other Times, Other Customs: The Anthropology of History'. *American Anthropologist*, 85/3. (Repr. Sahlins 1985).

—— (1985) *Islands of History.* Chicago, Ill.: Univ. of Chicago Press.

SAUSSURE, FERDINAND DE (1974) *Course in General Linguistics*. Trans. Wade Basku. Glasgow: Fontana/Collins.

SAWYER, P. H. (1982) *Kings and Vikings*. London and New York: Methuen.

SCHIER, KURT (1975) 'Iceland and the Rise of Literature in "Terra Nova": Some Comparative Reflections'. *Grípla*, I.

—— (1977) 'Einige methodische Überlegungen zum Problem von mündlicher und literarischer Tradition im Norden'. *Oral Tradition, Literary Tradition. A Symposium*, ed. H. Bekker-Nielsen, *et al.* Odense: Odense Univ. Press.

SCHREINER, JOHAN (1953) 'Bidrag til en datering af Kongespeilet'. *Historisk Tidsskrift*, 36.

SEATON, ETHEL (1935) *Literary Relations of England and Scandinavia in the Seventeenth Century*. Oxford: Clarendon Press.

SEE, KLAUS VON (1980) *Skaldendichtung*. Frankfurt.

SHORTER, EDWARD (1984) *A History of Women's Bodies*. Harmondsworth: Pelican.

SIGFÚSSON, SIGFÚS (ed.) (1922–58) *Íslenzkar þjóðsögur og sagnir*, i–xvi. Seyðisfjörður and Reykjavík: Víkingaútgáfan. (2nd edn., ed. Óskar Halldórsson, Reykjavík 1982: Bókaútgáfan Þjóðsaga, i–iv).

SIGURÐARDÓTTIR, SIGRÍÐUR (1982) 'Höfðu konur börn á brjósti 1700–1900?' *Sagnir*, 3.

SIGURÐSSON, GÍSLI (1960–3) 'Fornubuðir'. *Saga*, 3, pp. 291–8.

SIGURÐSSON, HARALDUR (1971–8) *Kartasaga Íslands*. i. frá öndverðu til loka 16. aldar. ii. frá lokum 16. aldar til 1848. Reykjavík: Bókútgafa Menningarsjóðs og Þjóðvinafélagsins.

—— SIGURÐSSON, JÓN (1951) *Hugvekja til Íslendinga*, ed. Sverrir Kristjánsson. Reykjavík: Mál og menning.

SIGURÐSSON, PÁLL (1971) *Brot úr réttarsögu*. Reykjavík: Hlaðbúð.

SIGURJÓNSSON, ARNÓR (1930) *Íslendingasaga. Yfirlit handa skólum og alþýðu*. Akureyri: Prentsmiðja Odds Björnssonar.

—— (1973) 'Jarðamat og jarðeignir á Vestfjörðum 1446, 1710 og 1846'. *Saga*, 11, pp. 74–115.

—— (1975) *Vestfirðingasaga 1390–1540*. Reykjavík: Prentsmiðjan Leiftur HF.

Skíðaríma. (1905), ed. Finnur Jónsson, *Rímnasafn. Samling af de ældste Islandske rimer*, i, pp. 10–42. Copenhagen: Samfund til udgivelse af gammel nordisk litteratur.

—— (1975) 'An Inquiry into the Written and Printed Texts, References and Commentaries', ed. Theo Homan. *Amsterdamer publikationen zur Sprache und Literatur*, 20. Amsterdam: Rodopi NV.

SMITH, HENRIK (1577) *Henrik Smiths lægebog*, i–vi. Fac. ed. Anna-Elisabeth Brade. Copenhagen: Rosenkilde og Bagger.

SOGNER, SØLVI (1976) 'A Demographic Crisis Averted'. *Scandinavian Economic History Review*, 24.

SOUTHWOLD, MARTIN (1978) 'Definition and its Problems in Social Anthropology'. *Yearbook of Symbolic Anthropology*, i, ed. E. Schwimmer. London: Hurst.

Speculum Regale (1848) *Konnungs-skuggsjá. Konge-speilet*, ed. R. Keyser, P. A. Munch, and C. R. Unger. Christiania: Carl C. Werner.

SPIESER, JEAN-MICHEL (1987) 'L'Histoire, le matériel, les immatériaux'. *La Pensée*, 257, pp. 81–6.

SPRINGBORG, PETER (1969) 'Nyt og gammelt fra Snæfjallaströnd. Bidrag til beskrivelse af den litterære aktivitet på Vestfjordene i 1. halvdel af det 17. århundrede'. *Afmælisrit Jóns Helgasonar, 30 Juni 1969*. ed. Jakob Benediktsson, *et al.* Reykjavík: Heimskringla.

—— (1977) 'Antiquæ Historiæ Lepores—Om Renæssancen i den Islandske Håndskriftsproduktion i 1600-tallet'. *Gardar*, 8.

Statistics of Iceland (1960), ii, no. 21. *Manntalið. Population Census 1703*. Reykjavík.

STEBLIN-KAMINSKIJ, M. I. (1969) 'On the Etymology of the Word Skáld'. *Afmælisrit Jóns Helgasonar. 30 Juni 1969*. ed. J. Benediktsson, *et al.* Reykjavík: Heimskringla.

STEFFENSEN, JÓN (1975) *Menning og meinsemdir. Ritgerðasafn um mótunarsögu íslenzkrar þjóðar og baráttu hennar við hungur og sóttir*. Reykjavík: Sögufélagið.

STEINDÓRSSON, STEINDÓR (1981) *Íslenskir náttúrufræðingar 1600–1900*. Reykjavík: Menningarsjóður.

STEINGRÍMSSON, JÓN (1945) *Æfisaga síra Jóns Steingrímssonar*, ed. Guðbrandur Jónsson. Reykjavík: Skaftfellingafélagið.

STENBERGER, MÅRTEN (ed.) (1943) *Forntida gårda i Island. Meddelanden från den nordiska arkeologiska undersökningan i Island sommaren 1939*. Copenhagen: Munksgård.

STORM, GUSTAV (ed.) (1881) *Samlede skrifter af Peder Claussøn Friis*. Kristiania: Det norske historiske forlag.

—— (ed.) (1888) *Islandske Annaler indtil 1578*. Christiania: Det Norske Historiske Kildeskriftfond.

—— (ed.) (1891) *Eiríks saga rauða*. Copenhagen: Samfund til udgivelse af gammel nordisk litteratur.

—— (ed.) (1895) *Historisk-topografiske Skrifter om Norge og norske landsdele, forfattede i Norge i det 16. aarhundrede*. Christiania: Det Norske Historiske Kildeskriftsfond.

STRATHERN, MARILYN (1987) 'Out of Context: The Persuasive Fictions of Anthropology'. *Current Anthropology*, 28/3.

STREET, BRIAN V. (1984) *Literacy in Theory and Practice*. Cambridge: Cambridge Univ. Press.

STRÖM, FOLKE (1942) *On the Sacral Origin of the Germanic Death Penalties*. Lund: Håkon Ohlssons Boktryckeri.

—— (1954) *Diser, nornor, valkyrjor. Fruktbarhetskult och sakralt kungadöme i Norden*. Vitterhets Historie och Antikvitets Akademiens Handlinger. Filologisk-filosofiska serien, 1. Stockholm: Kungl.

—— (1961) *Nordisk Hedendom. Tro og Sed i förkristen tid*. Lund: Akademi förlaget.

STRÖMBÄCK, DAG (1929) 'Banaþúfa och heillaþúfa'. In *Strömbäck 1970*.

—— (1931) 'Några drag ur äldre och nyare isländsk folktro'. *Island. Bilder från gammal och ny tid.* Stockholm: Skrifter utgivna av samfundet Sverige-Island, 1.

—— (1935) *Sejd.* Stockholm: Nordiska texter og undersökningar, 5.

—— (1943–4) 'Om Varulven'. *Svenska landsmål 1943–44.* (Repr. Strömbäck 1970).

—— (1970) *Folklore og Filologi. Valda uppsatser.* Kungl. Gustav Adolfs Akademien, 13 Aug. 1970. Stockholm: AB Lundequistska Bokhandeln.

—— (1975) *The Conversion of Iceland. A Survey.* Trans. P. Foote. London: Viking Society for Northern Research.

—— (1976) 'The Concept of Soul in Nordic Tradition'. *Arv,* 31, 1975.

Sturlunga saga. (1946), ed. Jón Jóhannesson, Magnús Finnbogason, and Kristján Eldjárn, i–ii. Reykjavík: Sturlunguútgáfan.

SVEINSSON, EINAR ÓLAFUR (1931*a*) 'Islandske Folkesagn'. In *Folkeviser, Folkesagn og Folkeeventyr,* ed. K. Liestøl and C. W. von Sydow. *Nordisk Kultur,* 9. Copenhagen, Oslo, and Stockholm.

—— (1931*b*) 'Islandske Folkeeventyr'. *Folkeviser, Folkesagn og Folkeeventyr,* ed. K. Liestøl and C. W. von Sydow. *Nordisk Kultur,* 9. Copenhagen, Oslo, and Stockholm.

—— (ed.) *Laxdœla saga.* Íslenzk fornrit, 5. Reykjavík: Hið íslenzka forn-ritafélag.

—— (1940) *Um íslenzkar þjóðsögur.* Reykjavík: Hið íslenzka bókmenntafélag.

—— (1944) 'Lestrarkunnátta íslendingar i fornöld'. *Skírnir,* 118.

—— (ed.) (1954) *Njáls saga.* Íslenzk fornrit, 12. Reykjavík: Hið íslenzka forn-ritafélag.

SYDOW, C. W. VON (1935) 'Övernaturliga väsen'. *Nordisk Kultur,* 19. Folketro: Copenhagen, Oslo, and Stockholm.

SYV, PEDER (1682) *Almindelige danske Ordsproge og korte Lærdomme.* Copenhagen.

TEITSSON, BJÖRN and STEFÁNSSON, MAGNÚS (1972) 'Um rannsóknir á íslenzkrí byggðarsögu tímabilsins fyrir 1700'. *Saga,* 10.

THOMAS, KEITH (1970) 'The Relevance of Social Anthropology to the Histor-ical Study of English Witchcraft'. *Witchcraft Confessions and Accusations,* ed. M. Douglas. ASA Monographs, 9. London: Tavistock.

—— (1971) *Religion and the Decline of Magic.* London: Weidenfeld and Nicolson.

—— (1983) *Man and the Natural World. Changing Attitudes in England 1500–1800.* London: Allen Lane.

THORODDSEN, PORVALDUR (1892–1904) *Landfræðissaga Íslands,* i–iv. Copen-hagen: Hið íslenzka bókmenntafélag.

—— (1908–22) *Lýsing Íslands,* i–iv. Copenhagen: Hið íslenzka bókmenntafélag.

—— (1916–17) *Árferði á Íslandi i þúsund ár.* Copenhagen: Hið íslenzka fræðafelag.

TILLHAGEN, CARL-HERMANN (1958) *Folklig läkekonst.* Stockholm: LTs Förlag.

TOMASSON, RICHARD F. (1976) 'Premarital Sexual Permissiveness and Illegitimacy in the Nordic Countries'. *Comparative Studies in Society and History,* ii.

TOMASSON, RICHARD F. (1977) 'A Millennium Of Misery: The Demography of the Icelanders'. *Population Studies*, 3.
—— (1980) *Iceland: The First New Society*. Reykjavík: Iceland Review/Univ. of Minnesota Press.
TROIL, UNO VON (1780) *Letters on Iceland. Made During a Voyage Undertaken in the Year 1772*. 2nd, corr. and improved, edn. London: J. Robson, *et al.*
TURVILLE-PETRE, GABRIEL (1964) *Myth and Religion of the North: The Religion of Ancient Scandinavia*. London: Weidenfeld and Nicolson.
—— (1972a) 'Liggja fylgjur þínar til Íslands'. *Nine Norse Studies*. Univ. College, London, Text Series, 5. London: Viking Society for Northern Research.
—— (1972b) *Nine Norse Studies*. Univ. College London, Text Series, 5. London: Viking Society for Northern Research.
—— (1976) *Scaldic Poetry*. Oxford: Clarendon Press.
TYLER, STEPHEN A. (1986) 'Post-Modern Ethnography: From Document of the Occult to Occult Document'. In *Writing Culture*, ed. J. Clifford and G. E Marcus. Berkeley, Calif.: Los Angeles, Calif.: and London: Univ. of California Press.
TYLOR, E. B. (1871) *Primitive Culture*. London: Murray.
UTTERSTRÖM, GUSTAV (1954) 'Some Populations Problems in Pre-Industrial Sweden'. *Scandinavian Economic History Review*, 2/2.
—— (1955) 'Climatic Fluctuations and Population Problems in Early Modern History'. *Scandinavian Economic History Review*, 3/1.
VIGFÚSSON, GUÐBRANDUR and UNGER C. R. (eds.) (1868) *Hákonar saga Hákonarsonar, Flateyjarbók*, iii. Norsk historisk kildeskriftsfonds skrifter, 4. Oslo: P. T. Malling.
VENDLER, ZENO (1967) *Linguistics in Philosophy*. Ithaca, NY: Cornell Univ. Press.
VETTER, DANIEL (1931) *Islandia* (1640), ed. B. Horák. Brno: Vydárá Filofická Fakulta.
VOVELLE, MICHEL (1982) 'Ideologies and mentalities'. In *Culture, Ideology and Politics*, ed. R. Samuel and G. S. Jones. History Workshop Series. London: Routledge & Kegan Paul.
VRIES, JAN DE (1956–7) *Altgermanische Religionsgeschichte*, i–ii. Grundiss der germanischen Philologie, 12. Berlin: Walter de Gruyter & Co.
—— (1977) *Altnordisches etymologisches Wörterbuch*. 3rd edn. Leiden: Brill.
VRIES, JAN DE (1976) *The Economy of Europe in an Age of Crisis 1600–1750*. Cambridge: Cambridge Univ. Press.
—— (1981) 'Measuring the Impact of Climate on History. The Search for Appropriate Methodologies'. In *Climate and History*, ed. R. I. Rotberg and T. K. Rabb. Princeton, NJ: Princeton Univ. Press.
WAX, ROSALIE H. (1969) *Magic, Fate and History. The Changing Ethos of the Vikings*. Kansas: Coronado Press.
—— and WAX, MURRAY (1955) 'The Vikings and the Rise of Capitalism'. *American Journal of Sociology*, 61.

WARNER, MARINA (1978) *Alone of all her Sex. The Myth and the Cult of the Virgin Mary*. London: Quartet Books.

WEBER, GERD WOLFGANG (1981) 'Irreligiosität und Heldenzeitalter. Zum Mythencharakter der altisländischen Literatur'. *Specvlvm Norroenvm. Norse Studies in Memory of Gabriel Turville-Petre*, ed. U. Dronke, *et al.* Odense: Odense Univ. Press.

WEBER, MAX (1970) *The Protestant Ethic and the Spirit of Capitalism*, trans. T. Parsons. London: Unwin Univ. Books.

WESTERGÅRD-NIELSEN, CHRISTIAN (1946) *Låneordene i det 16. århundredes trykte islandske Litteratur*. Bibliotheca Arnamagnæana, 6. Copenhagen: Munksgård.

WOLF, ERIC R. (1982) *Europe and the People without History*. Berkeley, Calif.: Univ. of California Press.

YOUNG, J. (1982) 'The Anthropologies of Illness and Sickness'. *Annual Review of Anthropology*, 1982.

ÞORSTEINSSON, HANNES (1924-7) 'Séra Jón Jonsson gamli á Staðarhrauni'. *Blanda*, 3. Reykjavík: Sögufélagið.

ÞÓRARINSSON, SIGURÐUR (1949) 'Tephrochronological Contributions to the Volcanology and Glaciology of Iceland'. *Geografiska Annaler*, 1949.

—— (1956) 'The Thousand Years' Struggle against Ice and Fire'. Reykjavík: Bókútgáfa menningarsjóðs.

—— (1971) 'Nokkur orð um Íslandslýsingu Odds Einarssonar', Oddur Einarsson. *Íslandslýsing*, ed. Jakob Benediktsson. Reykjavík: Menningarsjóður.

ÞÓRARINSSON, STEFÁN (1793) *Tilraun til að ákveða gagnsemi heyskaparins á Íslandi í samlíking við kornafla þann sem er mögulegur*. Copenhagen: Rit lærdomslistafélagsins, 14.

Þorgils saga ok Hafliða. Sturlunga saga, i, ed. Jón Jóhannesson, Magnús Finnbogason, and Kristján Eldjárn. Reykjavík: Sturlunguútgáfan.

ÞORKELSSON, JÓN (1884-91) 'Háttalykill Lopts ríka Guttormssonar'. *Småstykker*. Copenhagen: Samfund til udgivelse af gammel Nordisk litteratur.

—— (ed.) (1922-7) *Kvæðasafn. Eptir nafngreinda íslenzka menn frá miðöld*. Reykjavík: Hið íslenzka bókmenntafélag.

ÞÓRÓLFSSON, BJÖRN KAREL (1934) *Rímur fyrir 1600*. Safn Fræðifjelagsins um Ísland og íslendinga, 9. Reykjavík 1934: Hið íslenzka fræðafelag.

ÞORSTEINSSON, BJÖRN (1966) *Ný Íslandssaga*. Reykjavík: Heimskringla.

—— *Enska öldin í sögu Íslendinga*. Reykjavík: Mál og menning.

—— (1976) *Tíu þorskastríð 1415-1976*. Reykjavík: Sögufélagið.

—— (1980) *Íslensk miðaldasaga*. Reykjavík: Sögufelagið.

—— (1985) *Island*. Politikens Danmarkshistorie. Copenhagen: Politiken.

ÞORSTEINSSON, HANNES (ed.) (1902) 'Ritgerð Jóns Guðmundssonar lærða um ættir o.fl.'. *Safn til sögu Íslands og islenzkra bókmenta að fornu og nýju*, iii.

INDEX